The World of

the Swahili

John Middleton

The World of the S*wahili*

AN AFRICAN

MERCANTILE

CIVILIZATION

Yale University Press

New Haven and London

Designed by Jill Breitbarth.
Set in Sabon type by Tseng Information Systems, Inc., Durham, North
Carolina.
Printed in the United States of America by BookCrafters, Inc.,
Chelsea, Michigan.

Library of Congress Cataloging-in-Publication Data
Middleton, John, 1921–
    The world of the Swahili : an African mercantile civilization /
John Middleton.
        p. cm.
    Includes bibliographical references and index.
    ISBN 0-300-05219-7 (cloth)
        0-300-06080-7 (pbk.)
    1. Swahili-speaking peoples—Commerce. 2. Swahili-speaking
peoples—Kinship. 3. Swahili-speaking peoples—Social life and
customs. 4. Lamu (Kenya)—Commerce. 5. Lamu (Kenya)—Social life
and customs. 6. Zanzibar—Commerce. 7. Zanzibar—Social life and
customs. I. Title.
DT429.5.S94M54 1992
306'.089'96392—dc20   91-31617
                                                               CIP

The paper in this book meets the guidelines for permanence and
durability of the Committee on Production Guidelines for Book
Longevity of the Council on Library Resources.

10 9 8 7 6 5 4 3 2

C o n t e n t s

Illustrations

Preface

　　This book is about the people known as the Swahili, the "People of the Coast," who live along the coast of eastern Africa and on the nearby islands. Today they are known outside Africa largely because their language, which is widely used in eastern Africa, is learned by many people outside the continent who wish to identify themselves as having African ancestry. In fact, virtually no Swahili went to the Americas as slaves, and those who were sent from East Africa by the Portuguese came from inland groups to the far south. The East African slave trade was controlled by Arabs and almost all of its victims were taken across the Indian Ocean to Arabia, Persia, and India. The Swahili themselves were involved in this traffic as traders and not as slaves.

　　The Swahili have stood apart from neighboring groups by virtue of having a literate and Muslim culture with economic and political ties both within Africa and across the Indian Ocean. Their civilization has a long history of unusual cultural efflorescence and character; it has been and remains unique, with a documented history as long as any possessed by those who came to conquer it. Yet we may see it as being doomed from its beginning. It has been subjected to continual colonial overrule, in various forms, for at least five centuries, a fact that has profoundly affected the formation and growth of the society and its culture. Swahili civilization was based on trade between Africa and Asia, the Swahili being the middlemen and always dependent on events and trends which lay beyond their own control. The centers of economic and political power lay across the Indian Ocean, in the far interior of Africa, and in Europe; the Swahili coast has been at the periphery of their concerns, valuable but in the end dispensable.

　　To the Arabs of Oman and the Hadhramaut, the coast and islands, with their gardens and perennial sweet water, must have appeared as did Spain to the Arabs of northern Africa, as a Garden or Paradise set on earth. And the Portuguese in the sixteenth century saw it as a land much like their own. All considered it as the gateway to the inland wealth of Africa. For the peoples of the interior it was likewise a place for overseas trade from which they too could become wealthy and powerful. The People of the Coast have never been mere passive participants in this international trade but crucial partners without whom it could never have taken place. This book is an attempt to provide a record of a people proud of their past and their present abilities and consciousness, who, although always aware of their economic dependence upon others, have recognized themselves as forming a culturally unique and autonomous society.

The coast of the Swahili is today a mixture of modern ports and cities, of remote fishing villages and semiruined towns. From the sea the voyager sees the Swahili towns and villages set along the water's edge, some of white lime-washed buildings above stone wharves and jetties, others of low houses set above the beaches and almost invisible beneath coconut palms. Behind are gardens and groves of coconut and mango trees, and behind those in turn fields and stretches of bush. The large ports of Mombasa and Dar es Salaam resemble tropical ports anywhere. In the former, although historically a Swahili town, Swahili civilization is now that of a small minority; the latter is relatively modern. The lesser towns and villages retain much of the traditional way of life, in which the ancient Swahili values of urbanity (*utamaduni*) and civilization (*ustaarabu*) are still meaningful. But there is not a great deal left: what industry and modern commerce have done to Mombasa and Dar es Salaam, the 1964 revolution and its aftermath have done to Zanzibar, and upcountry immigrants and culturally illiterate entrepreneurs and tourists are doing to Malindi and Lamu. For the outsiders change has been profitable; for the Swahili it has almost brought the end of their history. Yet they resist and quietly retain their own identity.

The Swahili number about half a million people living in a string of settlements along the East African coast and its islands from Mogadishu in the north to Mozambique in the south. They form a society of a type very different from other African societies studied by anthropologists, most of which used to be called "tribal" societies, with clearly definable cultural, linguistic, and political identities. Despite the fashionable and questionable argument that "tribes" were "invented" by colonial governments, most peoples recognized themselves as discrete units even though none was ever either totally autonomous, isolated from neighboring societies, or had very long-lasting social and cultural boundaries. Anthropologists have worked out models for these groups that have enabled sense and order to be made in analysis. But the Swahili, as a centuries-old mercantile society with an unusual social structure, cannot be fitted into them.

Generalization about Swahili society and behavior can be made only by analyzing the underlying social structure, the idea that the Swahili themselves hold as a means of conceptualizing and comprehending their society in space and over time. They define their society largely in terms of ethnic origins and composition, but it should be seen as an *oikumene*, a system of exchange of goods, people, and values, based on and validated by reciprocal and complementary expectations between its members. In this book I attempt to provide an outline description of the main Swahili institutions in order to suggest that they have meaning, both for the Swahili and for others, only as elements in a highly structured society that seems rarely to have been recognized as forming a single whole. I wish to present a descriptive analysis so as to suggest a new interpretation of this mercantile society that has endured for many centuries and that is comparable to other mercantile societies elsewhere. This book cannot be a definitive account, but is meant rather to set the stage for future research and writing. My interpretation is intended to make common sense of the data rather than to be a deep anthropological analysis. It is based on the facts that Swahili society is of an unusual kind that has virtually never been discussed by anthropologists, that it is complex and contains many variations, and that the published information on it is immense in quantity but weak and unequal in quality. The first thing needed is an ethnographic account to replace the earlier (and excellent) one by Prins (1967), and this is what I here attempt to provide. It may be taken as the first part of a longer study.

This is a historical ethnography. Obviously, all ethnography is "historical" in that it must take note of changes in institutions and social behavior, both within and surrounding a particular society. In addition, variations in space are often considered in historical terms as representing temporal forms, and this may be suggested for certain Swahili institutions as well. For the Swahili the described historical depth needed for any understanding of their institutions, and perceived by the Swahili themselves as an essential dimension of their present-day culture, is greater than for most African societies. The Swahili are often accused of being culturally nostalgic, bewailing the vanishing of past glories; this condescending view bears little relationship to the actuality of ongoing Swahili society. Pride in the past is used as a source of ambition and as a weapon of protest, and does not imply lack of concern or excitement for the present and future. Some Swahili see the present as a period of opportunity for advancement perhaps unparalleled in their history; others see it as a time of decline and of social and moral decay. As an anthropologist I wish to report both views and seek to explain the apparent disparity between them by reference to their social and historical contexts: I myself do not consider one more accurate than the other, and both are "true."

This book is written for two categories of readers. The first comprises the Swahili themselves, many or most of whom may read, and will I hope find interest in, this account of their civilization as an ongoing whole by an outsider who has both respect and affection for it. The second comprises students who may want to learn something of how a mercantile society has worked in the past and today. I have avoided both jargon and pedantic reference to "theory" as being unwanted and contributing little except the obvious: the theory is in the ethnography. I have concentrated on those relatively few aspects of Swahili civilization that my teachers on the East African coast have shown me are central to it: its history, commerce, descent, marriage, religion, and notions of honor and purity. I have contextualized these within the frame of world history, colonialism and postcolonialism, and the everyday expressions of Swahili values. It is Swahili men and women, living, working, hoping, and despairing, who are the subjects of this book.

We cannot understand the Swahili present without understanding their past, nor can we understand that past without an ethnographic knowledge of the present: I have tried to do both. It is difficult to estimate how the society has changed over the past centuries. Certain developments are obvious and can be documented: the coming of Islam, the advent of Portuguese, Omani, and European overrule, the destruction of forms of indigenous kingship, changes in the patterns of ocean and hinterland trade, the abolition of slavery. But information is scarcely available for changes in social organization such as forms of marriage and residence, patterns of authority in local and descent groups, patterns of internal ranking and moral purity in the various communities, or the identities of local corporate groups. A reanalysis of earlier accounts demands that we interpret these "documents" in a new light in order to extract information on these basic institutions.

There are three problems here. One is that of translation, of trying to understand the "other" in the same terms as understanding one's own society and thereby avoiding the moral differentiation between the self and the other. The second is the all too common reliance on simplistic explanation for complex patterns of thought and behavior. Examples from much past writing include claims that the Swahili reckon descent "cognatically," "patrilineally," or even "matrilineally"; that "preferred" forms of marriage are with cross-cousins or with parallel-cousins; that marital residence is "virilocal" or "uxorilocal"; that "divorce rates" are high or low; that "polygyny" is universal or rare; that Swahili society is tightly coherent or so fragmented and even "broken down" as to lack any overall pattern; and many other oversimplifications. Most of these contentions are correct with reference to one part of the coast or another, but they distort social and historical actualities. The third problem is the lack of quantitative and case material, and here I plead guilty to defects in my own research. A good deal of quantitative data exists for general trends in the nineteenth and twentieth centuries, which has ably been collected and analyzed by historians such as Cooper, Nicholls, and Sheriff. I have not copied their findings here and refer the interested reader to their works and others listed in the references.

The problem of reliability of historical and ethnographic evidence is central to any account of Swahili society. The published data are generally scrappy, written by outside observers in different parts of the coast at different periods. The observers themselves have been of many kinds and have had different aims, and their writings need careful and different interpretations. The earliest were mostly Arab travelers of the Middle Ages, followed by Portuguese colonizers of the period of Portuguese expansion. They were followed in turn by other European traders, missionaries, administrators, and naval geographers. Some observers have been Swahili interested in their own past who, by means of traditional poetic forms of description, used their experience as the basis for moral texts as much as for historiography in a "modern" sense. In recent years Swahili and non-Swahili linguists, anthropologists, archeologists, and historians have contributed important studies. There are accounts by Swahili, Arabs, Chinese, Portuguese, Germans, British, French, Americans, Japanese, and others.

This book has been many years in making. Its actual writing began in the mid-1970s, but much of the thought behind it goes back far longer. I was fortunate to spend a year in Mombasa in 1944, when it was still culturally largely a Swahili city. I spoke the Swahili language and there were no hindrances to my walking in Old Town, Mji wa Kale, and in what were then (before tourism) sleepy towns along the coast, and talking with their courteous inhabitants. I was not then trained as an anthropologist and so missed much of what was to be learned, but the flavor of Swahili civilization was clear and seductive enough never to be forgotten.

In 1958, as a social anthropologist, I was invited by the government of the Sultanate of Zanzibar to undertake a study of systems of land tenure with particular reference to the "indigenous" population of the islands of Zanzibar and Pemba. This research resulted in the publication of two books, *Land Tenure in Zanzibar* and (with Jane Campbell) *Zanzibar: Its Society and Its Politics*. In 1986, as a recipient of a Fulbright-Hays Faculty Research Abroad Fellowship, I was able to spend several months in the towns of Lamu, Mombasa, and Pate. The main subject of my research was the systems of marriage in those places, which I selected because of the great differences between them and rural Zanzibar.[1] More recently I have made short visits with the support of the Yale Center for International and Area Studies. This book is based largely upon my own research in the two very different and contrasting Swahili communities of Zanzibar and Lamu islands.

Most of what I have gathered from conversations with many Swahili men and women has been considered by them as either confidential or as normally private talk, and I have not followed the fashionable habit of giving the names of the sources of every item of information. My "informants" were mostly friends and as such trusted me in their houses, and I learned much that I prefer not to put directly into print: I see no reason to embarrass those who were so generous with their time and knowledge, and without whom I could of course have done nothing. One point worth making is that in Lamu I have been lucky enough to have been accepted as an elderly scholar and as such have been able to discuss with both men and women anything other than personal psychological, medical, or financial matters, or certain aspects of modern politics. Swahili friends have told me that they would most certainly not talk about anything except in superficial terms with younger visitors, male or female. (The notion *siri,* "secret," is central in everyday behavior in the Swahili towns.)

I should like to mention a few people whose help has been especially valuable. I was able to thank those in Zanzibar and Pemba in the foreword to *Land Tenure in Zanzibar*. In Kenya I wish particularly to thank those who have helped me because of their love for and pride in their own civilization: the widely respected Sheikh Ahmed Sheikh Nabhany of Pate, Lamu, and Mombasa; Bwana Athman Lali Omar, Sheikh Athman Basheikh, and Ustaadh Harith Swaleh, all of Lamu; Sheikh Mwalimu Dini of Pate; Bwana Bakari Mwalimu of Siyu. Where I have misunderstood their views I apologize: I have a very long way to travel before I can earn the title of *bingwa,* a scholar knowledgeable in many fields. I thank also the late Mr. James de Vere Allen of Kwale, and Dr. Chacha Nyaigotti-Chacha and Messrs. Kimani Njogu and Justin Willis of Nairobi. I owe much to

Messrs. Leonard Scard and Kjell Nordenskiold. In Europe and the United States I am especially grateful to Thomas Beidelman, Ann Biersteker, Ivan Dihoff, Linda Donley-Reid (who has also allowed me to use several of her photographs), G. S. P. Freeman-Grenville, Mark Horton, and Ivan Karp. I thank Leon Yacher for drawing the maps, and Cynthia Bogarad and Barbara Munck for unfailing help in the preparation of the text. I am very grateful to my editors at Yale University Press: Ellen Graham, who has continually encouraged me and shown almost superhuman patience, and Harry Haskell, who has seen the book through the press with skill and good humor. Above all I thank Michelle Gilbert, who, with Werner Forman, first encouraged me to write this book and who over the last several years has made substantial and perceptive comments on the manuscript as I have written and rewritten it.

I have mentioned that I first visited the Swahili coast in 1944. There I was shown and taught much by my friend the late Dr. G. W. B. (Dicon) Huntingford, who after many years of working among the Nandi of highland Kenya came to work on the early history of the Swahili coast and Ethiopia. He showed me, with enthusiasm and generosity, much that was at that time little known to and even unobserved by outsiders. He died in London in 1978. This book is dedicated to his memory.

A NOTE ON SWAHILI WORDS

The language of the Swahili is a Bantu one, although it has a high proportion of loanwords from Arabic and other mercantile languages. One of its features is the use of prefixes to indicate noun classes. The people are properly known as waSwahili and one individual as mSwahili; the language is called kiSwahili. Unlike most ethnic names in Bantu-speaking Africa, there is no simple locative form for the place where the people live, which would be uSwahili: this form carries the connotation of a political entity which is lacking in the case of the waSwahili. There is the double form uSwahilini, which lacks political connotation but refers to the Swahili homeland. In this book I do not use these prefixes for proper names. For ordinary words I add the plural form only when it is needed in the text.

The Swahili People and Their Coast

THE PEOPLE CALLED SWAHILI

The first question conventionally asked in any ethnographic account is, Who are the people? In a sense this question is the main theme of this book. It has been held that there is no society that can be called Swahili, there being only coastal settlements whose populations have been so called by others, and in which those of higher rank have referred to those of lower rank as Swahili while refusing the name for themselves. The name itself is generally taken to come from the Arabic *sawahil* (coast), so that the Swahili are the "People of the Coast." [1] It seems not to have been used as an ethnic name before the eighteenth or nineteenth centuries, when the Omani Arab rulers of Zanzibar referred to their local subjects along the coast as Swahili, while calling themselves Arabs or Omani. [2]

In everyday talk the Swahili use local names such as waPemba, the people of Pemba island, or waMalindi, the people of Malindi town, but they recognize themselves as being Swahili in contradistinction to others. They form a complexly organized plural society composed of many elements of disparate origins that have for centuries intermingled, intermarried, and interbred. The socially superior—those generally referred to as "owners of the town" (*wenyeji*) or similar terms—find many idioms with which to distance themselves from those whom they regard as socially inferior, who although not wenyeji are nonetheless members of Swahili society: hierarchical difference is usually stated in terms of "ethnic" origins, but all may be referred to as "waSwahili."

Social and cultural difference between Swahili and non-Swahili is always recognized, even where the latter have today moved into the Swahili towns. The coastal peoples include many who have never been counted as Swahili. These comprise the groups known collectively today as the Mijikenda, and farther south the Zaramo, Zigua, and others. They are closely related to the Swahili in language, live next to them and indeed often intermingle with them on the ground, and have for centuries been linked to them by trade, clientage, and mutual military protection. Yet neither they nor anyone else have ever argued that they are Swahili, and intermarriage has been rare. There are also long-settled Indians, Somali, and

Europeans, who have never been called Swahili. On the other hand, some groups, such as the former Omani rulers and recent immigrants from Arabia, have clearly been considered members of Swahili society as soon as they have become socially and culturally incorporated.

Anthropologists and historians have often tried to produce a definition of a community or group whose composition and boundaries are more or less fixed at any moment in time, and which can then be compared with other communities or groups. But any such atemporal and fixed definition is lacking among the Swahili, who define their identity and those of their neighbors according to the historical moment. If it is useful or proper to be incorporated and counted as Swahili, then one is so counted; if it is not, then one is not so counted. At certain periods most people of the coast have called themselves Swahili; at others they have denied this identity and used other terms such as "Shirazi" or "Arab." But in a very real sense any such decision does not affect a person's membership of the entity that we may call "Swahili society." It is a polyethnic society, although this refers to the claimed diversity of origins of its members rather than to any actual racial differences, and these assumed distinctions play a large part in the Swahili world view.

The identity of the Swahili is a complex matter. Certain obvious criteria have been suggested, of which the most common is linguistic. There is a Swahili people, a cluster of speakers of Swahili dialects; and there is a language known as kiSwahili, both to those who speak it as a mother tongue and to those who have adopted it as a second language.[3] It is one of the so-called Sabaki group and related to the languages of the Mijikenda, Pokomo, and Comorians. KiSwahili differs from other Sabaki languages grammatically, by its high proportion of Arabic, Portuguese, and Hindi loanwords, and by the fact that it was for centuries written in Arabic script, the use of which has had significant overtones as regards social hierarchy.[4] In recent years, except for some religious and poetic texts, Roman script has been used.

There are also nonlinguistic criteria for defining the Swahili. The most important is that they have long been Muslims. This has marked them off from most of their neighbors and those of the interior, from their former European rulers, and from the present rulers of Kenya and Tanzania; and it gives them in their own eyes the status of a chosen people. It has linked them to Arabs, Persians, Somali, and Muslims from the Indian subcontinent, all of whom have played important roles in Swahili history. The Swahili, particularly the wealthier inhabitants of the older towns, have for centuries enjoyed a high standard of living and have constructed a clearly distinguishable Swahili culture. Their settlements are always marked by their architecture, the houses being square and in the larger towns made of stone. Swahili cuisine, clothing, adornment, poetry, naming, and many other traits are also unique in East Africa. However, there is much variation, each community on the coast having its own place within the wider whole in terms of dialect and detail of culturally diacritical behavior. Most studies of the Swahili have therefore considered their many settlements along the coast as distinct elements in a loose congeries defined in essentially cultural terms. This view is mistaken. Although never a single polity, the Swahili have for many centuries formed a single ongoing society possessing a single underlying structure. They conceive of themselves as a single "civilization" (ustaarabu) that belongs to them and to them only, and that has been unchanging over the centuries (although today it is in sad decline). Clearly it has changed continuously, but it has nonetheless retained its essential characteristics and has proved resilient in the face of external attacks and influences.

Swahili civilization is complex and subtle, containing many kinds and levels of conflicts and contradictions, and Swahili views of their world are filled with negotiations and compromises between opposites. One of the reasons for the tenacity of this civilization over the centuries within a generally hostile outer world has been precisely the fact that it is a middleman society. It has had to maintain a fragile balance between typically incompatible demands and expectations of trading partners who have met only indirectly through the mediation of the Swahili mercantile and cultural brokers. For many centuries the Swahili have been an exploited people within successive colonial systems. There is a widespread ethnocentric Western view that those exploited in colonial situations are not only subordinate but also victims without recourse except to accept that fate, but there are other sides to the picture. The Swahili have learned well how to use the greed, ambitions, and ignorance of their rulers and have played off one against the other. Their identity has been defined largely by this strategy, enabling them to survive centuries of outside contact and remain a viable and defiant people.

THE COAST, THE HINTERLAND, AND THE OCEAN

The life of the Swahili has revolved around the coast of East Africa, the boundary between the interior and the sailing routes across the Indian Ocean (see map 1). They have controlled this boundary as a place of trade exchange. The coast varies greatly along its length, and there are significant differences in the lands and peoples that lie behind it and so in the goods that have been exported. The northern half of the coast is backed by a long stretch of semidesert, the *nyika*, pierced by only a few routes for easy movement, and which limits the fertile coastal strip to a few miles. In the south the nyika lessens in aridity and the coastal plain grows wider, finally extending far into central Tanzania. I make a distinction between the hinterland immediately behind the coast and the interior, the vast heart of the African continent behind the hinterland. The Swahili settlements along the coastline have been dependent on the non-Swahili peoples of both hinterland and interior, have exploited them, and have been exploited by them in turn, throughout the past two millennia. They have dealt directly with the hinterland but only indirectly with the interior through the hinterland peoples. Just as there is a single Swahili civilization despite variations in detail, so there is a single Swahili coast that forms a unique land- and seascape. It comprises many

Map 1. The Swahili coast

lesser stretches of coastline, each of which differs from its neighbors and has its own name and physical, historical, cultural, linguistic, and mercantile features.

The eastern coastline of Africa consists of three great lengths. In the north, from the Red Sea to the Juba River and Ras Kiamboni, lies the eastern edge of the Somali desert. In the far south, from Cape Delgado, the northern point of Mozambique, to the southern tip of the continent, lies the sea-beaten coast of southeastern Africa. Between Ras Kiamboni and Cape Delgado lies the thousand-mile-long Swahili coast proper, tropical and fertile in most places, with many rivers, harbors, and offshore islands, part of both Africa and the Indian Ocean. In some areas the Swahili settlements are densely clustered, with large towns; in others there are only occasional villages along the shore.

In the far north is the Benadir coast of Somalia, from Mogadishu to the present Somalia-Kenya border. Here lie the towns of Mogadishu, Brava, and Kismayu, in all of which some Swahili in archaic forms is still spoken. Until a few centuries ago these were all important Swahili trading ports, but today the Swahili element has been overcome by that of the Somali. To most Swahili this is an almost forgotten part of their land.[5]

South of the Benadir lies the original heartland of the Swahili people, often referred to as uSwahilini ("at the place of the Swahili") and the Pwani ya Visiwani ("the coast of the islands"). In the north small islands provide a sheltered channel along which dhows can sail at most periods of the year. These are the Bajun islands, occupied by fishermen who speak the dialect of Swahili known as kiBajuni or kiTikuu. Formerly the Bajun also farmed on the mainland opposite, but Somali raiders have brought about their impoverishment and migration southward. The migrants are fishermen and laborers, often looked down upon as being willing to do unpleasant and low-paid tasks such as mangrove cutting. Until about the fifteenth century many slaves came from behind this region, and Ethiopian slave women remained popular as concubines until the present century. Later slaves sent for export from this area came from the south by coastal dhow traffic.

Southward the coast becomes green and watered, with many rivers, creeks, and islands, and with a reliable rainfall. The river mouths and estuaries provide routes to the interior and the small islands have been sites of settlements for centuries, protected from both the sea and the land. Long coral reefs offshore break the force of the sea along much of the coast. The northern part is flat, with long stretches of sandy beaches and extensive mangrove swamps. Its heart is the Lamu archipelago (see map 2). Many of its towns lack good harbors and the currents and sandbanks are difficult for shipping, but the towns are protected both from the force of the sea and in the past from raids by inland peoples. Somewhere on this part of the coast is the site or sites of Shungwaya, in myth and legend the original home of both the Swahili and Mijikenda. All Swahili have heard of Shungwaya, and it gives a focus to their more remote history and ancestry.[6] This region also contains the sites of towns from the beginnings of Swahili history: Shanga, Manda, Ungwana, Shaka, Ozi, and others. The main islands are Pate (Faza) and Lamu,

Map 2. The Lamu archipelago

on which were for many centuries the important towns of Pate, Siyu, and Lamu, each with its farming area on the mainland opposite. They have lost most of these lands which formerly provided the bulk of the food and oil grains exported to Arabia, as well as goods from hunting and pastoralist groups of the region, especially the Aweera (Boni) and the Somali and Orma (Galla). These included ivory, slaves, hides, skins, mangrove woods, gum copal, wild rubber, orchella, rock crystal, and other things. Lamu Town is today the most important settlement on the archipelago.

South of the Tana River lies the Nyali coast, centered on the ancient towns of Mombasa and Malindi. The former is today a large and important international port and the terminus of the Kenya-Uganda railway, but the latter is in decline except as a tourist center. Both had powerful rulers and have been seats of learning and poetry. Along most of this coast are cliffs and shallows stretching out to the reef; only a few islands and creeks offer safe harbors. At one time these towns held extensive grain plantations. Behind them lies a belt of hilly and fertile country occupied by the non-Swahili Mijikenda peoples. These farmers have enjoyed close trading and political relationships with the Swahili towns on the coast, protected by them but also giving them protection from the Orma and Maasai living farther inland. The Visiwani and Nyali coasts are the best-sited stretches to take advantage of the monsoons, and most sailing vessels of the past departed from their ports. Mombasa, in particular, was always the great prize for invaders such as the Portuguese and the Omani Arabs: whoever controlled Mombasa controlled the coast.

Near the Kenya-Tanzania border begins the fertile Mrima coast, with many islands, small rivers, and dense mangrove forests. This is the coast of the "Eight Cities," early Swahili petty states such as Utondwe, Tongoni, Mtangata, Pangani, and Vumba. Today there are the modern port of Tanga and a string of fishing settlements occupied by a melange of Swahili and non-Swahili groups. Behind, and intermingled with Swahili in places, live many closely related peoples such as the Digo, Duruma, Bondei, Teita, and Segeju, this last group almost certainly being "proper" Swahili. The Mrima continues southward past the old towns of Bagamoyo and Mboamaji and the modern city of Dar es Salaam, the capital of Tanzania, and then farther south to the vast marshy delta of the Rufiji. In the north of this coast the land rises to the highlands of Shambaa, Pare, and Kilimanjaro, all densely occupied by non-Swahili peoples. Southward lie the eastern plains of Tanzania, with many dispersed farming groups, Zaramo, Zigua, Doe, and others, who were trading partners of the coastal towns. The Zanzibar Sultanate decreed the Mrima as its monopoly and forbade foreign traders from operating there. It was the end of most of the main ivory and slave routes.[7]

The nineteenth-century slave trade was controlled by the Omani sultans from their capital of Zanzibar City. Zanzibar (known in Swahili as Unguja) lies just visible on the horizon from Bagamoyo. Over half of Zanzibar is coral and until the advent of the sultanate the settlements lay around the coast, with fishing, coconut products, and rice as the main productive resources. The Omani introduced clove growing, taking over the formerly little-used forested area in the western half of the island, where the clove plantations still exist. Cloves remain the main export of Zanzibar, although more are grown on Pemba Island to the north. Pemba, lying opposite Tanga, is more fertile, green, and densely populated. It is often referred to as Al-Khudra, "the green island," and was for centuries a supplier of rice and other grains to the coastal towns. To the south of Zanzibar lies the Mafia group, sandy and with a few areas of fertile soil.

South of the Rufiji is the Mgao coast, the site of the once wealthy and powerful Kilwa Kisiwani, "Kilwa on the Island." Kilwa's main exports remained much the same from the Middle Ages until the mid-nineteenth century: gold, slaves, and ivory. Its island site, with a good water supply and safe anchorage, provided the only good harbor on this long stretch of coast. Its hinterland was occupied by Yao, Ngindo, Makonde, and others, mixed farmers, cattle keepers, ivory hunters, and slave raiders. Finally, in the far south, in modern Mozambique, is the Kerimba coast with the Kerimba or Ibo islands, on which were once the southernmost Swahili communities of Sofala, Mozambique, and Chibuene. These ports exported the gold to Kilwa and Portugal that was produced far inland by Mono-potapa with its citadel of Zimbabwe, the target for the Portuguese invaders of the fifteenth century.

Across the Indian Ocean are the Comoro Islands, occupied by Swahili-speaking groups who have spread into the northwestern corner of Madagascar. There are strong cultural ties and ancient trading links between the Comoros and the coast proper, and today Comoro immigrants are found in most of the larger mainland towns. There are also Swahili settlements far in the interior, founded during the slave trade centered on Zanzibar, the most famous of which is Ujiji, on Lake Tanganyika.

The Swahili coast, although divided into these several ecologically and cultur-ally differentiated stretches, is nonetheless a single entity in which land and ocean are intimately linked. As Prins has stressed (1965), Swahili civilization is essen-tially a maritime one. The coast itself, as a fertile stretch of soil that can be used for productive farming, is very narrow, in most places no more than than ten miles wide. Most Swahili settlements have been in the same few fertile and well-watered places for centuries. Many settlements are towns in the sense of closely built-up places with permanent houses and streets; others are large villages, also usually closely built-up but with no more than a handful of permanent houses. Between settlements most soils are sandy or of broken coral, both of which carry crops, although only with continuous labor. Behind the coastline much of the land is not very fertile, although parts of it have supported productive grain planta-tions and have been a source of copal, orchella, aromatic woods and resins, and other export items. There are extensive mangrove forests in the tidal estuaries and mud flats, and sandy soils carry coconut palms. The areas of deeper and better soil, especially along the Nyali and Mrima coasts and on the islands of Zanzi-bar and Pemba, produce rice, grains, cloves, citrus, and many other fruits. The Swahili are gardeners and fishermen rather than farmers, and in the larger towns also traders. Their land has been closely cultivated for centuries, and except for the mangroves almost all its vegetation is man-made, most of the bush land being secondary woodland. A main factor in the recent decrease of cultivation and the decline in population in the more remote settlements was the abolition of slavery around the turn of the century. Almost everywhere in the now empty bush land, all that remain to mark the sites of former settlements are clusters of untended mango trees.

The ocean trade brought the Swahili wealth, luxury, and on occasions power, and the coast itself has produced enough for most everyday needs. Many of their food plants and trees came originally from Indonesia and India.[8] In return there was a reverse diffusion of African plants to India and beyond.[9] The staple food of most wealthier communities has been rice, grown on the larger islands and in parts of the mainland, using both natural swamps and some irrigation; today much is imported. Poorer people (and formerly slaves) depend on other staples, mainly sorghums, millets, maize, and cassava, grown in fields set outside the settlements under various forms of bush fallow.[10] Trees are economically of great importance[11] and the islands in particular grow spices.[12] Tobacco, kapok, and many other plants are cultivated, and various gums and resins are collected wild. Contrasted to the land behind the coast itself, mainly savanna bush, much of the Swahili coast is one vast garden that has provided a firm productive base for the merchant towns dotted along it.

Part of the coast is the sea: the two cannot be separated. The Swahili are a maritime people and the stretches of lagoon, creek, and open sea beyond the reefs are as much part of their environment as are the coastlands. The sea, rivers, and lagoons are not merely stretches of water but highly productive food resources, divided into territories that are owned by families and protected by spirits just as are stretches of land. The Swahili use the sea as though it were a network of roads. They have long known the compass, but a good captain of a sailing vessel relies more on his own skill and knowledge of the coast and its islands—and on magic—to make his ship fast and safe. The Swahili are, and seem always to have been, highly competent shipbuilders, and their sailing vessels and canoes are still made and repaired at several places along the coast.[13]

There has always been continual movement of traders and settlers up and down the coast. The coastline and sea provide a basic map in terms of which Swahili conceptualize their society and its history. The key to this map is the existence of the ocean monsoons. The monsoon winds cover most of the western Indian Ocean as far south as Madagascar, and the ocean trade has been organized around them as far back as historical knowledge goes. The northeast monsoon starts to blow in early November, is strong between December and February, and comes to an end by March. The weather is hot and dry, without rain. This is when the dhows come from Arabia and India carrying salt fish and many kinds of consumer goods. At the end of the monsoon come the heavy rains, and then a period of storms and turbulence when only coastal sailing is possible. The southwest monsoon begins soon afterward and is at its strongest from July until September, when ships sail north with grain, mangrove poles, and other produce, and in the past with slaves and ivory. Then there come light breezes until the beginning of the next northeast monsoon; the sea is calm but with winds that are uncertain for sailing.[14] The basic pattern is unchanging and reliable, summed up in the saying *Kasakazi mja naswi, Kusi mja na mtama* ("The northeast wind comes with fish, the southwest wind comes with sorghum").

The actual dates of the monsoons vary from year to year by several weeks, so that there is always the risk of ships becoming stranded at one end of the journey or the other. If the winds are seized at the right times, a large ocean-going dhow can sail the two thousand miles between East Africa and the Persian Gulf in thirty days or less. Careful planning is required for the cargoes to be ready in the ports most convenient for their particular destinations. There has therefore always been an important complementary coastal traffic between the ports up and down the coast. Goods from or to the southerly places must be carried to or from those from which sailing time across the ocean is shorter, so that the ocean dhows can come earlier to the coast and leave it later. These are the ports north of Zanzibar, and in some years even Zanzibar lies too far south for comfort. Some parts of the sea, such as the shallow waters between Zanzibar and the mainland and in the Bajun islands and the Lamu archipelago, can be used all the year round. But along most of the coast it is almost impossible (and certainly dangerous) for sailing vessels to make more than short local voyages at the "wrong" seasons. Today most larger craft are fitted with engines as well as sails, but even they try not to sail against the monsoon winds. Besides this southern limit to the use of the monsoons, the Indian Ocean between latitudes 10 and 30 degrees south and longitudes 60 and 90 degrees east is dangerous for shipping. This hurricane belt hardly affected East African coastal shipping directly, but by endangering direct sailing between India and the Cape of Good Hope it made ports such as Kilwa, Mombasa, and Zanzibar attractive to long-distance European shipping after the coming of the Portuguese.

The Swahili towns, set along this coast and its islands, have been the points of exchange between merchants who came by sea and by land. But the exchanges were virtually never direct transfers of goods between the two kinds of merchants. Merchants to and from Asia have carried their goods by ship, taking note of the monsoons, the need for ballast, and the internal organizational requirements of a merchant ship (the captain, the merchant himself, the crew, and water, food, and repair of ships). The owners of the very large ships have generally been Arab and Indian merchants, but Swahili merchants have owned vessels, using both Swahili and Arab crews. A trading expedition, which can take several months to cross the ocean and return, requires considerable financing that has not usually been available to the Swahili, whereas Indian and Arab merchants have been more readily given credit by Indian financiers. The African side of the trade was organized along much the same lines as the ocean side, with armed foot caravans, often of several hundred porters, taking the place of sailing vessels. It was run mainly by African traders from the hinterland and interior, not by the Swahili merchants themselves. (Many nineteenth-century caravans were an exception; they were run by Arab and Swahili traders from Zanzibar and used well-marked trade routes and permanent encampments in the interior.) Today, however, most of the traditional long-distance trade has gone and the middleman role of the Swahili towns has faded, although it is still remembered by older members of Swahili merchant families and remains the basis of Swahili views of their civilization.

ETHNIC ORIGINS

The Swahili have lived along this coast and its islands for over a thousand years, and there were communities before that which must have been very similar to theirs except for adherence to Islam and use of the Swahili language. Swahili society has derived its main characteristics from four factors: the nature of the coast; the trade between Africa and Asia in which the Swahili have played the role of middlemen; their long subjection to colonial exchange and political systems; and their ethnic composition and the complex historical formation of their society.

The formation of a society such as this raises many problems of obtaining and interpreting information about the past. There are gaps in the archeological record and few reliable figures for the Indian Ocean trade. The difficulties of interpretation are rather more subtle, but in general are based on the tensions within present-day Swahili society. As in any hierarchically stratified society, the members of the higher strata wish to see the present as validated by the past. A detailed historical analysis of the more distant past is outside my professional competence, and the reader is recommended to the works of historians.[15] Most have asked three important but sociologically somewhat inadequate questions: Is Swahili civilization an African one or a transplanted Asian one? In what ways do past historical processes of migration and incorporation relate to and so validate the distribution of present-day "communities"? And what has been the historical relationship between Islamic and pre-Islamic cultural elements? A fourth question, which is my main consideration in this book, is: What have been and are the social and cultural characteristics of this society?

Swahili origins, in the cultural rather than the racial sense, reflect the relations over a very long period between various African and Asian cultures. A problem is that Swahili notions of hierarchy and social difference are permeated by the view that race and culture are coterminous, whereas in social and historical reality they are not. Both outside observers and members of the socially superior Swahili groups have long held that Swahili culture was transplanted from Asia, and this view has been translated into terms of ethnic origins. More recently it has been suggested that the African component is far greater than had been thought, even though there have been many immigrant groups from Asia. Each has at first claimed to be different from those it found already settled, but over time these distinctions have become blurred through intermarriage, concubinage, and by the adoption of Swahili language and custom. In order to differentiate themselves, immigrants and those already settled have shown an intense concern with nuances of dialect and speech, religious behavior, deportment, dress, house adornment, and other cultural traits. Their settlements along the long and narrow coastal strip, often separated by many miles, have over the centuries grown to be very distinctive. Each part of the coast has its own name, its own traditions and myths of origin and ancestry, its own dialect, and its own set of moral values within the basic moral system provided by Islam. Yet together they form a single society with a single underlying structure, within which are several deep-rooted axes of contradiction: that between claimed and imputed origins in Africa or Asia appears to be the most pervasive, most internal competition being phrased in its terms.

We do not know when the ethnic and cultural amalgam that is today the Swahili people came into being, but by the first century A.D., the time of *The Periplus of the Erythraean Sea*, the first known account of this coast, one or two small

Arab trading posts had been established along it. In time trade became extensive enough to support the towns of the coast in their heyday from the twelfth to the eighteenth centuries. Besides overseas traders, the peoples of the hinterland have also played a crucial role in Swahili society, which was based largely on the exploitation of their resources.

Three categories of autochthonous peoples played a part—and still do so—in the Swahili world and form the main element of the population. The original peoples were presumably hunters and gatherers, still represented by a few small groups in the region.[16] The second category were ancient pre-Bantu Cushitic livestock keepers, represented today by groups such as the Orma (Oromo or Galla) and Somali.[17] James Allen has made a strong argument that these were the people who established the first permanent settlements along the coast (Allen [forthcoming]). The third category comprised Bantu-speaking groups, which migrated from the northwestern Congo region and probably reached the coast about the first and second centuries A.D. Descendants of these various peoples still exist in eastern Africa, and many of the present-day clan names found in the Swahili towns come etymologically from them.

Asia contributed other elements to the Swahili people and culture. The first in time were Indonesians, who settled in Madagascar between the second and fourth centuries A.D. They left traces behind them in eastern Africa in the form of cultivated plants and items of material culture. The influence of Persia must have been considerable, the Persian empire being the most powerful in the Indian Ocean from about 600 B.C. until the seventh century A.D. Many rulers of the medieval Swahili states (and their descendants to this day) called themselves Shirazi, to demonstrate a claimed cultural origin in southwestern Persia. Historically this appears unlikely. Coastal ruling houses seem to have claimed Persian ancestry in order to show that they were founded earlier than the houses of other local rulers with Arab origins. The name Zanj, Zinj, Zingion, and other forms, from which the name Zanzibar comes, may be of Persian origin.[18] One of the Swahili calendars is Persian; the Persian New Year festival, Nau Roz, is still celebrated in Swahili communities; and many of the technical terms having to do with sailing are Persian. All this argues for maritime contact, but hardly for political conquest.

The Arab influence on Swahili culture has been obvious. We may distinguish three main categories of "Arabs" (often so called and also self-proclaimed) in Swahili society.[19] The oldest claims to be the descendants of those Arabs who came mostly from the Hadhramaut and Oman before the arrival of the Portuguese in the late fifteenth century. They have for centuries been Swahili in speech and custom but retain their tribal and clan names. They include such ancient former ruling families as the Nabhany of Pate and the Mazrui of Mombasa. The members of the second category are descended from the Arabs who immigrated from Oman mainly during the eighteenth and nineteenth centuries, when the Al-Busaidi dynasty of Muscat subdued the Swahili coast and for a time ruled Oman from Zanzibar. The Omani made a distinction between those whose forerunners came from the coast of Arabia and those from its hinterland, only the latter always recognizing tribal and clan groupings. In East Africa each group accepted the authority of a sheikh who was both the chief of the local senior descent line and also the local representative of the principal tribal sheikh in Oman. The maintenance of the tie between Arabia and Zanzibar marked the Omani off from the "old" local "Arab-Swahili" families.[20] In Zanzibar, at least, many upper-rank Omani families clung to their Arabian identity: they were true colonial rulers and despised the local people, whom they exploited mercilessly. Yet the distinction was more apparent than real, and the Omani became inextricably linked to other parts of Swahili society. These Arabs are usually distinguished locally by the term *wa-Manga*, from the Swahili *manga* (literally, north) used to refer to the southeastern part of Arabia. The third category comprises those Hadhrami Arabs whose ancestors came from the Hadhramaut as petty traders mainly during the nineteenth century, prospered, and acquired wealth and high position.

Indians have settled in and traded with the Swahili towns for many centuries, and contact with India is clearly very ancient.[21] Both Muslim and Hindu Indians have been economically central as financiers in the ocean trade. The latter (usually known as Banyani) have been the more numerous, although some Muslim Indian groups such as the Bohra have been an integral part of the larger towns for many centuries. Unlike "Arabs," Indians are never counted as "Swahili."

People of slave ancestry are another important element in Swahili society. Even though slaves and their descendants have been marginal in social and religious terms, economically their presence has been crucial. In the northern areas slaves originally came from Ethiopia, whereas in the south they were taken from the interior as far as the Great Lakes and even beyond, and then kept as slaves along the coast or shipped overseas. There are also mainland Africans who have come to the coast and islands as free squatters. These last have rarely become Muslims and are not included as "Swahili."

The Swahili people contains other minor elements. In the Lamu archipelago the group known as Famao is said to be composed of the descendants of shipwrecked and marooned sailors (Portuguese, Chinese, and Persians) and local women; they are fully accepted as a very early component of the Swahili. Similar groups are found elsewhere on the coast, such as several "Portuguese" families in Pemba.[22] There are also Swahili from outside East Africa proper, of whom the most numerous are the Comorians from the Comoro Islands, as well as small numbers of Europeans.

Members of all these different groups inhabit the Swahili settlements along the thousand-mile coast, but their proportions and forms of incorporation vary from one settlement to another. No two of the several hundred settlements are exactly the same in their "ethnic" composition or history; and their varying forms of local, descent, and hierarchical organizations are linked to their ethnic composition. Those that have directly engaged in international trade have greater ethnic and hierarchical complexity than those involved indirectly or marginally; only the former had slaves, and they have been subject over the centuries to greater immigration and cultural influence from Asia. It is on this point that has hinged

the continual argument as to whether Swahili culture is "African" or "Asian."
Internal hierarchical distinctions are typically translated into ethnic terms, those
of higher rank being associated with mercantile wealth from the overseas trade;
with claimed Asian ancestry, Islam, and literacy; and with ever-changing sumptuary fashions of Asian origins. Conversely, those of lower rank are generally
associated with origins in Africa. Immigrants have come to the coastal settlements
from both Asia and the interior of Africa for many centuries.Although generally
small in numbers, the Asians' economic, social, and cultural importance has been
disproportionately large.

To attempt to enumerate these diverse elements in Swahili society would be
pointless, since most have long been intermixed and absorbed. The means of incorporation and assimilation have varied. Most immigrants have come to the hierarchically organized settlements, in which patrilineal descent is generally reckoned and they can form patrilineal groups side by side with those already there.
Settlements that comprise cognatic descent groups have accepted few immigrants.
The idiom of incorporation has been described in myth in terms of intermarriage,
and compatibility or incompatibility of modes of descent have been important
factors.

The Swahilis' Asian trading partners have been along the northern littoral of
the Indian Ocean, and the northern parts of the Swahili coast were the earliest to be affected by Asian trade and influence. The Swahili may be considered
to have become such with the coming of Islam, so that although pre-Islamic
settlements existed and contained some pre-Islamic Arabs, we should not call
them Swahili. Swahili identity spread from early sites on the Somali coast southward to Mozambique, a process that can be shown on linguistic, archeological,
and mythological grounds. The Swahili conceptualize it in terms of an actual
movement of groups of people, but this seems unlikely. The Swahili homeland
or place of origin was on the northern part of the coast and is always referred
to as Shungwaya. From there they are said to have moved down the coast during the first millennium A.D. Shungwaya is a central notion in the mythology of
the Swahili and their northern neighbors; from the Mrima coast southward it
plays no part in the myths of the hinterland peoples. Long conjectured to have
been at Bir Gao in present-day Somalia, Shungwaya is more likely to have been
farther south, on the mainland near the mouth of the Tana River. Some myths
mention Shungwaya as merely a stopping place at which immigrants from Persia
("Shiraz") landed and from which they sailed south to found various towns—a
view that supports the claim of non-African and pre-Arab ancestry. The Swahili
hold that in general their settlements moved southward from Shungwaya, and indeed certain elements of the population may have leapfrogged down the coast, as
once a settlement was established it would hardly have been abandoned except in
unusual circumstances.

There are three points to be made. Shungwaya was not a single settlement but
rather a region from which Swahili identity spread out; it was carried by traders,
in the sense that they brought existing settlements into the ocean exchange sys-

tem but did not themselves open them as new colonial settlers; and the name Shungwaya refers to the place of the earliest entrepots on which the trade was based, one of which was the famous Rhapta of the *Periplus* (see chapter 2). In this sense Swahili culture spread southward as part of the processes of trade and conversion to Islam. The Swahili were not composed of Asian merchant settlers, but they acquired their identity in response to the coming of Asian merchants—a very different matter.

In brief, the southerly "movement" of Swahili culture probably occurred not by the opening of new settlements but by the transformation of existing pre-Swahili settlements into Swahili ones as Islam moved south. Even if they were not "conquered" by Shirazi immigrants, existing settlements adopted Swahili culture so as to participate in a new, wider, and more profitable ocean trade that depended largely on the northerly towns, since it was only from them that ships could sail to Arabia and India directly with the monsoons. The adoption of a new identity and cultural elements is a more likely process than the actual migration of large numbers of people who either founded new towns or conquered existing ones by force of arms and ships. Such cultural adoption would explain some of the complexity of ethnic and "clan" mingling to be found throughout the coast, as well as the apparent age of lower levels of physical settlements, many of which show pre-Islamic lower strata covered by later Islamic buildings such as mosques and tombs.[23] Much the same process is visible today as Mijikenda, Pokomo, Zaramo, and other hinterland peoples, who wish to take part in the economic life of the coastal towns, become Muslims and so "Swahili."[24] We know little of the contemporary processes of conversion, but we may discern their material signs in the building of stone houses and town walls to make both physical and cultural boundaries against the "barbarians" beyond. All these matters remain the subject of continual and lively discussion among the Swahili themselves: as with any other multiethnic society, niceties of ancestry and hierarchy play a crucial part in the ever-changing rewriting of history to explain and validate the present.

THE MERCANTILE ECOLOGY

The Swahili have formed a middleman society in the two-thousand-year-old international mercantile system that has covered the northern Indian Ocean from the Red Sea to China and Indonesia. This system has been based upon the diversities between the African, Irano-Arab, Hindu, Indonesian, and Chinese regions, and upon the exchanges of commodities produced by one or two and required by the others. Most exchanges have been linked to clothing, food, housing, warfare, religion, labor, and precious metals.[25] Clothing includes an array of cotton, silk, and woollen stuffs, and such items as beads, ivory, metal wire, and animal skins; foods include the basic grains of rice, wheat, millet, sorghum, and sesame, the four "great" spices of cloves, nutmegs, mace, and cinnamon, and many palm products; housing and furnishing materials are mainly teak and mangrove woods, and with them may be included rock crystal, pottery, porcelain, copal, and orchella; military items include arms and gunpowder; religious needs are resins and gums for incense, and of course religious learning; labor needs were met by slaves; the precious metals include mainly iron, gold, brass, and bullion. East Africa is on the margin of the total trade area, but has been a necessary partner providing certain commodities that have not been easily obtained elsewhere. Its isolation and relative lack of financial sophistication (although this should not be exaggerated) made East Africa a region worth exploitation by outsiders, to its sad loss over many centuries.

This exchange system has been marked by international competition and cooperation of great complexity. The Swahili merchants in East Africa and their counterparts in Oman and India have been at its core, each group having its own continental forms of ecology, production, and transport. The nature of Swahili society has been determined largely by its ecology, but its trade needs have in turn determined ecological choices. An ecology is a social construct, and the coastal ecology and the modes of production and exchange based upon it have continually been reordered. A central factor in Swahili history has been ecological adaptation, the construction of ever-changing networks of productive and distributive complementarity in which different groups (whatever their ethnicities at different periods) together form a single exchange system, each occupying different niches. Each Swahili settlement has had to plan and achieve its own "portfolio" of resources that it controls, and of rights in and expectations of trade with external exchange partners. In addition, at any one time the whole must form a total balance between settlements in different parts of the coast, each of which may have its own trading partners and forms of production. This pattern must be translated into and buttressed by cultural and mythological complementarity, by intergroup relations couched in terms of forms of marriage, patronage, and joking relations or "cathartic alliance," and of ritualized mutual debts, obligations, and privileges. All of these are found both within Swahili society and in its relations with non-Swahili groups.

The Swahili exchange system has been based upon several main forms of production: gardening, fishing, grain farming, herding, hunting, gathering, mining, forestry, craft production, and slave raiding. Herding and gathering are important mainly behind the Benadir and Visiwani coasts; gold mining and slave raiding have taken place only in a few inland areas far from the coast itself; other forms of production are found in most parts of the coast and islands. Although they are not rigidly distinct specializations, each form of production has usually been limited to a particular section within the total system, typically defined in terms of ethnicity. They are linked by economic, political, and cultural ties centered on the entrepot towns, whose internal governments have typically included representatives of these various specialized groups.[26] Examples have been:

HUNTERS: Boni, Sanye, Makua, Kamba, etc.
GATHERERS: Boni, Sanye

HERDERS: Orma, Maasai, Somali
CULTIVATORS: all Bantu, agricultural Cushites
INTENSIVE GARDENERS: Swahili
FISHERMEN, FORESTERS: Swahili
CRAFTSMEN: all (ironsmithing: Makua, Maravi, Kamba)
MINERS: Zimbabwe Bantu, Kamba
SLAVE RAIDERS: interior Bantu, Zanzibar Swahili

All these peoples have at different periods formed part of sets of overlapping direct and indirect exchange relations, each set based upon a particular coastal trading town and often extending many hundreds of miles from the coast.

A basic and long-lasting characteristic of this system has been the imbalance in the kinds of goods traded. East Africa has until very recently exported almost all natural products, minimally processed to make them suitable for counting and measuring, storing, handling, and shipping: ivory, gold, rock crystal, mangrove poles, grains, hides and skins, gums, rhinoceros horn, and other items. Slaves were also counted as "natural," "wild," or "raw" products which needed some processing or domestication before being exported. Most of these items have come not from the Swahili settlements themselves but from the hinterland or interior. Some, including mangrove poles, spices, grains, and cowries, have come from the sea or from coastal plantations set outside the settlements proper; they have not been cut or grown by Swahili but formerly by their slaves and today by employed laborers.

Over a very long period this pattern of production and export has diminished the supply of African raw materials and human resources. Even if some of these have been naturally or potentially replenishable (ivory, human beings, grains), the incredibly large amounts taken have in the long run led in many areas to almost total depletion (for example, of elephants and human beings). The resulting stagnation of production, which steadily intensified during the period of Asian colonialism, was only stopped and regulated in the last few years of colonial rule and those of postcolonial independence.[27] One consequence was a perennial lack of political development in the African interior. The commodities from the Middle East, India, Europe and America have mostly been manufactured: cloth, beads, household furnishings and jewelry, weapons and firearms, and many more. Exceptions have been dried fish and coffee beans, but both of these are processed for export. The trade has thereby helped the establishment and profits of industries in Asia, Europe, and America and the enforced continuation of Africa's nonindustrial economy.

This trade has never been between two equal trading partners exchanging commodities at a central market and observing hypothetical rules of "pure" economic behavior. Goods from the interior have either been exchanged for imported goods directly at the Swahili towns or, more usually, have first been exchanged with intermediary non-Swahili traders of the hinterland who have in their turn dealt directly with the coastal towns. On the other side, goods have been shipped directly to and from the ports of Arabia, the Persian Gulf, and India, thence onward to inland Asia, China, the Red Sea and the Levant, and Europe and America. The Swahili have been the middlemen: as Alpers has written, "The [pre-European] trade of East Africa was governed by the congruence of different economic systems with different sets of perceptions" (1975: 203). The role of mercantile broker linked culturally to both sides has been filled by the Swahili.

Occasionally Asian and Portuguese traders ventured into the African interior, and of course African slaves taken to Asia were in immediate contact with those who bought them; but in general it was only the Swahili who had these contacts, and even then they made extensive use of intermediaries. The producers and consumers at the ends of the trading chain have determined the kinds, quantities, and values of items traded, and the Swahili middlemen have had to adapt to their requirements and demands. In addition, the Swahili have played a conflicting role in the trading chain: as exploiters of the peoples in the interior who have produced the commodities and the labor needed by the Arab and European colonialists, as allies of those very colonialists, and as the protectors of Africans of the interior as against the alien colonialists. Each side defines the role of ally differently. Until the rise of the Zanzibar Sultanate, both sides regarded the Swahili as necessary middlemen, and it was only during the later nineteenth century that the Swahili came to be feared and hated by many interior peoples.

An important part of the trading system has been transshipment between the coastal towns. The Indian Ocean trade has been dependent on the monsoons, which have determined the trading calendar. Since sailing ships require ballast in order to navigate the Indian Ocean safely, trade commodities that can act as ballast have always been in demand by merchants and captains: these bulk cargoes have included especially timber, grains, and slaves from Africa to Asia, and pottery, beads, and cloth in the reverse direction. Since all these have been of very great value, the African trade was important. Also, any ship would carry some of its cargo in the form of luxury items from Asia, such as porcelain, fine cloth, firearms, and bullion, destined for the Swahili towns themselves.

Rarely if ever has trade between the extremes of the network been direct. Cargoes have been made up, broken, and shipped by middleman merchants at the main transshipment market ports or emporia: Aden, Surat and the other Cambay ports, Malacca, Canton, and others in Asia, and the Swahili ports in Africa (where the merchants had the same role in breaking cargoes to and from the interior of the continent). However, the greater entrepots of the system were not in East Africa, with the probable exception of Kilwa as the transshipment port for gold, ivory, and slaves. Zanzibar later became the most important transshipment market and port for slaves, ivory, textiles, and firearms.

The interior exchanges, over which the Swahili could exercise little or no direct control, involved four categories of traders: the Swahili of the coastal towns; the intermediary traders of the immediate hinterland; the interior traders and caravaneers; and the original producers and consumers. This pattern occurred throughout the coast for most of its history, but changed during the nineteenth century with the intrusion into the interior by the traders of Zanzibar. The main productive regions in the interior have been central Ethiopia, the Kenya highlands, the lands around Lake Victoria and Lake Tanganyika, and the Nyasa-Zimbabwe region; each has been exploited by the Swahili at different historical periods. This picture must be qualified by adding that elephants have always been found in other areas without high densities of human population. Most of the ultimate producers and consumers were organized into kingdoms, the rulers monopolizing and organizing production and entering into forms of contract with the long-distance traders who exported and imported the trade goods. Control of the interior trade both demanded forms of centralized authority and in turn increased the power of the holders of that authority. However, they were not the actual carriers, who were specialist long-distance traders between the interior and the coast. The most important were the Kamba in the north, the Nyamwezi to their south, and the Yao in the far south.[28]

The peoples living immediately behind the coastal towns who have acted as intermediaries with the long-distance interior caravaneers have included the groups together known today as the Mijikenda behind the Nyali coast, peoples such as the Zaramo and Zigua behind the Mrima, and, in the far south, the Yao and Makonde. Their intermediary role has included economic and political partnerships with both the Swahili and the interior caravaneers, and the military protection of the Swahili settlements. Exchange of commodities between the Swahili ports and the interior producers has taken two forms. In one, intermediaries such as the Mijikenda made exchanges with the producers at permanent markets behind the coast, such as Changamwe and Kwa Jomvu behind Mombasa and Kao behind Lamu; the goods were taken to the ports (most of which were on islands) by slaves, who then carried import goods back to the markets. In the other form of exchange, the interior producers traded with Swahili representatives on mainland plantations owned by the lineages of the towns; the actual dealing was with free Swahili or trusted slave headmen, the goods then being shipped to the ports. These hinterland peoples were almost all culturally close to the Swahili, except in religion, but politically were kept at a distance as independent groups. For the ocean trade, the sailors and traders have been Arabs, Persians, Indians, Somali, Europeans, and Swahili. Just as the Swahili traders rarely went inland, so did relatively few of them enter the very long-distance ocean traffic until the advent of the Zanzibar Sultanate. But Swahili-built dhows, owned by Swahili merchants and captains, have always controlled the coastal trade and plied as far as southern Arabia and Madagascar. Money was not always used, standard barter values being recognized instead. The nineteenth-century Swahili of Zanzibar used money, as had the Portuguese and Indian traders of Mozambique a century earlier, as well as some early settlements such as Shanga and Kilwa. Financial brokers have been needed for both land and ocean transport. Most have been Indians, Arabs, and Europeans: the big profits, as in all colonial systems, have gone to outsiders.

All these elements were necessary for the formation and persistence of the coastal oikumene based on the Swahili towns. These urban nuclei grew by the continual cultural assimilation of groups attracted to their comparative wealth and security. This assimilation was accompanied by alliances with groups that chose not to enter Swahili society but to remain on its periphery.[29] Links between Swahili merchants and Arab traders have typically been by marriage and clanship, those with Somali, Indians, and Europeans being less personal.

A middleman society such as the Swahili has a fragile economy. The middlemen form separate communities with their own forms of social organization, provide the services of go-betweens, ensure the marketplace, and take their profit. But they are always at the mercy of the trading partners, who can at any time abandon or alter the patterns of trade and so weaken or destroy them. The trade has included the exchange of an immense number and range of commodities. These have varied from one part of the coast to another, depending on the availability of resources from the interior, and between parts of the Asian littoral at the other end. The Swahili have depended on these patterns of diversity of peoples, resources, and markets for the continuity of trade, but they could not themselves enforce them. The best they have been able to do has been to ensure that they have played their role as middlemen efficiently and predictably, and that the exchange routes have been safe and open as much as possible.

The Swahili have never formed a single state or empire but a complexly organized congeries of communities: no single town ever exercised total control. In the sixteenth and seventeenth centuries the Portuguese attempted to do so but lacked the power; in the eighteenth century the Sultanate of Zanzibar also tried but in the end failed. Later Europeans succeeded to some extent, and finally destroyed the Swahili as a mercantile society. Yet the internal structure of this society has persisted, and its mercantile history largely determines its form and the view of the world held by its members today.

A political state has a center and establishes a single political structure so that the outlying peoples and places are as much part of that whole as are those at the center. This process typically involves some forced movement and resettlement of both administrative personnel and subject and amalgamated groups, as well as the construction of the social illusion of a state ideology. Until the establishment of the Zanzibar Sultanate in the eighteenth century, the Swahili lacked the force to subject other peoples and form a state, but, more important, they did not have to. They have had no need to divide and rule, as the other members of the total system have been divided in any case. Swahili wealth has not been dependent upon taxes and tribute, but upon profits and commissions. The Swahili have been rich but politically and militarily weak, and thus an ever-tempting target for more powerful societies.

THE MIDDLEMAN SOCIETY

Swahili society has been shaped largely by the requirements of its place in international trade. The greater ports of the Indian Ocean have provided shipping facilities, warehousing, banking, legal facilities for enforcing contracts, military protection, and political neutrality and security, all necessary qualities of an "emporium."[30] How many of the Swahili port towns were true emporia in this sense is uncertain. Kilwa would seem to have been so, with its warehouses, its mint, and its internally powerful rulers. Not enough is known about the other medieval ports such as Mombasa and Pate; but early Arab and Portuguese records telling of ships and merchants from Brava in Malindi and distant traders in other towns point to extensive and secure movements of merchants over long distances (Freeman-Grenville [1962a]).

An emporium, or even a lesser port town, must provide many services. One is to accept imported goods and prepare them for export in either direction. The Swahili merchant lineages have acted as business corporations, processing exports and arranging for them to be ready for shipment on dates determined by the monsoons on the ocean side and by the rains and dry seasons on the landward side. Storage and breaking of cargoes have necessitated careful planning and organization. Most goods have required warehousing, although a few (such as mangrove poles) may be left outside at the waterfront. When most Swahili towns had kings, the ground floors of their palaces were used for storage, enabling the rulers to exert some control over the trade. This was the case in Kilwa, for example. But in Lamu, Mombasa, and Zanzibar, at least, more precious and less bulky goods have been stored in the Swahili merchants' stone houses.[31] Nineteenth-century Zanzibar slaves for export were kept in barracoons near the central slave market and the shipping jetties, but this was atypical. In addition, the Swahili have had to make complex mercantile arrangements: institutionalizing means for the exchange of goods and money, giving and getting credit, and honoring financial commitments and contracts with both sets of partners; ensuring the physical security of visiting traders; and maintaining facilities for victualing, watering, and repairing ships and caravans. They have also had to organize the exchange and consumption of imported luxury goods destined for their kin and townspeople. We do not know enough about the internal organization of the Swahili ports before the establishment of the Omani Sultanate in Zanzibar City to determine how they met these needs. One of the reasons for the success of Zanzibar City during the nineteenth century was that it could provide these services better than other Swahili towns; in particular, due to the size of its imports from the interior, from which caravan routes merged on Zanzibar, and due to its monopoly of the Mrima coast, its merchants could supply and accept full mixed cargoes. Zanzibar City also offered the protection of merchants' ships by the sultan's navy, and its excise and tax structure enabled it to charge relatively low customs dues on whatever goods it wished to favor.[32]

The Swahili have played the roles of brokers, taking their commissions and profits along with the risks involved in providing complex and often difficult services. But they have never controlled the actual trade. Merchant brokers in any societies have best flourished with a minimum of political interference and a maximum of political security and protection. The middleman role has typically been performed by various forms of narrowly exclusive corporations, whether unilineal descent groups and closely knit "families," business houses (often lineages themselves), or cooperative groups of agents (who again tend to become kin groups through the intermarriages of their partners). Societies permit these self-centered activities provided that the middlemen pay taxes, ensure that benefits trickle down to others, make charitable contributions, and purchase protection by exercising political ties with potential rivals and enemies. All of these factors have been a part of Swahili society and its civilization.

Relations between Swahili merchants and their trading partners have been personal rather than market-oriented. Exchange has been on an individual basis and the relationships typically have been long-lasting, often based on the marriage of an overseas merchant to a daughter of his host Swahili family. This pattern goes back as far as Swahili history can be documented: Ibn Battuta wrote of Mogadishu, then a Swahili town, that Swahili traders each had personal ties with Asian merchants, whom they entertained and accommodated in their own houses. His account makes several points clear. Both sides shared the common faith of Islam and its values of friendship, trust, and secure hospitality; these individual links, though based on exchange, were removed from public and commercial bargaining and concerned not with immediate payments but with credit and indirect financial ties; the ties were sanctioned by friendship and kinship (for marriage to take place, the two merchants should ideally share common clanship); merchants of both sides competed to create this tie with an opposite person of wealth, trustworthiness, credit, profitability, and honor; and finally, the ruler played a part by putting merchants together when he wished, as he was also a merchant and kept the most profitable deals for himself. Such matters as protection of harbors, provision of shipping facilities, and adjudication of claims may have fallen on local rulers or perhaps simply not been handled at all, but detailed information is lacking. Certainly merchants paid taxes and customs dues to rulers. The sultans of Zanzibar in the nineteenth century provided naval and military protection, legal and financial services, and took large sums in dues and taxes.[33]

Exchanges have involved commodities, yet the relations between traders and merchants have been based on ties of trust and modeled upon clanship and kinship. Friendship and interdependency have had to be translated into ties of "blood." This has been done by marriages between the families of Swahili merchants and Arab traders, on the one hand, and, on the other, by ties of clientship, fictive kinship, and blood brotherhood with African traders of the hinterland and the interior. Both sets of relationships have conflicted with the Swahili sense of their difference from non-Swahili and of the need for marriage partners to be of equal rank. Yet they also stress that a merchant patrician has in his very moral essence the ability to recognize the rights and dignity of others, and so to bend rules when necessary without losing his reputation and honor. Even today, after the demise of much of the trade, patrilineal descent groups in the mercantile towns have persisted over long periods as private corporations. They practice marriage between lineage kin and also use marriage to make far-reaching social and mercantile links with partners elsewhere. It has been a complex and effective system, paralleled by similar patterns in other societies on the peripheries of the earlier capitalist world.

PRODUCTION AND LABOR

The Swahili mercantile system has been based on certain kinds and modes of production and local exchange. The Swahili have produced goods both for their own consumption and in order to obtain commodities for exchange; they may not have produced most commodities themselves, but certainly they have organized, directly or indirectly, much of the actual production. Production, control, exchange, and use of labor have all taken the forms they have due to the Swahilis' role at the fringes of wide capitalist-controlled systems and to the ecological factors mentioned earlier.

Swahili settlements are of two main types, which I refer to as "stone-towns" and "country-towns." I discuss them in detail in chapter 3. Here I need say only that the stone-towns have in past centuries been inhabited by patrician merchants, recent immigrant Arab traders, and former slaves: these are the port towns of the ocean trade. Country-towns have been inhabited by fishermen and farmers, owning no slaves and taking no direct part in the ocean trade. I will discuss their economies later; here it is enough to say that country-town production has been and is essentially that of foodstuffs and some cash crops, which are consumed locally and sold at markets in the stone-towns. In much of the interior the mercantile investment in exports led to stagnation of indigenous food production in favor of hunting and slave raiding, but this has never affected the country-towns, which have had steady local markets for the items they have produced. Stone-towns have provided a relatively small part of their own food, formerly by slave labor, but most of that labor was used for growing export crops, mainly grains, cloves, and copra. In addition, stone-towns obtain some foodstuffs by local trade with non-Swahili hinterland groups. The pattern of Swahili society would obviously have been very different had there been no large-scale trade between Africa and Asia; and the complementary relations between stone- and country-towns provide the context for the differences in descent, marriage, religion, and other factors, the discussion of which takes up most of this book.

The term *production* is generally used to refer to food production, but other things are produced by the Swahili stone-towns, each of which has its own mode of production and forms of labor, planning, and exchange. Beside the organization of labor for farming, fishing, and seafaring, there is that for the stone-towns themselves and their buildings, sailing craft, furniture, utensils, tools, clothing, and forms of knowledge and learning. The reproduction of human beings has always been complex, the reproduction of free and of servile people following different jural procedures. Beyond production, the Swahili stone-towns have needed to process commodities for export and to store, guard, pack, load, and ship them. All three needs—production, processing, and disposal—have demanded a large and permanent labor force, although its composition has varied from one town and season to another. There has also been a marked division of labor in Swahili society: in general, women in stone-towns have not participated in either production, processing, or exchange outside personal tasks such as preparing cosmetics. In the past, virtually all the labor force consisted of slaves; in more recent years, slaves have been replaced by squatters and wage labor. It seems likely that there has long been a perennial shortage of free labor in the stone-towns. At one time this was mitigated by slave labor, but all labor requires housing, food, and clothing.

In the country-towns many of these needs have not arisen, because these tasks generally have been carried out by kin and neighbors. These towns have only very occasionally used slaves, squatters, or hired labor. Processing, storage, and exchange have rarely been technically complex: drying of fish, copra, and tobacco have been the most important requirements, but techniques and organization have been simple. Exchange has taken place at local markets and has also involved shipping by coastal dhows, canoes, and motor vehicles, usually owned by individuals or small groups of kin. Division of labor on the basis of sex and age has been recognized in the country-towns, but on the whole the economic roles of men and women have given them near-equality in production and exchange. The units of production have typically been nonspecialized and multiplex family, descent, and local groups.

Although slavery has ended, something should be said about its economic aspects: its aftermath remains crucial for understanding contemporary Swahili society.[34] Slaves were being exported over a thousand years ago, and the use of slave labor presumably was part of the coastal economy for the same length of time. The wealthier stone-town families kept slaves, and the rulers and other important men had large numbers of them. It is difficult to estimate how many slaves there were at various times and in various places, but the numbers were large. In the islands of Zanzibar and Pemba, the growing and export of cloves increased enormously after the 1820s, and by mid-century two-thirds of the islands' population were slaves. On the northern coast, the ruler Fumo Luti of Pate, who established the independent sultanate of Witu in the mid-nineteenth century, welcomed anyone who would settle with him, make farms, and help defend his state against outsiders. A European visitor estimated that some ten thousand slaves who had escaped from their owners lived around Witu, which would imply that there had been at least as many slaves as free people in the northern towns. Another estimate gives the number of slaves on the entire Kenya coast as a little over forty thousand, or 25 percent of the total population.[35]

The slaves used by the Swahili, as distinct from those shipped overseas, were rarely "chattel" slaves in the sense of being considered virtually inanimate things that could be used as the owner wished. Those shipped overseas were indeed chattels, hardly distinguished from animals, but for those kept on the coast there were categories of servitude. The two principal words for slave in Swahili are *mtwana* and *mtumwa*.[36] The former was generally used to refer to field and other outdoor working slaves, the lowest category who lived outside the towns in the fields and plantations. In the Lamu archipelago the plantations were on the mainland opposite the islands and produced large quantities of foodstuffs for export. Each slave was allocated a plot, the produce from which belonged to the owner; a hard-working slave might be given a second plot and receive part of the crops grown on it. He was also allocated a plot for his own food. In some areas a slave was allowed two or three days a week in which to work for himself. Many slaves used the proceeds from their own work to buy clothing and other items, and sometimes even to buy their own slaves. In Zanzibar Island the sultans gave out plantations, under freehold tenure, to their closer Omani Arab followers, and only they were permitted to grow cloves, using slave labor. On Pemba Island the system was a little different. There both Omani and Swahili (waPemba) grew cloves, only the former using slaves. The slaves' duties on the clove plantations were to tend the clove and other trees, to pick and dry the cloves in both the main season (August and September) and the lesser one (December and January), and to keep the owners' town and country houses supplied with food. Once these tasks were done, slaves were left very much to their own devices. They lived on the food they grew and could also sell their crops in the markets. They were therefore relatively free to move about the island: if they tried to escape, they risked being rounded up—their scarifications and clothing marked them out—and exported across the ocean, a fate far worse than living in Zanzibar. Other slaves were used on the rice farms, where labor was more continuous. An owner could also hire out his slaves to others as casual laborers.

The other category of servitude comprised the *watumwa*. The word *mtumwa* means literally "one who is sent or used," the connotation being that the slave was in some kind of personal relationship with his owner, and therefore used to perform domestic and other services within the town. Trusted slaves could also work on their own account and pay their owners hire or rent (*ijara*) equivalent to the wages needed for the owner to employ free labor. These slaves usually worked as sailors, fishermen, boatmen, artisans, hawkers, and port laborers; female slaves sometimes worked as prostitutes.[37] In some places—for example, Siyu—watumwa and poor people might be grouped together into the category *watwana*.

The second half of the nineteenth century was marked by changes in the place of the Swahili coast in the ever-widening capitalist world. Slavery was a crucial institution: its abolition not only spelled the near-ruin of many stone-town patricians but was also part of the process of bringing eastern Africa into the high colonial world. After abolition many former slaves simply stayed where they were, as subordinate members of Swahili households. These were more likely to be former house-slaves, who already had positions of trust, considerable security, and even respect, than former field-slaves who had never become members of their owners' households. The position of the plantation owners became financially difficult, as they now had to employ wage laborers in place of the slaves who had worked for nothing and had even fed themselves. This was a ruinous expense, although often necessary at clove harvest time, when many hands were needed. There developed the institution of "squatters," for whom the word *wageni* ("tenants") is used. Wageni refers to several categories of dependent or accessory persons: to "strangers," "guests," "tenants," and "squatters."[38] In many country-towns tenants are members of the cluster of settlements that comprise a particular "ethnic" group, such as Hadimu or Tumbatu: they are full kin who leave their natal villages elsewhere to reside with the "owners" (wenyeji) of the settlement, and their status is in no way servile. The squatters proper do not live in Hadimu and Tumbatu settlements but on the clove plantations; they reside and grow their own food there in return for an agreed number of days' work a year, without wages. The clove plantations of Zanzibar and Pemba were worked in this way from the turn of the century until the 1964 revolution. Squatters were both ex-slaves, often staying on the same plantations, and also "tribal" Africans from the hinterland, who were not so easily cowed or controlled. The term *wageni* is also used for immigrant wage laborers, who do not enjoy squatters' rights, but they are properly known as *wapagazi*. Such immigrants may in time acquire rights and even affinal ties with their hosts.[39]

I have mentioned the basic features of Swahili society: its long history of mercantile exchange and colonial domination, its multi-ethnic composition and the perennial conflict arising from claimed origins in Asia and Africa, its two main types of towns, its former reliance on slavery, and its powerful sense and knowledge of the past as people interpret it and see it manifest in the present. I turn to this history in the following chapter.

Chapter Two

The Merchants
and the Predators

THE PAST IN MYTH

Swahili society is literate, not merely in the sense that most of its members can read and write, but in the sense that they give high status to written documents that tell of their religious faith and past as a Muslim people. The Swahili view of this past, like that of any people, is encapsulated in both "myth" and "history"; but unlike that of most African peoples, it is founded in writing. This includes not only the Koran but also the "chronicles," which are essentially "myths" in the anthropological sense. They do not "explain" the coast as it was before Islam, since its acceptance was the factor that marked the acquisition of "Swahili" identity: Islam did not make a trading society, but it gave the society coherent cultural form and so "founded" it in the sense of the Swahili verb -buni (to construct), with the implication of giving the society an identity as a full and proper Islamic one. This identity is typically marked by the building of a congregational mosque. The myths refer not merely to the shaping of Swahili identity but also to the continual reformations of that identity over the centuries: once there has been a reformation, it subsumes the processes of any previous formation, so that most myths cannot be used to reconstruct "history" that is considered to be objectively "true," even though this is precisely what they are intended to do.

The histories of the incorporation of diverse groups to form the Swahili towns are a fascinating and tempting field to enter.[1] Instead, I will discuss how the Swahili themselves have envisaged the formation of their society. It has always been an amalgam of economically, politically, and socially diverse and unequal groups. We cannot now know for certain how the earliest immigrants were absorbed, but the main processes seem to have included occasional invasions by and assimilation of outsiders, and free and cooperative amalgamation of ecologically complementary elements. The latter was almost certainly the more usual until the coming of the Portuguese and their successor colonial rulers, the Omani Arabs. There have been certain idioms of incorporation: intermarriage, the forging of putative ties of descent, patronage, and conversion to Islam. These tell us how the process of societal formation has been recalled at later periods, and are mythopoeic rather than historiographical.

Myths are social constructs, and the intellectual problems that a society attempts to resolve by them throw light on the structure and history of that society. Swahili myths make order and coherence, and explain and resolve paradoxes in social experience that vary over time and from one town to another. At one period or place it has been important to show a pre-Islamic and "African" founding of a town, at another to stress Islamic and "Arab" founding, at yet another to stress an Islamic but "Persian" one. It is dangerous to generalize for the entire Swahili coast over many centuries. Anthropological analysis can show the main areas of contradictions and ambiguities in social process as the people themselves have seen them. These are the stuff of social history and can help us understand the society's past and present. Most Swahili myths are parts of written chronicles and are less fluid in content than oral traditions. As texts usually written in Arabic, they are given certain attributes of sanctity. They deal mostly with the founding and history of the ruling groups of the more important towns, and therefore with the origins of ruling families and their relations to those of lesser social importance. The same internal patterns are found in most of the myths, a sign not necessarily of common origins or links but of a common set of problems and meanings.

Together these myths, as they may be called even though many of the personages in them are actual historical figures, describe and validate the overall structure of Swahili society. Whether the actors are historical or not, the relations between them are expressed in particular mythopoeic idioms. Beside the idioms used, the selecting of certain events by the tellers and their ignoring of others show where they respond to and attempt to resolve basic social and historical paradoxes. These myths provide a categorization of Swahili social relations and the world in which they are situated, and also a morality by which conflicts and uncertainties in behavior may be resolved. They provide a moral schema or map of the society and its spatial, social, and historical surroundings.

Four main categories of Swahili myths can be distinguished. They include myths of the creation of the world; the poems of and about Fumo Liongo;[2] the written chronicles of certain towns, especially Kilwa, Pate, Lamu, Vumba, and Mombasa; and accounts, mainly in oral tradition, of the early relations between the towns and their external conquerors, the Portuguese and the Omani Arabs of Zanzibar.

The Swahili myth of creation—or the several local variants of it—does not need to be discussed here. Today it is obligatory to accept the "standard" Islamic myth, which has been well described and given a Lévi-Straussian analysis by el-Zein (1974: chapter 5).[3] Its main themes are the categorical social and moral distinctions between men and women, between free and slave, and between the realms of living people and the many kinds of spirits. As el-Zein shows, the theme of the myth and of the interpretations made of it in Lamu (we know little of the situation elsewhere) is essentially the moral distinctions between culture and nature, purity and impurity, and light (white), fire (red), and dust (black). El-Zein also suggests that free persons and slaves interpreted the myth differently; this seems probable, but his analysis contains little reference to any actual time period and has an air of historical unreality.

The chronicles of Fumo Liongo are important in the northern Swahili towns. The published materials are late variants of earlier versions that no longer exist. Fumo Liongo, the supposed author of the original poems, may not have been an actual historical figure, but he is always assumed to have been so.[4] He is generally taken to have been an "indigenous" ruler of the settlements north of the Tana River who resisted the immigration of strangers from Arabia and elsewhere anywhere from the twelfth to the eighteenth centuries. Today some scholars consider Fumo Liongo to have been a Muslim; others consider him to have been pre-Islamic; a few even claim that he was a Christian. Versions of the "histories" of settlements in the area are built upon these interpretations; these, however, miss the main points of the construction of this mercantile society.[5]

The scene of the Fumo Liongo epic is the Swahili "homeland," Shungwaya, the site of the earliest mercantile relations south of Mogadishu between "African" and "Arab" peoples. The people in the epic are the Swahili townsmen of the islands and mainland, the pastoralist Orma, and the hunting Boni. These categories together form a single system of the three ecologically complementary elements. Fumo Liongo moves between them, his behavior expressing the different facets of the complex of relations between the groups. He is part of each, born in the town of Shanga on Pate Island, driven out to the bush land of the Boni, and married to an Orma woman of the interior. In each situation he is an anomaly. In Shanga he is the sister's son of the ruler and so father sister's son to the latter's successor;[6] among the Boni a stranger and captive, yet also a hunter and a leader in a leaderless society; among the patrilineal Orma a "stranger" husband whose children could be neither fully Swahili nor fully Orma. The total system of three complementary ethnic groups, whose instabilities and ambiguities persist to the present day, is represented in the hero's unstable and ambiguous role. Behind lies the opposition of town/bush land and island/mainland, the first in each pair representing Islam and order, the second pre-Islam and disorder. By being part of all three communities, Fumo Liongo unites them by his person into a single, ecologically complete cluster; and by resisting the Arab immigrants, he gives the whole a Swahili identity. Many of the poems are wedding songs and refer to marriages of which the details are uncertain.[7] The weddings involve either Fumo Liongo himself or his sister, being either with a cousin, with a daughter or son of the ruler of the town, or with the Orma. The first two reflect the normal Swahili pattern of validating political authority, and the latter that of cementing ties of mercantile exchange with peoples of the mainland.

Four main themes are perceptible:[8] the opposition between the bush land and the town; the contradictory roles of the hero, a "wild" man caught in the context of "civilization," a hunter who is also a poet, the epitomes of the wilderness and of civilization; the opposition between pre-Islamic religion and Islam, and so between "African" and "Arab"; and the formation of the Shungwaya area as the original cluster of Swahili settlements that formed the earliest known trading area in East Africa. The hero stands at the conjunction of all these axes, which are basic to understanding Swahili society: its location, its occupations and ideologies, its origins, and its complex religious system. These spheres of ambiguity form the underlying themes of the Fumo Liongo poems, and since they are never resolved, the "historical" outcome remains unsettled. The "heroization" of the events validates the timeless identity of the Swahili people; and their being timeless means that they can refer to events of any period, including today.

Most myths of the making of Swahili society are part of the chronicles of the several towns. They include both myths of long-departed forms of Swahili society and accounts of more recent events. The chronicles are written documents, in Swahili, Arabic, or Portuguese. Most are copies, none seemingly older than two or three centuries, of earlier documents. The use of mythopoeic forms and idioms implies that they were composed (orally or in writing) as poems with mythical content and purpose, even though many of the events related in them have some historically "true" elements.[9]

As an example I give, in outline only, the myth of the founding of Kilwa, which exists in Arabic, Swahili, and Portuguese.[10] The chronicle is an account of the founding and rule of the so-called Shirazi kings of Kilwa, who seem to have settled there about the tenth century. The chronicle tells of the coming of the Shirazi in seven ships from Persia, each ship stopping at one of seven places where the kings established towns, including Mombasa, Pemba, Kilwa, and Johana in the Comoro Islands.[11] The chronicle states (I give only brief excerpts):

> When they arrived in the ship which went to Kilwa, they found it was an island surrounded by the sea, but that at low water it was joined to the mainland. . . . They disembarked on the island and met a man who was a Muslim. . . . It is said his name was Muriri wa Bari. They found there a mosque. . . .
>
> They asked the Muslim about the country and he replied: The island is ruled by an infidel from Muli, who is king of it; he has gone to Muli to hunt, but will soon return. After a few days the infidel returned from Muli and crossed to the island at low tide. The newcomer and he met together, and Muriri acted as interpreter. The newcomer to Kilwa said: I should like to settle on the island: pray sell it to me that I may do so.
>
> The infidel answered: I will sell it on condition that you encircle the island with colored clothing. The newcomer agreed with the infidel. . . . He encircled the island with clothing. . . . So the infidel agreed and took away all the clothing, handing over the island and departing to Muli. He concealed his real intention of returning with troops to kill the newcomer and his followers and to take their goods by force. The Muslim warned the purchaser. . . .
>
> So they set themselves to the task and dug out the creek. . . . The tide filled

it and did not recede again. Some days later the infidel came from Muli. . . . He saw the tide was up; and waited . . . for it to ebb until he could cross; but the water remained up and did not go down at all. Then he despaired of seizing the island and . . . went home full of remorse and sorrow. (Freeman-Grenville [1962b: 76–78])

This tale has three main characters: the autochthonous ruler, the Muslim go-between, and the immigrant Muslim from Asia. Muriri wa Bari presumably represents a trader already there, of unstated ethnic origin. He is given an "African" name and so he was not from "Shiraz." He is intermediary both as interpreter and also in ethnic, occupational, and religious terms, a trader who lacks political power. The tale makes it clear that there had been trade before there was political overlordship by immigrants. Muli refers to the "mainland" as distinct from the "island" opposite, Kilwa Kisiwani (Kilwa on the Island). The people of Muli are shown as hunters, the original "owners of the land." All three versions of the epic state that the island was obtained by an exchange of cloth, a major import. The immigrants considered that they had purchased the island, whereas the indigenes held that they had given only temporary rights of tenancy. The two parties required an interpreter, which implies that they differed in language and custom.

The process of settlement and incorporation is described in rather different terms in the Swahili version of the chronicle. Freeman-Grenville gives a succinct account of the incidents in this version:

The Swahili version [states]: "Then came Sultan Ali ibn Sulaiman al-Shirazi, who was a Persian. He came with his ship, his property, and his children. . . . They disembarked . . . and went to the headman of the land, Mrimba, and asked for a place to live in. . . . They gave presents to Mrimba of cloth and glass beads. This Sultan Ali married Mrimba's daughter, and lived peacefully in the town with his people. He took goods and gave them to the people . . . [which] were cloth and beads." The tale continues how Mrimba's daughter was persuaded to ask her father to cede the island to her husband. In return Mrimba agreed for such a quantity of cloth as would allow him to walk on it from the island to his new abode on the mainland. Once there, he repented and determined to make war on his son-in-law. But Ali had the Koran read in a magical manner so that the water rose and did not recede as it had done previously between the island and the mainland. Thus Mrimba was foiled and abandoned his warlike intent. He retired and settled on the river Rovuma to the south, but eventually made his grandson his heir, so that he inherited both Kilwa and his grandfather's mainland possessions. (1962b: 74)

This version adds to the Arabic one that the indigenous people were fishermen and farmers, not hunters: this was already a properly settled area. The name Mrimba (the same as Mrima?) may represent the people living along the coast. The immigrants both obtained a place of residence by the exchange of trade goods and also established marital ties. Mrimba then withdrew to the mainland. The

same idiom is used as in the Arabic version—the use of cloth to change its pos-
sessors from "barbarians" into "civilized" peoples,[12] and thereby to define and
measure boundaries and to establish a marriage. The affinal link was later transformed into a single patrilineal line of rulers. This was done through a visit by the
immigrant's son to his mother's father (an event that comes later in the account),
which may represent the negotiation for the son performing a correct cross-cousin
marriage with his mother's brother's daughter, who would have been a grandchild of Mrimba. The marriage would have recognized the superior position of
the indigenous group in terms of kinship, as being the first settled, and thereby
also in terms of ritual power over the local spirits of the land. But in terms of
political power as defined by patrilineal descent, the immigrants remained superior, the balance between the parties being formalized by the marriage and by
the acceptance of Islam.

We may discern certain principles. One is that, as in many myths of origin,
the events involve individuals and not groups. A second principle concerns the
idioms chosen to represent forms of incorporation and relations of alliance. The
main idiom is marriage, which implies a legitimacy of relationship that is lacking
in concubinage. Others include moral purity and impurity, as with the use of the
Koran against infidels; forms of political tribute and obligation, put into a kinship
idiom; and the use of cloth, which brings "civilization" to the formerly culturally naked.[13] All these idioms are statements about relationships of hierarchy and
social distance, and so of social boundaries. The myths of other towns, which I do
not have the space to discuss, use similar idioms and events with relatively minor
variations. There are either two or three protagonists: the autochthonous ruler
and the immigrant ruler, trader, or sailor; or the same together with an earlier
intermediary interpreter/trader. The simplest form of the mercantile relationship
has been that of merchants (the Swahili themselves) trading with both interior
and overseas partners. But in fact there were in most places three partners, none
of whom were properly yet Swahili: the interior and overseas ones, and also their
local hinterland intermediaries.

The attributes of the autochthonous ruler include controlling the mainland,
hunting, and bearing a non-Arabic name. The immigrant ruler is a person of
political account in his homeland overseas, with wealth in cloth, other trade
goods, clients, ocean-going ships, and an Islamic name. The protagonists meet on
an island that is also not an island, partially joined to the mainland and under the
control of the autochthonous ruler who controls the mainland proper. The spatial
distinction is very clear: the mainland contrasted to the ocean, with the island as
intermediate and liminal territory, not yet properly built upon and so not yet the
site of a properly founded "town." The protagonists are strangers, not as yet in a
proper social or moral relationship although linked by intermediary groups.

The immigrant asks the autochthonous ruler for rights to the island, to detach
it from the mainland both spatially and politically. The request is to make it not
part of the immigrant's original overseas realm but an intermediate and independent *tertium quid*. They come to an apparent agreement that the ruler will hand

over rights to the island in exchange for imported cloth or beads. Although still very different kinds of people, they are becoming more equal and are now in a social relationships by virtue of having made an exchange by a form of barter. The autochthonous ruler is no longer a "savage" hunter naked or wearing skins, because he has cloth. However, the exchange is unequal—manufactured cloth for unused or "natural" land. The autochthonous ruler leaves but intends to return to remove the immigrant: the island is still part of the mainland and the exchange is only a temporary one of cloth for usufruct, not for permanent alienation of the island. The contact is still between groups who are not yet wholly equal, who do not yet understand the other's intentions and motives, and time is still liminal: "history" has not yet begun.

The myths now come to the breaking of this paradox by warfare and magic. The first is an activity between members of different societies that must end by their being forcibly amalgamated or by one of them being destroyed: in either case they are no longer distinct entities. The second is a form of warfare at the mystical level. The autochthonous ruler attacks the immigrant, who responds by using Islamic magic to make the near-island into a proper island. Warfare is an extension of deceit, Islamic magic is an extension of sincerity; "tribal" warfare destroys the relationship between the trading partners, while Islam is by definition morally correct and all-powerful. The making of a canal between island and mainland creates a boundary, contrasted to the former lack of one and to formless spatial uncertainty. The definition of the island and its settlement by immigrant Muslim traders implies the creation of a town, a center of urbanity and religion.

The breaking of this part of the paradox leads to the establishment of a new political system controlled by the new rulers of the island—the first pattern of order, since the autochthon's realm was symbolically chaos. Now history is to begin, and there must be a recognized and validated relationship between the groups as equals. This is based upon intermarriage, and the remainder of the myths is devoted to that and to the orderly succession to the new authority by the legitimate heirs of both rulers. The immigrant ruler—or would-be and future ruler—marries the autochthonous ruler's daughter and receives the island as a marriage gift from her father. The son succeeds his father, and he is given a wedding gift by his father-in-law—the son of the original king—in his turn: this is the right to inherit the island and so to possess political power in perpetuity. The myths make the points that the immigrant ruling line acquires political legitimacy by marriage; that Swahili marriage is always between equals in rank (unlike concubinage), so that now both parties of the myths must be equals; that the mainland peoples remain as "mothers' brothers" to the Swahili town-dwellers, again an idiom that persists today; and that the islands become the permanent and legitimate sites of the coastal towns that face both ocean and mainland.

These accounts describe processes of social formation. One is the establishment of an ecological complementarity: overseas trade, hunting (for ivory), gathering (for gums and honey), agriculture (for food), herding (for hides and skins), and fishing. All these were found in the new Swahili settlements, but their complementarity in the myths had not occurred before, when each indigenous group had its own ecological niche. The myths define these roles: the indigenous peoples held rights over land, the immigrants had the right to engage in trade and to hold over-all political control, and the rights of the intermediaries were precisely those of intermediaries between the others. The myths tell of the marking of boundaries by walls or moats around the towns and so between them and the hinterland: a society without boundaries is one without orderly composition and structure. The idioms used to denote cosmological boundaries and complementarities, by which these relations were conceived and to some extent sanctioned, include war-fare, items of production and exchange, religion, and geography. The same binary structure occurs as in the myth of Fumo Liongo—town/bush land and island/mainland. The town of the island is now a "founded" entity, with on one side the waste of the bush and on the other the waste of the Indian Ocean.

From these myths we may again discern one of the basic contradictions that run through the structure of this mercantile society: the relations between the Swahili traders and their ethnically different partners in the interior of Africa and across the Indian Ocean. However, the two sets of relations have never been of equal content or weight. The former are seen as being with non-Muslims and the latter as with Muslims, there being a greater stated cultural gap in the former than in the latter, so that the relationship between Swahili and Africans involves an additional "ethnic" intermediary. The total pattern is not symmetrical, with the Swahili holding the balance in the center; the balance is asymmetrical and the problems inherent in this structure have been inherent in Swahili society through-out its existence.

The basic idiom of marriage in these myths of incorporation of diverse elements is repeated in later local traditions of the incorporation of Lamu into the Omani Sultanate of Zanzibar during the later eighteenth and nineteenth centuries.[14] There are certain differences between the two sets of accounts. The first deals with the establishment of a mercantile society, the second with the weakening of that soci-ety when it is subjugated by the politically superior colonial regime of Zanzibar. The first is told by the claimed descendants of the original newcomers; the second is told by the descendants of those who were subjected by later newcomers.[15]

The Omani extended their sway from Zanzibar by conquering the towns of the coast, and appointed local governors (*liwali*), who were members of the ruling al-Busaidi clan. The more important military expeditions were by non-Omani mercenaries, Baluchi, British, and others, who could not be made into royal rep-resentatives lest they build up local support that might later threaten the sultanate. But the liwali had to gain local support and legitimate their authority based on purely military force exercised by mercenaries. The locally acceptable idiom for achieving this was marriage: the then ruling families regarded this as the only means of making effective links. It is told in Lamu that the liwali and their fol-lowers wished to marry the daughters of local patricians but were invariably re-fused. Although Muslims, they were Ibadhi and not Shafe'i; the al-Busaidi clan, however powerful, was not accepted as socially or morally equal to the patricians.

Also, since the ideal mode of marriage was with paternal parallel-cousins, these marriages were not only undesirable but virtually proscribed. Finally, marriage was seen as closing potential antagonism, which the patricians did not wish to accept. We are here in the realm of recent history and the names told are those of actual persons and clans: yet it is the mythopoeic marriage idiom, in a negative context, that is singled out for comment.

These Swahili myths are essentially means of understanding and attempting to resolve—they are long-lasting precisely because they cannot in fact resolve—the basic structural processes and ambiguities within Swahili society. The Swahili have been able to use their wealth to form clientships and occasional marriages with partners; to use Islam as a political weapon; and to define the relationships between hierarchical differences and ethnic origins. These factors feature strongly in the myths. The validation of the Swahili position as middlemen is the main message, using ethnicity, moral superiority, and divine will to show the legitimacy of their mercantile activities and aspirations. The myths construct social space and time where there were formerly none, and invest them with veracity by placing their actors and events within named and recognizable places.

THE FLOWERING OF SWAHILI CIVILIZATION

Swahili notions of their past and its societal and cultural forms are important for understanding their society today. The rest of this chapter offers a brief historical outline of the changing nature of Swahili mercantile economy and society, of which the underlying structure appears to have remained remarkably constant.[16] A crucial factor has been the network of economic, political, and cultural relations between the Swahili and their trading partners. Before the rise of Zanzibar, the first truly powerful Swahili polity, in the eighteenth and nineteenth centuries, the Swahili had been in the orbit of Indian Ocean proto-capitalism. Zanzibar became powerful when European capitalism was establishing itself in the region, which soon became a fringe economy providing raw materials for the industries of Europe and India. The Swahili coast came to supply materials to metropolitan industry and to distribute the commodities produced by it. However, the middleman position of Swahili society enabled it to be fairly autonomous and to monopolize local trade.[17]

The Swahili coast has been part of the Indian Ocean trading system for some two thousand years, but its place within that system has changed markedly: from the earliest known mention of it in the first century A.D., when it was a mere trading outpost at the end of the then Levantine and Arab world; to its flowering during the first half of the second millennium, which might be called the Middle Ages;[18] through several periods of alien colonial and imperialist overrule; to its present economic and political decline as one small corner of a new Africa. For much of their history the Swahili have been a politically subject people, but the degrees and idioms of their subjection have varied from one period and local community to another.

In the first century A.D. there was published in Alexandria a navigator's guide to the Indian Ocean, in Greek, known to us as *The Periplus of the Erythraean Sea*. This is the earliest account of the Azanian coast, then merely a remote place at the limits of the Mediterranean world where trade might be carried on by those daring or foolish enough to sail there. The passage from the *Periplus* that refers to Azania has often been quoted and I shall not do so again here. It lists the ports from the Red Sea to the emporium of Rhapta, the last known place on the coast, and something of the Arab traders and the commodities in which they dealt.[19] The identity of Rhapta has been the subject of much argument, but recent work places it somewhere to the north of the Tana River, probably on the mainland opposite Manda and Pate islands, the land of Shungwaya and of Fumo Liongo.[20]

The items of commerce listed in the *Periplus* have been traded for centuries: ivory, tortoise shell, rhinoceros horn, and copra for export, some of which would be collected locally, and others obtained from inland peoples. Imported commodities included iron weapons, tools, and glass from Egypt, Europe, or India, and wine and grain from Arabia. These are all trade rather than luxury goods, and the standard of living of the colonists may well have been low: the profits presumably were taken by entrepreneurs in Arabia and Egypt.

The Arab settlers recognized some kind of overlordship or at least trading monopoly of the state of Himyar in southern Arabia. Rhapta may have been quite large, as Ptolemy the geographer later referred to it as a "metropolis," the only one in Azania. There is hardly mention of the local inhabitants, who may at that time have been Cushites: they were simply there, as trading partners, wives, and concubines, but of no concern in their own right; they spoke an African language and not Arabic. The main points of interest are that trade was being carried on between the East African coast and Arabia, and that Arab colonies and a mixed population of African and Arab origins were found on the coast. That is all we know of this distant region on what was then the edge of the Mediterranean world.

By the very end of the first millennium there had developed the coastal society that has come to be known as Swahili. The people rebuilt old settlements into stone-built towns and established new ones; they adopted Islam, which marked them off from the neighboring peoples of the hinterland and linked them to overseas traders; and they developed the wide networks of international trade and the institutions of an effective mercantile civilization.

Evidence for this early history is in both archeological and written records. Thieves have been looting Swahili ruins for centuries, and only in the last few decades has there been professionally competent excavation.[21] Since the ruins were of stone buildings and the items collected mainly imported porcelain, it was held that these settlements had been founded by immigrants from Asia. Most archeologists were selective, investigating the remains of stone buildings and mosques but not those of more temporary materials, and dating Chinese porcelain but not locally made pottery. The picture presented in their reports was of stone-built towns occupied by non-African migrants, mixing over time with Africans and so becoming an Asian creole society in Africa. More recent work has revealed a different history, shifting the emphasis from palaces and art objects to nonstone houses and objects of everyday use.

The earliest well-excavated sites are Shanga and Manda, facing each other across Manda Bay.[22] Manda has large and elaborately dressed "stone" (that is, coral) buildings and a sea wall of enormous blocks, each weighing a ton or more: its leaders could call upon a large labor force. Shanga was occupied by about A.D. 800, flourished for some four hundred years, and was then abandoned. Its Friday mosque was built about A.D. 1050, by which time an effective adherence to Islam was likely to have been becoming widespread. Shanga's earliest buildings were of timber, set around an enclosure in the center of which was a well. Horton has suggested that until the ninth century the ocean trade was with the Persian Gulf area; ivory, rock crystal, gold, tortoise shell, and slaves were exported there.[23] By about A.D. 950 there were stone buildings of dressed coral blocks and fired bricks. There are the ruins of 185 stone houses dating from about A.D. 1320–1400. At this time the ocean trade shifted to the Red Sea and the Levant, with the growing demand in Europe for ivory and rock crystal. During the mid-eleventh century the trade shifted back to the Persian Gulf and the towns of the Lamu archipelago lost ground both to Mogadishu (then a Swahili town) to the north and to Kilwa, the entrepot for gold in the far south. Horton suggests that Shanga and other settlements resembled in plan the fortified and sacred settlements (*kaya*) of the Mijikenda peoples to the south,[24] and that until stone buildings were made, they may have been occupied by Cushitic pastoralists who held periodic markets on the islands. We may surmise that Rhapta itself, as an emporium, was settled permanently while its satellite markets were not. Building in stone was a sign of permanent settlement, of mercantile wealth, and of a considerable organizational complexity.

The earliest settlements were in the north, nearest to Arabia and the Red Sea, spread southward to the Mrima coast, Pemba, and Zanzibar, and then farther south again. Most early settlements were on islands and creeks, and very few faced the sea. Allen has listed 20 towns (from all periods) with populations of over eight thousand people, 36 with populations of about thirty-five hundred, and 116 with populations of about fifteen hundred.[25]

The population of the coast may be said to have become "Swahili" by the eleventh century, with a general acceptance of Islam and the appearance of modern forms of the Swahili language. From the flowering of this civilization until its decline during the nineteenth century, the standards of living increased steadily, although the Swahili towns were not equal in size, power, or wealth. Until the Omani Sultanate of Zanzibar in the eighteenth century, the main trading towns were at first Shanga and Manda and then Pate, Siyu, Faza, and Lamu on the northern islands; Shaka, Ungwana, and others on the mainland near the Tana River; Malindi, Mombasa, Vumba, Utondwe, and many others on the central coast, with Kilwa in the far south; and Unguja Ukuu and other places on Zanzibar and Pemba islands. For centuries the greatest trading centers were Kilwa and Pate, followed later by Mombasa. The most spectacular objects from the earlier sites are perhaps the coins of many kinds,[26] and plates, jars, and bowls of Chinese porcelain.[27] Most pottery found at these sites was locally made: not everyone used Chinese porcelain. The earliest yet found is known as Wenje ware, dating from the second century, followed by that known as Kwale ware. There were used for cooking pots, storage pots and jars, eating bowls, boat-shaped lamps giving light from a cotton wick floating in ghee, and other domestic utensils. The more elegant porcelain was also used as decoration on tombs and in mosques and houses. The other common materials excavated are beads, mostly small red, blue, green, yellow, or black glass beads made on the west coast of India and used mainly in trade with inland peoples. Other domestic objects include glass rose water bottles from Aden; molded and inlaid Levantine glass; and seventeenth-century Dutch bottles. There are iron tools from India and copper cosmetic and toilet articles from Persia and Arabia. It seems likely that the local crafts of the coast found in later periods—the making of inlaid ebony and ivory chairs, silver and ivory door locks, copper- and brass-ornamented chests, carved wooden doors, and other objects—also existed during the Middle Ages. The people on the coast also grew and wove indigenous cotton.[28] The Swahili have always been literate, and they imported paper and ink from the Middle East.

A picture emerges of small local communities that lasted for many centuries and produced and brought from the interior various natural commodities that, after some necessary processing, were taken by overseas traders in return for consumer items; many goods, both imported and exported, were "exotic" luxury objects. The domestic standard of living was comparable to that found at the same time in much of India, the Middle East, and Europe.

For knowledge of these communities we are also dependent on the accounts of Arab and Portuguese travelers. Although Arab traders and colonists had presumably been Muslims from the early days of Islam, the wholesale acceptance of the faith by the coastal communities marked a qualitative change, which can be dated fairly reliably to the eleventh century. Early travelers' accounts mention Islam mainly to show that these communities were divided into believers and nonbelievers. In the early part of the second millennium they distinguished "white" from "black" members of the communities, but these terms seem to refer rather to free and slave rather than to believers and unbelievers. An account by the tenth-century Arab writer Al-Masudi shows that at least some form of Swahili was spoken and that the coastal settlements had become self-governing, with forms of sacred kingship; they contained both Muslims and non-Muslims.[29]

Al-Masudi and later Arab authors mention that the coast exported ivory, slaves, ambergris, copal, spices, leopard skins, tortoise shell, iron and pearls, and gold from the far south.[30] This was largely a specialized luxury trade carried on with Oman and other places that had large ocean ships which the local people lacked.

A thirteenth-century Chinese account states that the Swahili produced and exported ambergris, ivory, rhinoceros horns, gums, and spices in return for blue cotton cloth. Azania traded with other Far Eastern states in Indonesia and Malaya, and with Indian states such as Chola, between the ninth and twelfth centuries: the latter may have introduced Maldivian cowries, used in Africa as currency. By the twelfth or thirteenth century this eastern trade was in decline, perhaps because of the rise of Arab seafaring power in the western Indian Ocean.

The main historical and social processes from the first to the sixteenth centuries are fairly clear. First there was a "proto-society" of petty Arab traders and pre-Bantu Cushitic settlements engaged in trade with the Levant, southern Arabia, and the East. By the end of the first millennium this trade had developed, and Bantu elements of the society became the majority and culturally preeminent as "Swahili." As the ocean trade increased, so must the field of interior trade, and it seems likely that this led to the development of towns independent of the earlier Arabian overrule, however slight that may in fact have been. By the eleventh century Islam had become the local religion, and the building of towns in coral had become widespread. These developments led to the efflorescence of late medieval Swahili society, with the emergence of the still-remembered great ruling families. We can get some idea of how the merchants lived from the most famous of the medieval Muslim travelers, Muhammed ibn Abdullah ibn Battuta, who visited the Swahili coast in A.D. 1331. First he stayed for a time in Mogadishu, then still a wealthy Swahili town. The ruler of Mogadishu knew Arabic but spoke "the dialect of Mogadishu," which was most likely Swahili. People went barefoot except for him, and he walked under a silken canopy in splendid clothing. He was responsible for welcoming merchants and important visitors, the former making personal ties with individual merchant families of the town. The food and clothing of the wealthy were clearly luxurious; the food (described in some detail) was very like what would have been served in a Swahili family of good standing in any of the coastal towns during the present century.[31]

The town on which there is the most information for the fourteenth to seventeenth centuries is Kilwa, from both ibn Battuta and the early Portuguese who reached it at the beginning of the 1500s. Kilwa Kisiwani, "Kilwa on the Island," had two harbors that could take large sailing ships for trade in gold, ivory, and slaves. This trade lasted for over five hundred years from the early twelfth century. The Portuguese weakened Kilwa during the sixteenth century, but it subsequently revived and in the late eighteenth century became an important slaving town for the French Indian Ocean islands. By the late nineteenth century it was little more than a village and its site today is one of ruins, mainly of large public buildings: three forts, the palace, and four mosques, spread over an area of about a square mile. The "Great Mosque" has eighteen cupolas and eighteen barrel vaults, the finest medieval mosque in any of the coastal towns. The "Palace," a double-storied building set in a walled enclosure of some five acres, must have been an extremely impressive building, with large storage rooms. Most of the ruins show traces of

luxury, with courtyards, interior pools, and walls once covered with inset porcelain. The buildings of the well-to-do that survive as ruins were likewise built of
coral blocks, and were almost certainly surrounded by the mud-and-palm-leaf
houses of lesser people.[32]

Ibn Battuta wrote:

> Kilwa is one of the most beautiful and well-constructed towns in the world.
> The whole of it is elegantly built. The roofs are built with mangrove poles . . .
> people are engaged in a holy war, for their country lies beside that of pagan
> Zanj. The chief qualities are devotion and piety: they follow the Shafi'i rite.
>
>   When I arrived the Sultan was Abu al-Muzaffar Hasan surnamed Abu
> al-Mawahib ("The Father of Gifts") on account of his numerous charitable
> gifts. He frequently makes raids into the Zanj country, attacks them and
> carries off booty. (Freeman-Grenville [1962a: 31])

The "holy war" and raids into the Zanj country, the hinterland occupied by indigenous peoples, could only have been for slaves. Raiding for slaves would have
inhibited normal peaceful trade, and Kilwa was essentially a port of transshipment for gold and ivory from Sofala to the south.

In 1502 Vasco da Gama visited Kilwa, and the chronicler of his voyage wrote:

> The city is large and is of good buildings of stone and mortar with terraces,
> and the houses have much wood works. The city comes down to the shore,
> and is entirely surrounded by a wall and towers, within which there may
> be 12,000 inhabitants. The country all round is very luxuriant with many
> trees and gardens of all sorts of vegetables, citrons, lemons, and the best
> sweet oranges that were ever seen, sugar-canes, figs, pomegranates, and a
> great abundance of flocks, especially sheep. . . . The streets of the city are
> very narrow, as the houses are very high, of three and four stories, and one
> can run along the tops of them upon the terraces, as the houses are very
> close together: and in the port there were many ships. (Freeman-Grenville
> [1962a: 66])

The last sentence could almost be a description of Lamu at the present day.

What is lacking in these accounts are data on forms of social organization other
than kingship. It may be assumed that the basic social units were clans and lineages. The larger towns are today still so organized; there is ample oral tradition
that these groups go back for many centuries; and it seems very probable that
this was so for the reason that until recently these towns retained the same basic
mercantile functions. It appears likely that descent groups may originally have
represented lines of diverse ethnic origins, and so almost certainly would have
been ranked; that marriage was used to build trade and political links; that pre-
Islamic religious elements played a larger part in the total religious life than they
do today; and that slavery came to play a crucial productive role.

KINGS AND QUEENS

To these features may be added that of kingship. The Swahili have never formed a single polity, except unwillingly under the Sultanate of Zanzibar.[33] Until then they formed a series of mercantile towns, most with a king (*mfalme*) or queen (*malkia*). Lamu was governed by its patriciate and had no single ruler, a system that lasted until the turn of this century.[34] Country-towns have had their own organs of internal government. Several Swahili words refer to government: *hukumu*, government in the sense of a system of order and justice; *ufalme*, royalty, kingship, or dominion; *utawala*, rule, reign, or discipline; *ezi*, power or might; and *ta'a*, obedience to a ruler. Most are used in both political and nonpolitical situations, and in the former refer to juridical and representative aspects of government rather than to the exercise of absolute power by a single head of state. Few rulers seem to have been very powerful; even though traditions tell of early rulers of great cruelty, this is regarded as an aberration from the proper exercise of authority and may well be an idiom to exaggerate their power or to describe new and unwelcome forms of overrule by immigrants. Local chronicles tell of continual intrigue and dispute between royal lines and factions, perhaps a sign that rulers' positions were never very firmly held and always vulnerable to rebellion. Many of their efforts were devoted to keeping peaceful relations with dangerous neighbors, with whom they traded and on whom they were in the end dependent, although the Swahili rulers were never strong enough to control them. All of the rulers were weakened by the Omani Arabs during the eighteenth century and finally destroyed by them during the nineteenth century.

It is difficult to discuss Swahili kingship because we know little about how it actually worked in any particular town. The literature refers to kings, sultans, queens, wazirs, shahs, and other titles for various political officials, many from Persian and Arab models. We can distinguish three main categories of officials: those responsible, respectively, for relations with outsiders, for internal order, and for religious and legal matters. The important posts of military and naval leaders and of advisers responsible for finance tended to be hereditary and attached to descent groups representing a balance between "indigenous" and "immigrant" groups; juridical and ritual authority at the higher levels was typically held by the same person,[35] perhaps appointed for talent as much as for family affiliation. Above them was generally a hereditary ruler, a sacred and largely titular figure whose office represented the unity and continuity of the town. An army or navy included both free and slave men; the ships were dhows carrying soldiers, and became armed vessels only after the advent of the Portuguese. The finances of a town were the contents of the "purse" (*mkoba*) or "treasury" (*hazina*) of the ruler, but there was official machinery both to accept tribute and on occasion to find tribute for a conqueror. These petty states were organized by patrimonial authority, and state officials were royal kinsmen or representatives of constituent groupings rather than bureaucrats. Subordinate settlements were typically controlled by governors who were usually royal kinsmen, and there were often widespread relations of tributary recognition and of blood-brotherhood. The tales of "empires" extending far along the coast are based on recollections of these fragile relations, which were largely devoid of actual political power; they were loose trading confederations, although certainly towns such as Pate and Mombasa did at times muster armies and fleets.

The traditional "Shirazi" kings are exemplified by those of the early towns of the islands of Zanzibar, Tumbatu, and Pemba. The Hadimu of southern and central Zanzibar Island were ruled by kings with the title mfalme, the word for supreme ruler. They were also called *mwenye*, "owner," followed by their personal names. These kings, mentioned in the Portuguese records, once reigned at Kizimkazi or Unguja Ukuu ("Great Zanzibar"); they moved to the site of the present Zanzibar City and were there when the Omani came; next they moved (or were moved) a few miles away to Bweni and then to Dunga, where the ruins of their palace are found. The last mfalme proper, Hasan II, came to an agreement with the Omani sultans that, in return for annual tribute, they would leave him with internal authority over his people and not enslave them. Hasan II was married to Mwana wa Mwana, the last queen of the people of Tumbatu Island; we do not know whether they were cousins, nor whether she was a royal widow or regent. Hasan was succeeded by either his brother or his son, who held the title of *Mwenye Mkuu*, "the Great Owner." It would seem that in this case he did not assume the title mfalme, perhaps because that might have made him appear equal to the Omani sultan. This Mwenye Mkuu, Muhammed bin Ahmed, ruled at Dunga until his death in 1865. His son, the last Mwenye Mkuu, exercised little authority and died after eight years, leaving only daughters who did not succeed. The ruler had a council of elders, apparently consisting of his senior kinsmen. These kings are remembered as having great powers of magic that they used to protect their people.[36]

Part of the governmental organization of Mombasa still nominally exists.[37] The Mombasa polity was not a single group within a bounded territory but rather twelve groups of Swahili composing two confederacies at the core, recognizing the political and religious influence of a ruler in whom was vested central but limited authority to act as their representative in dealing with external powers. The twelve groups are each known as *mji* or *taifa*, words meaning literally a "town" and here referring to peoples living as single units on and immediately behind Mombasa Island; none seems to have been more than a thousand strong. They still exist, known as "The Three Towns" and "The Nine Towns." At one level they have been independent units of self-government, each headed by a sheikh from a particular lineage. The two confederacies are known as Mvita (or Mombasa, comprising "The Nine Towns") and Kilindini (the area of the main modern harbor, comprising "The Three Towns"). Each is headed by a *tamim*, that of Kilindini acting as president of a council of all twelve sheikhs, with that of Mvita as his deputy. In the past no one person exercised more than delegated authority and then only in times of trouble, such as dealing with obstreperous foreigners, for which the council appointed the "king" from outside their number.

Outside this inner circle, immediately behind Mombasa Island yet part of the wider Mombasa polity, live the Mijikenda ("Nine Towns") peoples, most of whom have refused Islam and have retained their cultural autonomy. Each of the nine groups has a fortified military and a religious center known as *kaya*.[38] The Mijikenda are traditionally linked to the Swahili of the city as clients, each constituent group being linked to a particular taifa and given a say in the selection of the tamim of the two confederacies. The Swahili gave them protection and gifts of cloth, and in return they protected Mombasa against raiding Maasai and Orma and traded directly with the Kamba and other inland peoples. The Mijikenda took the risks but also made profits, sharing them with the Swahili, who then took even further profits themselves from the ocean trade. As with all the Swahili stone-towns, Mombasa was a nucleus of a sphere of trade and influence: trade is what mattered and not political power as such.

There were formerly four other powerful polities, those of Kilwa, Vumba, Pate, and Lamu, on which information has been published.[39] Except for Lamu, which I have mentioned earlier, all were basically similar to those I have just described.

The Mrima coast south of Mombasa has been the site of many other small merchant towns. All have had their own various forms of government, but none ever had much power. Whereas Mombasa, Pate, and Lamu have been inhabited mainly by Swahili only, on the Mrima coast there has been a different pattern. Local non-Swahili groups have also lived in and near the towns and regard themselves as their citizens. Oral tradition claims that they were founded by immigrant "Shirazi," who made pacts with and paid subventions to the local peoples for rights to build and trade. These towns were not so much "governments" as licensed trading enclaves. They were taken over in the nineteenth century by the Zanzibar Sultanate, which established governors (liwali) from the royal dynasty; *kadhi* (judges), who were typically Omani; and *jemedari* (military commanders), mainly Baluchi. Today little is left but traditions, some regalia, and ruins of larger houses; the settlements are little more than fishing villages and market and local administrative centers.[40]

The most powerful of all polities has been that of the Sultanate of Zanzibar. Although it must be counted as "Swahili," the sultans tried to preserve their own Omani Arab identity and scorned their local subjects as "People of the Coast." Zanzibar was essentially a trading empire based on the patrimonial authority of the rulers, who regarded it as a personal fief for their own profit. They subdued the coastal towns and then ruled either through local immigrant rulers who were originally Omani themselves, such as the Mazrui of Mombasa, or through appointed governors who were members of the al-Busaidi clan. There is no need to present any further account of them here.[41]

Despite differences between these traditional forms of government, the regalia associated with them (except for the Zanzibar Sultanate) were remarkably similar. The royal regalia seem usually to have been possessed by the citizens rather than by the rulers, who were merely allowed to use them on occasion in order to provide a sense of continuity and extra-human validation apart from the life spans of their holders. These insignia, considered historically to go back to the earliest "Shirazi" kings, symbolically contained the power of kingship and so were considered superior to merely human and frail rulers. They varied from one town to another but seem always to have included the *siwa*, the great side-blown horns or trumpets of ivory, bronze, or wood; drums; and chairs of state made of ebony inlaid with silver, the *kiti cha ezi* (chair of power).[42] Besides having the use of regalia, rulers wore special and rich clothing (particularly scarlet cloth); they were accompanied by retinues of officials, musicians, and specially clad and armed slaves; and they are said to have had large harems. Clearly there was much emulation of Arab models, as signs both of power and of long ancestry; but this does not mean that they were themselves Arabs. Little of this speaks of real power, and indeed we may see the rulers as merchants in their own right: much of their power may have lain in their right to allocate new traders to local merchants or to monopolize them for their own profit. The many variations in the actual organization of the polities have reflected differences in ethnic composition, kinds and frequencies of immigrations, wealth, and commercial relations with trading partners, with one another, and with the Portuguese and early Omani conquerors.

Pre-Omani Swahili kingship throws light on the nature of this mercantile society. Profit, not power, was what counted, and the towns gave their rulers as little authority as they could: they were merchant-princes whose main duties were to act as representatives vis-à-vis other states. These petty states were physically very vulnerable and soon collapsed once outsiders with naval and military power came to the coast and took their privileged mercantile position from them. Although tales of vast Swahili empires are in the realm of fantasy rather than history, these petty states were not isolated. They frequently made formal alliances that were written on fine leather in Arabic script and signed by the rulers or their representatives in a mixture of ink and their own blood: the oath of alliance was a solemn one. These treaties were for specific ends only and were rarely long-lasting, but they reveal a latent political consciousness that extended beyond individual settlements.

A final point deserves mention: the Swahili queens, who feature in many chronicles and myths as the earliest Swahili rulers. A basic problem in Swahili history has always been that of the relationships between "African" and "Asian" elements, and these queens, known always by the title *mwana*—meaning son or daughter, but normally used to refer to a senior woman of high rank (Sacleux [1939: 639])—were presumably the senior women of the autochthonous ruling lines of the towns. They are frequently reported as marrying immigrant male rulers and so effecting the necessary link between the African and Asian elements. Since the two are not mutually exclusive, a queen might be the last child of an autochthonous royal family, or even a royal widow or a regent, but it is surely significant that virtually all queens are personages of myth rather than of historical record. Certainly they are hardly evidence of a conjectural matriarchy, as is often assumed.

THE COLONIAL OVERLORDS

The Swahili trade finally aroused the envy of other mercantile powers, which realized that supremacy in trade required supremacy in military and political relations. After many centuries of independence these settlements were to be weakened, conquered, or destroyed by the Portuguese and the Omani Arabs. The Swahili medieval world came to an end. Swahili society has persisted, but for more than four centuries as part of the Arab and European colonial worlds.

The outlines of the Portuguese and the later Omani political hegemonies over the Swahili coast have often been reported. I wish to discuss the consequences for the Swahili towns of being incorporated into these colonial states, and here our information is sketchy and often lacking. Neither the Portuguese nor the Omani cared much about the Swahili except as people to be exploited and overcome by force when necessary and possible. Information comes from historians who have worked on the conquerors' records and have typically not interpreted the Swahili side. Nonetheless, we can perceive the steady economic impoverishment and political weakening, the development of a wider society, and the stubborn persistence of Swahili identity and civilization. Other aspects of social life such as patterns of marriage may not have been much affected until the present century; and at times parts of the coast have undergone economic and political revival. Swahili decline was brought about not so much by violent confrontation (although this did occur) as by the loss of the control of economic and political activities to the colonial rulers.

The Portuguese came to find gold and spices, to seek the court of the legendary Christian king Prester John of Ethiopia, and to replace Islam with Christianity. They rounded the Cape of Good Hope in 1497, and in the following year an expedition under Vasco da Gama sailed up the East African coast past Kilwa to Mombasa and Malindi, and then across the ocean to Goa. His reception was hostile at Mombasa but friendly at Malindi, events that were to have long-term consequences, since Malindi was later to have the Portuguese as allies against Mombasa. For the first time a powerful outside ally was to affect the balance between competitive Swahili towns.

There was a Portuguese presence on the Swahili coast from 1498 until 1729.[43] They brought about a decisive change in the entire Indian Ocean trade area. Except for Arabian pirates, the Portuguese were the first in the western Indian Ocean to undertake trade by naval force, using armed fleets whose firepower was at the time devastating, whether against other ships or local ports. However, the Swahili never completely lost their trading position, for four reasons: the Portuguese were very few; their administration was inefficient and corrupt; only the Swahili had the knowledge and experience to organize the trade with the interior; and, except in the far south, the Portuguese hardly penetrated beyond the coast itself. They soon realized that the spice trade was disappointing and devoted most of their efforts to the south, based on the island of Mozambique and the Zambezi routes into the interior; they built a fort at Sofala as early as 1505. This region was far richer in gold, ivory, and slaves than the north, and Mozambique lay directly on the safest route between Portugal and India. The Swahili presence here was relatively weak, and the Portuguese found it easy to displace the existing Swahili traders south of Cape Delgado. Except for Mombasa, the key to controlling the ocean trade, where they built Fort Jesus at the end of the sixteenth century, the Portuguese presence was weak and sporadic.[44] Their exploitation of East Africa never had the priority given to India, and they lacked force to carry out any sustained program of control. They could sack a town and did so on occasion, as much out of bad temper and a sense of Christian duty as for any other reason. They compensated for their military weakness by using some towns as allies against others, changing and manipulating these alliances to their own advantage; we know little of the other side to these alliances, in which the towns themselves manipulated the Portuguese.

The size of the ocean trade of the period is almost impossible to estimate, but it was large and not merely the exchange of petty goods across a local backwater. The main exports were gold, ivory, and slaves, most being shipped to Cambay, the then capital of Gujarat, and elsewhere in India. Sofala was only one port, although important: the total trade controlled by the Portuguese must have been very substantial.[45] To pay for these commodities the Portuguese, like the Arabs and Swahili before them, used cloth and beads, mainly from India. The Swahili imported other goods also, as much for their own use and for trading with other Swahili towns as for trading with the inland peoples. These goods included pottery and porcelain, incense (used both for ritual and for caulking boats), cloth, glass, and perfumes. They came from many places: China, India, Persia, Arabia, and the Levant.[46]

The Portuguese retained Mozambique until the mid-twentieth century,[47] but after many local revolts and the loss of Mombasa to the Omani, they finally left the main Swahili coast in 1729. They were the first representatives of international merchant capitalism to come to East Africa. Especially in the far south, they were more ruthlessly effective than any of their predecessors (although not holding a candle in that regard to the Omani Arabs who followed them) both in removing natural resources and also in switching much local production to supplying items for export.

In general the Portuguese did little on the Swahili coast except to destroy much of what they found there. They were corrupt, cruel, and incompetent, although at times also impressively courageous. They left behind them little but resentment, some loanwords in the Swahili language, and even today local remembrance of their presence. They left their remarkable forts, ruins of churches, wells, and farmhouses, and the navigational pillars that marked their claims of sovereignty. Otherwise they created little and destroyed much. A Swahili saying of the time, using the name Manoel by which they seem generally to have been addressed, runs,

Enda Manoel, ututukiziye,
Enda, na sulubu uyititiziye.

(Go away Manoel, you have made us hate you, go, and carry your cross
with you.)

The expulsion of the Portuguese led first to a revival of many Swahili towns,
but the entire coast was soon transformed by the Omani Sultanate of Zanzibar.
Oman had a long interest in East Africa as the source of slave labor for irrigation
works. Omani moved to Zanzibar during the eighteenth century following dynas-
tic conflicts in Oman, when the religious political element lost power to a new
economic elite. The capital was moved from Muscat to Zanzibar in 1832, and the
state was finally divided in 1856, at the death of Sultan Seyyid Said ibn Sultan
al-Busaidi. The Omani came to realize that opportunities for wealth were better
in Africa than in Oman, and the increased trade in slaves and ivory during the
eighteenth and nineteenth centuries was a response both to increasing mercantile
development in Asia and also to the spread of a world capitalist system controlled
by Europe. Zanzibar, with its pure water, good harbors, and central position on
the coast, was ideal; and it was there virtually for the taking. The growing domination by the sultanate slowly choked the trade of the other Swahili areas: first
Mombasa and the Nyali and Mrima coasts, then Kilwa, and finally the Lamu
archipelago. As Zanzibar assumed the leading role in the traffic in slaves, ivory,
and firearms, it left to other towns trade in grains and mangrove poles; but by
establishing customs posts along the coast and the Mrima monopoly,[48] the sultans
took their share of the profits.

The Omani colonial empire in East Africa lasted for almost two and a half
centuries. Many accounts of the Omani Sultanate of Zanzibar have been written, and there is no need to repeat them here.[49] The Zanzibar Sultanate was a
mercantile colonial state whose rulers realized that to control the economy required the political subjugation of local towns. They tried, as the medieval Arabs
had not, to remain aloof from the local Swahili, whom they ruled and regarded
as unorthodox Muslims lacking in Arab physical purity. But they soon came to
speak Swahili and became Swahili themselves: their dependence upon their subjects as allies against the peoples of the interior ensured that their first attitude
did not long persist. The process of Omani control of the coast was determined
largely by the fact that the autonomous Swahili towns were economic and political rivals with continually shifting alliances. They all traded in much the same
items and competition was endemic. The Omani, who were skilled at the policy
of divide and rule, could not merely conquer a single central Swahili town and
thereby control the entire coast, but had to deal with each town individually—
one of the problems that had finally defeated the Portuguese. They established
forces and customs posts along the coast, but hardly interfered in the internal
government of Swahili towns, placing their own local representatives and troops
to enforce at least a token domination. They left the towns a proportion of the
revenues and relied on them to keep the peace and to ensure the perpetuation of
the all-important trade.

The complex history of the defeat of the local ruling dynasties, especially the
Nabhany of Pate and the Mazrui of Mombasa, need not be repeated here.[50] The

Nabhany were controlled by the 1820s and the Mazrui subdued by 1837. In the south the prize was Kilwa. The sultan of Kilwa was left in office as a puppet under an Omani governor who was virtually independent and became a supplier of slaves to Bourbon, Réunion, and Nossi-Bé. Kilwa had an unremitting flow of slaves brought to it by the so-called *ruga-ruga*, marauding gangs of uprooted people disturbed by the Ngoni wars to the south.

The sultanate became the most powerful state in coastal history and the first to achieve an effective hegemony over the entire coast. After the division of the Omani empire between Muscat and Zanzibar, both continued to be ruled by the same al-Busaidi dynasty, and Omani Arabs moved freely between the two places until the middle of the twentieth century. In 1870 Seyyid Barghash ibn Said al-Busaidi became sultan, and during his eighteen-year reign the sultanate became a world-famous and wealthy state. In 1873, under British pressure, he signed a treaty prohibiting the export of slaves from his dominions; although the actual ownership of slaves was not abolished except in the case of non-Muslim British subjects, their legal replenishment was. Slaves were kept in ever-larger numbers to work the plantations of cloves, grains, and sugar along the coast, thereby changing the basic economy to one of plantation slavery rather than of slave trading. As Sheriff has put it, the mid-nineteenth century saw the internalization of slavery (1987: 34). With the increasing demand for ivory in the West, especially the United States, the ivory trade became ever more important, leading to weakening of indigenous farming in the interior and the decline of elephant herds. In the second half of the century the import of firearms, ammunition, and gunpowder became important both because it was profitable and also because the trade affected the patterns of control and extension of caravan routes in the interior.[51] The Omani-controlled trade became more diversified with the export of rubber, gum-copal, orchella, cloves, sugar, and many resins, oils, and grains. After some years the volume and value of these exports, many being plantation crops, surpassed those of the older trade in slaves and ivory, and the middleman role of the Swahili became less important. The larger ports such as Zanzibar, Mombasa, Tanga, and later Dar es Salaam flourished, especially once the means of shipping changed from Arab and Swahili dhows to European steamers. The lesser ports dwindled in importance and many once busy places like Kilwa and Pate stagnated. Finally slavery itself was abolished, in 1897 in Zanzibar and Tanganyika and in 1907 in Kenya. Despite widespread opposition from the Omani and the Swahili patricians, the basis of much of the wealth of the Swahili towns was destroyed as part of the movement from small-scale rural production to plantation production controlled by Omani, Indian, and European financial houses.

The second half of the nineteenth century saw a marked change in the social structure of the Swahili coast, with the establishment of a plantation-owning aristocracy; at first this comprised members of the ruling dynasty and the local Swahili patrician families, but by the end of the century they had given much ground to new plantation owners, most of whom were of slave and immigrant origins, and in later years also to European companies. These developments estab-

lished a new form of social hierarchy, with a class of large-scale landed proprietors and forms of immigrant labor from the poorer coastal areas and the interior.
Many ex-slaves had no land of their own[52] and became "squatters" on the plantations; others acquired plots near the towns, occupying an ambiguous social
position as *wazalia*, "those born in the country." Although the urban merchants
lost wealth and power to the plantation owners, until the abolition of slavery they
kept much of their position because the latter had to buy slaves through them.
But as the years passed slaves moved increasingly from the towns to the plantations as free laborers and even landowners themselves, and after the abolition of
slavery the slave-merchants' role was doomed. Swahili merchants invested capital
as loans to landowners, but by the end of the century had been ousted by Indian
financiers. This period also saw the greatest influx of poor Hadhrami immigrants
from southern Arabia,[53] who by hard work and willingness to trade with ex-slaves
and other marginal elements of society acquired wealth as traders. They are today
economically the most important sector of the total Swahili population.

Despite continual agitation against Omani overrule,[54] economic control by
Zanzibar grew increasingly effective. It was achieved largely by taking from the
Swahili patricians their rights in land and their control of the international trade.
The presence of Omani governors (liwali) and their Baluchi and other mercenaries was bitterly resented. The governors built forts but found it difficult to
do much more than make an uneasy accommodation with the patricians, who
steadfastly refused to allow the intruders to incorporate themselves into local
society by marrying their daughters. By 1886 Seyyid Barghash had established
120 customs posts along the coast and so ensured his control over the export and
import trade. But inland much of the immediate hinterland was largely depopulated by tribal wars and slave raiding, and it was beyond the military capability
of Zanzibar to control the more distant interior directly. Instead the sultans made
alliances with the rulers in the interior, and Arab and Swahili traders and their
caravans built up wide networks of routes to the coast and continued to provide
middleman services between the African continent and the outside world. The
Zanzibar-controlled Swahili state was a system of mercantile exploitation rather
than a political empire.[55]

The third quarter of the nineteenth century marked the apogee of the Zanzibar Sultanate in producing wealth for the sultans and their immediate followers.
Several factors led to its decline: the destruction of many of the natural resources
of the interior; the resentment of the Swahili towns at being left out of much of
the new prosperity and at the attacks on the slavery on which so much of their
wealth depended; and the moving into their preserve of European and American
merchants who were both allies and competitors of the sultans. This was a period
of great disruption, strife, confusion, and local economic stagnation, despite the
wealth and ostentation of Zanzibar itself.

The Zanzibar trading network broke down in the last decades of the nineteenth
century and the interior communities set up lawless and cruel petty areas of influence of their own. The slave trade had virtually ceased, leaving vast numbers of

local African slaves, war captives, and refugees to be exploited as local laborers and ivory carriers to the coast, with great cruelty and loss of life. This was the other side of the Swahili coin: their brief but brutal exploitation of the disorganized and demoralized interior peoples. It is little wonder that at the time the advent of European colonial rulers and missionaries appeared preferable to Arab and Swahili brutality, or that even today the names "Arab" and "Swahili" are abhorred in parts of the interior.

There is no need to retell the dismemberment of the sultanate by the European colonial powers, the Germans establishing their colony of Tanganyika and the British declaring a protectorate over the islands of Zanzibar and Pemba and a ten-mile-deep strip of the Kenya coast. It was a shabby story, in which the Swahili were given little part to play in their own land and were ignored in wider East African economic, political, and educational developments. They appeared politically lethargic and consumed with nostalgia: there was, after all, not much they could do except make this silent protest and so at least retain a sense of their own identity.

During the final decades of the last century the British ruled in East Africa from Zanzibar itself, under its titular sultan. But after the decline of the slave trade the wealth of Zanzibar gave way to that produced on the mainland. Both the British and Germans extended their spheres of influence into the interior. First they allocated tracts of land along the coast to concessionary companies which were given the duty of local administration. This system failed. The British then built up Mombasa to be a large port and the terminus of the railroad to the interior, to which they thenceforward devoted their efforts. The Germans built the little port of Dar es Salaam into a capital city, and their more forceful presence led to rebellions by Swahili fearful that they would abolish the profitable use of and trade in slaves. Revolts in 1888–89 were led by Arab-Swahili leaders, Abushiri and Bwana Heri, both soon put down with much brutality. In the north there was serious resistance by the independent "sultan" of Witu and then by the Giryama.[56] However, the Swahili had no allies and soon agreed to work with the colonial administrations against the peoples of the interior.

Seyyid Barghash died in 1888, to be followed by a series of short-reigning successors until 1911,[57] when the sultan became Seyyid Khalifa ibn Harub, a great-grandson of Seyyid Said ibn Sultan, and a much respected ruler. He reigned in Zanzibar until his death in 1960. The traditional patrimonial authority of Seyyid Barghash gave way to what the British considered a proper form of government: an administrative bureaucracy in which the ruler played the role of ceremonial head of state, real authority residing in the hands of European officials.[58] The red flag of Zanzibar flew over public buildings along the Kenya coast until the 1960s, when the reign of the al-Busaidi dynasty was ended in East Africa by the Zanzibar revolution of 1964.[59]

Both British and German administrations at first encouraged the plantation economy, strengthened the mercantile and financial roles of non-Swahili merchants, and introduced Western non-Koranic education to teach skills needed in a modern industrial and urban economy. All these steps further weakened the position of the Swahili. As the colonial rulers took over the interior, far richer than the Swahili coast, their erstwhile allies became something of a nuisance. The Europeans bypassed the Swahili who had controlled the interior trade, although their language became the lingua franca of the colonial states. Under the British the liwali, the governors appointed by the sultans, were retained and given formal powers and high prestige. But real authority was held by the Kenya and Tanganyika governors, the Zanzibar resident, provincial, and district commissioners, other officials, and legislative and executive councils. Beneath were retained systems of local government of chiefs, headmen, and many kinds of elected and appointed local councils.[60]

Initially, European rule brought influence and prestige to the Swahili: they were the first local people with whom the Europeans dealt. Like their Omani predecessors, the British and Germans regarded themselves as superior to their coastal subjects, but the same ambiguity in the use of power affected them. At first they stood with the Omani sultans against non-Omani; then, when Omani power declined, they sided with the Swahili against the peoples of the interior; and finally they deserted their former Swahili allies altogether.

The European colonial period at first marked the widening of Swahili society, but it was to be only a few years before the inland peoples themselves fully entered the new colonial world of trade, cash crops, local administration, education, and the Christian religion; and it was these who later became the masters of the independent African states. Under independence a considerable amount of the former colonial administrative machinery has been retained: regional and district commissioners, "chiefs," town and village councils, and the like. The Swahili, once favored by the colonial powers, have become increasingly marginal in national politics, although with the appearance of some highly educated Swahili in governmental and commercial circles, their political and cultural isolation may be lessening.

A crucially important factor that has united the coastal towns since the later days of the sultanate and the advent of European overrule has been the introduction of a comprehensive legal system. The operation of law has been important not only for the smooth working of everyday life and the avoidance of destructive internecine disputes but also as means for defining Swahili society. There have been three forms of jural process: descent group and ward arbitration, judgment given by Muslim kadhis, and judgment given by secular judges and arbitrators representing an overruling colonial or postcolonial government. Except for certain offenses such as those against colonial laws imposed from above, in which the government itself has brought criminal action, disputants have been able to choose which of the three means of arbitration they will use. The likelihood of winning a case by appeal to one kind of court or another is one factor in this choice; another is the definition of identity—of which "community," ethnic group, or rank a disputant wishes to claim membership. To appeal to a lineage or ward council implies that the dispute is personal and not the concern of outsiders.

Commercial disputes between lineages are taken to representatives of the groups concerned: this defines the parties as members of an exclusive rank. To go to a kadhi's court defines the parties as Swahili Muslims, as distinct from either other Muslims or non-Muslims altogether. And to go to the secular courts, whether colonial or postcolonial, likewise defines social status in secular rather than religious terms. This is true of both the plaintiff and the defendant, since by using the secular courts the former accuses the latter of not being a true Swahili Muslim.[61]

I can make no more than brief mention of the present-day political organization of Swahili communities. There is the formal organization mentioned above but also local party organizations of branches and cells, led by those who choose a political career rather than—or often in addition to—one in commerce, education, or religion, and whose duties include the representation of local groups, the arbitration of local disputes, and mobilization for party ends. Their importance has grown with the ever-increasing mobility of people up and down the coast and of immigration by non-Swahili from the interior, all signs of the normal growth of a modern nation-state.

Most precolonial societies in East Africa were largely "frozen" by colonial rule, their traditionally permeable boundaries being defined as "intertribal" and fixed, and in many cases new political systems being established by the colonial power. The situation of the Swahili has been rather different. The various dominant political authorities have never been able to organize a total hegemony and so could not impose "one exclusive principle of hierarchy which would reinforce their corporate interests" (Constantin [1989: 155]). Politically subordinate groups have remained within their own narrow hierarchies, and instead of accepting subordination and dependence on a central state have been able to organize forms of local resistance and near-independence. This may be seen as an example of unsuccessful divide-and-rule, the central authority being unable to impose total domination over a majority who were already divided. The British were more successful in imposing overrule than the Omani, and the newly independent governments of Kenya and Tanzania are more willing to exercise overriding power than were the British. The former scale of Swahili society has widened with increasing power held by non-Swahili bureaucracies; the growing economic power of some recent immigrant groups to the Swahili towns such as the Hadhrami and Kikuyu, and their nontraditional ties with national and multinational companies; the realization by many Western-educated Swahili men and women that power awaits them not in family ties but in impersonal contacts with economic and political entrepreneurs and developers outside the coast itself; and the rise of coastally based political parties and groups such as Mwambao in Kenya (Salim [1970, 1972]; Cooper [1987]; Harris [1976]). In the larger towns such as Mombasa and Dar es Salaam, the Swahili have been outnumbered by non-Swahili laborers and workers. As these latter have become part of a wider economy, they have formed new kinds of associations, trades unions, and political parties, controlled not by Swahili but by immigrants who care nothing for local Swahili culture, which has now been relegated to a few ethnic ghettoes. The recent labor history of the coastal cities has been a crucial element in the Swahilis' development but has had little directly to do with them (Cooper [1987]).

A final form of colonialism is the modern tourist trade, in which once again the Swahili are exploited by outsiders (Peak [1989]). The coast is the scene of intensive tourism controlled by European entrepreneurs and their African partners, who are virtually never Swahili. The profits are shared by them and the national governments, and any "trickle-down effect" is slight. Tourists and their hangers-on are despised by most Swahili as non-Muslims who bring new commercial and sexual mores and have a corrupting influence. This is the final and perhaps the most degrading exploitation of the Swahili coast.

The Swahili have undergone radical changes during this century; but, always conscious of their past, they see these changes mainly as yet another set of developments of the kind they have experienced for as long as they can trace back. Most of the intercontinental trade has widened in its range: the goods carried have not changed in essence, except for slaves and ivory, but they are now supplied by inland producers who no longer need coastal middlemen but deal with overseas partners either directly or through governmental agencies. Forms of financial support and types of transportation have changed, and the ocean monsoons are hardly a factor; the long-standing services provided by the small Swahili ports are little needed. There remains a considerable amount of coastal trading with Somalia and southern Arabia, but it is not sufficient to keep the Swahili mercantile houses in profitable business (and as soon as it is shown to be profitable, an outside entrepreneur usually takes it over). Also, it has moved almost entirely from the hands of the patricians to those of Hadhrami merchants, who can use their relatively recent clan links with southern Arabia to their advantage.

Most of the commercial raison d'être of the stone-towns has gone. Yet Swahili society has remained in its internal organization not all that different from what it seems ever to have been. Essentially, each town has remained self-defined and largely autonomous, although increasingly exploited by central governments. There has been no single Swahili polity to be destroyed, and the Swahili towns remain peripheral to the economic and political centers of power, whether Zanzibar City, Nairobi, or Dar es Salaam. The identities of their ultimate governors have changed, but not their own positions within the wider polities and regions. And their pride in themselves sustains them and is too strong to be taken away.

The long rise and decline of Swahili fortunes that I have briefly described is of course only one view of their history, based largely on the writings of European scholars. What these have ignored are the internal histories of individual towns, about which we have relatively little information. Two points are clear: that the identity and underlying structure of Swahili society have proved resilient enough to persist over many centuries, and that however extensive earlier social and cultural changes may have been, during this century they have been marked, especially in the spheres of local and kinship organizations, religious behavior, the roles of women and those of slave ancestry, and notions of social hierarchy and ethnicity. These are the themes of the following chapters.

Chapter Three

T o w n s

TWO TYPES OF SETTLEMENT

The Swahili have never formed a single polity but rather a congeries of structurally linked communities, each more or less autonomous although
rarely self-sufficient. The power and size of the larger and more ancient settlements such as Mombasa, Pate, Lamu, and Kilwa have waxed and waned, but in
general they have maintained an equilibrium over many centuries, their degree
of power and influence depending on the vagaries of the ocean trade and ever-
shifting alliances with one another, with the inland peoples, and with external
powers. The Sultanate of Zanzibar came the nearest to being a single state in the
region, but it was a colonial state established by an alien dynasty, imposed by
force, and included many non-Swahili. Swahili communities have always been
politically complex and rift by factions of many kinds. Their internal structure
has been a balance between various kinds of social groupings: between the spatial
units of towns and quarters, between moieties, lineages, families, and many kinds
of social categories and factions.

The Swahili are urban dwellers and their civilization has been an urban one. The
basic social unit of their society is and has been the "town" (*mji* or *mui*). Towns
vary greatly in size, from densely built-up centers such as Mombasa, Zanzibar
City, or Lamu to settlements loosely dispersed over a wide area. Many appear
as towns by any definition, but others are stretches of low houses among which
grow coconut palms and between which run narrow streets and alleys. Most of
the medieval towns, such as Lamu and Pate, still exist and are occupied; some,
such as Kilwa, have deteriorated into little more than hamlets sited among ruins;
others, such as Mombasa, Dar es Salaam, and Tanga, are either modern conur-
bations around an ancient core or are newly founded. The central areas of the
Stone-towns have often been marked physically and symbolically by being enclosed by walls. Besides providing protection, these walls have defined the central
areas occupied by the patrician merchants and closed to outsiders except those
carefully admitted as trading or marital partners; poorer people, most slaves, and
strangers have lived in palm-matting houses outside the walls.

All the towns have a similar underlying structure, although it is largely concealed by morphological features. Simplistic geographical notions that make a distinction of order between urban and rural communities have little relevance for the Swahili. Marcel Mauss suggested that relations of exchange bind together differentiated parts of a social network into an organic whole, and to understand Swahili society we must see the internally complex organic unity of Swahili society as being based upon the complementarity of its constituent settlements, each with its own forms of production and division of labor. As Wheatley has written, "If structural regularities [between various kinds of urbanism] are ultimately elucidated, then it is practically certain that they will be manifested in shared functions and in trends in systemic change rather than in form" (1972: 601).[1]

The Swahili terminology for these settlements is based on criteria of social structure rather than of size or density. Two types of town must be distinguished. To keep close to Swahili usage I shall use the terms *stone-town* and *country-town*. Stone-town is immediately meaningful since most of these towns, or considerable areas within them, are built of stone (that is, of coral blocks).[2] The country-towns are made of less permanent materials. Like the building of walls, the use of stone has social and symbolic as well as technological connotations. There are many variations within both kinds of towns, but the distinction is important and meaningful, and their social, economic, and symbolic functions are different and complementary. The distinction is that between two ends of a continuum, and both are essentially ideal types.

The stone-town is typically the larger in population.[3] It comprises a dense settlement of permanent houses and public buildings of many kinds, with main streets and connecting alleyways, and small gardens set among the houses and in ruined house sites. A stone-town has had particular mercantile functions and in former times either a single ruler or a patrician oligarchy. It is still characterized by marked patterns of hierarchical difference and competition that are expressed in spatial, ethnic, and genealogical idioms. A country-town usually has a smaller population but may be much more dispersed on the ground, with coconut palms and gardens between the houses. Like the stone-towns, country-towns are permanent settlements, with a few public buildings and a traditional form of internal political organization. Some existing country-towns were at one time stone-towns and have waned with the decline in the ocean trade, epidemics, or attacks by marauders from the interior.[4] Ordinary dwellings are rarely of stone and are not permanent, and in their everyday life these towns appear more rural than urban. I am using these terms to express the Swahili view of their society, and not necessarily to mean that all stone-towns are of stone and all country-towns lack stone buildings. Indeed, part of the dwellings in all stone-towns have been made of mud-and-thatch. The epithet "stone" refers to an assumed permanence of both houses and population, and to the fact that in certain situations Swahili wish to build in stone to demonstrate and symbolize permanence—of status, rank, proprietorship, and ancestry. It takes a great deal of labor, wealth, and organization to build a stone house; each of these factors presupposes the existence of the others.

Towns are composed of smaller spatial units known as *mitaa* (sing. *mtaa*). In its literal sense the word means "piece" or "portion," but when used for units of settlement it may be translated both as "ward" or "quarter" and also as "moiety" or "deme." In some instances wards are corporate groups, in others they are not: I will discuss corporation in the following chapter.

Most of the present-day towns have been on the same sites for centuries: Mombasa, Lamu, Pate, and other ancient places have not moved. In more rural areas, such as those on Zanzibar Island, most of the land may be semibarren coral rock, with only a few patches of deep soil on which are built the country-towns. Over the centuries these have become built up and higher than the surrounding countryside. Although their houses are typically not of coral and so impermanent, the town sites are permanent and occupation has been continuous, so that the towns of today are firmly anchored both physically and symbolically in the past. The towns are basic social and historical landmarks: the people themselves can move from one to another, both temporarily and over the generations, and still retain a sense of stability and continuity in an unchanging "map" of their society. There has always been movement between each category of town, and in recent years a more general drift to the larger places from smaller and impoverished settlements.

However large or small the town, it is still the mji and has certain main characteristics. It has its own name, often referring to marked topographical features, such as Makutani ("the place of walls") or Kizingitini ("the place of the reef" or "of the landing place"). The town has a central "Friday" or congregational mosque, where all townsmen worship together on Fridays, and there are usually smaller local mosques also. In the larger centers, where there may be members of more than one Islamic sect or school, each may have its own mosque, but the principle remains. There is also typically a Koranic school, a marketplace, hotels and coffeehouses, the official houses of government officials, and in some towns a fort. There are places for dances, religious performances, political meetings, and specialist activities such as rope making or storing mangrove poles. The town is a person's chief place of residence, rights in which cannot be taken away even if much of his or her working life is spent elsewhere. This sense of belonging is seen in the town's being the place where a person will be buried, and all towns have one or more cemeteries. Besides being places where people live and die, most towns are centers of exchange and local government; they are places of artisans and craftsmen, and the centers of religion and learning. A town, whether a stone-town or a country-town, and despite the many differences in size and form, is a single corporation. Each acts as the nucleus of a single socioeconomic region which includes the central town, its satellite settlements, and its townlands either surrounding it or, where the town is on an island, often on the mainland opposite.

These settlements are not isolated. The country-towns have been and are more or less self-sufficient, but the stone-towns are not so; all are linked by patterns of exchange of foodstuffs, labor, many kinds of productive, technical, and processing services, religious cults, marriage partners, and in the past kingly dominance, representation, and protection in return for tribute and taxes. Most observers have considered the economies of the various parts of the coast and its towns in isolation from one another: one settlement is said to be composed of fishermen, another of copra growers, another of sailors and traders, and so on. However, the entire coast should be considered in its totality, as a single oikumene. Today this characteristic is weakening and has in many parts of the coast fallen into desuetude as the ocean trade has faded and the coast has been "opened up" to peoples from the interior. But the traditional interdependence of the coastal settlements provides much of the underlying structure of Swahili society. Throughout their history the towns have had to ensure both their own supplies of foodstuffs, living materials, and labor, and also trade goods for shipment overseas or for exchange with peoples of the hinterland and interior. The relationships between the town and the hinterland have always been an object of vital concern to the Swahili towns, perched so precariously along the narrow coastal strip.

The stone-towns have been the international entrepots for the Africa-Asia trade and have provided the warehouses and the brokerage, financial, shipping, labor, and other services necessary to that trade. To them came the "raw" and "natural" trade commodities from the interior, and they possessed plantations on which were grown grains and other crops for export. They owned many of the ocean-going dhows and maintained mercantile and familial links both with their opposite numbers across the Indian Ocean and with rulers of the interior. However, they did not, and still do not, provide most of their own labor and food. The labor was until the early years of this century provided by slaves, and the food was in the main provided by the country-towns and neighboring non-Swahili farmers, with some local domestic production by slaves in gardens set near the towns. The pattern has varied from town to town. Lamu's food has come mostly from neighboring country-towns, and to some extent from its own gardens and from farms on the mainland, formerly worked by slave labor and today little used.[5] To the north, however, the people of Pate still grow their own food both on Pate Island (which, unlike Lamu Island, is fertile) and on stretches of farms far away on the mainland, and scorn those who must buy food at the markets. Mombasa has depended on food from elsewhere, both on Mombasa Island, from neighboring hinterland groups such as the Giryama, and in the past from Pemba Island. Zanzibar City has depended on food from the country-towns of Zanzibar and Pemba islands. Throughout the coast in recent years labor has been provided by various forms of hired and squatter labor, from both the country-towns and inland settlements of other peoples. Food has been provided by the same traditional means except that production by market gardeners from the inland peoples has in some areas largely superseded the supply of food from the country-towns.

I have stressed the mercantile role of the patricians of the stone-towns. But they have not only been merchants, and few are so today. They have entered many occupations, as free property owners and controllers of servile or hired labor. These have included construction of ships and houses, repair facilities for shipping, carpentry, weaving, shopkeeping, and religious and educational services. Certain towns have specialties: Pate today depends on tobacco production, and

Siyu has for centuries had a reputation for the production of books, leather, and furniture.

The country-towns have played very different economic roles. They are interspersed with stone-towns along the coast, from the Bajun fishing settlements in the north to the scattered settlements in the far south in Tanzania and Mozambique. They are found also on Zanzibar, Pemba, Mafia, and the Comoros. Some have been country-towns as far back as can be traced or surmised, others were once stone-towns that have lost their mercantile functions. All country-towns have been and remain to some extent satellites of nearby stone-towns. Their inhabitants are basically fishermen, gardeners, and small-scale peasant producers linked by petty trade to the stone-towns. They have never owned the ocean-going dhows, although some of them build them, but have been limited to small craft for fishing and coastal traffic. They have not in most cases had close trade or political relations with the non-Swahili peoples inland, nor have they had the once important patron-client links that the stone-town rulers maintained with those peoples. Their links with the stone-towns were also those of patronage and clientship, but of a different kind, based on the recognition of common ethnicity, language, and religion.

Exchange between the two types of towns starts with the production by the country-towns of foodstuffs (grains, fish, oil, fruit, and so on) and local export consumer goods such as copra, tobacco, coir rope and matting, and items such as small sailing craft. These communities consume much of what they produce, but exchange part of it with neighboring stone-towns in return for consumer goods such as clothing and domestic items, and in the past for protection from exploitation and military attack from other towns and peoples. Details of the total economic system have varied from one century to another and from one part of the coast to another; but the overall pattern has remained constant. It has been based on the distribution of socioeconomic niches and on exchange of goods and services at different and complementary levels. The areas of the coast that produce food in quantities great enough to allow the export of surplus are not numerous, and the same is true of those that produce commodities such as tobacco or coir ropes and matting. There has been some exploitation by the stone-towns, which have exchanged manufactured goods for mostly natural products; the stone-towns have typically held greater wealth and power than the country-towns. This has buttressed their relationship—an internal subcolonialism.

Besides production and exchange of commodities, there is exchange of people, both as farm, maritime, and other forms of labor, and as marriage partners. Marriage exchanges have a different pattern from those of commodities and labor, not being random or "free" but consistent with rules of rank and descent. Families of different stone-towns exchange partners with one another, subject to rules of preferred marriage, and members of different country-towns also intermarry. But marriages are not common between members of the two categories of towns. Another important area of exchange is educational and religious services and duties, as Islamic scholars move from one town to another, establishing schools and religious beliefs and opinions. Admittedly, the greatest number of Islamic scholars has come from the larger stone-towns such as Zanzibar, Mombasa, and Lamu, but a glance at the history of Swahili Islam (see, for example, Pouwels [1987]) shows many from lesser stone-towns and country-towns. The exchange network forms the organic whole that is Swahili society, in which the rights, obligations, and sanctions in the exchange system are those of Islam and of Swahili "civilization" (ustaarabu). Economic exchanges (and more rarely other kinds) are made with neighboring non-Swahili groups but with different sanctions.

The trading system as a whole has never been symmetrical: even if some of the interior peoples were at times more powerful than the Swahili towns which were under the perpetual threat of being raided by them, the trading partners across the ocean were usually even more powerful. Both sides were in symbiotic relationships with the Swahili stone-towns as regards the exchange of commodities, but the centers of political and military power on both sides were beyond the control of the Swahili. On the other hand, the ties of religion and claimed ethnicity with the Swahilis' Asian partners have always had a strength lacking in their relations with hinterland partners. The nearer of these, however, were in various kinds of patron-client relationships with the Swahili stone-towns. All these economic requirements entailed complex social arrangements and sanctions. The nuclei or points of articulation of the system have been, and remain, the stone-towns. As the ports of trade they have carried on five kinds of direct exchanges: with the country-towns that have supplied them with everyday foodstuffs for their own consumption and with a few trade items; with other stone-towns, as in the medieval gold trade between Sofala and Kilwa or the later transshipment traffic in slaves between the southern towns that brought them to the coast and the northern ports that shipped them across the ocean; with partners on the other sides of the Indian Ocean; with the peoples of the interior, although this seems to have been limited mainly to the activities of the coastally based slave and ivory caravans of nineteenth-century Zanzibar; and with the non-Swahili peoples of the immediate hinterland, who were themselves the intermediary traders between the interior and the Swahili towns. All these types of exchange—and of course they have shaded into one another—have necessitated different kinds of social institutions. They have included patron-client relationships, alliances by marriage and fictive kinship, formally defined mercantile relations, and force, all controlled by former rulers and by individual trading families and lineages. Modern tourists who view the Swahili as romantic and perhaps quaint figures fail to appreciate that they are the successors and descendants of lines of entrepreneurs in networks of international business and finance of quite bewildering complexity.

MOSQUES, TOMBS, AND HOUSES

Each Swahili town is a unit in a complex system of production and exchange. It holds together as a single unit by means of its economic and political self-interest within this system and by its sense of unity and particular sets of symbols. There are many such sets, each pertaining to different levels of organization and representing heritage and ancestry, inclusion and exclusion, and "civilization" and purity. Among these symbols are mosques, tombs, houses, and forts and palaces, all physical buildings imbued with notions of ancestry, purity, honor, and reputation. In a sense, the remainder of this book is concerned with these notions: in this section I will discuss only the physical buildings and the urban space in which they are set, which provide the material setting for the utamuduni (urbanity) that is one of the basic characteristics of Swahili society.

One of the main distinguishing marks of Swahili civilization is the material and symbolic construction of its buildings, the most important and perduring of its forms of property. Swahili architecture has changed hardly at all over the centuries: the buildings of stone-towns of today such as Lamu and Pate are similar to those of the ruins of Shanga, Kilwa, Gedi, and other early settlements. The building tradition can be traced back to at least the twelfth century, up to the great eighteenth- and nineteenth-century houses of present-day Lamu and a few other places. There are similarities with the architecture of Islamic societies elsewhere,[6] and it may be asked whether these towns are uniquely Swahili or mere transplantations or copies of the towns and houses of the Arab world. A proper Near Eastern or North African town is traditionally defined by the possession of a congregational mosque (*jami*), a public baths (*hammam*), and a central market (*suq*): the Swahili towns all have the first, none the second, and the third in only a marginal sense. They must be regarded as sui generis.

The towns are defined and ordered entities that form spatial and temporal structures. Stone-towns are highly exclusive units, whereas country-towns are widely inclusive ones, and this distinction is represented spatially. Stone-towns have traditionally been surrounded by walls penetrated by named gates that enclose their patrician residents from the world outside; country-towns have not been walled but metaphorically extended into the outside world. In the stone-towns most male slaves, other than trusted and high-status domestic slaves, had to sleep at night outside the walls; it was in the evenings that free women could walk outside the houses in which they were largely secluded by day (and even today most ceremonies involving women are held after dark). Both kinds of towns are traditionally divided into moieties, which are both separated spatially and united symbolically by a central congregational or Friday mosque, the *msikiti wa Ijumaa* ("the mosque of gathering together" or "of Friday"). Towns are seen by their inhabitants as oases of purity and urbanity set in a barbarian wasteland, and at the core of each is its congregational mosque. A settlement without a mosque is not a "founded" town (*mji uliubunika*).

Mosques are found in every settlement along the coast, and in all but the very smallest there are more than one (large towns such as Mombasa and Lamu each have twenty or more). Except for a few recent grandly built ones, mosques are rectangular buildings constructed on the outside not unlike an ordinary house. Except for the *kibla* or *mihrab*[7] jutting out at the northern end (the alcove inside that is the focus of the seating plan, the congregation facing it), and the ablution places on the eastern or southern walls, it is often difficult to distinguish a small mosque on the outside from the houses that surround it; only the interior plan sets it apart. Mosques have two main patterns: one has aisles separated by an internal wall that is pierced by arches and pillars to support the wide roof down the center; the other has two or more rows of pillars to support the roof, without aisles, and here the view of the kibla is not obstructed for the congregation.[8] Near the entrance are paved ablution places and stepping stones into the building. The larger mosques have cisterns, but smaller ones have merely a few jars of water placed by the doors. A larger mosque has an anteroom for its *imam*. Perhaps due to Ibadhi influence, no Swahili mosques have minarets: the muezzin (*mwadhani*) calls the faithful to prayer from inside the mosque, these days often by an outside loudspeaker. Women are not usually allowed inside mosques, but in some of the older settlements they worship either seated at the back behind a screen or divided from men by a curtain or screen down the center of the building. A few large mosques have separate annexes for women.[9]

The town, as distinct from its houses, is public space, the physical representation of the town community and the public weal, both spatially and symbolically centered on its congregational mosque.[10] The mosque, the focus of the purity of the town, is a link in both time and space between the town's own historical purity and the center of the world's purity, Mecca. Those entering it must wash their head, hands, and feet and so leave impurity outside. Its immediate spatial tie is to its adjoining Koranic school (*madrasa*) that in most cases forms the other part of this spatial religious complex and links it with the wider and the future Islamic community, the *umma*. The cemetery, also a part of every town, analogously provides a link with the town's Islamic past. A pious man spends much of his day between mosque, madrasa, and cemetery (where he reads the Koran and prays for his dead kin).

Tombs are found in every town and are important buildings in their own right, those of the ninth to sixteenth centuries, the period of the greatest flowering of Swahili civilization, being remarkable monuments of architecture.[11] Tombs are built both at the northern ends of mosques, elsewhere both in towns and cemeteries, and standing on hills and headlands along the coast. The greatest from the past are the pillar tombs, in which the rectangular walls, usually highly complex in shape and design and adorned with stone carvings of geometrical forms, contain tall stone pillars.[12] Others have no pillars and are smaller, both with and without arched roofs and doors. Tombs often have niches for displaying porcelain, although most have been plundered and the plates removed or broken. Most graves are marked merely by small piles of stones or by small upright stones, and these usually vanish after a generation or two. Everywhere there are also larger and more elaborate stone tombs than the normal, built for famous holy men who are venerated both by local people—who may burn incense, say prayers, read the Koran, and leave small offerings there—and also by pilgrims who may come from great distances.[13]

The larger tombs of the past were probably built by members of wealthy patrician lineages as "the tangible manifestations of ancestry and symbols of residence in and commitment to the community for the descendants of the entombed" (Wilson [1979: 34]). Since the interiors have hardly been excavated, it is not yet known whether they were built for individuals of great fame, wealth, or saintliness, or for powerful lineages who might use them over many generations. Certainly a great stone pillar tomb, like a great stone house, has been associated with high patrician status and ancient and immaculate ancestry. But all tombs provide a link to the past, of both the town and its component descent groups.

The unity and continuity of the town are represented in its congregational mosque and tombs, those of its constituent descent groups in its houses. The Swahili distinguish three main types of domestic dwelling: a multistory stone house (*kiungu*); a stone house of any kind, including the former (*jumba*); and a mud-and-thatch or mud-and-palm-frond house (*nyumba ya udongo*, or merely *nyumba*, which is also the general word for a house). Stone-town houses have certain general features. They have the same kind of axial placement and internal design; they are enclosed from the streets of which they are part; formerly they had separate areas for free and slave occupants; and their room size is dictated by the technical limitations of the materials used in their construction. Three main factors must be considered: the materials, the internal organization of space, and the symbolic nature of the houses.

The basic materials are coral and wood. Coral is easily worked and found throughout the coast. It may be soft or hard. Soft coral is found under water level and can be cut and carved for jambs, lintels, and other decorated parts of the buildings: it hardens after being carved. Hard coral is found on the surface of much of the land area and is used for foundations and walls: it is cut into large blocks that are light to carry and are bound together by a mortar made from weathered or burnt coral and sand; the same material provides plaster and plaster-wash for internal decoration. Rough coral rag or rubble is also used for outside walls; it is bound by lime cement, then plastered smooth, and can last for up to two hundred years. It has been and still is proper in towns such as Pate for a patrician, on the birth of a daughter, to start the making of the lime (*chokaa*) for the house in which she will live after her marriage. A pit is filled with lime, which after long weathering becomes finely broken down and leached of its salt, making a high-quality and long-lasting cement. Most woods used in building are various kinds of mangrove, used either as round poles or as squared beams for joists for the floors and as rafters for the plastered ceilings. The use of mangrove poles limits the width of the rooms to about three meters, which is thus the standard module in building. Country-towns and poorer settlements, although they usually have stone mosques, contain mostly houses made of mud and coconut-palm leaf matting.

As an example, I will discuss the architecture of the more ancient and unchanged of the northern towns, such as Lamu and Pate; that of Mombasa has changed markedly over the generations as a consequence of many sackings and burnings; and Zanzibar City and Dar es Salaam are essentially nineteenth-century towns with little traditional architecture.

A typical stone-town dwelling house covers an area of something under 250 square meters. Houses are usually oblong and built around a small central open courtyard. The houses in the few remaining very traditional (and in the recent past poorer) towns, such as Pate, are single-story buildings, but in a wealthier and crowded town, such as Lamu, most are two-storied and many have three stories, the structurally safe limit. A story is typically added when the occupying family expands by the marriages of its daughters, residence for the first marriages of women being uxorilocal. In some grander houses the ground floor was occupied by slaves and used as a warehouse, and the family members lived above. Drainage is an important consideration: houses have flat roofs and house drains send the often heavy rainfall into the street drains, which empty into the sea. The traditional Swahili stone-built houses are complex structures, and here I give only the barest outline, to show the house as part of a wide symbolic schema that lies at the base of Swahili notions of purity, ancestry, and status. I discuss mainly the houses in Lamu, where the moiety of Mkomani has some four hundred such houses set in about ten hectares, the greatest number in a single place on the entire coast.[14]

The axis of a typical house runs north and south. The entrance to the courtyard is properly at the north end and the owner's private rooms are at the south end. The vagaries of street layouts mean that a staircase from the front door may twist and change directions so as to end up in the right place. The northern end is referred to as *upande wa kibla* (the side of the kibla), the northern and sacred end of a mosque. Houses and mosques should have the same orientations. In Lamu and Pate, at least, great efforts are made to have the rooms in the correct alignment: a visitor knows that by having his or her back to a rear wall of a gallery, he or she is facing Mecca. In places such as Mombasa Old Town this is by no means so, and a visitor must be shown the proper direction.

The traditional house is a very private place, its outside walls having only holes for ventilation. Light comes from the open courtyard. The entrance is through a large seat-lined porch (*daka*) raised a foot or two above the street, with a double wooden door traditionally elaborately carved and decorated with geometric or floral and leaf patterns and Koranic inscriptions. The double door opens directly onto an inner porch (*tekani*) on the ground floor; in some two-story houses one half of the door opens onto the inner porch and the other half onto a flight of stairs leading up one side of the courtyard to the upper floor. The porches are the limits of entrance to casual visitors. The inner porch gives onto the main inner courtyard (*kiwanda*), a word used for any open working place. In larger houses, at least, there is a well in the courtyard, and a bathroom and toilet in a small room off one of the corners. The main rooms are set to the south of the courtyard: in Lamu rain almost never comes from the north. In single-story houses there is typically a guest room (*sabule*) directly off the courtyard on the northern side of the inner porch, so that it is far from the main living quarters into which a guest cannot look. In larger houses the sabule is typically at the top of a staircase separate from the main family staircase, and has its own bathroom. In the absence of guests (who are usually visiting kin or trading partners), the head of the family may often sleep in the sabule, particularly when his wife has close female kin staying with her; they sleep with her in the main bedroom, the *ndani*.[15] There is also typically a staircase leading up the north wall to the roof. Formerly slaves would sleep under the staircases, the space known as *sarambi*.

On the southern side of the courtyard, facing north and Mecca, lie the living rooms of the owning family, opening directly off the courtyard. There are no separate living, eating, or sleeping rooms (beds are merely placed in curtained alcoves [*ngao*] when needed). The rooms are arranged in a series of galleries (*misana*, sing. *msana*), set transversely between the east and west walls.[16] Each inner gallery, farther back from the courtyard, has its floor set a step higher than the preceding level. Doorways set in the intervening walls mark them from the courtyard and each other, so that to a visitor each is set higher and is darker than the nearer one. There are formal ways of being invited farther into the interior of the house. The first of these galleries is a daytime area mainly for sitting and conversing; this is the *msana wa tini* (or *chini*), the "lower gallery." Behind, except in smaller houses, is a second area, the *msana wa yuu* (or *juu*), the "upper gallery." Both galleries have high painted poles at the ends for the curtains of the sleeping alcoves. Beyond the upper gallery is the most private area, the ndani, "inside" (occasionally called the *msana wa kati*, "central gallery"), where the wife and husband sleep. This is par excellence the wife's room. Some writers refer to it as the "harem quarters," but this romantic view is misleading: patricians have rarely been polygynous, and concubines did not sleep there in any case. In the grander houses these galleries are extremely high and cool, and often have small window-niches at the ends, in which are placed pieces of porcelain for show.

Behind the ndani are the *choo*, the bathroom-cum-toilet of the ndani, and a smaller space or room, the *nyumba ya kati* (center of the house), sometimes called *chumba ya kati* (central room).[17] The bathroom is usually on the left side facing from the courtyard, the nyumba ya kati on the right: the left is polluting, the right not. Each may have its own doorway from the ndani. The latter room has (or has had) two main functions. It is properly the place for childbirth, the preparation of corpses, and the seclusion of widows; and it was a place for storing the more precious trade goods and valuables. It is furnished merely with a bed of the kind called *ulili*;[18] it may have an exit, a hole blocked with loose removable stones, for passage of the corpse for burial, and a small side door or opening to the bathroom so that water can be brought into it easily. This room is found only on the main family floor.[19] The roof above is traditionally flat and on it may be a small penthouse kitchen (*jiko*), with its own narrow internal staircase; or the kitchen may be placed in a corner of the courtyard below.

A father should give his daughter at her first marriage her own separate living accommodation linked to his own: either a story may be added, each story being occupied by a separate elementary family, or he may build or buy an adjoining house. When this is across a street, a bridge (*wikio*) is built to link the two houses:

women can pass from one to the other without being seen from the street below. The working definition of a separate accommodation for each family is that it has its own bathroom-cum-toilet. Water comes from wells and cisterns.[20] The toilets are dry pits, vertical ducts set inside the walls; so long as they are kept dry, they are extremely effective and require only very occasional cleaning out. The walls are thick and lime-washed, and the ceilings are very high: these houses are cool and relatively dry even though the coastal climate is often very hot and humid.

These houses are not merely "machines for living in": they are as much symbolic as technical structures. They represent the permanence, stability, credit-worthiness, and purity of the owning lineage. These qualities are expressed both in the solidarity and layout of parts of a house, and in its external and internal decoration. The outside walls are plain and undecorated, although properly lime-washed, except for the carved outer doors. These imposing gates cut off the outside public world from the private family world within and symbolize the disdain of patrician owners for all others of different rank and ancestry. The internal decoration may be extremely elaborate. There is a marked increase in privacy from the outer porch at one end to the main wife's room, the ndani, at the other, with the nyumba ya kati even more secluded behind that. This is associated not merely with the seclusion of women but essentially with the ndani as the ritual center of the house. The first two galleries are separated by internal walls, each having two doorways; the wall of the ndani has only one central doorway, so that its interior cannot be seen from the first gallery or the courtyard. Walls have rows of wooden pegs for hanging rugs and tapestries. Walls, pillars, and parts of the walls, as well as door jambs and lintels, are carved and decorated in plaster. The back walls of the msana wa yuu and particularly of the ndani are set with rows of niches, *vidaka* or *zidaka* (diminutive forms of daka, the outer porch of the house), set into the plaster (see fig. 1). These niches are arched and so shaped that their roofs are sloped higher at the back, so that the observer cannot see the join between roof and back; the backs are also slightly angled relative to one another, so that there is only a single central place from which the entire wall panel can be viewed in proper perspective. James Allen (1979: 14) points out that the panels of niches are designed to be looked at by only a small group of people at a time, on occasions such as weddings, standing in the doorway to the ndani. The niches are for displaying porcelain, manuscripts and writing materials, copies of the Koran, and other treasures. Beneath the rows of niches, in the center, is typically a blank rectangle where is placed a bed called *kitanda* or *samadari* on which a bride is presented at her wedding. The observers stand in the upper gallery, from which they can best see her seated and surrounded by the beauty of the niches and their contents. In the past the rooms occupied by slaves were not plastered but those occupied by free persons had to be, even if they lacked niches: plaster is associated with purity.[21]

The various rooms contain furniture: beds, chairs, stools, rugs, cushions, and wall hangings. Properly the furniture in a gallery should be arranged symmetrically: a sleeping alcove and bed at each end, and chairs (which are made and

Figure 1. Wall niches *(zidaka)* of the inner room of a patrician house, Lamu. Photo: author.

sold in pairs) arranged so that each half of a gallery is a mirror-image of the other. However, the panels of niches are not shaped symmetrically (J. de V. Allen [1979: 14]). This pattern of the stone-houses has both great symbolic importance and is also of great antiquity, as may be seen in the ruins of Shanga, Ungwana, Pate, Gedi, and other sites.

The house has several degrees of privacy and purity. The outer porch is open to anyone, although it is not part of the interior proper and is literally liminal. The inner porch and the main courtyard are open to those who live in the house or are invited to enter it. Men, other than the senior male members of the owning lineage, may enter the lower gallery only; women, other than the chief wife, and kin invited by her alone may enter the upper gallery but no farther; the ndani is normally reserved for the owner and his wife. Formerly, domestic slaves (as non-persons) could enter various galleries as part of their normal tasks: there were stairs inside the house but outside the galleries for them to reach the roof and the kitchen. Prepubertal children are permitted everywhere except in the ndani and the rooms behind it. Much depends on the size of the house and the number of its galleries and rooms. The whole forms a structure of degrees of purity and impurity that reflects the wider schema of relations of age, gender, descent, and rank.

Not all stone-houses in a place such as Lamu are of this pattern. Some are what are usually called "verandah houses," which form the majority of buildings in larger and ethnically more mixed towns such as Mombasa and Zanzibar City. These are the houses of Indian and other non-Swahili merchants and officials, being shops and offices as well as dwelling houses. Their internal layouts are different and need not be discussed here.[22]

I have described the older stone-built houses of Lamu, although today at least half its houses are either small mud-and-thatch dwellings or of modern concrete blocks: but almost all the houses of Mkomani moiety are of stone. I do not thereby imply that these are in any way "traditional." Their having two or even three stories is a consequence of overcrowding and shortage of land for building: instead of building sideways, patricians of Lamu have had to build upwards. The former wealth of the houses' proprietors and the fact that they have not been pulled down to make way for more "modern" Indian or Hadhrami houses, as has happened in Mombasa Old Town, have ensured their greater and longer complexity and material elaboration. The underlying symbolic significances are more clearly obvious, but in many ways Lamu is a town sui generis.

The more traditional type of stone-houses, however, is represented by those of Pate (and of ruined sites). In Pate all houses are stone-built, usually roofed with coconut fronds. They are virtually all of one story, with two or three galleries, the nyumba ya kata and choo behind, the ndani and choo having rows of niches and being decorated and plastered as in Lamu. The sabule is merely a separate room-cum-bathroom at the edge of the courtyard. Pate houses are each occupied by only a single nuclear family, with a few attached kin such as widowed grandmothers; in Lamu it is a story that is so occupied. The population of Pate has declined during the past century or two, so that empty plots are available within and at the edges of the town; Pate today may represent the basic and "traditional" Swahili stone-town more accurately than does Lamu.

In the country-towns and in the peripheral parts of most stone-towns, the dwelling houses are both simpler and smaller, and lack much of the symbolic content of stone-houses. They are also oblong, but typically of one story only. A few may be of stone but virtually all consist of either walls of a mixture of coral and mud smoothed with lime and whitewashed, or merely of palm-leaf matting. These houses are strong and can last for a good many years, but not for generations, as can the stone-built houses. The pent-roofs are traditionally of coconut-palm matting but today may well be of corrugated iron or flattened petrol tins, which, although uncomfortable in hot weather, are fireproof and long-lasting. Extra walls are made with palm fronds to provide outbuildings, kitchens, wash-houses, and toilets. Usually a palm-frond screen is built around the whole complex for privacy and to mark it off as a separate building for a separate household. These houses have something of the same internal arrangement as the stone-town houses. An outside verandah takes the place of the porch. Then there are the single entrance door of coconut matting, and inside a men's reception room, and then one or two transverse rooms. Rooms are always smaller and much lower than those of the stone-towns. Outside this central cluster of rooms are the out-buildings. Even the simplest of these Swahili houses are different from those of neighboring peoples.

There are many social differences between these two main kinds of house, refer-ring mainly to forms of stratification, to the position of women, and to mercantile wealth. The stone-towns have been characterized by marked differences of rank, both between free and slave and between patricians and commoners. The large stone-built houses that I have described are those of patricians. In the country-towns there are no patricians. But in all the stone-towns patrician lineages have at times become poor, perhaps regaining their wealth later. If poor, they may live either in single-story stone-houses (as in present-day Pate and Siyu, for example) or in palm-matting houses.[23] It has sometimes been thought that palm-leaf houses on the peripheries of stone-towns were those of slaves, but this is incorrect: the kind of house built is a function of wealth as well as of rank. Country-towns have lacked these distinctions and their single-story dwellings lack the associated complexity of rank and gender distinctions and boundaries. In the stone-towns the patrician families observed, and still observe as far as they can, the house-seclusion of women. In the country-towns women have always been far more equal to men and have rarely practiced seclusion. The possession of a stone-built house expresses a family's sense of permanence and prosperity. Their wealth is seen to be permanent in their possession of the house and also in the treasures displayed in the niches of the walls of the main rooms. The patrician house is one of the category of inalienable objects that Mauss called *immeubles,* which remain attached to their original owners even if temporarily transferred to other people. They validate a person's or group's present identity by encapsulating their history of ownership and identity: their permanence is transferred to their owner and the owners' lines of descent.

James Allen has written that to live in a double-story stone-house

> implies an awareness of one's family descent going back many generations and a confidence of many generations to come. It implies a pride in one's lit-erary and cultural heritage. And it implies . . . such things as secluding one's women, dressing in prescribed ways, involving oneself in certain ritual func-tions connected with mosques and in certain financial commitments to the community, and showing business acumen and an understanding of the long term in financial matters. People who live in mud-and-thatch either do not feel constrained to share these values and this way of life or cannot afford to, and the step from one condition to the other is a very clear and decisive one.[24]

The patricians of present-day Lamu and Pate hold on to their houses, however dilapidated they may have become in recent years: without them their lineages would effectively end, even if living descendants remained.[25]

COUNTRY-TOWNS

        I wish now to describe the two types of towns, using actual examples and not presenting ideal types; I stress again that no two towns are the same. I will first describe the country-towns of the island of Zanzibar, occupied by peoples who refer to themselves as Hadimu and Tumbatu, and where I have lived myself. The life of these settlements has been deeply changed by the 1964 revolution and its aftermath. I will therefore describe them as they were in 1958, and use the "ethnographic present" tense to do so, even though I imagine that some of my account is now outdated, particularly since the pattern as I found it has been complicated by the influx into the Hadimu towns of recent non-Swahili immigrants from the mainland, many of whom worked as squatters on the clove plantations.[26]

Zanzibar Island is divided into two main ecological zones. The hilly western part of the island was covered by rain forest until it was cleared by slave labor for clove plantations in the eighteenth and nineteenth centuries; the remainder of the island is of soils where cloves will not grow. The former areas were little used except for some farming, hunting, and timber until the coming of the Omani Arabs; the latter have been occupied for as long as is known by the Hadimu over most of the island and by the Tumbatu in the north.

The Hadimu and Tumbatu are mainly subsistence farmers and fishermen, but the export of cash crops and labor is also important, and much of their present staple, rice, is imported. The main exports are coir, copra, fish, poultry, chillies, citrus, goats, and kapok; in some southeastern settlements tobacco is an important crop, sent to Somalia; and in the southwestern settlements the export of mangrove timber is valuable. The towns are mostly large and flourishing and unable to accept more residents due to shortage of building and gardening land. They vary in size[27] and are dispersed because only a few places have fertile soil deep enough to support trees (Middleton [1961: 10–11]). Most are near the coast and typically separated by several miles of land on which are scattered fields under shifting cultivation. One may see quite clearly when looking across the flat coral landscape that the towns are built up upon higher areas of good soil that have been occupied for generations. Houses, of coconut matting and with coral and mud walls, are arranged in clusters, with streets and alleyways between them. Some settlements are a mile or more across; most are more compact.[28] The central building of every settlement is the congregational mosque. There are typically small shops, formerly leased by urban-based Swahili from the citizens, coffeehouses, meeting halls, markets, wells, and washplaces. Dwelling houses are single-story, rarely of stone, the streets are of sand, and the general impression is one of large and rather untidy villages, very different from the stone-towns. This impression is due partly to the permanently cultivated gardens (*mashamba*, sing. *shamba*) between the clusters of houses. They are used for planting what may be called "permanent" trees—those in which private rights are held— as distinct from those that grow wild, although both are of economic importance (plantains are not considered "trees"). The most important permanent trees are the coconut palm (grown for copra, coir, cooking oil, wood, building fronds, matting, and other uses), mango (for its wood as well as its fruit), and many citrus.[29] The "wild" trees, which grow in the bush land but may be deliberately planted, are mostly palms[30] and timber trees, especially mangroves for building poles and dyes. Plantains are planted in most gardens.

The main food crops are grown in fields (*makonde*, sing. *konde*) in the bush land outside the settlements. The bush is cleared and patches of soil in the coral loosened. In these are planted millets, maize, cassava, sweet potatoes, pulses, and cocoyam; sesame, chillies, tobacco, and vegetables such as eggplant and tomatoes are widely grown as cash crops, occasionally in gardens as well. Double cropping is general and fields are left fallow for various periods depending on the soils (Middleton [1961: 14ff]). Rice is grown in the few large low-lying and wet plains that are owned by wealthy men in Zanzibar City; they should be classed with the clove plantations as being legally outside the Hadimu townlands.

The main unit of settlement is the "town" (mji), a self-contained unit with its own sense of identity, its own proprietary citizens, its own lands, and its own organs of internal self-government. A part of the town that is spatially separate may be referred to by the diminutive form *kijiji* (pl. *vijiji*); this may be translated as "village," but it remains a section of a town, which is thus a cluster of villages. In each town there is an original founding village, such as Kae Kuu ("the great settlement") in Makunduchi, from which men founded daughter villages "as they went out to look for places to plant their cassava." This village is surrounded by the villages established later by the founder's descendants. The whole town is surrounded by its townlands in the bush, which reach as far as the mutually recognized boundaries with neighboring towns. The distribution of the founding and later villages, gardens, and townlands represents in spatial form the town's past history. Towns are divided into moieties (*mitaa*, sing. *mtaa*). In many country-towns these are no longer important, but they remain so in the more isolated ones, such as Nungwi in the far north of the island, Nganani-Makunduchi in the southeast, and Gomani-Kichangani on Tumbatu Island. Moieties are typically separated by an open stretch of land on which stands the congregational mosque. Towns are divided into wards or quarters, for which the word *mtaa* is also used. Most villages of a town contain more than one ward. A ward is an area occupied by a single kinship cluster (described in the following chapter), but the criteria are also spatial and demographic, a ward being large enough to be represented by a single elected elder who acts as an adviser to the more formal town organ of local government known as the "Four Men," *Watu Wanne*. Towns, moieties, villages, and wards are all given their own names.

Most Hadimu settlements have dense populations. There is perpetual competition for valuable resources with continual readjustments of population. These are slow at the level of the town, the structure of which remains stable for long periods. But at the ward level a critical increase in population can occur very suddenly, and an increase of a dozen people can lead to a serious shortage of its better planting and building land. Although the populations of these traditional Hadimu towns have not increased greatly during the past half-century or so, local shortages of land occur regularly. These may lead to secession of individuals or groups of siblings, who move away to be tenants with other kin, to Zanzibar City, to the plantation areas, or to the mainland. But most people do not want to leave their natal towns, and it is thought good that a kin group should gain in population, importance, and prestige. People say that long ago settlements were small and the land plentiful with room for everyone to build, plant trees, and cultivate. But as population has grown there has been competition and fragmentation; first the town and village land is divided into ward lands, and then these last are themselves divided. A settlement must be seen as constantly changing in size and composition, although as a corporation the town remains more or less permanent.

The internal composition and layout of these towns are built around the concepts of *kiambo* and *kitongo,* both difficult to translate.[31] Kiambo refers essentially to an occupied piece of land, whereas kitongo refers to an aspect of ownership, to an inalienable plot of land belonging in perpetuity to a kin group; it is spatially usually part of a kiambo. The main residential area of a village, containing houses, other buildings, and gardens, is its kiambo (pl. *viambo*). The word may also be used loosely to refer to the whole settlement area of a town or to that of a single ward, but properly it is the residential area of a single village. A kiambo is planted with permanent trees, beneath which are gardens. The word *kiambo* connotes residential building, permanent occupation, the planting of trees, and in some places the deserted sites of ancestral buildings (the more ancient places, such as Unguja Ukuu, have wide expanses of the ruins of stone-built houses). It has the implication of "home," the place where live members of the kin groups whose members "own" the village.[32]

The kiambo of a village is typically divided into areas each belonging to a ward, the basic corporate group in these towns. This ward land may also be called kiambo, as in the phrase *kiambo cha mtaa* (the kiambo of the ward), but it is properly said to be the kitongo of the kin group whose members are the "proprietors" of the ward, and on which are their houses and their ancestral graves. The rest of the ward's land, on which are neither graves nor houses, is its garden (shamba). A kitongo is inalienable and held jointly by the descendants of its founder, who first planted trees on it. It is said to belong to a *shirika* and to be "like *waqf.*"[33] Shirika is a closed association of people, usually kin, who jointly own land or an enterprise that is inalienable without the agreement of every member; the word is often used to refer to the property itself that is held in perpetuity by the group.

The kiambo and the kitongo are key features of at least the southern country-towns. They express the notions of an inalienable piece of land defined by permanent trees and buildings which gives identity to those who live on it. These are kin, but the basic notion is not that of a self-perpetuating group of kin but of a place, settled, built upon, and planted with trees that are "permanent," unlike the annual food crops that are grown in the fields outside the kiambo. The tie with soil and locality is the essential one.

These Hadimu towns of southeastern Zanzibar Island may be placed typologically at one end of a spectrum, the other end of which is occupied by the larger stone-towns. The southeastern Hadimu and the Tumbatu live in mostly flourishing towns, with sufficient lands and fishing resources to be self-sustaining in most years. The same is true of the remoter country-towns of Pemba Island. But elsewhere in both islands the situation is different, due to economic and social changes brought about by the introduction of cloves in 1818, by land infertility and sporadic shortage, and by reliance on wage labor.[34] In general there has been a partial breakdown of the tightly bounded traditional Hadimu system based upon the residential and productive kiambo. Some of the same process would seem to be true in northern Mafia, the Mrima coast, and more markedly in the impoverished Bajun settlements in the far north of the coast.[35]

The northern country-towns are in many ways different. Their general economic role is similar but their political relations with local stone-towns have varied considerably. Most are long-settled Bajun towns, some of which may have once been stone-towns but have become impoverished in recent centuries; a few are more recently founded as political offshoots of nearby stone-towns. Little is known of the former category,[36] and my own brief study of the town of Matondoni on Lamu Island is the only source on the latter.[37]

Matondoni is a mainly Bajun settlement some five miles northwest of Lamu Town and closely tied to it as supplier of foodstuffs, sand for building, ship and sail making and repairing, palm-frond mats and baskets, and unskilled labor (see fig. 2). Matondoni is a place of about a thousand people, divided into two moieties (*mtao* in kiMatondoni) separated by the wide central street, in which stands the congregational mosque. The Bajun of the town control the crops, the mangrove forests, and the sea products (fish and sand), and retain a traditional form of internal town government. The inhabitants say that they are all equal, with no differences in rank; a few people of wealth who come from Pate or Lamu have owned slaves and ocean dhows, but they are not true citizens. Each moiety comprises a number of wards. Each is a clearly marked area of the town, bounded by sandy alleyways between the houses, most of which stand in small and inalienable plots known as viambo (sing. *chambo*), the same term as the Hadimu kiambo. Other than the mosques, few buildings are made of stone. Each ward has a central plaza of unbuilt land in front of a mosque and school, where the ward has them. A ward also has its own well. The town is built round two creeks that are used for building and repairing dhows, most belonging to patrician families of Lamu. It covers perhaps a quarter of a square mile and behind it lie its fields and palm groves, the latter stretching as far as Lamu Town itself. Each elementary family has a *kiwanda*, or plot, of land and another kiwanda of water offshore for fishing. Matondoni is basically similar to the country-towns of Zanzibar and Pemba. It has become neither impoverished nor depopulated, although it is hardly a wealthy

Figure 2. Launching a new dhow, Matondoni. Photo: Linda Donley-Reid.

place. The essential distinction between stone-town and country-town persists on the northern Swahili coast as well as on Zanzibar Island far to the south. The patterns are those of social and economic factors and functions rather than of ethnicity or of crude geography.

Government in the country-towns is in the eyes of the people themselves essentially egalitarian, a view that has reflected their economically and politically subordinate role in relation to the stone-towns. The governmental offices correspond to the usual distinction between the administrative and political aspects of government. One comprises local officials whose duty is to organize internal order within the town and to maintain peaceful relations with mystical forces believed to affect it. The other once comprised officials whose main responsibility was to maintain relations between the town and the nearest stone-town, the sultanate, and non-Swahili polities. This second category was the first to be weakened by Omani impact and it is difficult now to reconstruct. The former type has persisted in most areas, even if many of its functions have faded.

The form of Swahili government still operational today in the Hadimu areas is fairly representative of all country-towns, although details and titles vary widely. The town has a single council of elders, known as the Watu Wanne (Four Men), or often merely as *wazee* (old men) or *wakuu* (great men). They are elected and must have local personal reputation, some degree of wealth, and some Islamic learning. In close association with them are two other officials, the *sheha wa mji* and the *mzale* or *mvyale,* who is often a woman.

The sheha wa mji (often referred to as *mjumbe,* headman) accepts and controls tenants and places their dues in the town purse (*mkoba wa mji*), which is under his control and used for such matters as sacrifices to the spirits and the upkeep of the town mosque. Each constituent ward has a head, the *mkubwa wa mtaa* (big man of the ward). The "big men" do not form a council but they may represent their wards at meetings of the Watu Wanne. Each controls the influx of tenants into ward land and controls the "ward purse" (*mkoba wa mtaa*), used mainly for bridewealth contributions and funeral dues for ward members. These towns are jurally corporations, but the degree of corporateness is weak, and the internal officeholders have little formal authority, with diffuse and mainly ritual sanctions. The other official, the mzale, has the duty of placating the various spirits of the locality when fields are being opened or tilled; to treat sickness and to counter witchcraft and sorcery by sacrifice and the use of medicines; to organize the Mwaka, the annual rites of the New Year; and to open and close the planting seasons.

Until the middle of the nineteenth century these Hadimu towns were subject to the authority of the Mwenye Mkuu. The ruler appointed an official in each country-town from the local townsmen, known as the *sheha wa serikali,* "shah of the government," or simply as sheha, whose duties were to collect tribute and labor for the mwenye mkuu. The appointment seems to have been made by some kind of consultative process. The mwenye mkuu is said to have supervised matters of succession and inheritance, but the meaning of this is obscure: his duty may have been to ratify the succession of local town officials and possibly the granting of tenant rights and so the movements of people from one town to another. This official is still known as sheha and is the link between the local town and the central administration at Zanzibar City. The offices of sheha wa mji and sheha wa serikali were conflated and in colonial times translated as "headman." The modern sheha has taken over many of the traditional responsibilities of the Watu Wanne, but these still sit in their councils and play an important although often informal role in the everyday life of the towns. In the Swahili towns of the modern Kenya and Tanzania coast, there are today also elected officials known as "chiefs," elected district councils, and district commissioners and other officials appointed by the central government.

The organization of the country-towns is consistent with their traditional economic and political roles, subjected to the demands of the mercantile stone-towns. They are culturally distinct and indeed enclosed, and rely largely on their social isolation and traditional ritual sanctions to retain their identity and internal cohesion, which remain strong even today. They often regard themselves as exploited and seen as socially backward by the more powerful stone-towns, and translate this largely into ethnic and religious terms.

STONE-TOWNS

The stone-towns were for many centuries those of the middlemen in the international trade, and still show that history in their social structure and memories of past wealth and power. The greater stone-towns such as Mombasa, Lamu, and Pate have all been effective ports of trade, as safe deep-water ports with adequate resources both for their own populations and for revictualing ships. Except for the Zanzibar slave market under the nineteenth-century sultanate, goods were not exchanged at central markets but between Swahili lineage-based business houses and individual overseas merchants. Most needs for credit were met by lineage treasuries, and Indian financial brokers were available. The exchange with the African interior was dealt with largely by hinterland intermediaries, whose own exchange relations were also with individual Swahili lineages. Today, after the decline of most of the trade—although a surprisingly large volume is still carried on, mainly with Somalia, Arabia, and Zanzibar—these towns are still largely maritime. Ships are still built and repaired, but most revictualing and financial services have been taken over by banking services outside Swahili control, and the towns have lost much of their former wealth and elegance of life. Although Mombasa and Dar es Salaam today contain industrial areas, these are outside the Swahili enclaves: the Swahili towns themselves remain nonindustrial settlements.

Much of the internal organization of Swahili towns has vanished or been severely weakened during the present century. But a good deal of the traditional pattern is still found in the more remote stone-towns such as Lamu and Pate. In the far north of the coast and far from Zanzibar, they escaped some of the turmoil brought by the Omani sultanate; being the northernmost major ports, they continued to trade with Arabia, whereas ports farther south had much of their trade taken over by Zanzibar; also during this century they have escaped most of the raids of the Orma and Somali. These towns have not declined into mere shadows of their former glory. It is true that much of Lamu's fertile lands on the mainland have been taken away in recent years to accommodate favored settlers from inland areas, and many houses and farms have been seized by rapacious non-Swahili officials for their own use; these actions have led to deep resentment. But the Swahili are merchants, able to take advantage of new opportunities, and they have both adapted themselves to "modern" life and fiercely retained their traditions, although many young people are increasingly becoming Westernized. Swahili Mombasa remains a center of business and learning, Pate has become a wealthy tobacco producer, and with the advent of new roads and air traffic Malindi and Lamu have become centers for tourists. Farther south, in Tanzania, impoverishment and stagnation are today widespread.

Here I discuss mainly Lamu, as I have greater knowledge of it than of other towns (see map 3).[38] It lies on the northern shore of Lamu Island, on an arm of the sea entered some two miles to the southeast. On the island are also the stone-town of Shela and the small country-towns of Matondoni and Kipungani. The

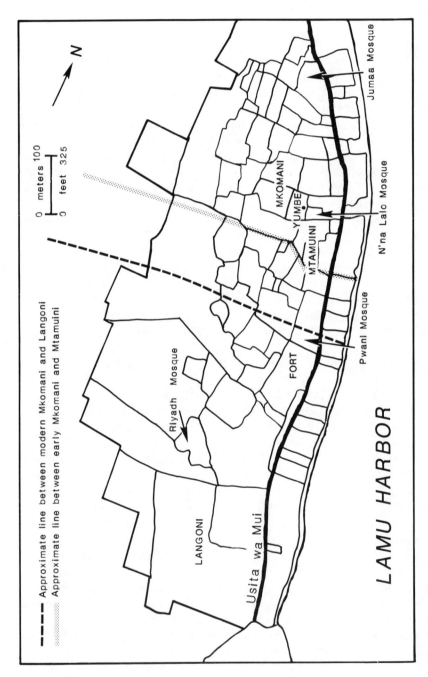

Map 3. Lamu Town

interior of the island consists of sand dunes which are of crucial value: through them the heavy rainfall is filtered into natural "tanks" of sweet water that have for centuries provided Lamu with a reliable water supply.[39] Lamu has held large plantations on the nearby mainland, which were highly productive in the eighteenth and nineteenth centuries for the export of grains to Arabia. The island provides coconut, mango, and tamarind, and town gardens grow betel, spices, jasmine, roses, and other items. Fish, the staple protein, is caught by Bajun fishermen, who although Swahili are not patricians. Today most of Lamu's other food comes from the mainland, grown by Kikuyu and other recent immigrants, an updating of traditional forms of production by slaves.

Lamu has a population today of some twelve thousand people, almost half of whom are immigrants from the impoverished Bajun settlements to the north.[40] The patricians, who wielded political authority for many centuries, are now in a numerical and political minority, but the "traditional" values of their culture are still considered to be the epitome of Swahili civilization.[41] Mkomani, the ancient stone-town proper in the northern part of Lamu, is the largest stone-town on the Swahili coast. The southern part, Langoni, today houses most of the more recent immigrants. Mkomani has houses, most of two or three stories set in a general grid pattern of many narrow streets that branch off the Usita wa Mui (Street of the Town), which runs the length of the town one block behind the waterfront and along which are small shops, workshops, eating and lodging houses, and some mosques. Until early British colonial times the Usita wa Mui was open to the sea, but during the nineteenth century it was separated by a line of large Indian-style "verandah" houses, mostly occupied by Zanzibari and British officials and traders, which cut the town off from the waterfront. Many of the four hundred stone buildings of the town are of considerable size and elegance, although more are falling into decay. Mkomani is still a very secluded and private place, its tall houses turned inward from the streets. Almost all its houses are occupied by the *waungwana* (patricians), who wish to keep out any nonpatricians, however rich: it gives the impression of a fortress whose families, each in its own inward-turned stone house, see themselves as linked together over many generations to retain their exclusivity and keep the outside world at a distance. Virtually all Mkomani's nonpatrician residents live there as clients of patricians, mostly being descendants of their patrons' former slaves. In Langoni are the large cement-block houses of Hadhrami and Omani businessmen, and behind are the smaller and usually mud-and-thatch houses of the lower-born and poor. The extremes of the town are occupied by people of known slave and stranger ancestry. As with many ancient towns, the elegance of its facade hides a good deal of poverty and squalor (see fig. 3).

The main buildings of the town are the great central fort (begun in 1809 and completed in 1821, for long a prison and now a museum), the many mosques, and some of the finer houses along the waterfront. To the southeast of the fort, in Langoni, only the Riyadh and the newly completed Safaa mosques are outstanding.

Figure 3. The main street (Usita wa Mui), Lamu. Photo: Linda Donley-Reid.

Lamu has two cemeteries, one at each end of the town. The northern one is the older and less cared for today, mainly because of the decline in the fortunes of the patricians, who used it before the nineteenth-century immigration of other groups from Arabia. The latter are buried in the southern cemetery, which is better cared for and divided into areas each associated with a particular descent or "ethnic" group.[42] A person may decide by verbal bequest (*wasia*) to be buried near his or her father or mother, although for patricians this has little meaning due to the prevalence of intralineage marriage. Most grave plots of particular lineages are defined by waqf of a forebear, so that direct patrilineal descendants of the founder are buried there as a mark of lineage honor and reputation.

Lamu is divided into twenty-eight wards or quarters (mitaa). They vary in size, some with only twenty or so large stone houses and others with up to perhaps a hundred small mud-and-thatch houses. The wards do not coincide with the blocks that are outlined by the streets, so that neighboring houses, even when sharing a joint wall and with their porches and doors adjoining on the same street, may belong to different wards. The wards are named but the streets are not, the former having much greater social and topographical significance.[43]

The descent groups of the town live dispersed among the wards, the two group-ings not being coterminous. Pouwels (1987: 33) states that each descent group has, or had, its own ward, but this is certainly not so today. This may be due to continual past immigration of diverse groups who occupy whatever space they can find: those groups that become wealthy or numerous may then claim par-ticular subclan status and a particular space within the town that does not fit preexisting ward boundaries. It may also be due to the processes of providing houses for daughters at marriage, the new houses needing to be adjoining those of the fathers; the density of population is so high that ward boundaries must be ignored.[44] There is, however, a general congruence between ward membership and the cluster of effective kin and neighbors known as *jamaa*: kin and neigh-bors form overlapping clusters that provide for a highly cohesive structure. Those people who are concerned with their own neighborhood and have lived there and been accepted by other residents for a very long time are known as the *wenye mtaa* (owners of the ward) and know and care little about those in other neigh-borhoods, except for their own kin.

Ward names give the flavor of how the inhabitants regard, or have in the past re-garded, their town. Many names refer to trades and crafts, but today they have no relevance as far as actual occupations are concerned; other names refer to places of origin of original occupants.[45] The names give a sense of continuity: they refer to places that were once important and are still so as landmarks in history, and also to the actual land on which the town is built and to the believed traditional uses of the various places and kinds of land.

Most other stone-towns are structurally similar, although the depth of their adherence to Swahili "tradition" varies. The best known is Mombasa Old Town, as it is called. Today merely a small section of Mombasa, it has a population of some two thousand living in a network of narrow streets lying between the dhow harbor and the modern commercial city. Old Town is defined not only geographically but by the fact that its inhabitants see themselves as an enclave of Muslims and reckon many ties of common ancestry and kinship both among themselves and with other Swahili towns. It is divided into moieties, Mji wa Kale (Old Town proper) and Kibokoni, the former having eight wards and the latter three. As with Lamu, most of its seafront houses are of the nineteenth century, and few traditional Swahili houses remain. To the north of Lamu, on Faza or Pate Island, are the ancient towns of Pate and Siyu occupied by Swahili still adher-ing to "traditional" Swahili culture, although perhaps only Pate could properly be called a stone-town. Other towns of the island are mainly Bajun; Faza and

Kizingitini are much larger but should be classified as country-towns. Siyu today is rather tumbledown, but Pate forms a close-knit and exclusive town in which every house is stone-built, although few have more than a single story. It is surrounded by the remains of a wall and has a wide expanse of ruins from its former days of wealth; the town was once at least a mile across. It has moieties, Mtayuu and Kichokwe, the former containing patricians only and the latter various categories of nonpatricians, each moiety properly being endogamous. Pate and Siyu, and other northern towns such as Ndau, are far more ethnically homogeneous than Lamu or Mombasa, both of which have received heavy immigration during the last and this centuries. Other stone-towns of the coast are today little more than remnants of their former selves. Zanzibar City is not a "traditional" Swahili town, but built mainly in the eighteenth and nineteenth centuries by the Omani sultans. Dar es Salaam is not a traditional Swahili town in any case, being a late nineteenth-century German administrative and Indian commercial center.

All towns have in the past been divided into moieties, and in several these are still recognized. Accounts of them are generally both confusing and confused, mainly because moieties play little part in town life today. The accounts disagree as to their nomenclature, whether mtaa, mkao, or chama, all three terms seemingly being used haphazardly. However, a pattern is discernible, there being essentially two forms of organization, one of territorial settlement and the other of government and hierarchy.

A stone-town is divided into two spatial divisions or moieties. The boundary between them moves over time but is always marked by the situation of the congregational mosque and often by an empty space or street. In Lamu local tradition tells that at the beginning of its known history the town was divided into two halves known as Vuyoni and Hedabu, which stood on or near the two hills north and south of the present town; they ceased to exist as named entities when Hedabu was covered by sand dunes. The town then moved to the lower area between the hills, and, known as al-Amu (the place of reconciliation), consisted of two mitaa known as Mkomani (the place of the hyphaene palm) or Yumbe (palace or city hall) to the north and Mtamuini (the moiety of the town) to the south.

The boundary between the two halves has altered with changes in demography and political power, and concomitant changes have taken place in the identity of the particular mosque considered as the Ijumaa or Friday congregational mosque. At the beginning was the division between Vuyoni and Hedabu, with an unoccupied space between them in which people say must have been the then Friday mosque. This was followed by the differentiation of Mkomani and Mtamuini, with the Jumaa mosque (founded about 1500) between them. Together these filled the area known today as Mkomani, which extends to the area of the present fort. The area north of the Jumaa mosque has declined but is still filled with stone dwellings. Beyond both moieties were areas of small mud houses of the poor and strangers. With the decline of the northern end of Lamu, the freeing of slaves, the immigration of many newcomers from Arabia in the last century, and the building of many houses for them to the south of the then town, the boundary moved south again to its present position at the fort and the Msikiti wa Pwani (the mosque on the beach, as the seafront was not yet built up), and the division became that between Mkomani and Langoni (at the gate). Today the Msikiti wa Pwani is the "official" congregational mosque, but each moiety also has its "own" congregational mosque, the Msikiti Nnalalo (replacing the Msikiti Jumaa) in the northern part of Mkomani and the Msikiti wa Riyadh in the center of Langoni. Which mosque people attend is a matter of political adherence, convenience, and competition. Other stone-towns have similar moieties, although unlike Lamu they mostly appear to have been stable for long periods. In most of them one moiety is essentially that of patricians and the other of nonpatricians (recent immigrants and wazalia). The two are thus hierarchically unequal, and marriage is rare between them: only at the congregational mosque is there at least formal equality. But before the abolition of slavery the situation was somewhat different and, in Lamu at least, the moieties were of equal "free" status, the wazalia and recent immigrants being few and attached to patrician lineages by ties of clientship.

In Lamu (I am uncertain about the position elsewhere, and there may be other examples), the town has also been divided into two groups known as *mikao* (sing. *mkao*; literally, those who live together) or as *vyama* (sing. *chama*, association).[46] I call them "demes." The members of one mkao mostly lived in their own moiety, but many lived in the other, mainly for reasons of commercial convenience, because they married women from the other moiety, because they had quarreled with their own close kin, or because they feared sickness or witchcraft. The demes were not corporate groups. They possessed their own names and provided the structure of town government: they are known as Zena and Suudi.[47] Lamu has been distinguished from other stone-towns by having been ruled by a patrician oligarchy. Until the system of government ended early in the present century, the patrician subclans lived in the two mitaa of Mkomani and Mtamuini before the latter was superseded by Langoni. The patrician subclans were divided between Zena and Suudi, each deme including members of all, or virtually all, the subclans of the town. Zena was associated with the north, the *upande* (side) of Mkomani, and Suudi with the south, the side of Mtamuini. More from Mkomani claimed affiliation with Zena and more from Mtamuini with Suudi.

Zena and Suudi formed the town government, the Yumbe (the same word as for town hall), each "reigning" (*kutawala*) or being given "power" (*ezi*) for a four-year period in alternation. Each mkao had its own elder, known as Bwana Zena and Bwana Suudi, respectively, selected for both genealogical status and ability. Each elder selected from among his mkao's members the *Mwenye Mui* ("Owner of the Town") to act as head of government for four years, assisted by the Council, the Yumbe, composed of one representative for each subclan, chosen mainly by genealogical seniority.[48] The handing over of power every four years was marked by festivals of poetry and dance competitions; today the youths' associations of Mkomani and Langoni still compete in musical competitions and football matches, and have been known as *beni,* from the English "band" (Ranger [1975]).[49] Zena and Suudi are remembered today but have had no political significance since the beginning of this century. The British after 1890 changed this traditional ruling system from the alternation of the Yumbe to one of representation by ethnic and hierarchical criteria; they established a nonalternating council with one member each from Zena, Suudi, the Bajun, the Indians, the Europeans, and a category known as "African." Zena is still the place of sacrifice of an ox that is part of the main annual town purificatory ritual. But the Yumbe itself, the "palace," is today in ruins.

There were until only a few years ago other town officials, whose titles are known and who were attached to particular subclans, even if today they have little or no authority. They were particularly the *mkuu wa pwani* (senior man of the seashore) and *jumbe la wakulima* (headman of the cultivators); the latter still exercises a role in Pate, at least. They were also found in country-towns, and the mkuu wa pwani remains an important person in Matondoni. These officials were responsible for deciding the auspicious times for launching sailing craft and for opening cultivation, and so were concerned with astrology and divination. Where they are found now, they are usually merged into the category of *walimu* (teachers).

The populations of the stone-towns form small plural communities, each different from others yet all with essentially similar structures. They include groups that have lived there since the towns were founded and also groups that have entered them at different times in more recent history; all define themselves by different ethnic origins, whether historically accurate or not. These elements have formed the urban populations but have also retained their own claimed identities within a particular town. Towns are divided not only into moieties but by ethnicity, ancestry, hierarchy, occupation, wealth, and sense of cultural identity. The relations between these factors are many-sided and their patterns vary from town to town. In the distant past we may assume that the basic principle of ancestry was that described by early Arab travelers, in which light-skinned Muslims held higher status than darker-skinned non-Muslims and slaves. The last categories might have been one, and the linking of skin color to religion and cultural norms seems to have been cultural and linguistic rather than physical. Under the British many people were permitted to define themselves as "Arab," and so of high rank and entitled to special privileges, whatever their physical appearance.

K i n s h i p ,   D e s c e n t ,

a n d   F a m i l y

THE COUNTRY-TOWNS:
DESCENT AMONG EQUALS

The internal organization of Swahili settlements is based on relations between members of local or territorially defined groups on the one hand, and of groups defined by descent and kinship on the other. Those who live in a particular town or ward (except for temporary labor migrants) do so because they are members of one of its families or can trace kinship to one of them. They may distinguish themselves from their neighbors in several ways: by the house and ward in which they live, by kinship, by ultimate ancestry, by rank, and by ethnicity, which are all in various ways interconnected.

The spatial patterns I have described are long-lasting and provide a sense of societal and cultural permanence, stability, and historical continuity, and they have had great functional significance for the mercantile oikumene as such. But the Swahili consider their descent groups to be those through which are organized most of their everyday relations and obligations outside the household. There are important variations between the forms of descent groups in stone-towns and country-towns: they are also elements in a single system. They are not so in the sense of being alternating, as are those described by Leach for highland Burma (1954), but in the sense of being linked to the complementary modes of production of the different settlements.

I shall first consider the Hadimu country-towns.[1] These include virtually only Hadimu, with a handful of people of other ethnic ancestries who live as individual families on the social margin of the communities and are not accepted as full citizens. The citizens of the towns are the "proprietors" (*wananchi*, sing. *mwananchi*, or *wenyeji*, sing. *mwenyeji*: literally, owner of the land and owner of the town, respectively). Others are known as *wageni* (sing. *mgeni*), strangers or tenants, who are "proprietors" in other Hadimu towns but have come to live in their present place of occupation as wageni. Only the proprietors of a town, who are all kin to each other, have full and inalienable rights (*haki*) of settlement and

Figure 4. A woman of Vumba, Kenya-Tanzania border

landholding; tenants exercise rights at the pleasure of the proprietors. But all are of the same rank: there is no hierarchical difference, except that very wealthy or pious men may be given great prestige as individuals.

The widest Hadimu kinship group is the *ukoo* (pl. *koo*). It is a bilateral group of the kind usually called a kindred or, more accurately but clumsily, an unrestricted nonunilineal descent group. The ukoo consists in theory, and almost invariably in practice, of all the descendants through both men and women of a common great-grandfather. The Hadimu usually define it by saying that all the members of an ukoo recognize common descent as far as a great-grandchild (*kilembwe* or *kiyukuu*).[2] The descendants of any pair of great-grandparents down to those whom the present generation call great-grandchildren typically form a single ukoo. The name of an assumed founder is known and gives his name to the ukoo; but this is used mainly to refer to *koo* other than one's own. A person sees his or her ukoo in terms of a cluster of cognates with whom can be claimed ties of obligation: *Fulani ni ndugu wa ukoo wangu* ("So-and-so is my ukoo-sibling"). Most people know eight great-grandparents; and due to the high incidence of divorce in the country-towns, many can recognize more than that number, as divorced spouses may remain included as classificatory kin. Since marriages are typically between cross-cousins, the various grandparents are usually of a single descent group. An individual can claim a right of residence or at least of agricultural use in the lands of any of those senior kin, and these links are carefully made and nurtured. In everyday affairs stress is laid on the greater importance to the individual of the *upande* (or *ufungu*) *wa kuumeni*, the "male side," over the *upande* (or *ufungu*) *wa kuukeni*, the "female side," and distant matrilateral kin tend to be forgotten more quickly than patrilateral kin.

The ukoo is not a residential unit as such, but the "proprietors" of a town, of whatever size, are of the same ukoo. Ukoo membership may also extend to residents in other towns, but the status of proprietor is limited to the town in which most of one's ancestors have lived; if one moves elsewhere, one remains a proprietor of that town but becomes a tenant where one actually resides. Proprietors contribute toward *uzawa*, the money given at funerals and certain other rites, and toward bridewealth; they have the full rights of building and cultivation in their own town's land without payment called *ubani* (incense), which must be given by a tenant who is member of another ukoo. There are other and less important reciprocal obligations between members of an ukoo. The recognition of the duty to contribute to these payments, and to those of marriage in particular, is a sign of men's sharing rights in and obligations toward the women of their common descent group, that is, of their shared concern for its perpetuation. The expected amounts of contribution vary with the genealogical distance between the members, those closest to the segments concerned in a marriage or funeral contributing the most; but every member, however distant and wherever resident at a given time, contributes something. These towns have high rates of divorce, and family genealogies can show great complexity; the formal recognition of these obligations between large clusters of kin constructs wide networks of exchange and so helps to give all Hadimu a single cohesive identity. The recognition of obligation between ukoo members over great distances is a means of retaining rights of residence for a future occasion by people who have moved temporarily from their "home" town in which they will be buried and to which their children can retain the right to return.

The genealogical depth of an ukoo is more or less constant, so that its membership may change at every generation. Descendants of a common great-great-grandfather typically do not form a single ukoo and the tie of siblings (*ndugu*) is not recognized between all his descendants. Hadimu say that the number of generations (*madaraja,* sing. *daraja*) should be seven, as a very old man will recognize his ukoo founder as his great-grandfather and will also have great-grandchildren living. Much depends on demographic factors. A small ukoo that has not increased in recent generations may include more than four or five generations in its genealogy. A factor here is the availability of land: the more land available, the greater the number of recognized generations. The number of generations depends also to a large extent upon the reputation of the remembered founder, since members like to keep a famous name as that of their ukoo founder. As far as I know, remembered founders are always men, although the intergenerational links include both men and women.

A person is only recognized as an ukoo member both if he or she can trace descent by "blood" (*damu*) from the founder and if his or her skin color is neither too light nor too dark, as these may indicate non-Hadimu ancestry and so not be acceptable. This applies particularly if one of the parents was an Omani Arab who may have married a Hadimu woman in order to obtain land rights.

Within the ukoo are recognized two smaller segments that are of more immediate everyday importance. These are known as *tumbo* (pl. *matumbo*) and *mlango* (pl. *milango*). The word *ufungu* (pl. *fungu*) is sometimes used, but essentially it refers to a small corporate unilineal segment within a cognatic cluster.[3] The tumbo (literally, womb or stomach) is a bilateral group like the ukoo. A person has several matumbo. In theory, a person might recognize six: those of his or her father, mother, father's father, father's mother, mother's father, and mother's mother. But in any generation these kin were typically cross-cousins as well as spouses, so that the actual number of matumbo recognized by a single person is usually two or three, and occasionally only one. A tumbo segments every other generation or so, so that the descendants of a single pair of great-grandparents will typically divide into closely linked but different matumbo. When a person refers to "my tumbo" (*tumbo langu*), he or she is referring in particular to those members with whom he or she is living at the present time. He or she maintains rights in the property of the others, but exercises the rights that attach to the status as a proprietor only in that in which he or she resides. Factors of distance, trust, and friendship are important. Marriage is typically virilocal, but the husband has the choice of attaching himself to the household of any fellow tumbo member; which he chooses usually depends upon availability of land and on degree of trust between the parties.

The tumbo is that part of a person's ukoo within which close cooperation, rights, and obligations are recognized and put into action in many situations. These are consequent upon living in the same ward: farming, building, inheriting rights in a particular piece of land, assisting in payment of bridewealth and funeral dues, and so on. The composition of the tumbo is defined in everyday usage by the particular situation in which it becomes relevant. It may be dispersed, but this is unusual and is a sign that it is about to segment: its members maintain their mutual rights and obligations wherever they may be unless they sell these rights, which they can only do to another member.[4] Cross-cousin marriage tends to be within the tumbo if there are valuable rights in property that should be kept within it and not dispersed.

The composition of matumbo shows an immense diversity of kin, linked in many ways; it is rarely uniform in terms of descent or number of generations. Its genealogically senior member may be either male or female, although authority is more likely to be held by a man and it is more effective for the group to be represented in public matters by a man. I have come across no two matumbo of quite the same genealogical composition. If a tumbo becomes too large for its available building space, it tends to divide, small groups of kin hiving off to become new matumbo in time. The use of the term *tumbo* for the residential group obviates any need for numerical or genealogical parity between wards. It also obviates the need for consistency in ways of tracing descent from the founder to the present members. The groups of ward proprietors are merely referred to as matumbo of equal status. Matumbo are referred to as "the tumbo of so-and-so" and, like koo, have no permanent names. Although the people may discuss this organization in terms of descent, in actuality it is shared membership of a ward that that defines that of a tumbo: rights of residence are given precedence over those of descent.

Those members of a tumbo who have managed effectively to limit and consolidate their holdings, even for a generation, form the group referred to as *mlango*. Mlango means "door" and is said to "show the way" into the ukoo. It is a descent group of three or four generations only, differentiated by paternal origin from coordinate milango. It is not a patrilineal lineage as it is not corporate, and its patrilineality is not stressed; but its women's children whose fathers come from outside it are said to lack "strength." Since marital residence is usually virilocal, the mlango is essentially a cluster of men related by common grandpaternal origin and their wives and children, who live, build, farm, and fish together. It is a residential and working unit that is the patrifocal core of the small cognatic descent group called tumbo. It is said that it is through his or her mlango that a person knows his or her position in the wider groupings that form the totality of his or her kin, for which the word *jamaa* is also used.[5] On occasion, a particular tumbo may be identical in composition with a mlango, but it is more usual for there to be several milango within a ward "owned" by single tumbo. All these small groups have slight differences in composition, size, and spatial layout. It is precisely in their looseness that lies their effectiveness and the perception of consistency.

Authority within these groups is minimal. In societies in which rights in land and other property are restricted to unilineal descent groups, the very exclusiveness of the group means that a person fears to lose membership, and this fear may provide adequate sanction for the authority of the elders. But in Hadimu society a person can almost always move to live with members of other related matumbo, who rarely refuse him or her entry: a person takes care to have kin of the wider ukoo to fall back upon for help should he or she quarrel with fellow tumbo members. A related factor is that of the status of women. Sisters are regarded as full and equal members of a tumbo with their brothers, although under Islamic law they formally inherit only half-shares in property rights. A woman is likely to live with her husband's tumbo, but she retains her rights in others and is usually accepted in them.

A similar system is reported by Caplan for the Mbwera, the Swahili of Mafia Island (Caplan [1975]). The terms for these groups used by the Mbwera include *kikao* (pl. *vikao*), tumbo, mlango, and the form *koo* (pl. *makoo*). All are used slightly differently from among the Hadimu (and kikao is used also for the ward, the mtaa of the Hadimu), but the overall pattern is similar. It permits enjoyment of land and residential rights over a wide area during a person's lifetime. People retain most of the rights open to them as members of more than one descent group and do not restrict their claiming of rights merely to the land of the group within which they are residing at any given time. The system is very open. This may be due, as Caplan points out for Mafia, to the fact that there is little scarcity of land. In Zanzibar, where good land is scarce, there is nonetheless plenty of poor land; it is sites for building and gardens that are sought after.

These communities are rural, country-towns or sets of country-towns which are the satellites of a stone-town. In the case of the Hadimu this was the capital of the "king"; after the death of the last ruler in 1873 it became Zanzibar City, the seat of the Omani sultans. In the case of the Mbwera it was at one time Kilwa, to which the island of Mafia was then subject, and today is Dar es Salaam and to a lesser extent Zanzibar City. The pressure exerted by these stone-towns to produce foodstuffs has always been considerable. Land suitable for food production has great value and is often scarce: this holds for both the Hadimu and for the "six towns" of the northern part of Mafia.

The members of the Hadimu settlements face two contradictory problems because of the shortage of good land: to keep a plot for each small group, and yet to keep open rights for its members (including future rights for its children) in the widely dispersed lands of the Hadimu country. They could use one of two strategies. They could severely restrict residence in a particular settlement by observing strictly unilineally claimed rights only, or they could open up residence to all cognates of the settlement's residents, who would in turn be given reciprocal rights in other settlements. They have chosen the second alternative. This is consistent with the facts that the available sites for opening fields are not of high fertility; sandy areas along the beaches are suitable for coconut palms but virtually nothing else; and the areas of sea that can be fished with seine and other nets are widely dispersed (each is owned by particular towns and by wards within them). Since productive land and water are usually limited, it might be expected that the inhabitants of country-towns might adopt patriliny as a means of keeping these resources to themselves, as a scarce good. The reason that they do not appears to be that soil types and water are both distributed unevenly in relation to the relatively few sites with deep soil where permanent gardens, wells, and settlement may be made. Most towns are on the coast and each needs both inland resources, stretches of sea, and stretches of sandy soil for palms. It is more efficient for families to have widely dispersed rights in these resources than to limit them to a particular locality.

There are various ways of limiting the enjoyment of land and house rights to those members of a tumbo who do actually choose to reside together, including the buying out of rights of sisters and their descendants, except for the right to be buried in the graveyard of their natal tumbo. On the other hand, no effort is made to restrict the range of membership of the ukoo, as it is precisely in the unrestricted nature of its membership that its value lies. What becomes clear is the link between the enjoyment of rights in property and the skewing toward patrilineality: among Hadimu the smallest kin group is the mlango, holding close residential and garden rights; the tumbo is wider, with less narrow rights; and the ukoo is wider still and often holds potential rather than presently enjoyed rights. This skewing is marked in some areas, such as Pemba, where milango or fungu may own rice marshes and clove trees, a group of patrilineal kin having bought out rights from others who could claim shares in them. Another factor is relevant: where property is new and of the kind that produces commodities for exchange outside the tumbo, such as cloves, it becomes likely that the tumbo will be replaced by the ufungu or mlango. Emphasis in these groups is placed on patriliny, excluding distant nonpatrilineal kin who could otherwise claim rights in profitable exchange products. A group of close kin may hive off and open stands of trees on their own, or they may simply register the existing stands as waqf for the benefit of patrilineal descendants only.

The country-towns strictly limit the immigration of stone-town and non-Swahili "strangers"; and the disapproval of intermarriage with people in these categories ensures control of the enjoyment of land and water rights and any possible inheritance outside the local ethnic group. The sense of solidarity against the stone-towns and their historically rapacious and powerful inhabitants has led to the recognized obligation of sharing resources among all Hadimu in order to present a powerful presence and make it difficult for the stone-towns to take over the country-towns and their lands piecemeal. Besides the use of force, as with the nineteenth-century seizure of the Hadimu ricelands by the Omani, this takeover has been achieved more subtly by intermarriage. This has happened to some extent in Pemba, but the endogamy of the Hadimu, their insistence on an ukoo member being of the "proper" skin color, and their refusal in past years to allow Arabs as tenants prevented this from happening in Zanzibar Island. This argument was presented to me on many occasions by Hadimu who were fully aware of its necessity and its implications; it is not limited to them, but provides a meaningful pattern that is found throughout these rural Swahili communities. The functional tie between ecology, production, territorial distribution, patterns of descent, and a leaning toward patriliny is very clear and would appear to have persisted for a long period (although the postrevolutionary situation in Zanzibar is uncertain).

THE STONE-TOWNS:
DESCENT AND HIERARCHY

The patterning and ideology of descent and descent groups in the stone-towns are very different. Here I discuss the situation mainly in the northern town of Lamu. The structure of stone-town territorial units is simple and consistent, but that of descent groups is less so. The Swahili coast has been the site of immigration of many groups of different ethnicity, ancestry, population size, rank, and occupation for more than a millennium. Most have come to the stone-towns as merchants, accepted as representing the potential for increased fields of exchange. As part of the process of incorporation and hierarchization, claims have continually been put forward to Arabian provenance even where this is clearly historically inaccurate. Intermarriage, lineage affiliation, adoption, and clientship have been continual, so that ancestry claimed at one period by a particular group may later be changed. Descent groups are ranked according to many often contradictory criteria: wealth, ancestry, date of immigration, size of membership, Islamic devotion, and moral reputation and purity. Their hierarchical order is continually contested, and the apparent confusion and internal contradictions in documentary and oral traditions are real, and not due merely to uncertainty on the part of members of a particular town about what they consider a properly ordered pattern. This does not mean that there is neither order nor pattern: but they are in the underlying structure and not in temporary organization.

The original inhabitants of these towns were possibly Cushites, but that is irrelevant to this discussion. The oldest elements of the present populations are those who have generally referred to themselves and have been referred to by others as *waungwana* (sing. *mwungwana*), whose subculture is considered to be quintessentially "Swahili." The word is usually given the meaning of either "free person" as distinguished from a slave, this being the common usage in most country-towns, or "patrician," this being the common usage in most stone-towns.[6] They have been merchants and have not formed a land-owning aristocracy, although many of them owned plantations worked by slave labor. The word might also be translated by the English word "gentleman": it is used to refer not so much to rank as to moral behavior, that of being "gentle" in the sense of accepting the legitimate claims of others while standing up for one's own, of being just, fair, and honorable. I have heard it said that one or two men of personal moral distinction but of slave ancestry should nonetheless be counted as waungwana, and that those who are reckoned as waungwana by birth should not so call themselves, because this would imply unfitting criticism of the behavior and standing of others. Properly it is the moral behavior associated with great pedigree that matters, not the pedigree in itself. Among waungwana themselves there have always been elite categories, often based upon religious scholarship. In Zanzibar they were basically courtiers; in other stone-towns they were clearly associated with the ruling houses; in Lamu, which had no ruling house but a ruling oligarchy, the patricians themselves formed the ruling body. Although the distinction be-

Figure 5. A patrician elder, Lamu. Photo: Michelle Gilbert.

tween patricians and others is rarely expressed in behavior, in a few towns such as Pate and Siyu patricians are freely distinguished in everyday conversation, and in Siyu, at least, patricians and nonpatricians do not sit or eat together at weddings.

There are other elements in these towns' populations, both more recent ones from Arabia and Zanzibar, such as Hadhrami and Omani Arabs, Baluchi, and others, and also immigrants from other parts of the coast, the hinterland, and the interior; but however wealthy and powerful, they are not referred to as waungwana. In Lamu the patricians live in the northern moiety of the town, Mkomani, whose "old" families regard themselves and are generally regarded by others as the "true" citizens, the waAmu (Lamuans), an elite category within the Watu wa Lamu (people of Lamu). Those latter who are not waAmu are sometimes called (perhaps not very politely) the wageni, "strangers" who have entered the town more recently than the patricians, even if over a century ago. Of these the economically most important and politically most powerful are those Hadhrami who came in the nineteenth century and have become wealthy merchants themselves, and of course non-Swahili government officials. In the past there were various categories of slaves, but their descendants are never so called. The usual word used, although discreetly, is *mzalia* (pl. *wazalia*), meaning "one born in the country." Formerly this referred mainly to the free children of manumitted concubines who were given a marginal identity.

The patricians of the stone-towns are divided into various kinds and levels of descent groups, which have different but complementary functions. There are first the groups known as *kabila* (pl. *makabila*) or *taifa* (pl. *mataifa*). Both terms are usually translated as "tribe," "clan," or "town."[7] Taifa also refers to the "townspeople" of all the waAmu, whereas kabila has a greater implication of descent. I refer to them as "subclans," generally claimed to be segments of clans whose members are found elsewhere in both Arabia and East Africa. Those clan members living in any particular town form a subclan: some subclans are today very small but are structurally coordinate both with other subclans living in the same town and also with subclans of the same clan living elsewhere. Clans are dispersed and not corporate groups, and certainly in most cases the genealogical links of ancestry to the founders of long ago are claimed rather than historically accurate.[8]

Subclans are said to be branches of the *shina* (root or trunk) from which they sprang, which possess the *nisba* or *nasiba* (family names) that are known throughout the coast. Some patrician patronyms are those of clans found in southern Arabia; others are clearly originally either place names or epithets. Properly, only the first of these should be referred to as nisba, the publicly accepted possession of which by a descent group demonstrates Arabian rather than African origin, its older link with Islam, and so its higher status in the society at large.

The subclans comprise a basic and relatively unchanging structure of a stone-town such as Lamu, Pate, or Siyu. The patrician subclans of Lamu are properly known as the Makabila Thenashara, the "Twelve Tribes," as the phrase is usually translated.[9] The Twelve are divided into the "Three Tribes" (Makabila Matatu) and the "Nine Tribes" (Makabila Tisa). The Three comprise today the groups named waFamao or al-Famii,[10] the Wayunbili (with whom are included the Kinamte), and the Waungwana wa Yumbe. The last is the first in rank and it was their representatives who sat on the governing council of the town: the name means literally "the patricians of the town-hall" or "of the place of government." The Waungwana wa Yumbe are composed of nine subclans, the Nine Tribes: the Three and the Nine are thus neither genealogically nor structurally coordinate. The Nine are usually said to form a single exogamous cluster; their marriage with the Wayunbili is discouraged, although that with al-Famii is permitted. However, each subclan tries to ensure that at least the marriages of its first-born daughters should be within it, "to preserve the blood"; those of later daughters should not be outside the Nine, although this is not always observed today. These subclans are divided in another way by the use of Arabic or Swahili prefixes to their names.

The Arabic prefix *al-*, as in the name al-Bakari, is said to demonstrate a clan origin in Oman, and the other Arabic prefix *Ba-*, as in the name Basheikh, a Yemen or Hadhramaut origin (and so an earlier one). The Bantu prefix *Wa-*, as in Wayunbili, points to an African origin. The Famao, of believed mixed Asian and African origins, are referred to with either prefix.

The order of subclan ranking varies at different periods and in different accounts, whether written or oral. One that fits the accounts I have been given myself is that presented by Prins (1971: 14).[11] They and other groups are generally ranked by categories or clusters that refer to traditional town statuses and functions, each subsuming those preceding it:

WENYE MUI: The Owners of the Town
BANU LAMII: The Children of Lamu
WATU WAKUU: The Great People
WENYE EZI: The Owners of Power
WAAMU: The Lamuans
WATU WA LAMU: The People of Lamu

The first five categories comprise the patricians of Lamu; the sixth includes all others except for recent up-country immigrants, who despite holding political power today are in general despised by the "People of Lamu" and are not included as other than temporary residents.

The "People of Lamu" are ranked according to accepted ancestry and in terms of categories of inclusivity and exclusivity. The pattern is represented in table 1, based on a diagram by Prins (1971: 20–21).[12] To the members of any one of the categories shown (Banu Lamii, waAmu, and the others), those of any category higher are not differentiated: a member of subclan 10 sees all higher subclans as undifferentiated WaYumbe; one of subclan 7 sees all higher subclans as undifferentiated Watu Wakuu; and so on. The boundary of the waAmu marks a distinction of a different order than merely degree, as it is only the waAmu who should be referred to as waungwana (patricians). However, matters are neither as simple nor so formally rigid as the diagram might imply, due mainly to anomalies in antiquity of settlement and ancestral provenance. The "lowest" in status are the Wayunbili and Kinamte, yet they may also be included as Banu Lamii, although not of "true" patrician status decided by pedigree as are the Banu Lamii as usually defined; they may be referred to together as al-Makhzumi. They are earlier settled than other subclans included as Banu Lamii and may be considered autochthonous, but were conquered by later immigrants. They did not provide members of the government, and today are few.[13] The two Sharifu lineages, Ahdali and Husseini, are peripheral, because their claimed dates of settlement in Lamu are later than the others and also because all maSharifu are socially marginal.

The main groupings of inclusion and exclusion presented above permit local citizens to conceptualize a "map" of Lamu that permits internal changes and uncertainties of affiliation. The groupings are relatively unchanging over long periods, whereas the identities of the lineages (not shown in the diagram) within each

SUBCLAN	RANKED CATEGORIES						
	A	B	C	D	E	F	G
1. Bereki	*Wenye Mui*						
2. Miraji							
3. Bashekh		*Banu Lamii*					
4. Bakari							
5. Maawi (including Bauri)							
6. Madi			*Watu Wakuu*				
7. Ahdali							
8. Husseini							
9. Jahadmy			*Wenye Ezi or Wa Yumbe*				
10. Famao							
11. Kinamte							
12. Wayunbili					*waAmu*		
13. Alawi							
14. Hadhrami							
15. Omani, Baluchi, etc.							
16. 19th-century Sharifu immigrants							
17. Bajun						*Watu wa Lamu*	
18. Pokomo							
19. Mijikenda							
20. Kikuyu and other new strangers							Total residents

1–9 = The Nine, or Wangwana wa Yumbe
1–12 = The Three (i.e., Wangwana wa Yumbe; Famao; Wayunbili plus Kinamte)

Table 1. Lamu descent groups

subclan may change fairly rapidly, with new immigration, the increase, decrease, absorption, fusion, and even dying out of descent groups, all of which processes have occurred in local oral tradition. In addition, the paradigm permits ignorance of groupings other than one's own without destroying the view of the system as a functioning whole in which changes can be ignored even though they occur continually.

The system of ranked subclans has today lost most of its former basis in political and economic power, but it is remembered and discussed on many occasions, especially weddings. Subclans still hold certain ritual duties: they jointly "own" the Friday mosque; have the right to elect every four years from the Watu wa Lamu (including the Hadhrami, but not the Bajun) the mosque officials; their heads have the prerogative of occupying the right hand bay during the *khutba* sermon and of praying behind an imam chosen from their number (a right seldom exercised). Most of their public responsibilities no longer exist, so that the complexities of structure cannot be observed in action: the blowing of the great horn (siwa) at patrician weddings, the duties of the hereditary offices of prison warden, keeper of the town treasury, and warden of the sea.

The traditional form of government in Lamu has been by the alternation of the two demes Zena and Suudi. It is in this context that the lack of congruence between ward and subclan boundaries may be seen not as an anomaly due to change but instead as a functionally necessary principle of organization. Each reigning council contained representatives of each subclan, and therefore each subclan had to be divided between Zena and Suudi. While the demes are not territorial groupings as are the moieties Mkomani and Langoni (or earlier Mkomani and Mtamuini), Zena is still associated with the north and Suudi with the south; the houses of each subclan are distributed likewise, even though there are no strictly drawn boundaries between them. For the system to work, each subclan has to have at least two lineages each with its houses in different parts of the town, and this was so in the past when the patrician population was larger. But the pattern is—or has been—more than one of political alternation. On ritual occasions the two sides were both involved by virtue of the ritual functionaries being from the deme opposite to where the ritual was actually performed, so that there was ritual complementarity between them. The Friday mosque is in Zena but the lineage of its preachers is a lineage of the al-Maawi living in Suudi; the ritual expert of the sea (no longer functional) should be from the Zena members of the al-Bakari, who live mostly in Suudi; and there have been other examples.[14]

In brief, the system of subclans provides an overall structure for the town; provides in socio-spatial and hierarchical terms an understanding of the history of that town; and places Lamu within its wider social and historical context by linking its subclans with claimed origins and clan ties in Arabia (although not all such claims are publicly accepted). Although the main order of ranking seems not greatly to change over time, its validation does so in the sense that new genealogical claims are continually made to add weight to tradition. Detailed genealogical links are not always recognized within subclans, so that changes in claims to membership may easily be made merely by claiming new or different ancestry. El-Zein (1974: 54ff) adds another classification based on ultimate descent from the two branches of Arabs, known as Adnan and Joktan. My informants have disclaimed this classification, although the names are known: it appears to be one held by certain maSharifu groups with recent ancestry in Arabia.

Within a subclan there are constituent segments of lesser genealogical depth, for which many terms are used, the most usual being *mlango, tumbo, ukoo, nyumba,* and *uladi.*[15] In Lamu they refer to effective patrilineal groups of kin that are continually being founded and later replaced by newly formed successor units. They comprise kin descended from a recent ancestor or ancestress and are of relatively shallow genealogical depth. Tumbo (womb) is defined by a single founding "womb," by having a single ancestress, usually only two or three generations back; it is referred to by the name of its living head. Ukoo, mlango (door), and uladi are used loosely for a small lineage of greater depth descended from a common male founder, and may therefore include several matumbo. The terms

refer to the same groups, and the difference is that ukoo and uladi are collective nouns meaning "the descendants of so-and-so" and cannot be used without
the eponymous founder's name; whereas mlango is more usually referred to by
the name of its senior living member. Uladi, from the Arabic *aulad* (lineage),
is mainly used by those who perhaps more loudly than most claim Arabian provenance, the Hadhrami, Omani, and Sharifu subclans. Although the usage is loose
since these small groups change in size and composition fairly quickly and the
term is not then always altered, in general mlango, ukoo, and uladi refer to a lineage, while tumbo is used for a small noncorporate segment of a lineage. Nyumba
(house) is used for a household, that segment of a subclan which actually occupies
a stone house.

Stone-town lineages, of whatever span and depth, are not unchanging but
undergo regular cycles of development, although the subclans retain the same
basic structure for several generations. However, today they may dissolve by emigration due to impoverishment and because the great stone houses are too costly
to maintain. Variations and permutations have abounded with normal vagaries of
demography and profit. A lineage will segment every few generations if more children are born than can fill the lineage's houses or if the lineage has been increasing
its wealth. Segmentation is marked by a paternal parallel-cousin marriage which
establishes a new segment within which close cross-cousin marriages can then be
arranged for three or four generations. The existing lineage may then divide and
its name fall into desuetude.

A lineage that in a given time in its history is not occupying a stone-built
house is unlikely to acquire the status and name. Lineages are corporate groups:
each has a name, its members share certain property rights, and it is represented
by a genealogically senior male member. Ownership of a lineage stone house is
the essential criterion rather than genealogical position within a subclan. These
groups do not form units in a "segmentary lineage system" of the classic type,
there being no balance of segments in complementary opposition. I shall discuss
the ownership of stone-built houses below; here I need say only that although certain rights in houses may be exchanged under certain conditions, most are subject
to past waqf and so their disposal is extremely limited if not legally prohibited.
Most houses are occupied by members of lineages whose eponymous founders
left them as waqf for their unilineal descendants, and it is especially these that are
referred to as *uladi wa X*, "X" being the original maker of the waqf.

The pattern of authority within subclans is that each lineage has its own head.
There is today rarely more than a single level of segmentation, but in a few large
subclans the uladi are divided into segments, matumbo or nyumba. The head of
whichever lineage is considered at a given time to be the senior group, properly
by virtue of the genealogical position of its founder, is thereby also the *mkuu wa
kabila* (head of the subclan), although today the title has little meaning. Formerly
the mkuu wa kabila was important and would represent his subclan in the governing council of the town; today his cluster of kin, his jamaa, still plays a key
role in the marriages and funerary rites of his subclan members.

In the case of lineages that are generally not recognized as possessing Arabian origin (despite frequent claims), the word *uladi* is less often used than *utandu* or *utanzu* (branch). Prins mentions this (1971: 27) but does not explain that for other patricians to deny to the Famao, Kinamte, and others the courtesy of claiming the epithet *uladi* is unfitting the behavior of a proper mwungwana.[16]

I have been describing the patrician half of the town, Mkomani. There is also Langoni, the other moiety and an integral part of Lamu. It has markedly increased in population during the present century, while Mkomani has decreased in both population and financial and political importance. Most of the dwelling houses in Langoni are small and of only one story, but there are also a good many modern concrete-block two-story houses. One reason for this last development has been the determination of the patrician families of Mkomani to have little to do with non-Lamuan immigrants ever since the coming of the Omani Arabs in the eighteenth and nineteenth centuries, and they try not to permit these immigrants to settle in Mkomani.

Langoni's population has six main elements today. One comprises the wealthier and now politically important families of mainly nineteenth-century immigration from Arabia, some directly and others indirectly through Zanzibar or the Comoro Islands; they claim Arabian and high-status Islamic origins. They include the descendants of the Omanis sent from Zanzibar to administer and oversee the coastal towns, and those of Hadhrami traders (often referred to by the local patricians as waShihiri)[17] who came from the Hadhramaut during the nineteenth century. Despite their social importance, the more traditionally minded among the Mkomani patricians still regard them as nouveaux riches and disapprove of marriage with them. A second category comprises families of *ungwana* origin from other towns, representatives of "old Arab" lineages such as the Mazrui, from Mombasa; although ancient in origin they are not included as WaAmu proper or as waungwana of Mkomani. A third category is composed of Bajun, many of them immigrants from the impoverished coast to the north; some have become wealthy but most are poor, their men working as laborers and fishermen. The fourth category is that of the descendants of former slaves, many or even most of whom preferred to remain in Lamu and still retain many patron-client ties with their former owners and their descendants; they are commonly merged with the Bajun population. A fifth category is mixed, comprising several anciently established trading families of Bohra Indians, and the descendants of nineteenth-century immigrants associated with the Zanzibar Sultanate such as Baluchi soldiers, most of whom have become absorbed into other categories. A final category consists of recent immigrants from the mainland who are not Muslims (as are all the categories just mentioned) and so not Swahili but Pokomo, Mijikenda, Kikuyu, and others; they remain apart as newcomers, socially and culturally.

The patrician subclan and lineage system retains importance because it still provides an assumed standard for proper Swahili "civilization" and "urbanity," to which all others aspire. As Prins writes: "The social structure [of Lamu] lingers on when the social organization has already largely vanished" (1971: 17).

The patrilineal descent groups of the Hadhrami and al-Busaidi groups in Langoni are essentially similar in overall structure, although they differ in patterns of marriage and marital residence.[18] Some Bajun groups, especially the wealthy and better-educated, whose members claimed to be "Arab" during British rule, have also organized themselves in this way.[19]

The names and relationships of the patrician subclans of all the Swahili stone-towns are confused and confusing, due partly to the loss of political and economic power by these groups during the present century. Similar complexities of descent group organization can be found in all of them, and the ethnic composition of these towns is one factor that distinguishes them from most country-towns. This composition is, of course, congruent with their histories both of social formation and of their patterns of rights in property. Prins lists the "clans" found on the Benadir coast, among the Bajun, and in the stone-towns of Faza, Siyu, Pate, Lamu, Shela, Mombasa, and Vumba (1961: 82–83). Some of these places have become very small and unimportant, and some of his lists refer to almost vanished communities. Yet the names are remembered and their historical interrelations are discussed at length in the towns themselves.[20]

Visiting, which essentially means the recognition and expression of ties of kinship between members of subclans of the same clan in the many towns along the coast, is frequent and involves both many people and considerable distances. The network of subclans forms permanent links between the towns and is important in maintaining Swahili identity. In addition, ties of marriage are widespread and obligations of visiting and gift giving are based largely upon them. The relationships between the patrician subclans and nonpatrician descent groups may best be considered historically, and have been mentioned in the section on myth in chapter 2 above. The historical pattern as held by those local scholars who have written on Swahili history reflects the belief that the first occupants of the Swahili coast were Bantu speakers and other "African" groups, many of whose names (or those of their descendants) are remembered, although many no longer exist as distinct groups. In Lamu these are represented by the Wayunbili, Kinamte, and Famao, and there are similar groups elsewhere, such as the waChangamwe and waTangata of Mombasa. They were "swallowed up" (as one local scholar expressed it to me in English) by immigrants from Arabia, mainly by marriage and occasionally by conquest and enslavement (as with the waNg'andu of Manda, who were subjugated and absorbed by the patricians of Pate). Marriage is always mentioned as a means of absorption. The process is seen as that of autochthonous groups being "swallowed" by immigrant patrilineal subclans, a privatization of resources by those able to acquire wealth by commerce. Demographically it is more likely that the swallowing was the other way, but the history is seen as one of commerce and political power. Each stone-town is today divided into moieties, one of which is inhabited by makabila ya waungwana (patrician subclans), the other by nonpatricians, descendants of the first category mentioned above: Bajun, wazalia, and recent Muslim immigrants. Individual patricians may in fact live in a "nonpatrician" moiety, especially when they marry there. In Zanzibar and Dar es

Salaam, the ancient coastal subclans are largely lacking, the rulers and merchants being of Omani Arab immigrant stock (until the 1964 revolution, at least) and the others being Hadimu, Zaramo, Zigua, and various marginal groups as well as the descendants of slaves.

A category that should be mentioned here is that of the subclans and lineages known as maSharifu,[21] who claim and are attributed direct patrilineal descent from the Prophet. They are found in both stone-towns and country-towns and are considered to be possessed of an innate spiritual virtue and grace; they hold high prestige and are given special forms of greetings and precedence. Some Sharifu lineages have been members of the stone-towns for many centuries, others since only the nineteenth century. The former, in particular, are counted as patricians, although their status is ambiguous: they have substituted spiritual qualities for ancestry, and yet their ancestry is more immaculate than that of anyone else. The maSharifu are usually (but not exclusively or necessarily) endogamous, and marriages between them and non-Sharifu hold many problems of behavior and rank for the spouses and their children insofar as there would be a contradiction between the authority of the husband (if he is not Sharifu) and the moral superiority of the wife. However, "secret" marriages between Sharifu men and nonpatrician non-Sharifu women are frequent, and often a subject for much disapproval and malicious gossip.[22]

I need say little about other stone-towns, whose descent systems are essentially the same as that of Lamu. Lamu is the largest stone-town with a still functioning descent system: elsewhere, as in Mombasa Old Town, the numbers of constituent groups remaining are far less and the complexity of Lamu is no longer found.

A final point concerns the nature of stone-town descent and descent groups. *Patrilineal* is a blanket term under which is conventionally placed a cluster of traits largely because they are often, although not invariably, found together: mode of descent, use of descent names, residence, forms of marriage and succession, group membership.[23] Stone-town marital residence is properly uxorilocal, a trait not usually classed with patriliny; but the recognition of the patriline provides an effective basis for the other traits listed, and the Swahili themselves have words for the kin groups and categories formed around it.

A peculiar assumption in some studies of the Swahili is that they are or have been a matrilineal people. This has been made in reference to the past by Knappert (1979), Nurse and Spear (1985), and others. I use the word "assumption" because there is no evidence for it. It may be based upon an outmoded ethnology, or upon a misinterpretation of Swahili myths in which a ruler is said to have transmitted his authority to an immigrant through marriage to his daughter; but this is patrilineal and not matrilineal descent. Many early Swahili towns are said to have been ruled by queens, but queens may rule in patrilineal societies. More important, these queens are essentially mediatory personages of myth, symbols of autochthony in contrast to male immigrants, of indigenous society in contrast to new mercantile and political power.

Shepherd (1977) bases much of her argument on the position of a patrician daughter at her marriage. Among the Comorians a first-born daughter, at least, is given a house at her marriage by her father that is afterwards hers to dispose of as she thinks fit.[24] If she leaves it to her daughter, and that daughter leaves it to her daughter in turn, then it appears that the line of matrifiliated women have perpetual rights of ownership over a piece of immovable property. But in this case the "father" would not give the house to his daughter, as is said to be his duty: his wife would already own the house in which he resides, and it is she who would pass it to the daughter. Certainly, in a town such as Lamu the houses are owned by lineages and not by their individual members, although the individuals enjoy limited rights of residence that might cursorily be considered "ownership." In any case, a matrifilial line is not a matrilineal lineage, as it is not corporate, it has no name, and it has no presumed perpetuity. In matriliny the successor to a man who holds authority is a sister's son, but among the Swahili patricians the head of a lineage is the head of a corporation and his successor is always the son thought the most likely to succeed in business. The head of the lineage lives with his wife in the ndani of the main house. She is responsible for the care and purity of the house, he for its wealth and reputation among men. The ownership of houses remains patrilineal and consistent with the mode of paternal parallel cross-cousin marriage.

Another argument, also advanced by Shepherd, is that the smallest descent group among the Comorian Swahili is the *inga*, a descent group of two or three generations that springs from a single woman; this is clearly similar to the tumbo of patrician society. But the tumbo is not a matrilineal group among either Lamuans or Hadimu, nor does the inga appear to one among the Comorians. These groups are small-scale segments of wider patrilineal descent groups, differentiated by maternal or grandmaternal descent from a male progenitor-ancestor. It is not an example of matriliny but of matrifiliation.

Several observers have suggested that people of Lamu and elsewhere who are of slave ancestry trace their descent matrilineally.[25] Genealogies may at first appear to be examples of matrilineal descent, but even though the intergenerational links run from woman to woman, they are not so. They are examples of people related by mother-daughter links over several generations, but there is no property or office in which rights are transmitted. The links are those of mother-daughter only, one generation at a time. There are many such genealogies in Lamu and other stone-towns, but the people involved do not form corporate descent groups of any kind. Their women's names are in the form of X *binti* Y, with no clan or lineage names. A patrilineal lineage is surrounded by a maze of links of affiliations of this kind (and most people of slave ancestry recognize father-child links also), but these do not add up to a complementary matrilineal organization. Finally, the system of naming of women shows the emphasis placed upon the patriline. A man is known by his personal names and those of his father and grandfather, with the addition of the name of his subclan; a woman is known by her personal name and those of her father and father's father and her father's (and so her own) subclan.[26]

DESCENT AND CORPORATE GROUPS

The recognized mode of descent among the Swahili varies from one settlement to another between descent reckoned in the direct patrilineal line, mainly in the stone-towns, and that reckoned cognatically or bilaterally, mainly in the country-towns. The fact that the Swahili terms for descent groups include both those of Arabic and those of Bantu origins allows the variants to be seen in terms of different ethnic origins. The Lamu patrician pattern is similar in some respects to that found in southern Arabia and has often been taken to be a reflection of or borrowing from that region; the Hadimu pattern has often been taken as being in some way more "African" (although in fact such bilateral systems are uncommon in Africa); and since the Hadimu and others often refer to themselves as "Shirazi," it has even been thought that this pattern has a Persian origin. However, such "historical" explanations do not get us very far: it is of greater use to consider the functional aspects of these organizational variants.

The relationship between the two forms of descent is historically and socially complex. They should be considered as linked, as subtypes in a total continuum of Swahili "descent"; but this is not to force them into a simplistic evolutionary pattern, nor should any one variant be considered as "typically Swahili." Neither mode of descent is determined entirely by ecological, historical, or psychological factors, but by people taking those factors into account—particularly, as with all cultural choices and decisions, those patterns of which a society has some experience from its own past. The inhabitants of Swahili settlements have always made these decisions as to what is most beneficial to each community, whether a stone-town or a country-town. They have done so while maintaining a generally similar vocabulary of terms for local and kinship groupings. They use these terms in different ways, yet by using the same terms they are aware of themselves as being members of a single culture with a single underlying structure, and make it easy for members of one town to settle in another. Indeed, the variation in usage of the same basic terms is an indication of the nature of Swahili society: as a middle-man society it has had continually to adapt to ever-changing threats and demands from its external partners, while at the same time it has had to retain its sense of single identity over many centuries. This adaptability is expressed, among other ways, in its organizational looseness and variation between its many constituent communities. The basic traditional structure of a stone-town such as Lamu is one of mutually exclusive patrician subclans, each being endogamous at least as far as first marriages of daughters are concerned, but with a slight degree of hypergamy permitted for marriages with other patrician subclans. Marriages with nonpatricians are rarely approved, although they are increasingly frequent. These patrician descent groups are multiplex organizations which have controlled their own activities of production, residence, marriage, inheritance, and business exchanges, and have permitted relatively little individual independence of action. The same pattern is found in all the stone-towns, although in recent years, especially with the spread of Western-type education to women as well as men, individuals have become increasingly able to acquire new roles and new mobility. The cognatic groups of the country-towns have also been multiplex organizations, but the lack of exclusivity of these descent groups, of whatever span, means that individuals are permitted greater freedom for independent action, with greater mobility.

Descent groups do not stand in isolation but are part of wider systems of exchange and alliance. The economic and political relationships between stone-towns and the other towns are traditionally those of a nuclear settlement and its satellites. This relationship is reflected in the pattern of terminology used for descent groups and in the actual composition of the groups even where designated by the same Swahili term. Their composition is related to patterns of land and property holding, of inheritance, of succession to political and other office, of marriage, and of residence.

The most important distinction between the two types of recognized descent is that among stone-town patricians (and among Hadhrami and Omani lineages also) the recognition of the patriline alone enables property rights to be limited to members of the single line and the group formed around it; whereas in country-towns rights in property may be dispersed to all descendants of a great-grandfather through both men and women. The observance of the patriline in the stone-towns means that direct ancestry to clan founders, usually claimed to have been in Arabia, ensures that a distinction can be made between those with that ancestry and those without it. In country-towns such as those of the Hadimu, unilineally traced ancestry is not recognized and so no such distinction can be made. However, as I have mentioned, in Pemba (and elsewhere) among many families owning clove trees there is a greater emphasis on the mlango, a small patrilineal descent group, so that rights in these profitable trees are retained over the generations; marriage follows the typical rules exemplified by the Hadimu, but the significance of this definition of mlango is obvious.

Another interpretation is to see the essential contrast between stone-towns as "traditionally" composed of business houses, and the country-town as composed of peasant gardeners and fishermen. In both the main territorial unit is the "town" (mji), of great duration and occupying the same sites for generations. But it has very different meanings for its inhabitants. The stone-town, formerly walled, is a fortress in the waste of "barbarism" (*ushenzi*) and is considered the place of long residence of people of Islamic "civilization" (ustaarabu) claiming descent from ancestors in Arabia. The country-towns mark the only fertile sites of residence and gardening set in less hospitable coral wasteland, and the ideological links with descent lines of great depth are not found. The association with past time that is so much a part of the unilineal subclan is lacking in a cognatic system of descent. For the stone-town merchants the town has been the port of trade, finance, and profit from providing services to others; for country-town peasants the town is a residential base for occupations—including provision of food and labor to the stone-towns—most of which involve seasonal movement from one set of fields and one stretch of ocean to another, and from home to abroad as migrant laborers and clove pickers. The distinction runs through the differences in corporation and in notions of descent and of rights in property between the two kinds of towns.

In terms of property this distinction is between rural and urban "real" property (as apart from personalty), especially land and houses but including such productive resources as slaves, ships, and profitable trees. This is consistent with, indeed perhaps consequent upon, the system of production and distribution of foodstuffs and other commodities. The areas of food production both for local consumption and for trade were in the past worked either by free Swahili or by slaves (today by squatters or hired laborers). The pattern of ownership of the "free" and "servile" productive areas was and still is different. The former is by the citizens of the country-towns and the latter is by those inhabitants of the stone-towns who owned slaves and today use other labor to work their plantations. The former is by farmers who form largely egalitarian communities with complex methods of ensuring suitable distribution of land rights over a wide range of different soil types and among a wide range of cognatic kin. The latter is by urban-dwelling proprietors who do not traditionally farm themselves but use various other kinds of labor. Hadimu land is subdivided among and thrown open to all the citizens of a settlement, whereas a stone-town plantation, however large it may be, has been owned by a single lineage and kept exclusively for that lineage's use and inheritance. The same process has been developing in areas such as Pemba, where indigenous groups have come to share in small-scale plantations themselves. Another example was during the nineteenth century in Malindi and on the mainland around Witu, where ex-slaves and others opened up new plantations to grow grains for export overseas: the new entrepreneurs (some of whom were women) reckoned effective descent in the male line only, neither ethnic nor original town affiliation being considered important. Another factor is that the stone-towns include many patrilineal descent groups that claim by their names to have moved from other places on the coast. To enter a hierarchically ranked urban structure, an immigrant group would need to be patrilineal and not cognatic: a cognatic group could not fit into the internal structure of a patrician community. Likewise, intermarriage between families of different types of descent is extremely difficult, and this provides another barrier between them. The situation has not, of course, prevented concubinage or clandestine marriage.

In all societies the framework for cohesion and continuity lies in the structure of corporate groups. There is a considerable literature on corporate groups in nonindustrial societies, and the definition of corporation is generally accepted by anthropologists: a corporation is a single unit (or a single person as a corporation sole) in the sense that from the outside its membership is undifferentiated; it is a single body for jural purposes; it has a single and exclusive membership; it has presumptive perpetuity; it has an internal authority structure the control of which is in its members' hands; it has a single representative who acts vis-à-vis other groups; and it has a name or title.

The main function of a corporate group among the Swahili is to ensure clear definition of the inclusive identity of its membership and of its rights in particular kinds of property, and clear exclusion of nonmembers from the enjoyment of these rights.[27] Both inclusion and exclusion are assured through time, although there are always means by which the members may include new members or exclude present ones. It is in this particular sense that we may say that corporate groups provide the cores or skeletons of towns and segments of towns. Property rights are held over material and immaterial objects and resources by both groups and individuals as members of groups. The main material rights include those over resources such as land, stretches of beach and water, trees, crops, houses, sailing craft, tools, and other objects of personal use and consumption, and also over people of various kinds, of whom the most obvious have been slaves. The main immaterial rights include the right to marry, rights of political, familial, and religious authority, the right to claim particular ancestry, and the right to define who are fellow citizens. Rights of all kinds are usually vested in corporations aggregate or sole. An obvious exception may be that of rights given at least temporarily to new religious leaders, but this does not invalidate the general rule, since their status is accepted as one that is ideally devoid of any rights in property. And in any case most religious innovators among the Swahili have been maSharifu, who are members of property-owning lineages.

It is useful to summarize the differences between the territorial and descent groups of the various settlements. The Hadimu and Lamu patricians may again be taken as the extremes of a spectrum along which other settlements lie at various points. A main difference is in the identity and composition of the corporate groups. In both stone- and country-towns the largest corporate group is the town itself. It is a settlement for habitation and as such a discrete spatial unit; it has its own townlands that form its exclusive property for the enjoyment of its citizens (the boundaries of the townlands are often open to dispute with neighboring towns, but at any given time they are recognized); it has its own personnel, whom its members appoint themselves, responsible for internal government and the control of town affairs and finances; it has an official responsible mainly for external relations with other towns and superior states (in the latter case the various colonial states took upon themselves to appoint these representatives, but it is significant that by so doing they recognized the identity of the towns as corporate entities); it has a name and presumptive perpetuity validated by its claimed history and physical permanence; it has a recognized membership in its citizens or "proprietors" and they have the right to accept or refuse other people as various categories of tenants.

The small descent group that forms a household, whether with its own or sharing a homestead, is known as nyumba. It has the right to select its own head with internal authority over other members and to represent it vis-à-vis other household and groups, to own its own accommodation and its contents, and to control the use of land and water that are allocated to it by superior authority in the town. However, the household as such is not a corporate group; it is, properly speaking, the lineage segment of its head that is corporate and not the cluster of residents, some of whom are typically of other subclans or lineages.

Beneath the level of the town there is significant variation in the composition and identity of constituent corporate groups. They include both descent and local groups of various depth and span. In both the two main types of town there are moieties, but these are not corporate: they have neither presumptive perpetuity nor autonomy other than spatial discreteness; their internal authority structure is temporary only, in that they are given responsibility for the organization of New Year and other rites. The same holds for the demes of traditional Lamu government. There are also the wards or quarters. Here a distinction needs to be made: in the Hadimu towns the wards are the corporate groups; in Lamu the corporate groups are the patrilineal subclans and lineages. Among the Hadimu each ward is associated with a particular tumbo, a cognatic descent group, but although rights in land, houses, and personnel are allocated to the townspeople as members of particular matumbo, it is the ward that remains corporate. The ward has presumptive perpetuity, whereas the tumbo does not. The ward has a name, whereas the tumbo does not. The ward has a publicly recognized head, the mkubwa wa mtaa; although he is also an elder of a tumbo, the statuses are distinguished and they are acquired quite differently. The ward has a "purse" (mkoba wa mtaa) for the use of all its members as a group, which stands for its corporate interest and identity. The ward is a closed group and has the right to accept or refuse additional members and tenants, whereas tumbo membership is potentially very wide: but actual or effective residential membership of a tumbo by a tenant, that is, a member from elsewhere, can be given only by the mkubwa wa mtaa and not by the members of the tumbo alone on their own initiative.

In Lamu, by contrast, although the town is divided into wards, the houses of the descent groups of the town are not congruent with ward boundaries (and indeed could not have been in the past, when the alternating governing role of Zena and Suudi was operative). In Lamu, and also in Mombasa and Pate, it is the unilineal descent groups that are corporate (even though the term *tumbo* may be used for segments of them, its composition and meaning are very different from those of the Hadimu settlements). Subclans and lineages have presumptive perpetuity; each has a head and an internal authority structure; each manages its own internal affairs; each has its own houses, lands, and rights over its own persons (and formerly its slaves); each has a name. The subclan has no "purse" to correspond to that of the country-town ward. Money and valuables are kept by individuals, but the head of a house (that is, of a lineage) and his wife are expected to have their own place for safekeeping, either a large jar, a locked chest, or a form of safe built into a wall. The word *hazina* (treasury) has been used for such wealth, especially in commerce, there often being need for considerable sums of money (today most people keep their money in commercial banks). Each subclan formerly had responsibility for certain offices connected with the town government, each having the right to select the actual holders of these offices. One consequence of the discrepancy between subclans and wards, of course, is that the ranking of subclans may change over time without changing the pattern of town layout provided by the wards.

A central difference is that of the drawing of social boundaries or closure of these corporations. This is consistent with and may be seen as a consequence of ecological factors and the kinds of rights in productive resources that are recognized. Among the Hadimu settlements there is relatively little ecological variation other than in spatial terms: in some areas the ecologically complementary resources are closer together than in others. In Pemba Island there is greater ecological variation and fertility, and a greater reliance upon cash crops in the form of both rice and cloves. In Mkomani the main items of property are the permanent houses, possession of which gives not only shelter but also prestige and the reputation of sharing in the highest form of Swahili civilization. Productive resources in land were, and still are, both highly fertile and usually far from the town, many miles away in the hinterland and limited in availability. Formerly the possession of slaves, who were in a relationship of personal dependence and attachment to their owners, was linked to the subclans and lineages, much of whose social standing depended in turn upon this very ownership. These three patterns are marked by an increase in exclusivity of ties of kinship and marriage and a widening of the range of situations that involve corporate groups. The corporate groups hold and are partially defined by rights in inalienable property. In both Hadimu and Pemba wards and Lamu patrician lineages, the widespread institution of waqf with regard to these properties is an important aspect of corporateness. Among the Hadimu the kitongo-owning group is a small unit in a wide-reaching system of exchange relations, whereas the patrician lineage is both tightly bounded and also responsible for virtually all the relations of its members, unlike the Hadimu situation.

Other towns fall between these extremes in this regard: those of Pemba, the country-towns on Pate and Lamu islands, the towns of the Mrima. An illuminating example is the account of northern Mafia Island by Caplan, who refers to the cognatic descent groups as corporate (1975). The term for them is *kikao*, which is used also to refer to a ward, most of whose members are of the same cognatic descent group. It would seem, and I think would be expected, that the system as far as incorporation is concerned would be not unlike that of the Hadimu. But there are certain differences. Despite variations in usage of the same set of kinship and residential terms, the kikao of Mafia seems to be structurally equivalent to the ukoo of the Hadimu: each has about the same generation depth and each is subdivided into a number of lesser and overlapping cognatic descent groups, each of which is in turn of about the same number of generations in each place. The word for this lesser segment is tumbo among the Hadimu and koo and other terms on Mafia. One difference between the two places is that it would appear that pressure on land is greater on Mafia, as is also pressure from non-Mbwera elements of the total island population. It would follow that emphasis would be placed more on descent groups than on the territorial units. And there is recognized on Mafia a more complex ranking system and a greater ethnic intermixture than among the Hadimu. The Mbwera of Mafia appear closer in these respects to the country-towns of Pemba than to the Hadimu of Zanzibar; but the situation is not quite clear.

Finally, another category of corporation is found in any town. This is the *shirika*, a group that holds waqf on a property or that is established as a property-owning enterprise. The term *ufungu* is used for such groups. I have mentioned them above in connection with property in country-towns, and shall discuss them in chapter 8 as an aspect of the process of privatization. Shirika might be translated as "company," referring to a corporation aggregate or sole that holds property or acquires and sells property, whether material or immaterial. Such enterprises may be registered legally, as a proprietor of a house, mosque, or any trading company in the usual capitalist sense of the term. This notion, a key one in contemporary Swahili society, can be found in Swahili history as far back as it can be traced.

FAMILY AND KINSHIP GROUPS AND CATEGORIES

Swahili descent and kinship form a complex topic because of the many variations between towns and between groups of different rank. However, all towns and groups choose from a common set of kinship terms to define certain domestic and kinship ties; they are idioms that express rights and obligations of many kinds. Little material has been published on Swahili kinship terminology: a list of terms is given by Prins (1956); the fullest account is by Landberg (1977). However, a set of kinship terms is not a kinship system, and we need to ask according to what principles and in what situations the terms are used. The terms themselves vary little from one part of the coast to another, but the situations of usage, and so their precise meanings, vary considerably. Swahili marriage is a means of defining and redefining boundaries of inclusivity and exclusivity, and the use of kin terms and categories is linked to these processes.

Two basic terms refer to clusters of kin without reference to descent as such: nyumba (house, household, or homestead) and jamaa, usually translated as "family" but more accurately "cluster of effective kin."[28] Households are of varying composition. The relationship between the actual house, the household, and its general social position is an important and close one, rather more so in the stone-towns, with their traditionally more sumptuous and sophisticated way of life, than in the country-towns. There are still in the stone-towns great variations in materials and sizes of houses, their upkeep, furnishings and ornaments inside them, division of labor within the household, forms of clothing, diet, and personal possessions such as jewelry, all of which express variations in status and reputation; these variations are fewer in country-towns.

The size and composition of households vary between towns and within towns over time, according to stages in their cycles of development. Control of these variations is managed by various strategies. In the country-towns the average size of a domestic group occupying a typical dwelling house is about 3.5 persons. A marked feature of country-towns is the immense variation in household composition, even though the sizes are much the same.[29] Many factors are involved, including high divorce rates, wide dispersal of fertile plots of land, much individual spatial mobility, and widespread fostering of children. Country-town houses can easily have a room or two added, so if there is garden space, a family can increase the size of its residence. Where garden space cannot be increased for a ward, individuals and their elementary families try to move elsewhere as kin-tenants. The composition of households varies among settlements. The fullest account for the country-towns is for Mafia Island, which agrees reasonably well with that among the Hadimu and Tumbatu of Zanzibar Island. In northern Mafia Island half of the households are grouped into clusters, each averaging three households and usually having a focal household with a male head (Caplan [1975: 51]). The Bajun of Tundwa on Faza Island have households most of which lack men living in them permanently, and the household heads and house owners are mostly women. A woman and her children provide the only relatively long-standing unit in that community (J. Bujra [1968]).

In a stone-town, such as Lamu, the situation has been and is different. Among patricians corporateness and authority lie in the patrilineal lineage, and the group occupying a house includes both one or two segments of the owning family and other kin and nonkin integrated to varying extents, as with slaves in the past and servants today. Among patricians there is need both to ensure the continuity of the lineage occupying its permanent house and to form collateral links to related subclans elsewhere. Both are accomplished by careful marriage planning for the lineage's daughters. The principle is that the eldest daughter should marry one of her father's brother's sons and live in her father's house; younger daughters may marry other parallel- or cross-cousins and may move elsewhere. The average figures for stone-house occupancy depend largely on how many floors a house has, and this in turn may depend on whether houses are physically joined. Figures for Lamu houses show an average of 4.5 persons to a household and 2.1 households in a single house (Siravo and Pulver [1986: 67ff]). Stone-towns show more uniform and stable household composition than country-towns. Most households have male heads, and these towns show features that are the opposite of those listed above for country-towns: they have low divorce rates, less dispersal of fertile land, less mobility, and less fostering of children.

The jamaa, a word of wide usage, is essentially a cluster of kin, both cognatic and affinal, centered on ego; but it may include friends, neighbors, and others with whom ego may interact in specific situations. There is a qualification in that the Swahili jamaa seems rarely to include persons of higher, or at least of markedly higher, rank than ego. Ego calls his or her jamaa into operation, that is, he or she may invoke ties of obligation from those junior, as clients, but usually not from those senior. When a particular jamaa has been recognized for a long time, this qualification may no longer apply, and the junior may expect more assistance from a senior.

The composition of the jamaa is a function of the content and limits of the links between its members, both related to the composition and range of an individual's social networks, which are not unbounded. These networks' limits are those of named ethnic and same-rank groups where these exist and, where they do not, of the relations of economic and social exchange centered on a town. In most country-towns the ethnic group is coterminous with an individual's network, as with the Hadimu or Tumbatu of Zanzibar Island, or, in the case of the Bajun, the kin dispersed over a small cluster of islands. In the stone-towns the network is defined as centered on a particular town, family, or kin group, but includes members of the same agnatic ancestry elsewhere, who live in stone-towns but only rarely in country-towns. Both kinds of networks may overlap with others and may include non-Swahili.

Within such a wide network an individual's jamaa depends on his or her general social importance. The more important a person is in terms of seniority of age, influence, religious purity, and moral reputation, the wider are its limits. The system depends on fluidity for its effectiveness. An important factor is the proportion of kin and nonkin in a particular jamaa in a particular settlement, which is linked to the identity of the corporate groups in that settlement. The jamaa is never corporate, but since every settlement has as its basic social groups those that are corporate, they are functionally complementary: obligations that are not placed upon the corporate group fall on the jamaa. Among the Hadimu an individual's jamaa is almost always identical with the joint membership of his or her various descent groups and wards in which he or she can claim some form of residential right. Jamaa members are selected from these groups because there are virtually no people with whom an individual comes into personal contact except for other Hadimu. The difference between the jamaa and the cognatic descent group is that an individual chooses certain members of the group as being those with whom he or she maintains relations of trust and obligation to form the jamaa. Among the Bajun of Faza Island, where descent groups of any kind are weak, the jamaa may be the only unit outside the household (which is here small) on which an individual can rely on everyday situations. It is therefore composed of selected kin and neighbors, links of common descent being of little or no importance. In the stone-towns the corporate groups are patrilineal lineages and the jamaa is a cluster of kin and neighbors with whom an individual has ties of friendship and of patron-client obligations. Here the jamaa is relevant largely in membership of political and religious factions; also, these towns have many kinds of nonkinship associations which often take the place of jamaa elsewhere. The jamaa is an operative cluster of persons called together in specific situations by a given individual or household. The most important situations are those of participation in mortuary and wedding rites, but there are many others: although usually seen as social occasions, essentially they have jural significance. In all of them the members of the jamaa are formally invited, the invitations defining the properly constituted jamaa at that period in an individual's or household's history. Those invited are expected to attend and to contribute moneys. Others may attend as a sign of respect, friendship, or recognition of distant kinship, and, by implication, of a wish to be included more formally. A death is followed by mourning (*matanga*), by visits, and by the payments of mourning gifts by the jamaa of the family's senior member. The death of a wealthy and important person may be followed by visits of several hundred people, mostly kin, not only from the particular town but from towns up and down the coast. Since marriages are typically between close kin, the jamaa members show their obligations both to the deceased and to his or her immediate family.[30]

In the situations involving the jamaa, the often ambiguous, even contradictory relations of equality and inequality are balanced; the situations refer to the exercise of power and authority, and the decisions whether to invite someone's jamaa are made carefully and with an eye to the future. But some situations are more charged with power than others, and are correspondingly more public and formal. The most important formal occasions include marriage, death, and inheritance, all of which concern the transition and transformation of persons and groups. This formal expression and definition of transition and transformation involves the publicly witnessed transfer of money and commodities such as food, cosmetics, and cloth, all things of high symbolic content. In both types of towns the definition of a jamaa is essentially strategic, part of the search for power, land, wealth, prestige, and reputation. In the search allies are acquired and competitors must be defined, and kinship usage provides one means of doing so. This remark is of course something of a simplification: Swahili are dealing with situations of ambiguity. But the ambiguity must be resolved, by definition and redefinition of categorical boundaries between people and groups.

Swahili descent groups are never very clearly bounded or restricted. Variations in range are linked to generational depth and the emphasized mode of descent. The main features of the kinship terminologies proper are that emphasis is placed upon generational solidarity and intergenerational difference, with the frequent merging of alternate generations; on the recognition of seniority of others by juniors; on the frequency of merging affines with cognates; and on the recognition of ambiguously marginal kin by the use of joking relationships. Some of these principles are at times contradictory, and the fluidity of usage and reference resolves this.

I turn now, very briefly, to kinship usage. In the country-towns members of the same generation are usually addressed and referred to as *ndugu* (sibling), although there are formal terms for older brother, for sister, and descriptive terms for more distant cousins when they need to be distinguished. Those cousins who are potential spouses may also be referred to as *mkoi* (pl. *wakoi*; Landberg [1977: 107])[31] and as *mtani* (pl. *watani*, joking partner: see below). Members of alternate generations of the same ukoo or lineage may be referred to as *babu* (grandfather), *bibi* (grandmother; also wife or senior woman), and *mjukuu* (grandchild), but the latter is not used in address and the others only rather formally. The more personal form of address is simply "ndugu," stressing the solidarity of alternate generations; and a grandparent may jokingly address or refer to a grandchild as *mchumba* (fiancée) or *mume mwenzangu* (co-husband), as both grandfather and grandson share the same bibi (Landberg [1977: 115]). The picture varies in the stone-towns, but essentially the same terms are used in the same situations. The main difference is in the far narrower range of ndugu, which here is less used for members of patrilineally related subclans in other towns, except in a rhetorical manner (such as brothers of the town or of Islam). Also, the usages between alternate generations mentioned above are uncommon, although understood. It is important that the linguistic use of all these terms expresses relations of seniority, juniority, and equality.[32]

With this goes a difference in the depth of genealogies, which is closely linked to the relative importance of ancestry as means of ensuring either exclusion or inclusion of others by a property-owning group. Genealogies in country-towns are typically shallow, rarely of more than four or five generations; the exceptions are genealogies for the claimed Shirazi founders of people such as Hadimu who wish to claim earlier origins than Omani so as to preserve rights in land. But the general shallowness of genealogies is consistent with the wide-spreading nature of the ukoo and its strategy of inclusivity. The opposite holds in the stone-towns.[33]

An area of great ambiguity is the position of cousins. The ideal pattern of marriage is between cousins, for strategic reasons. For stone-town patricians the paternal parallel-cousin is preferred, in particular for a first-born daughter, and in country-towns cross-cousins as well as paternal parallel-cousins; marriages with maternal parallel-cousins are disapproved. The ambiguity arises in the nearness of cousins to the prohibition against incest. Actual paternal parallel-cousins are almost siblings, and first-degree cross-cousins may be almost as closely related. In addition, since in all Swahili towns marriages should be between those equal in rank, the basic principle of respect for seniority cannot be brought into play to help resolve ambiguity. One obvious way of doing so is by institutionalized familiarity, the "joking relationship" or *utani*.[34]

The Swahili distinguish two kinds of utani. One form is between cognatic and fictive kin, and the other is between the Swahili towns and the different ethnic groups with which they have come into trade relationships. However, besides treating others with familiarity, watani (those who practice utani) may threaten to disrupt the normal and proper behavior between kin and affines, especially in ritual; they are considered to be in a contractual relationship that is rather different from, or is additional to, that of cognatic kinship. Watani include cross-cousins, the mother's brother and the sister's child, and lineal cognates of alternate generations. The first category comprises kin among whom marriage is permitted or preferred; the other categories comprise those between whom marriage is prohibited. All these relationships are ambiguous, although in different ways. Landberg describes the ambiguity between cross-cousins as "an alliance between those who are members of the same generation, yet, ideally, members of different but related kin groups" (1977: 129). The mother's brother (mjomba) is both a cognate and also a potential parent-in-law; the same is true of the father's sister (shangazi), but in this case the relationship to her is seen as one of *stahi* (respect), the form of behavior contrary or complementary to that of privileged familiarity. Grandparents are those who hold authority over those who hold authority over oneself, and part of the ambiguity resides in this; also nonlineal grandparents and grandchildren may intermarry if the age differences are not marked, as can be the case with classificatory kin.[35] The situations in which joking behavior may, or even should, occur are those of birth, marriage, and funerals. All may involve efforts by joking kin to interrupt proceedings unless they are given small sums of money, as well as forms of verbal sexual insult. In these rites of transition, the underlying patterns of cognatic and affinal kinship are changed and validated. To quote Landberg again: "Both the social categories and rituals involve a mixing of qualities which ought to be kept separate. Further, *watani* can behave in ways which are otherwise not appropriate to the proper social and moral order. None the less, it is precisely the ambiguities inherent in transitional states and symbolized in these social categories which provide the basis for *utani* ritual action. *Utani* ritual activities provide a context for the presentation of certain basic conflicts in Swahili society" (1977: 130).

These formal and informal relations between groups and persons change continually with changes in economy, governmental authority, educational achievement, and other factors. They are formed into the accepted patterns and perpetuated in ordered and expected ways by the redefinition of relations of descent and alliance that are part of all systems of marriage. The patterns of Swahili marriages reflect the underlying need to perpetuate particular groups and forms of power. Because of the internal complexity and variance of the Swahili towns, there is great variety of marriage patterns, although they present an underlying coherence and all express the central notions of descent, rank, wealth, and purity. The main difference is that the marriages of the wealthier families of the stone-towns are more elaborate and contain greater degrees of formal Islamic validation than those of the families of country-towns and the poorer members of the stone-towns. This distinction affects both the identities of spouses and the nature and function of marriage payments. In planning marriage strategies, the Swahili divide kin and neighbors into certain categories. The membership of a category at a particular time and place changes in particular situations: in this way there can be constant shifts and adjustments of personnel in a category while the overall schema itself remains stable. These categories must be distinguished from descriptive and classificatory kinship terms: the latter may cross the categorical boundaries. The categories that are here significant in both stone-towns and country-towns (as contrasted with differences between them in kinship terminology itself) include:

1. cognatic kin with whom marriage is forbidden;
2. cognatic kin with whom marriage is preferred or permitted;

3. affines, who may also be cognates;
4. nonkin with whom marriage is permitted although not preferred;
5. nonkin with whom marriage is forbidden or strongly disapproved.

The first category include "siblings of one womb" (*ndugu wa tumbo moja*), that is, siblings of one father or one mother, the smallest family group; and all members of adjacent generations, although certain stepchildren are not included.[36] The second category comprises all those kin of the same and alternate generations other than direct lineal kin. Preferred marriages are with cross-cousins and the paternal parallel-cousin; marriage with a maternal parallel-cousin is not approved but does occur in later marriages of divorced women. Kin with whom marriage is permitted are also included as watani. The category of affines need not be discussed here, except that many affines are likely also to be ego's cognates and watani. The fourth category includes all others who are Swahili; and the fifth comprises strangers of different ethnic affiliations and those of markedly lower rank.

AMBIGUITIES OF GENDER AND SERVILITY

The populations of the Swahili towns are divided by boundaries of local propinquity, descent groupings, and kinship relations. They are also divided by what the Swahili see as basic and divinely ordained categories of humanity: men, women, servile, and infidel groups. The relationships between these categories are complex and ever-changing, providing cross-cutting patterns of a kind that have often been considered elsewhere in Africa as stabilizing mechanisms but which may equally be considered as divisive. Although people of servile rank (including manumitted slaves) have never become full members of free descent groups, they have been closely linked to them and usually considered as nonkin members of households. The view that slaves and those with slave ancestry are inferior is virtually universal and is held by both men and women of free ancestry. Some writers have sought to show that men of free ancestry class women and those of slave ancestry together. This is a superficial generalization: men may regard each category as in some respects inferior, but not as forming a single one. The relationships between difference and complementarity are subtle, and the views held by men and women are also different.

The Swahili refer to any human being as "a child of Adam" (*binadamu*). But within this universalistic category (stated by men who claim Koranic validation for it) there are subcategories, each defined in contradistinction to others: men and women, "civilized" and "barbarian," free and slave. The Swahili world is one of deep contradictions and ambiguities. In one dimension free men stand firmly at the center and women and servile categories are placed on the margin; in another women are placed at the very center as holders of the moral purity on which depends the perpetuation of the society. Behind these categorizations lies the perennial ambiguity of origins in Africa and in Asia that is reflected in these categorical pairs. And as in all societies the roles of men, women, slaves, and barbarians are never defined clearly and irrevocably: they change, they merge with one another, new roles are accepted and old ones allowed to fade.

The previous chapters have presented a general view of the place of men in Swahili towns. They hold general authority, and most formal political and other roles are played by them and are on the whole well defined and straightforward. The nature and place of women are more ambiguous. There is a general Swahili belief that women are both different from men and (in the view of men) inferior to them. Not all "modern" Swahili women accept these beliefs, and indeed I know many who refuse, as far as they are able, to live by them and try to change them.[37] But the basic tenets of Swahili civilization reinforce them and their implications run through everyday behavior.

The status of Swahili women is contingent on certain factors: mode of descent, forms of marriage and residence, rules of inheritance and rights in forms of property, forms of hierarchical differentiation, and ability to acquire their own wealth. Among Swahili communities there are variations in all these factors and the position of women varies accordingly. The ambiguity of women's status has traditionally been based upon three kinds of differentiation: between the roles of men and women; between those of women in stone-towns and country-towns; and, in the past, between the roles of slave and free women. This last distinction was greatly affected by the ending of slavery: the difference between women who had held authority over slaves and those who had themselves been slaves became less certain, although it still affects much everyday behavior. Also, differences in education, individual wealth, and occupation of women have introduced new forms of differentiation between them.[38]

The role of a woman differs according to whether she is a patrician member of a stone-town, a member of the poorer groups in a stone-town, or a resident of a country-town. Women in the country-towns have always played a productive role in farming, petty trading, and coir making that is substantially equal to that of men. The wide network of cognatic kin ties that provide an individual's jamaa comprises links through women which are equally important as those through men. By Muslim law a women inherits only half the share of property that comes to a man, but she can take her inheritance and her right to future inheritance, as well as that to leave it to her children, wherever she chooses to live. She is a person of considerable formal social and economic importance in her own right, and plays a role equal to her male kin in most of the affairs of her kin groups. The poorer categories of stone-town women not of slave descent have something in common with those of country-towns.

The traditional position of a patrician woman in the stone-towns is based on the principle that she is and has always been the means by which the lineage perpetuates itself, with the qualification that slave concubines could also bear children for their owners. She holds certain rights in the house and other property by her marriage and is able to acquire wealth (for example, by petty trade) and keep it as her own as she thinks fit; and she controls the everyday life of the household. On the other hand, she is traditionally subject to many personal constraints that are intimately linked to Islam and to the moral purity of the lineage, and so strictly enforced by her male kin. They include the observance of house-seclusion for much of a woman's day, the necessity to be a virgin at marriage, the inability to sue for divorce coupled with the possibility of being divorced by her husband without formal trial or appeal except in unusual circumstances, and the need to be veiled when she goes outside the house. Although the effects of these constraints may be mitigated by participation in primarily women's events such as weddings and picnics, patrician women traditionally have suffered what they often claim to be irksome rules.[39] Today these restrictions have lessened considerably as these towns have become more "modern" in an economic and political sense and as their children acquire a more "Western" education. Increasing numbers of young Swahili women take to modern careers, mostly in the lower commercial, educational, and health spheres. There has also been in recent years a marked change in the position of younger men, with the opening of employment opportunities in the oil states of the Persian Gulf. Some better-educated young men have been able to earn large sums of money to use for very high marriage payments. The men who do not go to the Gulf states have become relatively poor and cannot possibly find the sums needed for an expensive marriage, and the opportunities for young women to follow a traditional marital career have become fewer. The uncertainties of a woman's role have doubtless increased in recent years because of this.

A central factor that concerns women is the concept of *usafi* (purity), which I will discuss further in chapter 8. "Purity" is best considered in relation to a particular social structure, which in turn reflects the Swahili view of the world as a whole. Although both men and women are descendants of Adam, they differ morally and physically in many respects. The most important is moral purity, although as always the moral is linked to the physical. Purity appertains to both individuals and descent groups, as well as to houses, towns, and other places and things. All are seen as interlinked and the purity of one reinforces that of others. The purity of a group is paramount in ensuring its proper place in the hierarchy of descent groups, and it depends particularly on the purity of its women.

In all Swahili towns men worship in the mosques, and may enter them and sit on the seats usually built in the street in front of them whenever they please. The practice for women varies: in some towns they may not enter a mosque at all; in others they may sit behind the men, separated from them by a screen; in others they may sit on the left side of the mosque, with the men on the right side. But usually they may neither enter the mosques, nor sit on the seats outside, nor clean themselves with water from the mosque cistern. Men are continually being purified by attendance in the mosque and at its prayers and other rites. They perform ritual ablutions before praying and after sexual intercourse; they should wear cleanly laundered white robes and *kofia* (the white embroidered Swahili men's cap); they wash before and after eating, observe proper rules for eating, defecation, and other bodily activities, and so on. All of these (and of course the preparation of men's clothing and of cooked food) demand a fairly high standard of living and a modicum of work by others, and these notions and behavior re-inforce social hierarchy. These physical acts ensure both physical cleanliness and also moral purity. In the past most polluting activities were performed by slaves, whose purity did not greatly matter.

The purity of women is more difficult to evaluate and achieve than that of men, which is consistent with the greater ambivalence in their social status. Relevant here is the complex relationship between women and the world of spirits, which sets them apart from men in the moral sphere, and the importance of a woman's puberty rites, her wedding, and her virginity. The role traditionally played in these rites by slave women is important, as are the emphasis on sexuality and the lack of male actors. Certain moral qualities were attributed to female slaves, especially a lack of Muslim purity and morality, voracious sexuality, and a symbolic link with fire—altogether the opposite of the desired moral purity attributed to free patrician women. Initiated women are ambiguous. They are guardians of lineage and house purity, and to become such a guardian a woman must lose her "nature" and so resolve the ambiguity that is part of her as an individual. In this resolution lies the importance of female initiation at puberty: men do not need to do this. Women become more pure, responsible for their own prayers to God; yet they also become associated by their training with sexuality rather than with lineage procreation. The moral ambiguity of a newly adult woman is concomitant with her ambiguous status within the lineage, and also with her ritual ambiguity in being both related to lineage ancestors and associated with spirits. This ambiguity is also reflected in other aspects of a woman's life: her wearing of a veil; her at times very real sexual freedom in a formally male-controlled society; the popular belief (at least among men) that both married and divorced women are always ready for extramarital affairs; and her right to various kinds of property given at her marriage.

It has been held that women are peripheral members of Swahili society. This seems to be based on the fact that that more women than men live in real poverty. In the outlying parts of the northern coast, in particular, the recent impoverish-ment of the area has led to severe female poverty. The women tend to move south and may need to become laborers and at times prostitutes in the larger towns. Not being patricians but mostly Bajun, such women become merged with those of slave descent and join a subclass of the urban poor.

The values and cultural influences of slavery remain important parts of Swahili culture.[40] Slavery has contained a basic ambiguity in that for those who claimed some Arab ancestry, the "Africans" who were also among their ancestors were considered to be the descendants of Ham and as such divinely condemned to servitude. The slave was recognized as a "son of Adam," but as also a "son of Ham" he shared in Ham's disobedience to his father, Noah; and as an infidel he was marked by his refusal to honor the promise made by Adam that humankind would obey God by accepting Islam. Slaves were made into Muslims, they were taught the basic prayers and shown how to pray, but were not taught about such matters as Islamic rules of inheritance and marriage. These were considered too difficult for them at first, and it was feared that if they knew too much they might expect to be treated like free people.

A newly acquired slave was considered to be only just above the level of an animal. He would be referred to as *mjinga* (stupid person), *mshenzi* (barbarian), or *mateka* (war captive or booty). A new slave was washed by an old slave who also trimmed hair and nails and who taught what was demanded of a slave, including some grasp of the Swahili language. A man was circumcised if he was to work as a domestic slave, since he would then be unpolluting and able to handle and prepare food. He was then given a name. Slaves could not be given ordinary names such as Muhammed since these were "owned" by the patricians. Instead they were called by a name referring to the day of the week when they entered the town or by names such as Sa'idi ("happiness") or other attributes that they lacked. Slave women were given similar names, whereas free women were given the names of women related to the Prophet. A new slave was thus symbolically reborn and transformed into a member of Swahili society. But a slave never became a full member of that society; even if freed by the owner in later life, his or her origin was not forgotten. Slaves were distinguished also by their dress. Men could not wear the patrician turban or woollen clothes, nor carry arms unless told to do so by their owners; they wore merely a loincloth.[41] Slave women wore either a *kaniki* (a black cloth) or a colored piece of cloth that left the shoulders uncovered: they were regarded as sexually promiscuous and described as being like "fire." When a slave died, mourning was not observed; the corpse was referred to by the word for the carcass of an animal and was not washed with perfumed water, as was that of a free person.

Slaves were frequently freed by their owners, usually as *sadaka*, a voluntary religious act of charity or of penance. These were in some areas known as *wahadimu*.[42] Usually a *mhadimu* recognized an obligation to remain a member of his previous owner's household and was entrusted with personal matters as his former owner's agent. He would be given a slave woman as a wife: the offspring of such a marriage were known as wazalia (home-born persons).

Slaves were owned by lineages but were not absorbed into them. They underwent a process of demarginalization and a degree of absorption in local town society, but that was all. The status of slave was a highly ambiguous form of dependence. When slaves were freed, or escaped, they had to construct a new and always ill defined status for themselves.

The treatment of slaves varied considerably according to the whims of their owners and their value on the market. It is a duty in Islam not to be brutal to slaves who work well and do not try to escape. But there are many records of slaves escaping and setting up settlements of runaway slaves on the mainland, both to escape harsh treatment and to make a profitable living.[43] Female slaves retained on the coast were referred to as *mjakazi* (female newcomer) or, in its diminutive form, *kijakazi,* and were allotted both domestic and field tasks. Many became concubines (*suriya*) to their owners or their owners' sons. The son of such a union bore his father's name and was a member of his father's patriline, but although free, he was given lower status than his half-brothers whose mothers were free.[44] He would not usually marry a freeborn woman but only a former slave who had been given her freedom. The daughter of a concubine by her owner remained a slave in theory, but since it was proper for a concubine who bore her owner's child to be given her freedom, the practice was not clearly defined. Slave women were also married to freed slaves or given as mates to other slaves without marriage.

Swahili society was profoundly affected by the abolition of slavery. The descendants of slaves were free in colonial civil law but not according to the *shari'a* (Islamic law), since in Islam a slave may only be freed if the manumission is made voluntarily by the owner. Until today a stigma has been attached to descendants of slaves; and although a member of a formerly free family may marry a woman of slave ancestry, until very recently a man of that ancestry could not properly marry without permission from the family of his former owner and having paid them a due known as *kilemba* (literally, turban), a payment made to a teacher by a student or apprentice at the end of a course of instruction. Without this payment the marriage would not properly be recognized at law and the children would be counted as illegitimate.

From the mid-nineteenth century runaway slaves and those captured by British antislavery patrols came to form groups living on the fringes of Swahili society, in particular between Mombasa and Lamu. Many, perhaps most, were Muslims and known as *mahaji,* who looked down on local non-Muslims; others accepted Christianity, which also marked them off from local peoples. An example is the waMisheni ("mission people") of Rabai, who played an important economic part in early colonial days as traders, mechanics, railwaymen, and coconut producers (Herlehy and Morton [1988]). They have provided links between the Swahili towns and the local mainland peoples at the interface between Swahili and the interior. They are peripheral to the Swahili proper, but it is important to stress the permeability of the Swahili settlements by local non-Swahili, even those who have not adopted Islam.

The abolition of slavery did not cause long-held views as to the nature of slave women to die away immediately; indeed they are still held to some extent today. But it has led to a marked change in the axis of differentiation, in that the descendants of both formerly free and formerly slave women have come to regard themselves as belonging to a single category of women.[45] Much writing about Swahili women emphasizes the unity of women of free and slave ancestries and distinguishes between men's and women's "cultures," especially in the stone-towns. Some writers have held Islam to be especially the religion of men, while that of women comprises forms of spirit possession; this shows a misunderstanding of Swahili religion. It has also been suggested that both during and since slavery, women of both free and slave ancestry have seen themselves as having common concerns distinct from those of men; that the traditional "patrician" culture of the stone-towns has been a male and largely Arab one; that the culture of women has originated in the behavior and memories of the cultures of indigenous "African" societies from which slave women came; and that, unlike male slaves, many female slaves lived in the actual households of the patricians and so passed much of their own cultural behavior to free women and their female children. In brief, the pattern of male, urban, "Asian" culture has been contrasted to female, originally rural, "African" culture.

Interesting though these suggestions are, it is a simplification to assume that male and female areas in Swahili society are separate from each other: they are complementary and neither has ideological or religious existence or meaning apart from the other. There is also the factor of historical time. Discussion of the historical link between Swahili women's subculture and those of the societies from which many slaves were drawn centers around the origins and nature of this "mixed" African-Asian people, since it has been suggested that the female slaves brought with them certain traits from the interior and that these have persisted to form part of women's subculture.[46]

One problem with this suggestion is that not all women in the stone-towns were slaves. The views of patrician daughters about nonpatricians were equally "patrician" as those of their brothers and husbands, and these views are held today by many older Swahili women in towns such as Pate and Lamu.[47] Although several writers mention marriages between patrician men and slave or ex-slave women, these were highly unusual. Unions with concubines were frequent, but concubines did not live in the same houses as their masters and their wives, so their cultural influence was minimal. Female slaves and concubines did bring with them many traits from their natal societies, but certain factors militate against the diffusion of these traits. Slaves were taught the elements of Islam and were encouraged to disavow non-Islamic beliefs; there were deliberate efforts to remove traces of "barbarian" behavior from slaves so as to increase the social reputation of the household as one of believers; concubines (suriya, a formally defined status) were almost always women who had taken pains to become educated and Muslim, were both socially and sexually adept, and had separated themselves from their fellow slaves and their own cultural origins; and, finally, non-Islamic items of ritual were incorporated into the corpus of religious behavior known as *mila* and so permitted under Islam. Mila is part of permitted Swahili religious practice, and efforts to regard it as forming part of a distinct female subculture are unfounded: both men and women accept and practice it.

Chapter Five

Perpetuation

and Alliance

THE STRUCTURE AND RANGE
OF MARRIAGES

Of all Swahili institutions, perhaps marriage has been the most badly described. Most writers have considered it unimportant, part of a pattern of sexual looseness in everyday life demonstrated by the high divorce rate. There is no truth in this view. Marriage patterns vary from one town to another, as do rates of divorce, forms of marital residence, transfers of property, and everyday sexual behavior. Perhaps this diversity has confused observers.

A wide range of male-female unions is recognized in the Swahili towns, although not found in all of them. It runs from forms of marriage regarded as "proper" and lawful in Islamic and customary law by their definition as *ndoa*, the consequence of *kuoa*, the verb that is (correctly) translated into English as "to marry";[1] to concubinage, which is lawful but not ndoa; to unions defined as unlawful (*harimu*), which are also not ndoa. The lawful unions include the "official" marriage, known as *ndoa ya rasmi*,[2] properly registered by *kadhi* (judge), *khatibu* (preacher), or *mwalimu* (teacher);[3] the so-called secret marriage (*ndoa ya siri*); and concubinage. Both forms of marriage involve a wedding (*arusi* or *harusi*), while concubinage does not. Unlawful unions include intercourse with a recently deserted or divorced woman and with prostitutes. These are either given a euphemistic gloss or regarded as immoral and perhaps requiring ritual purification, but are not specifically condemned as sins. In addition, although permitted under the law, cases of excessive serial polygyny are disapproved: these are almost invariably cases of secret marriages. Other forms of sexual union include casual heterosexual love affairs that are condemned if too frequent or indiscreet, and homosexual unions. Homosexuality is said to have been tolerated between slave owners and slave boys, and today during Ramadan when heterosexual intercourse is prohibited. It is frequent between visiting sailors and local males, and with tourists, although this last is strongly disapproved if the union becomes permanent (many of the local men and boys involved are not Swahili but "beach boys" from upcountry groups). Homosexuality is often but not necessarily associated with

mashoga, male transvestites who act as drummers and musicians at women's festivities. In Lamu and rural Zanzibar, at least, it is disapproved if between adults
or close kin, and I know of cases where continual homosexual behavior has led to
ostracism and even banishment.

Unions vary in certain main respects. These include the kin and rank relationships between the partners; the degrees of affinity concerned in and created by the
union; the transfer of forms of property and wealth; the patterns of residence; the
formal establishment or not of a household (nyumba); the duration or expected
duration of the union; the modes of public and legal recognition of the union; the
affiliation of children born of the union; and the kind of wedding rite performed.
Marriages may be considered part of long-term strategies pursued by corporate
groups, whether lineages or wards. Strategies concerned with rights in property
and acquisition of power largely determine the choice and range of spouses; concern with purity and reputation largely decides the contents of the marriage rites;
and the wealth and ambitions of individuals also affect the choice of particular
forms of marriage and of spouses. As it is said, *Mtu haowi mke huowa ukoo* ("A
man does not marry a wife, he marries a descent group").

I will first discuss forms of marriage among the patricians of Lamu, and then
those of the Hadimu of Zanzibar, as examples from the ends of the spectrum between stone- and country-towns.[4] In all Swahili marriages there are elements of
Islamic law and also nonjural elements, some of which are found in other Muslim societies and others not. While marriage is an important rite of transition for
both men and women, it is far more so for women, especially in the case of a first
marriage; elaborate and costly weddings are rarely performed for later marriages.
I will discuss the notion of purity later; it is central to an understanding of the
position of the bride. For her the marriage marks the transition from young girl
(*msichana*) to pure wife (*mwanamke*); her purity is the basis for the purity of her
lineage. The wedding itself is thus a rite of transition for the entire lineage, a corporate group that is renewed and perpetuated by the first marriage of an eldest
daughter.[5] The complexities of the transition from girl to wife make sense only in
this context.

Underlying the pattern of patrician marriages in Lamu are certain characteristics of Lamu itself. A limit is placed upon physical expansion, so that new houses
on new sites can be constructed only with great difficulty, and the expense of land
purchase may be prohibitive. Houses themselves may be subdivided, rebuilt from
and on the sites of ruined buildings, and very occasionally bought and sold; they
are valuable and treasured resources. The ownership of the main productive resources has until recently been limited to and controlled by the patrician lineages
of the town, and marriage has as one of its principal functions the validation and
maintenance of the ownership of these resources and other property.

Patrician marriages, and to a lesser degree nonpatrician marriages also, are
based on certain rules of endogamy and of preferred and prohibited degrees of
marriage: the first involves a system of intergroup relations, the latter one of interpersonal relations. Endogamy concerns those relations expressed in terms of the

notion of *kufu*.[6] Kufu means "rank" or "social level," as in *Fulani si kufu wetu* ("So-and-so is not of our level" or "So-and-so is not our social equal"). A proper or lawful wedding (arusi ya rasmi) should take place only between those of the same kufu. The word refers to the distinction between free and slave, between patrician and nonpatrician, and between one patrician subclan and another since these are also ranked, although in a somewhat indeterminate and fluid manner. It refers also to personal manners and to Islamic scholarship, so that at times a free man and a slave, or a patrician and nonpatrician, might be said metaphorically to be of the same kufu in those senses: but their families would not intermarry. In effect the usage means that marriages between paternal parallel-cousins have been and remain the preferred form for a woman's first marriage in Mkomani.

Paternal parallel-cousin marriage means that both spouses belong to the same lineage and so rights in lineage property are retained within it. Most such marriages begin with the betrothal, the agreement between the two elementary families concerned that their children should be betrothed for a later marriage when they come of age. There is a general congruence between the importance of devolution of rights in property by marriage, the incidence of close-cousin marriage, and the frequency of betrothal. Betrothal is closely linked to the ongoing status of a lineage as a property-holding corporation. The arrangement of a paternal parallel-cousin marriage is not made for every first-born daughter. It is associated particularly with the de facto establishment of a new segment of a subclan or lineage, one that has begun to assume operative identity due to business success, the building of a new house or additional part of a house that physically marks off the growth of a new segment, or merely the sudden appearance of a new segment due to the birth of one or two generations of many successful children. It is found also in situations of paternal and fraternal trust and affection. It involves verbal agreement between the parties, but no registration beyond formal statements to other subclan members and to close friends who act as witnesses. The marriage and marriage payments for a marriage with betrothal are the same as those for a marriage without it. The betrothed know that they are so, especially when they go to school and then reach puberty. The age of first marriage varies greatly today. Traditionally a girl would be married as soon after puberty as was practicable, and a boy some years later. Today first marriages take place later: a groom needs to have earned enough money to make the heavy payments needed as gifts to the bride's kin, and both may need at least to finish school.

A series of cross-cousin marriages, if made following a paternal parallel-cousin marriage, are within the same lineage. When the initial paternal parallel-cousin marriage is lacking, then they would not be, as is the situation described later for the Hadimu of Zanzibar. But this is not a common strategy among the Lamu patricians with reference to the first marriages of most elder daughters and sons. It is the marriages of younger children that are used to spread marital links more widely. Most marriages of virgin women other than first-born daughters among patrician families are with the mother's brother's son and the father's sister's son. Marriage with the mother's sister's daughter is legal but widely considered as harimu (ritually impure or forbidden), since sisters may often suckle one another's children and so the marriage may be said to be incestuous.

From genealogies I estimate that some 65 percent of patrician first-born daughters' first marriages during this century have been with paternal parallel-cousins, 25 percent with first and second cousins, and 10 percent with men whose kinship relationships are more distant or nonexistent. The relevant factors are the size and span of the lineage concerned in a particular marriage, and the importance given to the establishment and maintenance of family links with other towns. If there is a "useful" cousin living in Mombasa or Zanzibar, then that cousin may be considered highly suitable for betrothal and marriage.

Paternal parallel-cousin marriages are said to have been highly stable and rarely to have ended in divorce. One rather cynical old lady told me that of course a husband might persuade his wife to let him take a concubine, or he might find one without first telling her. This, she assured me, was very much better than his taking a second wife, which appears to have been rare among the patricians of Lamu[7] and might lead to divorce. There have been cases of patrician polygyny in Lamu: the co-wives would not live in the same house, the husband moving from one house to another. However, all those of which I have knowledge have been cases of secret marriages (see below); otherwise the practice would raise many difficulties.

A woman's later marriages differ from her first marriage mainly because she is no longer a virgin and her status is no longer so closely linked to the purity and continuance of the lineage. Whereas for the first marriage she is likely to have been betrothed, this is not so for later marriages. For her first marriage she must obey the wishes and the authority of her parents, who are responsible for the wedding rites. But for later marriages she has greater freedom to make her own choice. Individual mobility between the coastal towns is considerable, and a young divorced woman or widow may visit kin in another town and there find another husband. In addition, she may now have her own property from her earlier dowry. If she has children, she is reckoned more likely to be a mature and responsible woman, but she now has the responsibility of providing for them. The choice is much more open to personal factors—two cousins choosing each other—although usually with the agreement of at least their mothers and close maternal kin. The official bridewealth (*mahari*) is still payable; the divorce rate for these marriages is higher than for a first marriage; and relatively few are legally registered. Such out-marriages create new interlineage links, which in following generations may the more easily be strengthened by further marriages.

An institution that has often aroused a prurient interest and a good deal of argument among patrician families is that of "secret marriage" (*ndoa ya siri*) or "secret wedding" (*arusi ya siri*). It is reported especially from the older stone-towns such as Mombasa and Lamu. A better translation would be "clandestine marriage."[8] It is a marriage in which there is consent between the partners but not the parents, and it can end in a divorce by repudiation as can an "official" marriage. Significantly, a nuptial agreement may be made before a *mwalimu*, with two witnesses, although neither the bride's nor the groom's families are informed or play any part. It differs from an official marriage also in that no property is transmitted and any gifts made are from the man to the woman only and are not displayed or transferred in public.

I have earlier mentioned the notion of equality of rank (kufu). In most marriages of other than first-born daughters and in later marriages of divorced wives and of widows, hypergamy is acceptable and perhaps usual. It is particularly associated with clandestine marriages and with marriages of patrician men with nonpatrician women of the Bajun towns, who can thereby become at least partly incorporated into patrician groups.

Clandestine marriages are frequent. They are institutionalized and sooner or later become known and recognized: they are "secret" in that they are kept from the man's immediate family and first wife if he is already married. These marriages are often made when the families concerned have not agreed to them, so that the partners choose one another. They are almost always made either with young divorced women, who may own some property and jewelry of their own, or with women of lower rank who would not be approved by patrician families.[9] Wives in patrician families do not usually approve of their husbands' later marriages to co-wives, as I have mentioned, and the "secret" is therefore revealed to them only slowly. A clandestine marriage does not create proper ties of affinity. However, the marriage is itself legitimate, as are the children from it, and according to informants who have themselves made clandestine marriages, it is usually after the birth of a child that the first wife is told. Those of which I have knowledge were with secret wives both in other towns and also within the same town, and in the latter case the secret soon became open knowledge.

Many clandestine marriages are between Sharifu men and non-Sharifu and nonpatrician women, the men being serially married to many women, each union lasting only a day or two (el-Zein [1974: 156f]). Children of such a marriage may be taken by the Sharifu fathers, who thereby build up their own subclans and acquire more adherents for the modern Sharifu mosques. This form of marriage does not include a wedding (arusi) and is close to *kukaa na hawara* (to stay with a paramour). It is hypergamous in a ritual sense, in that a Sharifu is ritually higher than any non-Sharifu.

Divorce is common, but its incidence varies considerably from one town to another according to rank, mode of descent and residence, wealth, occupational mobility, and the position of a marriage in the life-history of a given man or woman. Divorces among patricians and the wealthier Hadhrami and Omani families are far less common than among other and poorer families. But in all Swahili communities divorce is generally accepted as a normal part of most marriages other than traditional patrician ones.[10]

Divorce is acquired easily by the husband. The most common grounds are a wife's adultery, her believed sterility, and persistent quarreling. The husband has merely to inform a kadhi or mwalimu that he wishes a divorce; a man's word is legally reliable and no evidence of behavior is required. Or he may pronounce a triple repudiation (*talaka*). The first and second permit him to take back the wife if he does so before the end of her period of seclusion (*eda*) after the separation, which is three months as a separated woman. (If she is pregnant when separated, the eda lasts until the birth of the child.) The third repudiation makes the divorce irrevocable. The husband may then reclaim the wife only after she has undergone another proper marriage and divorce with a new husband. It is said that a husband may arrange a nominal and short-lasting marriage for the woman and then arrange a divorce for her so that he can remarry her; but this remarriage must be a correct one and is not merely a revival of the original union, and the practice is more in the realm of popular gossip than of actuality. A formal divorce occurs in general only in the case of a first or perhaps second marriage, as these are likely to be the only ones registered and involving property; later marriages, which are usually unregistered, may be ended merely by verbal repudiation.

Under Islamic law a wife finds it much more difficult to institute a divorce, as she must produce detailed reasons and evidence, although she may bring various pressures upon her husband to divorce her. Her main grounds are the husband's failure to perform certain legal and conventional duties: to give his wife adequate accommodation, food, clothing, money if he is away, and sexual satisfaction. She may also sue if he acquires a loathsome or venereal disease, is physically deformed, becomes insane, or beats her leaving severe scars. She may obtain a divorce, known as *fasikhi*, if the husband abandons her for more than three months (although if he reappears the divorce may be annulled); or she may acquire the divorce known as *khuluu* by repaying the marriage payments, and this divorce is irrevocable. Women may taunt or provoke their husbands to divorce them, a method that appears to be generally successful.

By contrast, the high rate of divorce in the Swahili country-towns might suggest that marriage is not considered to be of great importance there.[11] However, marriage, although very fragile, is not entered into lightly in the case of women's first marriages, which are almost invariably between betrothed cross-cousins. Marriages are tied to considerations of rights in property and so are the affairs not merely of the groom and bride but of their wards and families over several generations; the difference in form of descent groups in the country-towns from that in the stone-towns provides a quite different context for relations of exchange and alliance between them. In the country-towns the range of cross-cousin marriage is much wider than in patrician marriages. One reason for this is that the residents of country-towns recognize only minor hierarchical differences—those having to do with age, education, and religious probity, but not with ancestry; and there is also greater equality between men and women. The distinction between wife-givers and wife-takers is more marked than it is among patricians, where the notion of kufu is so important (it makes little sense in the country-towns). In lineage-endogamous patrician marriages, the distinction between wife-givers and wife-takers is not as clearly expressed in behavior as it is among Hadimu and others, marked largely by the frequent symbolic demands for money by the wife-givers (see chapter 6). The distance between cross-cousins may not always be significantly greater than that between parallel-cousins in terms of interpersonal kinship, but it is very much so when they are members of different wards or villages. I am referring mainly to Hadimu marriages, but these are similar enough to those of other country-towns to be representative.[12]

In the country-towns the preferred form of marriage for a man is with the mother's brother's daughter and the father's brother's daughter, both of which are frequent; marriage with the father's sister's daughter is approved but less common; that with the mother's sister's daughter is not approved. Few men are polygynous. A man should not marry close "sisters" either simultaneously or serially: his wives should come from different wards. Much depends on the kinship distance in these various categories. Marital choices are made as part of strategies by members of kinship groups, wards, and villages. The marriages of men are typically arranged by their fathers, who are usually related as brothers or as brothers-in-law, the former of the same mlango and the latter of the same tumbo. Marriages between close kin are used to strengthen those groups and to unite the fathers' enterprises. It is common for marriages to be arranged between the children of men who are particularly close friends or (I think more usually) partners in fishing, ownership of sailing craft, or other activities: I know of several such cases between men who were partners living in different towns. If only distantly related, they may appoint each other as foster parents of one of each's children so that "proper" cross-cousin marriage may later take place and the partners' property kept together in the following generation. Later marriages of a man or a woman are frequently extended more widely to cousins living elsewhere, to disperse potential rights in property that will be held by the fathers' grandchildren. Today most men and women get married in their mid-teens. Betrothal is frequent for a woman's first marriage, the girl remaining with her parents until she undergoes initiation at puberty. This arrangement is especially common between families within the ward, since, as the parents say, it ensures that the girl will not reach puberty and then willfully marry someone outside it, an action that would later have repercussions on the inheritance, through her, of rights in the ward's property.

It is generally assumed in these towns that marriages will end in divorce. If there are no children, this is of little account. If there are children, it is said that the siblings a woman bears by different husbands will have the advantage of being able between them to claim inheritance from the members of all the several wards concerned, so that as adults they will have a wider choice of residence and farming rights than they would otherwise have had. It is often said that every wife "runs" with at least one other man than her husband. The husband is said often to know of these affairs and, at least in 1958, expected to be given about a hundred shillings by each of the men involved when the husband brought the matter up in public. Men often said cynically that husbands encourage their wives to sleep with other men, because the wives will do so in any case, they may then get a "return" on their bridewealth, and they will have reasons for divorce should they later want it. On the other hand, several Hadimu women told me that a woman continues after marriage to "own her own vagina" and to be on the lookout to "meet a penis" on the path as she goes to farm, or to market, or to the beach to make coir and look for shellfish. Most divorces take place during the dry season, when there is less money about and men can claim back their bridewealth if they initiate the divorce. Marriages usually take place after the clove season, when most men have their earnings as clove pickers in the plantation areas. Most children remain with their mothers after a divorce; in many households that have more than four or five children, they will have different fathers and so links with different wards and villages. The same situation with regard to divorce appears to be found among other country-towns along the coast.

MARRIAGE PAYMENTS

Swahili marriages are arenas for the complex playing out of the relations between groups, of their perpetuation, of allocation of rights in property and persons, of exchange of and succession to those rights, of notions of hierarchy, and of the wishes of individuals. Marriage and inheritance, closely linked, are the principal means, with sale and charitable bequests, for the orderly devolution of rights in property between persons and groups of the same and different generations.

In both country-towns and stone-towns, marriage may be said to be endogamous: in the former with regard to the ukoo (or its equivalent), in the latter with regard to the subclan. Exogamous marriages are permitted under certain circumstances and do occur; and the range of units within which marriages are preferred is a situational rather than an ideal one. However, *endogamy* and *exogamy* are anthropological observers' terms, and we need to see how the Swahili themselves state and practice the various rules to which they refer.

Marriage choices in the various Swahili towns are decided both by culturally decreed rules of preference and also by the immediate interests of kin groups. The rules determine the basic patterns, and group and individual interests determine the incidence of various kinds of marriage at a given time. Rules may be broken with changes in the interests of a community or group. The Swahili have two essential marriage rules: that marriages should take place only between those of equal rank and between those related as cousins (except maternal parallel-cousins), and that marriage patterns must meet the rules of the shari'a, which refer to individual kinship relationships only. There are almost certainly more breaches of the former rule than of the latter. Marriages among stone-town patricians, on the one hand, and among members of country-towns, on the other, differ from one another in two ways. The aim of the former is mainly exclusivity, that of the latter mainly inclusivity; and the key factors are the notions of property and of purity. I use the word *aim* deliberately: marriages are arranged, both formally and informally, as parts of long-term strategies.

The consideration of property exchanges in Swahili marriages is a complicated matter for several reasons. First, Swahili marriage transfers must follow the rules laid down in the shari'a, even when functionally these do not "fit" the particular set of social conditions in which a marriage occurs; second, there has been a great deal of change in recent years, due mainly to the inflation brought about by the emigration of Swahili to earn wages in the oil-producing countries of the Middle East; and third, an inquiry into these transfers involves many confidential matters that families not unnaturally prefer to keep to themselves.

In the stone-towns there are five categories of marriage transfers, three from the groom or his family to the bride or her family, and two made within the bride's family. Those in the country-towns are basically the same but often conflated. The first category is that laid down in the shari'a and known in Swahili as *mahari,* usually translated into English as "bridewealth," the transfer that marks the legality of the union. It is a payment transferred by the bridegroom's lineage to that of the bride's father or guardian, and is made directly to the latter. The transfer is properly registered by a religious official competent to perform the marriage rite, and its amount is stated in the official certificate of registration. The mahari varies within narrow limits; today it is about eight hundred shillings, or a little more among patricians and wealthy families and rather less among most others. This is a small sum for many, although often beyond the ability of poor families to find easily. Although it is the jurally stated transfer, it need not be made at or before the wedding, and is often made several years afterward. If it is not transferred by the time of the wedding, this should be registered on the marriage certificate. It is in fact not always transferred by the time children are born or even by the time the couple are divorced; in the latter case the certificate of divorce will mention the nontransfer, and the money should sooner or later be transferred to the divorced woman's father or guardian. It is said that nonpayment leads to "shame" and loss of "respect," but there seems to be little other sanction, legal or otherwise. It seems that the payment is always transferred eventually.

The second category of payment is not laid down in the shari'a, is not necessary in any religious or jural sense, and is not officially registered; it is found mainly among patricians and wealthier groups. It is transferred between the same parties as is the mahari but is a separate item. It is referred to in colloquial speech merely as *kitu* (thing). I have heard English-speaking people call it a "donation" and so I shall refer to it by that term; it derives from the Latin *donatio,* which Goody, referring to similar payments in the European Middle Ages, calls "indirect dowry." [13] This payment is much larger than the mahari. It amounts these days to between three and six thousand shillings, but there have been cases in recent years of payments as high as fifty thousand shillings, given by wealthy salaried men returning from the Middle East. The "donation" should be given before the wedding [14] and is provided by the groom and his immediate family, the exact contributions depending on their wealth. Today, at least, a large part comes directly from the groom if he can find the money from his earnings. This effectively makes most "good" marriages impossible for those men without such income. It is given to the bride's father or guardian, who uses it partly for the wedding itself (and expenses for a grand wedding are very heavy) and partly, if he wishes, toward the dowry that he will give his daughter. A small part, about 5 percent, should be given to charity; this is the *zaka* (tithe or alms).

The third category of transfer comprises the many smaller payments and gifts made by the groom to the bride, her kin, her chaperon, and her assistants during the wedding. These mark the various stages in the process of changes of status of the groom and bride relative to one another and to their families. Even where the pair are close kin and so of equal status, the groom is seen as the supplicant and the bride and her close kin as the givers who can delay the wedding at any stage.

The fourth category is the dowry, the "gift" (*hidaya*) made to the bride by her father. In the northern stone-towns, at least, this is composed of household goods of all kinds, furniture, clothing, and especially gold jewelry. All become the bride's own property absolutely. Jewelry is always mentioned as the most traditional and essential part: she may choose it or order it from goldsmiths, who will make it to her specifications. Later she may pawn it to the goldsmith, sell it, or dispose of it as she wishes: the proper way is to leave it to her daughters unless she depends upon it if widowed or divorced.

Finally, there is the transfer to the bride of certain rights in a stone house. This is not part of the dowry, not being a hidaya, but is her father's paternal duty. This transfer is properly made to her at the beginning of the period of *fungate*, the honeymoon. Ideally a daughter should be given rights in either a house newly built or purchased for her by her father, or a portion of the father's own house, by subdividing it, by adding on a higher floor, by building a new section across the street and joined to the original house by a bridge, or by purchasing other accommodation. The criterion for the portion defined as a separate dwelling space is that it has its own bathroom and pit toilet. The father should begin this process at his daughter's birth by preparing a pit of lime for the house building. This is still done in Pate, where there is space to build new houses, which are of one story only. It is not possible in Lamu or Mombasa due to overcrowding and scarcity of land, so the bride's quarters may comprise only part of the father's house; even so we may speak of it as her "house." The father should also make a marriage gift to the husband at the beginning or end of the honeymoon, usually of clothing or other personal items.[15]

I am writing here of the situation at the first marriage, assumed to be that of a virgin bride. For a woman's later marriages the payments will be much smaller, except for the mahari (if paid at all), since that is registered with a religious official (which is not always done for later marriages) and is considered as more or less a standard payment laid down by modern interpretation of the shari'a. Much depends on the social standing and reputation of the woman and her family, whether she has been the guilty party to a divorce or is a widow. The other payments typically will be small. She has already received dowry for her first marriage and so has her own furniture, clothing, and jewelry, and perhaps residential rights in her house. Thus, in a future marriage these may be mere token transfers, or may not even be made at all.

None of these transferred items need be returned in case of divorce instituted by the husband, but they may be so if instituted by the wife. However, both payment and return are subject to demands of pride and reputation. A woman for whom mahari has not been transferred may well use its nonpayment as an excuse to demand that her husband divorce her, saying that he need not now trouble to pay it as his refusal to do so shows that he did not consider the marriage legitimate in any case. A man who divorces his wife is expected to say that she should keep the mahari as a sign of his wealth, social status, and generosity. The other items are not returned at divorce, there being a direct congruence between their size, the wealth of the parties, and the expectation and incidence of divorce: it is the poor who have high rates of divorce, rather than the wealthy.

The situation in country-towns is essentially similar. Here there are neither patrilineal mercantile corporations, permanent stone houses, nor productive or mercantile resources other than stretches of land and sea and the labor of their inhabitants. Marriages may disperse the inheritance of rights in these last, but only to a certain degree: marriages are still preferably with cross-cousins. One strategy is to have children with widely dispersed rights of residence or farming, both in their natal towns and in neighboring ones, and parallel-cousin marriage limits this. The emphasis is not on ensuring the continuation of exclusive lineages but rather on ensuring a wide proliferation of cognatic ties. In the country-towns all forms of property other than small personal items are dispersed at every generation. In Lamu, stone-town inheritance excludes rights in houses, certain of which are transferred by a father to his daughters before his death, and the same applies to her jewelry and clothing. Property remains within the lineage and is rarely dispersed. In the country-towns a house is not regarded as the property of a lineage, to be occupied by a senior daughter who becomes a wife, but is owned individually by its builder. Marriages must observe the interpretations of marriage payments as stated by the coastal kadhis. This applies to the mahari, the bridewealth proper, and other payments are made according to considerations of family wealth and the likelihood of divorce.[16]

Negotiations for a marriage are formal. The position of wife-giver is higher than that of wife-taker, and efforts may be made to marry her as a negotiable good to the highest "bidder" (provided he is a cross-cousin), unless she has been betrothed as a child. Formality increases when the pair are members of different wards and especially if distantly related, and then a negotiator is used between the respective fathers. He, properly a ward elder (mkubwa wa mtaa), bears a gift from the groom's father to the bride's father, the former being in the position of supplicant. Bridewealth is transferred at marriage in the form of cash. Among the Hadimu in the late 1950s it was typically three hundred shillings. The groom's father contributed a hundred shillings, his mother fifty, and his brothers another fifty; he found the other hundred shillings himself. If the husband later divorces his wife, bridewealth is not returnable. In theory it is returnable should the wife initiate the divorce by leaving him, but if she has borne children, the husband usually will waive the payment. The payment of three hundred shillings was divided in the ratio of two hundred to the bride herself and one hundred to her father, who would give half of that to her mother. Her full siblings would expect a small share also; the husband might give each of them twenty shillings, either as a gesture of his sincerity toward the bride and her kin, or as a token of appreciation if they held out for a long time before allowing the marriage to take place. These payments applied when a man married a mother's brother's daughter or father's brother's daughter; if he married the father's sister's daughter, the bridewealth was less, perhaps only 150 shillings.

PROPERTY AND MARITAL RESIDENCE

The patricians and the wealthier Hadhrami and Omani immigrants from Arabia practice marriage between patrilateral parallel-cousins, as well as between cross-cousins. Cross-cousin marriage is generally preferred in the country-towns. Ladislav Holy writes that father's-brother's-daughter marriage in Middle Eastern societies "represents a striking exception to the principle of exogamy and, because it unites people who are already united and between whom there is, in a structural sense, no sociological difference, it plays precisely the opposite role from that played by marriage throughout most of the world" (1989: 1). Here I shall widen consideration of this particular form to include that between cross-cousins, as both forms are parts of a single pattern and to consider them separately leads to misunderstanding of their functions. Father's-brother's-daughter marriage is often called "Arab" marriage, but although the Swahili are culturally influenced by the cultures of southern Arabia, they are not Arabs; and although a society may borrow forms of clothing or furniture (usually changing part of their symbolic meanings in the new context), to borrow forms of marriage is a more complex phenomenon. Marriage patterns may be borrowed anywhere. But when the societies are economically and culturally very different, as with the Swahili and Arabs, then we must look closely at both the functions and symbols concerned in their social contexts, especially the part played by exchanges of forms of property. There are also certain pitfalls in analysis: in the relationships between a society stating a preference for or a probability of cousin marriages, their statistically measurable practice, and their overt and latent functions. None of these "explains" the others.[17]

Most Middle Eastern societies that practice father's-brother's-daughter marriage see it in terms of marrying the closest possible kin, the father's brother's daughter being considered closer than the father's sister's daughter. This view is also held by the Swahili. Patricians in particular hold the view that the marriages of a lineage's daughters should first be within the lineage, then within the sub-clan, and then with members of other patrician subclans. The relative incidence of marriages with the actual paternal parallel-cousins, with classificatory paternal parallel-cousins, and with cross-cousins depends mainly on the stages reached in lineage cycles of development, on factors of wealth and business, and on the actual availability of partners, as these lineages are rarely large in numbers.

Most studies of marriages in Africa stress the importance of marriage payments as functionally linked to the procreation of legitimate children. Among the patricians there is another factor that is crucial in the eyes of the people themselves: the purity of the descent line, which may be considered a form of immaterial property. A young woman who is a virgin is regarded as a morally and spiritually pure person, and provided that she contracts a licit marriage with a husband of proper descent and equal rank, her children will in turn also be morally and spiritually pure. The most effective means of ensuring this is by a paternal parallel-cousin marriage. Both she and her children then belong to the same lineage and her purity and ancestry are safely transmitted to the next generation. The purity of the line is continued by a marriage of a virgin woman to a cross-cousin provided that they are of the same lineage or subclan, as occurs if they are descended from an earlier paternal parallel-cousin marriage. At the same time some fathers have felt the need to marry their daughters to men who were effective business partners elsewhere. In many such cases the husband and wife were unrelated and so children begotten by them might become "lost." Therefore, the mahari demanded would be greater than normal and the marriage would not be that of a first-born daughter but of a later-born one who could be "spared" for the purpose. If she were given housing by her father, then the trading partner would need to regard it as his local home and his children would be brought up there. The system tended to work a little differently than these remarks might imply, since distant Arab trading partners were themselves often ultimately members of the same clan that the patrician family reckoned to be its own, and so could be considered cousins.

Swahili society recognizes rights in four main categories of property: productive and immovable, reproductive, personal and movable property, and trade goods. The boundaries between them are not clearly defined, and I have grouped them thus because the Swahili do so themselves, not explicitly but rather implicitly in various forms of transactions. Productive and immovable property includes land, the sea within the reefs, creeks, wells, and houses; reproductive property includes people—siblings, children, domestic slaves, and livestock; personal and movable property includes the things on land, such as crops, ships and canoes, money, jewelry, furnishings, clothing, heirlooms, and many smaller personal items; trade goods traditionally include ivory, nondomestic slaves, gold, timber, and many others exchanged between the interior and Asia. The fourth category stands apart from the others in that the objects had only money value. Whereas some of the others may today be given money values, this is still considered immoral and they are subject to ritualized forms of exchange only. Added to this difference is that of personal identification with the owners. Objects in the first category are owned by and identified with the "personality" of a lineage; those in the second are similar, but rights in them are vested more clearly in individuals; and those in the third category are owned by and identified with particular individuals. Not all of these categories of objects are transmittable by or in marriage, but all are heritable, many being transferred by marriage in expectation of the future. Those rights transmitted by inheritance are, most important, those in productive and immovable property; those transmitted by or in marriage and later inherited include the second and third categories. However, certain rights in houses are transmitted at marriage; and rights in most of the others may be sold, although usually only by forms of transfer between certain limited kin and in carefully ritualized situations that typically involve mutual gift and feast giving. Much of the significance of the incidence of polygamy, of prescriptive and pre-ferred marriages, of divorce, and of modes of descent and marital residence may be seen in the light of ensuring orderly devolution of rights in property across and within kinship and other groups and between generations. Polygyny may dis-perse rights widely, so that a descent group may be unable to retain them over the generations; the choice of marriages between categories of kin controls the range of devolution of property rights among them; a high divorce rate may limit the devolution of rights in personal and some movable property only and not those in productive and immovable property; and the choice of marital residence, within a certain mode of descent, will affect the devolution of property of all kinds.

Rights in immovable property are affected and often created by legal mar-riage. The acquisition and inheritance of immovable property refers particularly to rights of residence in stone-built houses and are related to the complexities of the relationships between patrilineal descent and uxorilocal marriage. These relationships can be understood only within the overall context of a mercantile society in which the descent groups are, traditionally, business corporations.[18]

The stone house of the patricians has great economic and symbolic importance. It has been reported that stone houses are "owned" by wives who are given them by their fathers and transmit that ownership to their daughters, or may even sell the house to strangers: this is a simplification and a misunderstanding. For tra-ditional and wealthy patrician subclans, the approved form of marital residence is uxorilocal.[19] Not every daughter is, or could be, given right of residence in a "house" by her father at her marriage: a first-born daughter is given that right, as a duty of her father. And that house should be lived in by her eldest daughter. Rights in it are often said to belong to her for her to dispose of as she wishes, but any transfer is hedged with many conditions. The house is and remains part of the total lineage property and should not pass outside it; but rights of user in it are given to the daughter and she may indirectly transmit them to her own daughter provided the (male) lineage head agrees. Since the marriages of first-born daugh-ters, who are those to whom these rights are strictly transmitted, should be with paternal parallel-cousins, both the succeeding spouses will be of the same lineage as her father. Although it has been reported that she may carry these rights of user with her to her new husband if she is divorced and even married to someone outside the subclan, my informants all say that this never happens in the case of patrician women who are first daughters, for whom divorce is rare. Residence is uxorilocal, so a new husband would have to move to a house not of his subclan, which is considered highly improper;[20] and those women who contract serial marriages are rarely patricians. In the Bajun towns of Faza Island and elsewhere, women are indeed known to purchase houses with the proceeds from trade or prostitution; but this is a different pattern altogether, as the houses are not stone houses of the Lamu type and lack the connection with lineage property.

For some years a husband of a first-born daughter typically lives not only with his wife but with his wife's mother (his own father's brother's wife), although each woman lives on her "own" floor. The mother is responsible for running the domestic affairs of the house as a single unit. She should treat her son-in-law as though he were one of her own sons, over whom she also maintains effective control in domestic matters. Should a woman go to live virilocally in her husband's house, which will be under the domestic control of his mother in her turn, the women are so likely to quarrel that divorce is almost inevitable. There is here, however, an important qualification. When the father of a set of siblings dies, the senior man of the next generation, who is a son of one of the preceding generation's set of fraternal siblings and has married the father's daughter, should properly move into the deceased father's living quarters; he may already live on another floor of the same house or in a neighboring house, but he succeeds to the deceased's lineage position and so to his "house" as well. It is clear that should the various married couples consist of previously unrelated spouses, the system outlined above cannot easily work. Many houses would be needed, for one thing, which would be impossible in the crowded stone-town of Lamu. And problems of lineage and family authority, formal and informal, would become difficult of resolution. The system "works" because a majority of the marriages are between parallel- or very close cousins. Polygynous marriages are difficult because the husband has to live uxorically, in two residences;even so, occasional polygyny does occur. If both wives are in the same town, each must have separate accommodation: they should not be "sisters" of the same lineage, and the second wife is both the junior and the more distantly related (or not related at all) to the husband. Each wife will have her own accommodation from her father, and the husband will provide her own servants (in the past, slaves). Other cases of polygyny are usually either when the husband has wives in different towns between which he moves (for example, as a trader), or when the second marriage begins as a clandestine marriage, the second wife not having a house of her own from her father but being provided with one by her husband. (Again, if such a marriage is lasting, the wives usually live in different towns.)

The basic principles of the system are simple. The head of a patrician lineage is, or has been traditionally, the head of a business corporation; he is succeeded in that office by a chosen son, usually but not necessarily the eldest. The office of lineage head is also attached to a particular house in its sense of an actual building, in which the ndani is occupied by the holder of that office and his wife. In time the lineage head has a daughter: at her marriage she is given accommodation, but at the death of the father she, if married to the lineage successor to her father (her paternal parallel-cousin), will move into the ndani hitherto occupied by her parents, and her husband will move there with her. The accommodation that she has been occupying, provided by her father, may then go to her daughter, so that her husband merely transfers that accommodation to the daughter and need not find other accommodation for her; or it is used by a younger sister and her husband. The mother may move into another part of the house, as the "grandmother." Remember that the original father obtained the accommodation through his wife, who was given it by *her* father, who was properly her husband's father's brother. The house is the property of the lineage but rights of accommodation in it are given to daughters. Among other things, this avoids the application of the Islamic law of inheritance, which would lead to the rights in the house being dispersed among all the deceased's children: being a pre-death transfer, it is not subject to the rules of inheritance.

The mode of inheritance of stone houses is complex and shows how inadequate in some respects are the conventional notions of patriliny and matriliny. Stone houses are owned by patrilineal lineages, corporate groups in which the ultimate right of possession is vested. Right of residential occupation is vested jointly in a daughter and her husband: it is she who is "given" a unit of accommodation by her father, but it is the husband who will in turn "give" the same accommodation to her daughter, so that both the wife and her husband hold different rights in the same property.

The institution of waqf is crucial for the continuation of the patrician system of property. In almost all cases these houses are subject to waqf and so cannot in any case be given, by a wife or husband, to anyone outside the descent group (or whatever other group or category comprises the beneficiaries under the waqf). A waqf may be made by any Muslim "for the maintenance and support, either wholly or partly, of any person including the family, children, descendants or kindred of the maker" (Anderson [1954: 93–94]), by the making and registration of a written testament (*wasia*); it is under the trusteeship of government-appointed waqf commissioners, who, should the originally listed beneficiaries die out or not be found, may use it for charitable purposes. This is in law the *waqf ahli*; the *waqf khayri* is a benefice made for religious or charitable purposes only, such as maintenance of a mosque or cemetery. My information is that the great majority of stone houses in Lamu, at least, are part of waqf ahli and so cannot be "owned" or "sold" by a daughter or wife merely because she might wish to do so. A house waqf, which corresponds closely to the "entail" of English law, is typically made as benefice for a named patrilineal descent group, individual names not being necessary. Many waqf were made as acts of piety in benefice for a husband's freed slaves and their descendants; even today efforts of national governments to use such property for resettlement schemes have failed at law.

This process of marriage, succession, and inheritance must be seen over several generations, in the context of the ongoing process of lineage development. The marriages of first-born children should be between paternal parallel-cousins who, belonging to the same lineage, have lived in adjoining or neighboring houses, or even in the same house. In the history of these lineages the headship passes to a selected "son" of one of the "brothers" who compose the senior generation of the lineage. Headship tends to rotate among the segments of the lineage: the allocation of rights in houses could not work without such rotation, as a man's own daughter cannot marry his own son—her full brother—as would otherwise be necessary. Finally, the continuity of purity of the subclan depends on the purity of its houses and of its senior women, who form lines of mothers and daughters living over time in the same ndani of the same house. It is the right to occupy the ndani that is transmitted to first-born daughters, a form of succession that bestows informal domestic authority but not formal lineage authority, which is retained by the women's husbands. Which daughter is selected to occupy the ndani depends upon the selection of her husband, although there should properly be congruence between his selection to be head and his marriage to the first-born daughter of the sibling set of daughters: the choice is made early in a man's life by lineage elders and marked by betrothal in childhood.

This account gives a rather too formalistic view of the complexities of the system, in which factors of personality, individual ability, affection, trust, dislike, distrust, and simple demography must all be reckoned with. The pattern can best be illustrated by an actual series of marriages that took place in Lamu in the late 1930s and early 1940s (see table 2). It involved seven children, four male and three female, of two well-to-do sons of the same father. The brothers (A and B) arranged the marriages of two of the sons (C and E) to two of the daughters (G and D), the marriages taking place in 1937 and 1939, respectively; the other two sons were married in 1941 and 1944 to two cross-cousins of different lineages of the same subclan; and the third daughter (I) was married in 1946 to a cross-cousin living in Mombasa. All these marriages were arranged by betrothal when the children were between six and ten years old. Before any of the marriages occurred the elder brother died, the other becoming thereby the sole "father" of the seven children and, with his wife, responsible for seeing through the actual marriages. Daughters D and G were each given houses or accommodation in existing houses of the lineage, the sons went to live uxorilocally with their wives elsewhere in Lamu, and daughter I went to live in Mombasa.

The occupational and property aspect of this set of marriages is significant. The remaining brother (B) of the senior generation was the head of the family, and with his wife's agreement supplied the three daughters of the succeeding generation with housing, furniture, clothing, jewelry, and other property, as well as prestigious weddings. He and his wife had also to arrange the distribution of business responsibilities among the men of the succeeding generation. The men would inherit formal responsibilities, and the informal responsibility of their wives was also considerable. Traditionally, one son would be—and still is—chosen to become a religious practitioner and scholar: cynics say that a more able son is typically given business responsibilities, while a less able one becomes the learned man. Other sons would be allocated responsibility for various parts of the lineage's productive property: its plantations, its dhows, its lands behind the town on Lamu Island, its shop in the main street of the town (if it had one), the upkeep

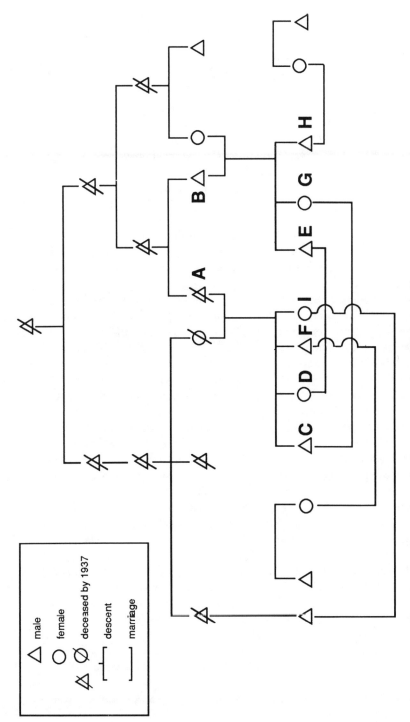

Table 2. A Lamu business corporation. Letters refer to order of birth; later children not shown.

of its houses, and other forms of property. Properly, a senior son should take over the formal headship of the lineage and in time occupy the same accommodation as his wife's father after the latter's death. In this case the senior son C was confirmed as successor to B, and he and his wife G, B's daughter, were given rooms at their marriage in B's house. He was given responsibility for managing the lineage's small store in the main street of the town. F was considered the most proper to assume religious duties and was sent to a Muslim college in Mombasa, where he has stayed. E was put in charge of the coconut palms and crops in the lineage's gardens behind the town; formerly his duties would have included managing a plantation on the mainland, but it has long been abandoned for lack of labor. H, the youngest, seems to have been given no specific responsibilities except those of a general family assistant. He went to a "modern" school and it was thought that he might later travel elsewhere and set up trading links in another town. In fact, he has hung around Lamu, little regarded in general and making a living by hiring out donkeys; this seems largely to have been due to the decline in the family fortunes, so that there remained little business that he could have done by staying with his brothers.

This example is not atypical of patrician families. It is not representative of poorer Bajun or other immigrant groups in Langoni, who have neither business interests, wealth, nor permanent houses. I am unsure as to how close it is to the pattern found in Hadhrami trading lineages.

At the basis of the system is the identity of the corporate groups of the various towns. In a stone-town such as Lamu the patrician lineage is a mercantile corporation, or has been so in the past. Such a corporation must make wealth, use that wealth to acquire and retain social rank and prestige, and if possible use it to acquire more wealth. There are means to achieve these ends. I have mentioned trade, but today this is of little importance. Rank and prestige are acquired competitively also, by transforming wealth into position by the building of a great house; by providing hospitality, alms, and pious works such as building a mosque; and by demonstrating the moral purity of the line (which is typically claimed to have begun in Mecca, Yemen, or the Hadhramaut). The purity is seen in that of the lineage's women, who spend their lives in the physical purity of these great enclosed buildings and wield great informal authority over lineage matters; and in that of its men, who acquire *heshima* (reputation or honor) by scholarship, business integrity and skill, and piety. These last do in fact lead to the acquisition of yet more wealth, as I will discuss later, as do skillful "diplomatic" marriages of the younger and "spare" daughters. The emphasis is always on ensuring the continuation of exclusive patrilineal descent groups.

Ties based upon marriage and kinship extend beyond the boundaries of individual towns. These extensions must be considered within the context of the functions of the corporate groups, that of exclusivity in the stone-towns and of inclusivity in the country-towns. There is much variation in these groups along the stone-town/country-town continuum, and the actuality is never tidy and clear-cut. This variation and uncertainty in definition and operation express the paradoxes in the notions of exclusive and inclusive groupings. If an exclusive group has one important function, the more exclusive it is, the less well can it perform other necessary functions; and the same applies, mutatis mutandis, to inclusive groups. On the other hand, the uncertainty enables any group to choose from the options available to it, since it is often doubtful whether exclusivity or inclusivity is at at any given time the more favorable. A socially and financially more secure and self-confident group may prefer exclusivity, but another, less secure and self-confident one may prefer inclusivity. Or the former, if its fortunes decline, may come to appreciate the greater value of marital links with related lineages elsewhere.

The endogamy of subclans is still properly observed, particularly within each "ethnic" grouping in the sense that the traditional rules are followed. What change there has been lies in increasing marriage between these groupings. A patrician man may marry a Hadhrami bride, but if he marries a patrician woman, he tries to observe the endogamy of his subclan. A few patricians still refuse to allow their first-born daughters to become wives of wealthy nonpatricians. If their sons marry Hadhrami and other wives, this is not so serious, as it does not affect the purity of houses and women; their children will still be patricians. In addition, the range of "equals" is widening: a patrician will marry a Hadhrami (formerly regarded as socially inferior), although he will rarely marry a Bajun woman. However, patrician and Hadhrami women are beginning to marry wealthy and well-educated Bajun men, although cases are still few and usually accompanied by long argument and disapproval.

A factor of growing importance is Western education, of both boys and girls, and with it the greater choice of occupations open to them that are unconnected to lineage businesses and familial control. The education of Swahili girls, in particular, has a large impact on patterns of marriage (Le Guennec Coppens [1983]). Whereas traditional education was essentially for boys and consisted mainly of Koranic study, this is no longer so, and Western education places as much emphasis on English as on Arabic. The change has been greater for girls. Young Swahili women can enter many careers in business as well as more conventional women's occupations in teaching and hospital work, and they do so with enthusiasm and success, often traveling widely as well. They rarely marry non-Swahili and family links remain all-powerful, but marriage choices are more open and made more independently than before. Swahili see their civilization as under threat by non-Muslim agencies and take care not to lose family members to the world outside.

As Lévi-Strauss has written:

The primacy of the exchange relationship over the unilineal criterion and of alliance over filiation explains that groups practicing exchange can, if they like, practice both exogamy and endogamy simultaneously or successively. Exogamy enables them to diversify alliances and to gain certain advantages (at the price, however, of certain risks); while endogamy consolidates and perpetuates previously acquired advantages (though not without exposing the momentarily more powerful line to dangers in the form of collaterals who have become rivals). This is a twofold dynamic of opening and closing, whereby one movement corresponds to a statistical model, and the other to a mechanical model: by means of the one, a group opens itself to history and exploits the resources of chance; while the other assumes the preservation or the regular recovery of patrimonies, rank, and titles. (1984: 94–95)

Chapter   Six

Transformation

of the Person

INITIATION AND WEDDINGS
IN THE STONE-TOWNS

Swahili marriage patterns may be seen as strategies to maintain
or improve the position of descent groups over time within the ever-changing
wider society. They involve the transfer of property and the transformation of
individual members into holders of new statuses: both processes are aspects of
the continual definition and redefinition of the social and moral identities of persons and groups and the relations between them that form the internal history
of Swahili society. These processes are ritualized as parts of rites of initiation,
marriage, childbirth, and death. They construct a person, defining and redefining
attributes and qualities that vary during that person's lifetime according to sex,
age, and moral position considered appropriate to their standing. There are four
main transition rites among the Swahili. Initiation makes a child into a marriage-
able adult, and a wedding completes the process to social adulthood; initiation
and wedding rites together form the *arusi,* a word that is usually translated into
English as "wedding";[1] having a child makes a woman or man into a mother or
father; and death changes that status into widowhood or widowerhood and into
ancestorhood.

No man or woman can be married until he or she has been through the rites
of initiation, which show wide variations from one part of the coast to another
in content, complexity, and the ages of initiands. The rite for males is based upon
circumcision, but its elaborateness varies considerably from one town to another.
The simplest form is that of patricians, the wealthy, and those more "modern"
than most in their general outlook; most of these today perform the rite on the
eighth day after birth, and certainly not later than five years. It is a family rite only,
culminating in reading of the *maulidi*[2] by an Islamic teacher. Women undergo the
rite known as *unyago.* This is relatively slight among patricians, and is private and
informal; it is said merely that a girl passing through it is *unyagoni* (in the phase
of instruction). However, it is an integral part of the total process of marriage.

The traditional large, costly, and elaborate weddings of the stone-town patricians of Lamu are the officially witnessed occasions known as *arusi ya rasmi* (legally correct weddings)[3] and often as *arusi kuu* (great weddings), those of first-born daughters that mark the transfer of rights in lineage houses. Although today grand patrician weddings are infrequent, those of first-born daughters provide the highly formalized pattern on which others are modeled and evaluated, and I present an account of this pattern even though it may never be seen today in entirety. There are variations elsewhere, although they are slight among wealthy patricians in places such as Pate or Mombasa. Poorer patrician and nonpatrician families have probably never held these splendid weddings; today, wealthy families of Hadhrami and other origins also emulate them, but new details are constantly introduced. As a long-time resident of Lamu said to me, "There are as many kinds of wedding in Lamu as there are families." Every person who describes his or her wedding, or those of kin, gives a slightly different account: each is ethnographically correct and makes perfect "sense" to the participants. Factors that make for variation are several but the most important is wealth: it is said, *Inategemea uwezo wa mtu* ("It depends on the wealth of the person"). The costs of a fine wedding are high, for purchasing and preparing food and furnishings, paying musicians, and decorating the house. Weddings of later-born daughters, second weddings, and those of nonpatrician women are basically similar, although the structural implications of the marriages of which they form part vary from one town and social rank to another.

Marriage comprises certain stages. It begins with the proposal (*posa*) and betrothal (*uchumba*) of the partners (*wachumba*, sing. *mchumba*), followed by visits between the families, which include discussion of and agreement on the marriage contract (*ahadi*).[4] There follows the wedding proper, which should be held in the month preceding Ramadhan.[5] It effects the transformation of a female from a girl to a recognized and legitimated married woman and of a boy to a recognized and legitimated married man. The rite of personal transition for a woman is the more complex and has a more clearly marked structure: the rite of separation, the period of seclusion of the girl as a virgin, the rite of aggregation as a bride whose virginity has been demonstrated and who may now enter a second period of seclusion, and finally that period's rite of aggregation that validates her final status as a married woman. If there is no divorce, widowhood (*ujane*)[6] marks the last stage of the marriage.[7] The most elaborate rite effects the transition of the bride from a virgin girl into a fully married woman. The transition of the groom is far less elaborate. Today his role has often faded into one with little ceremony, whereas that of the bride remains filled with as much pomp and public display as can be afforded.

A patrician wedding, however attenuated it may be these days, is a dramatic performance of considerable complexity. There are certain sets of performers: the groom and bride, referred to during it as *Bwana Arusi* and *Bibi Arusi*, respectively, denoting their central and yet transitory roles; their parental guardians, who arrange the details of the rite and the transfers of marriage payments; the groups of female kin of either side, each of which acts as a chorus and comments on the changing relationships of the bride and groom by means of dances and songs and thereby bears witness to an external structure of time and place; musicians, food sellers, and other providers of services; and the public of the town, who attend some parts of the rite and who, represented by a Muslim official, ensure the legal registration and witnessing of the union.

Several functionaries oversee the activities that make up the arusi. The two most important are the *mpambaji* (pl. *wapambaji*) and the *somo* (pl. *masomo*).[8] The mpambaji ("she who adorns or decorates") is properly an older woman of the lineage, ideally a sister of the lineage head, and the role may be inherited from mother to daughter.[9] She is also responsible for the ritual care of the house (which she "adorns") and for ensuring the proper and continued physical and moral purity of its women.[10] Her role includes preparing the daughters of the lineage for their weddings, supervising the ritual preparation of the corpses of dead members of the lineage, and purifying a widow. All these forms of preparation involve the ritual bodily lustration that marks rites of separation and aggregation. Today only one or two patrician families still have their own wapambaji, most hiring practitioners of lower status. The somo should also be an older kinswoman (mother's mother or mother's sister), and is appointed at the time of the betrothal for the particular wedding.[11] She is a personal teacher and guardian of the girl, with whom she is on intimate terms, and is essentially responsible for the bride's morality, sexual behavior, and purity. She plays an important role in all Swahili groups along the coast (Strobel [1975, 1979]).[12] A crucial role is that of the *mwalishi mke* ("the woman who invites"), who will be in charge of relations with wider kin and neighbors on behalf of the bride's family. There is also the *mwalishi mume* ("the man who invites"), who does the same for the groom's side. The former is properly the bride's mother, mother's sister, own elder sister, or maternal grandmother, and should be a woman of reputation and popularity; the latter is the groom's father or another close male kinsman. The inviters play structurally important roles as they determine the memberships of the respective jamaa of the two families. There are also several *waandazi* (servitors), female kin of the bride's mother who assist with the guests, handing food, burning incense, and anointing with perfume.

At her first menstruation, a girl tells her grandmother and her somo, who teaches her to purify herself of the impurity of menstrual blood. She is now no longer *mtoto* (child) but *msichana*[13] or *mwanamwali*. She retains this status until her betrothal, when she begins sexual instruction and the transition to the status of a married woman. As soon as she begins the transition she becomes *mwari* (neophyte or initiand) and goes into seclusion in her house. While she is mwari, she sleeps on the bed called *ulili* in the ndani ya kati, and may leave only to visit the adjoining bathroom; she may be visited only by close female kin. She may not plait, trim, or adorn her hair, trim her eyebrows, wear kohl or other cosmetics, or use henna; nor should she wear elaborate or attractive clothing. She is liminal, neither girl nor woman, denuded of all marks that signify female sexuality. Until this time she is properly ignorant of sexual matters, which she will learn now from her somo. Her sexual instruction should properly be given only after her betrothal, as were she to receive it before then, it is said that she might be tempted into sexual affairs and so lose her virginity.

At the time of the proposal, the groom's family investigate the bride and her family—*kuchunguza, njia ya siri* ("to investigate, by secret ways"); the women, in particular, exchange *maneno chini kwa chini* ("deeply hidden words"). And the men of the bride's family investigate the groom and his family. When the pair are in fact close cousins, this may be rather perfunctory, but details are sought about the bride's virginity and the groom's financial standing and moral reputation. The groom's men then visit the bride's family one evening to propose the marriage. No answer is usually given at first and the groom's family, as the supplicants, must wait for a reply; the bride's family will properly send no word until in time the groom's family return and formally ask for one. If the pair do not know each other, various stratagems may be used to permit them to see each other without its being "officially" recognized that they are doing so. Both tell their immediate families whether or not they agree to the choice. If the proposal is accepted, the groom's side may agree to give the bride's guardian a sum of money, sometimes as much as five thousand shillings, to "tie" her so that no other proposals may be accepted. (This is not obligatory and is not one of the proper transfers made at marriage.) The bride's family then begin to invite female kin to spend a day or two with the bride to help prepare food, decorate the bridegroom's chair, sew silken pillows for the bridal bed, plan the vigil that will later occur, and so on; these are tasks for married women, and young girls are invited to sing at nighttime in the bride's house.

The date for the wedding is then arranged so that the end of the honeymoon will be on a Friday morning to allow the groom to attend midday prayers at the congregational mosque. The number of days needed varies but is usually about ten. There is in practice a good deal of variation, as some elements may be conflated or omitted: again, much depends on wealth.

The bride's preparation normally requires three days, and involves first the conclusion of the period as mwari and then her physical transformation into a bride. First is the ritual lustration that marks her separation from the liminal and impure status of mwari. This is called *kutiwa chooni* ("to be put into the bathroom") and involves the washing and shaving of her body except for her head. It is done by the mpambaji in the bathroom attached to the ndani of her parents, the central place of purification of the entire house. By it the impurities, physical and moral, of the period of puberty are removed and the mwari is left in a state of symbolic and moral nakedness. She moves from her ulili bed in the nyumba ya kati to a usual sleeping bed placed in her sleeping alcove at one end of the *msana wa juu,* the room or gallery immediately adjoining the ndani. She moves from the individual seclusion and nullity of the nyumba ya kati to the more public rooms of the house, a move reflected also in the change of bed. Over the following days the mpambaji prepares her body as a bride. This is the period of *jiwe la tibu* ("stone of perfume"), when there are ground the perfumes of sandalwood, aloes, cloves, and other spices with which she will be adorned. The house has also to be cleaned and decorated (*kupamba nyumba*), especially the plaster work of the ndani. The main events after the washing of her body are "washing the hair" (*kuosha nywele*), which is then pressed and straightened, and the slow and painful *kutinda sikini* ("to shave the edge of the hair into a straight line"; Sacleux [1939: 804]), which involves the removal of hair with melted sugar and lime juice. All downy hair is removed from her forehead and the nape of her neck, and her eyebrows are trimmed. Her neck and body are rubbed with *liwa* (a species of sandalwood) and perfumed with aloes. Henna is applied, properly for the first time in her life, on her feet (including the soles, which are entirely painted), as well as on her hands. The application of the henna takes two or three days. During this time she stays at home, sitting on a bed behind her sleeping alcove's curtain, dressed in two *khangas* (square cloths worn as women's apparel) over a simple dress. In seclusion she becomes liminal in both location and in appearance, while her body is transformed from that of a presexual girl to that of a physically adult woman, the process known as *kufuga ukuti* ("to bring out her beauty").[14]

There now begins the *kesha*, or "vigil," that ends with her defloration. During the *kesha ya wanawake* ("vigil of the women"), the bride plays no part at all in the complex sequence of meetings between the two sides but remains in seclusion. The main activities all take place at night, and the women of both sides begin to perform their role as chorus as the activities now move into the public sphere. The groom has his own *kesha ya wanaume* ("vigil of the men"), but he is hardly secluded, although the events occur at nighttime.

Before the kesha there is an intercalary day, that of *kualika* ("to invite"), when the girl's female kin visit her: these are part of the effective jamaa of her parents. The visit should take place in the afternoon in the courtyard of the bride's father's house, but these days it is often in an enclosed place nearby, on a dead-end street, or on the roof of the house (which is not properly part of the house itself). Those formally invited unveil themselves (as though in their own houses) and are given tea and the pastries of spiced meat known as *samosa*; other women may be spectators and remain veiled. If the visiting is in the house, the women should dance the *ngoma ya ndani* ("dance of the inner room") or *msondo*, but if outside they usually dance the dance known as *vugo*. These dances are performed only at weddings and contain sexual references and comments on the stages of the wedding.[15] They are danced by mature women who vie with one another in their words and movements; men and very young women do not attend.

On the following day there should begin the kesha,[16] held late in the evening and lasting into the early morning. During the early part of the night, until midnight, the bride's female kin and invited jamaa members decorate a *kitanda cha samadari*[17] with special covering cloths and hung on its top and side with golden jewelry.[18] The younger women sit with the bride and the somo. They should not hear the conversation of the older women in the courtyard below who perform the *chakacha* dance. During the night the dancers are given tea, sambusas, and the sweetmeat known as *halwa*. These days the vigil may start on the day of kualika, and the entire period be shortened.

The lives of the bride and groom are becoming joined, and this is marked by the exchange of personal wedding items between the two sides. Times of day vary, but the first exchange takes place the following morning, at any time after the first prayers. The older female kin of the bride, singing vugo songs, take a gift to the groom; this is *kupeleka msuaki* ("to send the toothstick"). He gives them a small gift of money in return. The "toothstick" usually comprises several trays of "delicious" foods, made with flour, eggs, honey, and other "soft" ingredients.[19] The emphasis is on their being "delicious" or "soft," in contrast to the meal later given to the groom when he is taken to the bride, which will consist of "hot" and "hard" food. The party is met outside the groom's house by his female kin and the two groups compete in singing vugo songs. The food is eaten by the groom, and the men of his vigil and the bride's party return home. Later in the day the female kin of the groom send part of the *kitu* ("donation"), consisting of the bride's trousseau, to her, parading through the streets singing vugo songs; this is the *kupeleka begi* ("to send the bag"). The remainder of the donation is taken by the groom's guardian to that of the bride at this time.

The same day, in the afternoon before the five o'clock prayers, the male kin and friends of the bridegroom perform various dances in one of the public places of the town; these include the *kirumbizi*, or stick dance, the *ndonge, uta,* and other dances, and there may be poetry competitions between men who aspire to high reputation by their skill. The groom is seated in an ebony and ivory chair (*kiti cha mpingo*) dressed in fine clothes, including turban and embroidered waistcoat. The participants must be offered food and refreshments by the groom's family. The audience is mostly of men of the town, the public thereby being brought informally into the process.

That day also the groom's male kin and his invited guests dress him in great finery, and his group proceeds to the bride's house, led by men playing *zumari* (a kind of clarinet) and in former days the great siwa horn. They are followed by the groom and then by his female kin singing vugo songs. The groom is welcomed and seated on the decorated kitanda cha samadari placed in the msana wa chini, as he has men with him who are not of the bride's house.[20] The proceedings are organized by the senior men of the bride's family, properly her father's brother. Her father should not attend: it is said that he would gain "shame" (*haya*) by being where his daughter will later be deflowered. The bride's father's brother and the kadhi or mwalimu enter the ndani formally to ask for the bride's consent to the marriage, the *idhini*: it is known for a bride to refuse at this late stage. When she has agreed, her close female kin spray the groom with aloes and perfumes and put a garland of roses and jasmine around his neck, the somo gives him betel leaf and drink, and kin of the bride fan him with palm-leaf fans. This adornment marks his change of role from being a suitor to being the fully accepted bridegroom who will later enter the bride's sleeping alcove. He is anointed with perfumes used by women, a symbol of the later physical union by which they will become one. Meanwhile, the older women of both "sides" sing chakacha and other songs in the open courtyard. The "competition" is becoming muted and the notion of sexual complementary stressed.

On the following morning the *nikaha*, the formal agreement of marriage, is signed and witnessed; this is performed by the kadhi or mwalimu (who here formally represents the town) either at the mosque or at the groom's house. The former is usual if the family is wealthy enough to offer coffee and sweetmeats to two or three hundred guests at the mosque, and the latter if they are not rich, as then only twenty or thirty people will attend. The bride's father attends the nikaha, as it is a legal matter, and he offers the guests halwa as a token gift from his side to theirs, a sign of recognition that they are now formally linked.

That night between nine o'clock and midnight, after the final prayers, there is the rite of *kutia nyumbani* ("to put [him] in the house"), after which the two sides are physically conjoined. It begins with *kupiga kilemba* ("to tie the turban") in the groom's house, when he is dressed in finest attire of white *kanzu*, turban, embroidered waistcoat, and other items that represent male authority and high status. He is then taken in procession, accompanied by his close female and male kin, to the bride's house. His party is met outside the house by a group of the bride's female kin; women of the two groups sing and dance highly competitive vugo songs. The bride's group is accepted as "winning." The women then all enter the bride's house together; the groom enters with only a few close male kin and friends. All sit in the lower gallery, where he is seated on the kiti cha samadari.

The rite known as *kutia ndani* ("to put [him] inside") begins. Light food is served, without rice and so not a proper meal; the groom eats only a mouthful or two, and his kin then leave except for two or three close and honored male kin. The mwalishi mke comes out from the bride's room wearing a khanga, only her face showing, and gives the message that the groom is awaited. As he makes to enter the upper gallery, the door is shut in his face or, if there is no door, the curtain is closed and his way barred by the somo (in former days by a female slave) and he is asked for the "key"; he must give an *arishi,* a small gift of money or a jewel, to be allowed to enter. He is taken inside, properly by the bride's father's brother, representing the inmates of the house, and is seated on a kiti cha samadari, alone except for his host and the close female kin of the bride. He is perfumed by the somo to prepare him "to enter inside." From outside the curtain of the bride's sleeping alcove he gives a *jazuwa* (gift), a small sum of money or a jewel, into his bride's hand (*kupa mkono,* "to give the hand") while she is hidden inside. The somo first lifts the curtain and brings him in so that he and the bride are together, hidden by the curtain; she then lifts the very fine veil (*kihoshi*) that covers the bride's face so that the groom may actually see her—this is properly the first time he has done so. He places his right hand on her head and blesses her by reading an appropriate verse from the Koran. The couple are now sitting close to each other on ordinary chairs, known in Lamu as *viti vya mdodoki.* The groom returns outside the curtain, and his turban is taken by the *mwalishi mke* and placed on the bed in the alcove, leaving his head covered by a white sewn cap (*kofia*) only. His head and shoulders are covered with the bride's veil and a khanga, to show that "he has a wife." This symbolic exchange of clothing is said to represent the future sharing of their formerly separate identities, but also marks their shared liminality during this part of the rite de passage. The somo calls the groom to reenter the alcove, gives him betel leaf (which he spits out into a bowl) to "give him strength," and hands him a cup of milk, which stands for softness and purity: he drinks and hands it to the bride. The somo serves the two of them food, again without rice. He is given dove meat (*nyama ya ndiwa*), considered to be a very "hot" meat, again for "strength" for his coming duty (*kazi*). The bride eats "soft" food such as bread made with egg and milk with almonds and cardamom. The sharing of food and drink also represents the sharing of identities. The somo then conducts the groom to the bride's bed and remains nearby, usually on the other side of the curtain, later to witness the bride's blood as sign of her virginity. The groom and bride talk together and may eat a little. She is seated or lying on her bed, adorned with jasmine but with no cosmetics. When ready, he penetrates her—often against her will, it is said: statements made to me show the difficulties expected by both of them, and emphasize that the groom may have to use force as the bride is apprehensive, a remark that may reflect stereotypes of expected rather than of actual behavior. The somo waits and may enter to "help" the bride if she calls. When penetration is effected, the groom may knock on the bed or wall, and the somo enters. First she takes the bride to the bathroom, where she undergoes a second ritual lustration (*kutiwa chooni*) by the mpambaji, to remove the "impurity" of intercourse.[21] The somo then takes the sheet (*kasarwanda*)[22] with blood on it as evidence of the bride's virginity and shows it to the women of the family, who are waiting outside. It is proper for the groom to give his bride a further gift of a jewel or money, the *haki* ("a just share"), as a sign of his pledge to her now that she has been shown to be a virgin. The groom also goes to wash. Later the somo should visit the houses of the bride's female kin to tell them of the virginity and perhaps show them the sheet as evidence. The *kuingia ndani* involves only the physical penetration of the bride by the groom. If he should ejaculate, her blood will be mixed with semen and be unsuitable as physical evidence of her virginity. It is widely held that the penetration may take some hours or even days; in that case the groom is given additional "hot" food, betel leaf with a Koranic verse written on it, and other means to reassure him and give him "strength." The physical defloration is the culmination of this part of the total rite of transition: it is said, *Arusi imejibu* ("The initiation has [been] repeated or answered").[23]

The bed is tidied (the kasarwanda has now been removed) and the groom returns to effect full intercourse. The couple may be given tea and more "hot" and "soft" foods as before, and they remain there until the following day.

The following day is the occasion for the wedding feast (*lima*) given by the bride's family in the courtyard, or today even in a public hall. Later the groom's family will give a feast to his kin also. These are *karamu* (feasts) and *sherehe* (rejoicing).

Meanwhile, the mpambaji and the bride's sisters prepare her for the rite called in the kiAmu dialect *ntazanyao* ("[to see] the tips of the toes"); it takes place in the evening.[24] The bride is elaborately adorned by her mpambaji: her face is heavily made up, she is anointed with unguents and perfumes, she wears golden jewelry and silken clothing of great ornateness given to her as part of her hidaya. These days her face and hair may also be adorned with gold coins and jewelry and little of her actual face may be visible at all. She sits on the decorated kitanda cha samadari placed in front of the blank space in the rear wall of the ndani, with the whitewashed *zidaka* alcoves above and of either side of her. Her "beauty" is seen in conjunction with that of the center of the house, both she and the house being linked in their purity.

The term *ntazanyao* refers to her position while sitting, with her feet together and her hands placed on her knees, both feet and hands being elaborately painted with henna and her feet being placed on an ornate cushion. She remains in this position for about an hour. She should move neither her body nor her head, and should not look at those observing her: indeed, it is common for her to have her eyes closed. She becomes masked, her individual personality being irrelevant. If she shows signs of recognizing people, it is said that "she has no shame" (*hana haya*). In the past a proper ntazanyao would take place three times, each for a different "audience," but as far as I know this has not been done for many years. (Today there is only a single performance.) The first occasion was for the bride's close female kin only, the kitanda being placed in the center of the rear wall of the ndani, the observers standing in the doorway to the gallery. Traditionally, the rite was repeated on the following two days, for more distant kin and then for neighbors. The kitanda was placed in a lower room each day, so that on the third it could be seen from the courtyard. These days the ntazanyao may be held in a public hall: few stone houses are today in fine condition, but, more important, they are no longer used as sites for corporate commercial activity and so have lost much of their erstwhile significance. Many women attend, both kin and neighbors, care being taken to invite the socially important women of the town (so as to include them in the bride's parents' jamaa). They are seated, discarding their veils, facing the dais where the bride will be shown; the bride's younger kin, also unveiled, are seated behind on mats; those who attend but without invitations stand at the back, veiled. There is dancing and singing of chakacha, and guests may pin money on the bride's dress. Sweet cakes and fruit juice are served and the guests are sprayed with fragrances and rose water. After being presented publicly, the bride is washed; this is not referred to as kutiwa chooni but is rather a personal cleansing of some of the heavy cosmetics, to any degree that she desires.

The groom returns to her that same night to commence the honeymoon (*fungate*, the old Bantu word for seven). Traditionally, the couple remained inside her sleeping alcove for a period of seclusion, fourteen days for her and seven for him. The final day for him is a Friday so that he can present himself as a newly married man at the midday prayers in the congregational mosque. He then pays a formal call on his wife's parents; the father should give him a gift, also called hidaya, in the past often a plantation or fine clothing, today usually money.[25] These days the bride is usually secluded for seven days and the groom often not at all. During the period of seclusion they continue to be referred to respectively as Bwana Arusi and Bibi Arusi, as the marriage is not yet completed. The bride is now legally married but cannot yet attend public affairs or rites such as weddings and funerals.

Acquisition of her final and full status is by her *kutolezwa nde* ("to be shown outside"). This occurs as part of a later wedding, that of the ntazanyao of another woman who should be a close kinswoman of at least the same subclan. This is not thought necessary today so long as they are of the same rank. She is adorned in her own house and taken, heavily veiled, to the scene of the rite by her mpambaji. She is seated below the chair of the other bride; she stays for only a short time and is less adorned, perfumed, painted, and beautifully clothed than the new bride, the center of attention. Since almost all marriages take place in the same month, most women can soon find an occasion for their kutolezwa nde, although some may have to wait. This appearance marks the completion of her transition to a formally and publicly recognized married woman.

Once fully married, a woman has the social standing and the degree of purity required of a patrician wife. She should carefully retain it and transmit it to her own daughters. Traditionally, she should live in house-seclusion; she may not go out during daylight, and only when accompanied by a kinswoman, servant, or, formerly, a slave. She is veiled, and until the British prohibited it, she might walk completely inside a tent-like covering, the shiraa. She must show herself a pious Muslim, and should say prayers and read the sacred texts in her own house. She performs acts of charity, and in the past and also today such a woman might become known as a poet or Islamic scholar. Today many younger patrician women are educated and enter various occupations, but this has become possible only with the decline of the patrician wealth and style of life. The position of a younger daughter is not as strictly controlled, and that of nonpatrician women has few such rules and conventions today.

Some elements of the arusi are today largely omitted or elided, and certain traditional rules are decreasingly observed, even among patricians. The elements that seem invariably to be retained include the kesha, or vigil, the nikaha, the kutia ndani, and the ntazanyao. There are always the processions of women through the streets singing vugo songs, to fetch the groom for the kutia ndani, and there is visiting by close kin of the bride and a degree of hospitality and gift giving. For later marriages of patricians and marriages of poorer women, however, these events may be compressed into a couple of days. Much is today conflated and specific details ignored, and certainly very few weddings follow anything near the full traditional pattern. But the logic and meanings are still accepted, even if only rarely put into practice, and they form a single coherent rite of transformation.

An essential point is that although the words *initiation* and *wedding* are separate in English, the Swahili combine them in the single word *arusi*. There is a single process, which begins with the boy's circumcision and girl's menarche and ends with the public recognition that the man and woman are fully married and socially complete adults. Several levels of transformation take place: from socially immature and symbolically impure girl into socially mature and symbolically pure married woman; from boy into married man; and from two lines, descent segments, or "sides" (those of the male and the female) into a single entity. The whole is an elaborate drama carefully staged by subtle plays upon sexuality and "beauty," movement in spaces of house and street, day and night, clothing, furniture, food, fragrances, and competitive songs and dances. The emphasis throughout is on the role of the woman; that of the man is complementary but far less prominent. The weight of symbolic meaning is placed on the woman's moral transformation. It is a counterweight to the mercantile role of the man, which is more public and easily perceived. Between them, the couple represent a balance between control of reproduction and that of material production.

The significance of the bride's virginity and "beauty" is central. What is important is not so much that she is or should be a virgin, but rather that she loses her virginity in this carefully bounded ritual situation by a deliberate act on the parts of both herself and the groom.[26] It is this programmed loss of virginity that transforms her into a full woman: hence the ntazanyao follows the defloration, when her newly completed womanhood is publicly displayed.[27] She is not merely an individual but is an exemplar of mature womanhood, in control of her own body and so a publicly defined and recognized person on whom the future of lineage and town depends. Kufuga ukuti is part of this element of the process. During the arusi her "beauty" is transformed from that of a child into that of complete adult femininity: wearing no cosmetics at first, at the end she is presented heavily adorned and painted, traces of her original individuality concealed beneath a form of masking. It is said, *Ukuti wake unaonekana zaidi*, "Her beauty is made more apparent," in the sense that the external expression of her inner maturity is now shown publicly. The "beauty" is essentially the social or public expression of an ideal quality of maturity and purity, shown by the deliberate loss of her previously deliberately retained virginity. The masking reaches its height at her ntazanyao and is lessened at the kutolezwa nde, after which the bride dresses as an ordinary married woman.

The uses of henna, cosmetics, fragrances, aromatics, and unguents are complex and important in Swahili culture in general.[28] They are used in many ritual situations and mark certain phases of liminality, masking the body while the social personality is undergoing a change of sexual identity and acquisition of physical and moral purity. The use of henna is most prominent at the ntazanyao, when the soles of the bride's feet are totally painted; her hands and feet are also covered with designs in henna, her face heavily painted with cosmetics, and the remainder of her body totally clothed. She is enveloped and concealed from impurity and is presented as the idea of "beauty," devoid of personality. In private with her husband she wears only the slightest of cosmetics: intimate sexual relations are the opposite of public expressions of social personality.[29]

Several symbols are used in the couple's transition from separate individuals to spouses. During the vigil both eat, separately, "soft" or "delicious" foods; at the kutia ndani the bride is given "soft" and "cool" foods, the groom "hard" and "hot" foods; during the fungate both share normal foods; after it they eat normal foods, but separately. The soft/cool and hard/hot foods are eaten without rice: they are neither proper meals nor feasts, but an exchange of symbolic items that represent the preliminary stages toward a complementary sexual relationship. The use of furniture is important: the groom is seated on a "chair of ebony" in his public role, on a samadari when he approaches the bride before a more restricted group, then on a kiti cha mdodoki when he is first alone with her. Finally he moves to her sleeping bed (kitanda). She moves from ulili to kitanda in her private role, and then to the samadari for her public appearance. The samadari is a seat of elegance and public appearance, but lacks the "power" of the "chair of ebony" that is also known as *kiti cha ezi* ("chair of power"). The symbolic use of clothing is important. The groom is dressed ornately in the clothing of high-status masculinity when in public places; later he is given items of female adornment and of his bride's clothing, first during the vigil when he enters her house and later when is waiting to enter her sleeping alcove, where his turban has been placed on her bed. His public image becomes that of inmate of the purified house and of participant in the privacy of marriage. This process is the complementary opposite of the bride's movement from privacy to the public image of marriage. Later they both play their proper complementary public as well as private roles.

Finally, we may see the arusi in terms of competition between the two "sides," moving from hostility to conciliation. This is especially noticeable in two dimensions. One is that of the competitive vugo performances of the women of each side. By the time of the ntazanyao, the women of the man's side play no separate part; those of the woman's side monopolize the scene, welcoming her as a newly and publicly defined mature woman who joins them in controlling sexuality and purity and so future lineage reproduction. The other dimension is that of the complementary roles of the mpambaji and the somo. The former deals with the bride's public "beauty," the latter with her personal and private purity, both united by the conclusion of the wedding. By the arusi two disparate and immature individuals become linked as a single entity. Its male aspect, as it were, faces the outside world of commerce and public social relations and the exchange of material resources that have been symbolized by the various exchanges during the arusi; its female aspect faces the domestic world of continuing moral purity of house and wife.

INITIATION AND WEDDINGS IN THE COUNTRY-TOWNS

Initiation and weddings in the stone- and country-towns differ in many details, although it is obvious that both are essentially variations on a common model.

In most of the country-towns, from those of the Bajun in the north to those of the Mrima and Mgao coasts in the south, initiation takes place at puberty. It is typically part of a cycle of initiation rites known as *unyago*, an important communal rite of concern to groups over a wide area. The unyago rites are similar to those known as *jando* among groups peripheral to the Swahili, and may take place in a circumcision "lodge" (*ukumbi*). The pattern consists of first the rite of separation, then the period of seclusion in the *ukumbi,* and then the final rite of aggregation. The rite of separation is that of the circumcision itself, performed by the circumciser (*ngariba*), who is typically also the local mwalimu or Islamic teacher: this is seen as an essentially Islamic rite. The period of seclusion, where it is still found, is under control of the functionary known as *kungwi*[30] and may last up to two or three weeks. The boys are secluded from contact with other people of their age, male and female, and taught adult moral and sexual behavior, sing initiation songs known as *manyago*, and are fed on liminal food such as half-cooked rice. The rite of aggregation is elaborate. The initiands are given adult names, ritually bathed in a river or the sea, and given symbolic feminine attributes. They are adorned with silver necklaces and beads, their faces painted with lime and kohl and the palms of their hands and the soles of their feet with henna, and covered with a woman's khanga cloth. During the seclusion they may be referred to as *mwari* (pl. *waari,* "neophytes," a word that refers primarily to girls), and their final adornment marks them symbolically as non-men;[31] the status of men is given at the final events, those of receiving gifts from kin and participating in a public feast, when they are dressed in new and fine clothes including turban and waistcoat, traditional attire of wealthy upper-class Swahili men. The series of rites is known as arusi, a word that also includes the subsequent weddings.[32]

Male puberty rites in the country-towns are often said to be more complex than in the stone-towns because of the greater degree of orthodox Islamization that has taken place in the latter. The country-town rites are said by stone-town dwellers to be unorthodox and relics of an "African" past. Another difference has functional rather than conjectural historical significance: it is associated with the distinctions between unilineal and cognatic descent and between the recognition of hierarchical ranking and the lack of it. The formal status of a stone-town patrician male is determined almost entirely by his position by birth within his subclan and lineage, in particular vis-à-vis his father and father's brother. The status of a male of a country-town is dependent rather upon his status vis-à-vis others of the same age within his widespread cognatic group, all of whose males are socially equal except in age.[33]

Women's puberty rites in country-towns are also of some complexity. As long as she is a minor (that is, until puberty), rights in a woman are owned and controlled by her father, who during her childhood may make arrangements for a marriage after puberty with a particular cousin or foster child of an appropriate kinsman. If such arrangements are not made, she is in theory free after puberty to marry whomever she wishes, although a young woman will typically bow to the wishes of her parents and members of her natal tumbo, since they are involved in the wedding feast without which the marriage is incomplete. As one young woman in the town of Makunduchi in southeastern Zanzibar Island said to me, "I do not really mind, since I can soon obtain a divorce if I want one and can then run with whatever men I like."

The fullest account of this rite is given by Caplan for the Mbwera of Mafia Island (Caplan [1976]), and the Hadimu of Zanzibar practice an almost identical one. As Caplan points out, an important aspect of the women's rites is that they stress the pleasures of sexuality; procreation is not given priority. Such writers as Burton and Ingrams imply that the seemingly "free" sexual behavior of Swahili women is a survival of slavery. This view has no truth: the behavior is an integral part of the whole system of descent and marriage and not a historical "aberration." Furthermore, and more obviously relevant, neither the Hadimu nor the Mbwera were enslaved.

Weddings in the country-towns follow essentially the same basic pattern as those in the stone-towns, but the rites are less elaborate. The fullest account is that by Landberg (1977: chapter 7) for Kigombe on the Mrima coast. There a woman's first marriage is the most important, any later marriages attracting fewer participants to the wedding. Also, many of the minor payments mentioned below may not be given or are transferred only very perfunctorily. Marriages include the Islamic requirements of the formal contract ceremony (*hutuba*) and the transfer of the marriage payment (mahari). Other payments are not required under Islamic law but are part of local Swahili custom (mila). Marriages begin with the proposal (*uposo*), the hutuba, and the presentation of the groom to the bride (*kuingia nyumbani*, "to enter the house"), which is accompanied by feasting and merrymaking (*sherehe*). Dates and times for the last two parts of the wedding are determined by divination. The proposal is made by a go-between (*mshenga*), a kinsman or close friend of the groom: he approaches a senior kinsman of the bride's father (not the father himself), who then acts as custodian for the many marriage payments. The groom's father gives the custodian a payment called *pesa kwa kosa* ("monies for error"), which opens the way for formal preparations for the match. The main payment is the mahari. This is not a proper bridewealth as found in many other African societies, but is used to purchase furniture, especially a bed, jewelry, and other household and personal objects for the bride. The mahari is registered with the government and is not usually returnable at divorce. In Kigombe most mahari reported by Landberg were between two hundred and six hundred shillings, but some were as high as two thousand. The mahari was often paid in installments. Other payments include the *kilemba* (turban), paid to the bride's father, and *mkaja* (literally, a belt worn by women during pregnancy and after childbirth), paid to the bride's mother and her siblings. Both take the form of money and not of actual clothing, but the names respectively symbolize certain aspects of the roles of the *upande wa kiumeni* (side of the male) and the *upande wa kiukeni* (side of the female). Small payments known as *dovuo* (saliva) are given to members of the bride's grandparental generation in recognition of the utani (joking relationship) between members of alternate generations. None of these lesser payments is registered, and they are not returnable at divorce.

These payments are made, or at least begun, before the central ceremonies of the hutuba and the groom's presentation to his bride. Other small payments are made in connection with the hutuba by the groom or his father to the government and Islamic functionaries who take part. These are the *ushahidi* (testimony) made to the two witnesses; the *haki yake* (just share) to the mwalimu who performs the ceremony; and the *kuozewa* ("to be married"), paid to the two witnesses who sit with the bride at this time. The *lima la mji* (wedding feast), given to the chief elder of the bride's village for the right to marry one of his members, is placed in the village treasury (*hazina*). If the groom is a "proprietor" of the village, he pays twenty shillings, but a "stranger" or tenant pays double that amount. Other payments pass from the groom to the bride's cross-cousins who had been eligible to marry her (this is the *peka mke*, "abduction of the bride") and to the bride's female cross-cousins (the *fedha za nzuia*, "monies of hindrance," as these women may otherwise debar the groom from entering his bride's house). These various cross-cousins may prevent the consummation of the marriage until they receive their shares.

The groom also makes payments to the bride or her chaperon (*kungwi*) before the consummation. These payments are *kono la arusi* ("the hand of marriage"), made so that he may take her hand, and the *kuosha miguu* ("to wash the feet"), so that the chaperon may wash his feet before the consummation. If the bride is shown to be a virgin, the chaperon announces it and then leads the women of the house of the bride's mother to announce it at other houses of the village, at each of which they are given small sums of money. The fungate traditionally involves fourteen days' seclusion for the bride and seven for the groom, but today the bride is typically secluded for seven days and the groom not at all.

More needs to be said about the main transfer, the mahari. This consists of two distinct parts: the mahari proper, which must be found by the groom even if he has to borrow the money, and the *sanduku* ("box," the bride's trousseau), which is the responsibility of the members of the groom's descent group and which may amount to many hundreds of shillings; it consists mainly of gold jewelry and items of clothing. These are displayed at the front porch of the bride's house on the day of the kuingia nyumbani festivities. The bride's mother and her female kin provide her with cooking utensils, linen, and similar items for her new home. Her family must also provide the *kombe la arusi* ("dish of the wedding," that is, the wedding feast), which should be held in the bride's village after the kuingia nyumbani, when the groom is presented to the bride. The groom and his close kin are fed first, then other male guests, and then the women. During the feast women sing wedding songs, make sexual jokes, fan the groom and wave a khanga, a woman's cloth, over him and his food. The feast may be very expensive, since all visitors must be given food by the bride's father and his kin.[34]

Before the kuingia nyumbani there is the preparation of the groom and the bride. The groom is massaged by a female chaperon (kungwi), assisted by other women of the same village. His body is rubbed with *msio*, a mixture of cloves, ginger, sandalwood and other perfumes; during the massage he is fanned and sexual jokes are made to him. Msio means "a white smooth coral stone" and is another term for the unguents used. On the wedding day the groom is displayed before his kin and other men, dressed in his finest clothes—if possible in a *kanzu* (a long white ankle-length, shirt-like garment), a *joho* (an embroidered waistcoat), a turban, and a garland of flowers around his neck. The bride is also massaged by her chaperon, and the palms of her hands and the soles of her feet painted with henna; henna designs may also be painted on her face and the backs of her hands. Women's dance groups also perform. There are many different dances and costumes. Dances and the songs that go with them undergo changes, with new fashions and the introduction of new dances from other parts of the coast and islands. Details need not concern us, but the reputation acquired by the performance of excellent dances, with new and expensive costumes, musicians, and paraphernalia such as microphones and lighting, is considerable and an important factor that helps makes a wedding memorable.[35]

My brief description is indebted to Landberg's excellent account, which should be consulted for further details. These weddings follow the pattern of those described in the preceding section, and there is no need to present an analogous analysis here.

CHILDBIRTH AND DEATH

The expected life of a Swahili woman after marriage includes pregnancy and childbirth, often divorce, then widowhood and death. All these processes, which are given the classic structure of rites de passage, affect both herself and her kin and neighbors. They also affect men, but the rites themselves concern women to a far greater extent. Variations are considerable from one part of the coast to another, but I lack space here to present more than an outline account.[36]

When a woman realizes that she is pregnant, the rite of separation is performed (*kutia hijabuni*, "to place [her] behind a veil or curtain," that is, to shelter her from envious glances and the evil spirits known as *shaitani*). She is covered by a khanga and sits facing Mecca while prayers are said over her by an Islamic teacher. In some areas she and her close female kin then share a meal called *tangalazi*, made of rice and other grains and coconut; in other areas the grains are thrown over her and her face, wrists, and feet are washed in coconut milk. The foodstuffs represent the controlled fertility of these crops when tended by their growers and so her own controlled fertility as a married woman. She is then taken to the bed where she will sleep and later give birth; an elder sister lies on the bed and simulates childbirth to "teach" the pregnant woman. She now moves into the period of seclusion and liminality; during the pregnancy she may not leave the house and is looked after by a woman known as kungwi, who will also act as her midwife.

The impurity of childbirth affects both the mother and her child, and the processes of purification and the rites of reaggregation of each, although different in detail, are coordinated. After the birth the baby has to be protected and is for eight days kept in seclusion; an amulet is tied to its arm and kohl painted round the eyes to ward off evil spirits; in some areas a grotesque effigy, known as *kinyago*,[37] is placed on the roof as mystical protection. On the eighth day the baby is taken outside the house and shown the sun and the corners of the house, to ensure its proper location in the social space in which it will grow up. The woman remains in house-seclusion for forty days, when she is washed, shaven, and given new clothes, to remove the impurity of birth. This is followed by a feast, known as *haramu, hitima,* or *arobaini,* that marks her reaggregation into the community. Haramu means "feast"; hitima is a complex word, used properly for the Koran, which is read on many ritual occasions, and in the phrase *kufanya hitima* ("to do [or make] hitima," that is, to conclude a reading of the Koran by giving a feast); arobaini means "forty." The child has its *akika*, when its hair is cut and its birth-name is formally given, followed by a closing feast to mark the end of the liminality and the impurity of its birth, on either the eighth or the fortieth day. There is wide variation, but today at least the fortieth day is the more usual, so that rites for child and mother can be performed together. By the rites the mother is brought back into society and the child is given a social identity.

Swahili mortuary rites are important, except in the case of very poor people, orphans, and formerly of slaves. They form a set of rites of transition that affect particularly the widow, those for a widower being of less importance. They are also the occasions for large gatherings of kin and so also have importance for the definition of the jamaa. Mortuary rites include both those defined as in accordance with the shari'a (Islamic law), which are performed throughout the coast, and those defined as part of mila (local religious custom), which vary widely. Those that are part of mila are more noticeable in the country-towns, as would be expected. Whatever the variations, however, the rites all comprise three main elements: first the burial proceedings (*maziko,* from *kuzika,* "to bury"); then the seclusion of mourning (matanga); and last the purification and feasting that marks the closure of the ritual series.

The most elaborate forms of the maziko are those of the stone-town patricians. In former great houses they were performed under the supervision of the senior woman known as mpambaji (the adorner), assisted by washers (*waosha*) and buriers (*wazishi*). The former were women—the deceased's wife (for a woman, usually a sister) and slaves—and the latter free kinsmen. In the past if there was no mpambaji, the corpse is said to have been prepared by members of the Wayunbili, a presumed autochthonous subclan. Today this is usually done by professionals, who are poor and of low status.

In patrician houses a trench (*ufuko*) is dug by close male kin in the floor of the inner room called nyumba ya kati, and a bed of the kind called ulili is placed over it; or a chair of the kind called *mwankisu* may be used, with a hole cut in the center of its rush seat. The corpse is laid on the bed, its head at the southern end so as to face Mecca. Female kin collect the articles needed for the preparation: charcoal, incense, cloves, dalia powder,[38] camphor, soap, and other perfumes. The corpse is washed with perfumed and camphored water, the stomach contents are expelled into the ufuko, and bodily orifices cleaned, closed with cotton, and perfumed. The washer uses gloves, and they and the pieces of cloth used in cleaning are placed in the ufuko. The sisters of the widow or widower send pairs of khanga cloths to help in washing the body. The cloths and bodily matter are later taken by a professional washer (formerly a female slave) to the seashore and there placed in a dug depression, also called ufuko, that will be cleaned and filled by the tides.

Meanwhile, the grave is being dug. The corpse is wrapped (*kukafini,* a word used in this context only) in a shroud (*sanda*) of twenty-four cubits of a plain white cloth known as *mafuta,* which is sewn by the male kin to wrap the corpse entirely. If the corpse is that of a women, it is tied around the waist with a *leso* or khanga, the women's cloths. It is wrapped in a sleeping mat (*mkeka*) borrowed from the deceased's usual mosque.[39] It is properly carried through an aperture[40] in the wall of the nyumba ya kati and not through the house itself, but today this is unusual. It is taken on a bier (*jeneza*) to the local mosque to be blessed by the mwalimu and for prayers to be read, then carried to the cemetery. Three male lineage members (or five, but an odd number in any case) stand in the grave to remove the khanga and mkeka;[41] they place the corpse in a recess, also called ufuko, dug in the floor of the grave (*kaburi*). This is then filled in and a jug of water (*mdahasini*) brought from the deceased's house (formerly by a female slave) is poured over it. At various stages verses of the Koran are spoken, so the deceased is alerted by the water to learn the proper responses for its later judgment.

The notions of pollution and purity are important throughout the burial. The corpse is prepared in the nyumba ya kati, the room where childbirth would traditionally also take place and where pollution by bodily substances can be controlled and removed. The corpse is polluting, and so is placed within another ufuko at the bottom of the grave, which is covered in to seal the potential pollution within the earth; the pollution is countered from leaving the soil by the sacredness of the cemetery itself. Within the house, meanwhile, the ufuko is filled in and the room occupied by the widow, until it is vacated by her and repurified; the ufuko on the seashore is filled in by the sea.

Visiting and weeping begin immediately after the death. Women wail in the house and while the bier is being carried to the cemetery. Wailing must cease after the burial. On the day of the burial begin the periods of mourning (matanga) and of the widow's seclusion (eda). The former comprises a set of public rites and the latter affects the inner purity of the widow alone. The matanga lasts for three days (in some areas for seven), during which the kin and members of the jamaa of the household head visit the widow or widower to offer condolences; the men read prayers while seated on mats on the floor of the *daka,* the outside porch of the deceased's house. Women should not wear bright or new cloths; the mourning is a rite of aggregation that marks the end of the period of immediate grief and of the symbolic seclusion of the family. The final day is marked by a feast, *karamu* or hitima, known also as *kukunja jamvi* ("to roll up the [floor] mat").

A widow's seclusion (eda)[42] begins on the day of the burial. Properly this lasts for four months and ten days; that of a widower lasts two months and five days and is not as strict as that for a widow. She sleeps on the ulili bed set over the in-filled ufuko where her husband's corpse was prepared for burial. She wears white clothing specially sewn for the occasion, without cosmetics or perfumes; she observes certain food taboos decided for her by divination, speaks only in a low voice or whisper, cannot cut her hair or nails, must cover her head (normally not done indoors), must wear wooden bathroom clogs, should remain in the same room as far as possible and certainly not leave the house, and may not speak with any man who might later marry her. During this period she is not yet a widow (*mjane*) but a *kizuka* (phantom or ghost). In brief, she is a nonperson, potentially polluting, and surrounded by taboos lest she pollute others. She is bathed on Thursday evenings and fasts on Fridays, and reads the Koran and certain prayers. For the bath she is taken into the adjoining bathroom, which is fumigated with incense, and there washed and her skin anointed with cloves and rose water.[43] Her hair and nails are clipped and the clippings collected; at the conclusion of the eda an old woman (formerly a slave) takes them to the seashore for disposal (*kuzika eda*, "to bury eda"). On that day the widow makes a final prayer for her husband, weeps, is given new clothing and adorned with cosmetics by her mpambaji. She may visit outside and, if she wishes, remarry; if she is no longer of childbearing age and the mother of the wife of her husband's successor, she may become the *nyanya* (grandmother) of the house.

The kin of the deceased make regular visits to the grave, and if the deceased was a respected and learned man, offerings of meat and rice may be made for him at the mosque, eaten there after the midday Friday prayer.

The structure of the mortuary and mourning rites in the country-towns are essentially similar, although not as elaborate, largely because they lack the stone houses, the centers of descent group purity and perpetuation, in which a "phantom" widow may be so deeply secluded.[44]

These rites have obvious similarities with those of initiation and marriage. In both, the rites for women are more elaborate and of greater structural importance than those for men. Initiation and weddings are means to form, increase, and retain purity in both women and the houses in which they live. But there is a reversal in this context between a bride-to-be and a "phantom" widow: the former must be kept from being polluted, the latter must be kept from polluting the house and those around her. Both occupy the nyumba ya kati and sleep on the ulili bed kept there; both are anointed with the fragrance called *tibu*, which removes or hides physical impurities. The bride-to-be is being prepared to commence her sexual and procreative career, whereas the widow is being prepared to end it by becoming the "grandmother" to her grandchildren, her role of holder of purity being given to her daughter. A "phantom" undergoes the period of seclusion known as eda, as does a divorced woman. But the period of seclusion for a bride is not so called. Eda is a period of cessation of sexuality and fertility. Once these have at least temporally ceased, the woman no longer contributes to the perpetuation of the line of descent and her duty and ability to perpetuate the group's purity are ended. If such a woman later remarries, her new husband will be of a different descent line in any case. It must be remembered that the most important patrician marriages, those of the first-born daughters of lineage segments, are typically without divorce. When divorce is frequent, as in country-towns and among the poorer members of stone-towns, then a line of "purity holders" loses significance. There is also the importance of food sharing: both periods of seclusion end in purification and then a feast (karamu), to which are invited members of the jamaa as defined by the hosts; a wider cluster of kin, friends, and neighbors may also come to demonstrate their sense of recognition of and solidarity with the host group. This recognition is both cooperative and competitive: people are proud to contribute as much as they can, and at least try to offer as much as others of the jamaa. At the same time, segments compete with each other by offering more money and help and by doing so immediately without having to wait to raise the money by loans or gifts.

The arusi and matanga form a process of the redefinition and relegitimization of lineage, kin group, and jamaa. The many symbolic actions, however seemingly free and overtly ad hoc, are essential stages in the process and should be performed in the "correct" order. The strictness and elaboration found among "traditional" patrician groups are part of the core importance of ongoing corporate business houses. When this is not so—as in country-towns and today in many stone-towns also—then the details lose their structural meaning and may be elided or performed in a different order. For example, the ntazanyao may be performed before the kutia ndani, but this obscures the full significance of the bride's virginity. The traditional forms of chair may not be used at specific points in the wedding, or a widow may fail to sleep on the ulili bed. When the redefinition and relegitimization of groups are no longer important, the symbolism loses force and the rites become trivialized, although they still have the function of activating the jamaa, a function that is congruent with the lessening of importance of descent groups and the corresponding increase these days in the importance of ego-centered kin clusters.

P o w e r,   R i t u a l,

a n d   K n o w l e d g e

THE ACCEPTANCE OF ISLAM

The Swahili coast has been part of the Islamic world from the eleventh century. The earliest ruin identifiable as a mosque is at Shanga, and the oldest known inscription from or on a mosque is the Kufic one at Kizimkazi on Zanzibar Island, dating from A.D. 1106. The existence of a mosque does not mean that a town's entire population many centuries ago were practicing Muslims, nor that its social functions were the same then as they are now. Many historians have considered that Islam was brought to the coast by Arab traders from southern Arabia; others argue that Islam was brought from Ethiopia and northern Somalia by groups of Zaidites; still others claim that Islam came from Persia, especially from "Shiraz," a claim that gives historical priority to non-Arab Muslims.[1]

Swahili Islam is Sunni, most of the population being Shafi'i, although the former rulers of Zanzibar and their kin from Oman were Ibadhi. The religious distinction helped to maintain Omani ethnic and political superiority, especially since Ibadhi can only be born and not converted. In the larger towns there were until recently kadhis for both Shafi'i and Ibadhi, the former usually disliking the latter for their strictness and exclusiveness as well as for holding much of Shafi'i behavior as unorthodox, although in fact the Ibadhi sultans showed great tolerance.

Adherence to Islam has meant more than the observance of Muslim rites and the acceptance of Muslim religious beliefs; it has also meant the acceptance of Islamic law, which has often been in conflict both with local law—especially relating to inheritance, land tenure, and marriage—and also at times with laws introduced by colonial and national governments. It has also made the Swahili conscious of being part of the total Islamic community (*umma*) centered on Mecca and the Prophet's teaching. The Swahili see themselves as historically and morally separated from the impure peoples of the interior and as linked to the remainder of the Muslim world. In addition, each Swahili town sees itself as being on another level a separate umma, a sacred center set in the wilderness of unbelievers. Its sacredness is maintained not only by the behavior of its people but also by the guidance of those who possess knowledge and spirituality.[2] The most important values that have supported Swahili society are those of Islam, in giving a sense of cultural identity and in validating Swahili notions of rank and social and scholarly difference. Islam may be considered, at least as it is practiced among the Swahili, as based upon a corpus of knowledge established by God through His Prophet and shared and "owned" by living Islamic scholars and functionaries. The living need not "understand" this knowledge, and indeed relatively few Swahili are able to discuss its theological and jural qualities in any depth. Merely to possess it by reciting verses of the Koran in Arabic, by hearing a mosque teacher doing so, or by physically owning Koranic verses in written Arabic, is to possess the identity of a responsible member of the umma. Although both men and women can be members in this sense, the transformation of knowledge into formal power is virtually limited to men.

In this chapter I will discuss certain aspects—sociological rather than historical or theological—of religion among the Swahili.[3] In order not to perpetuate what I consider a misleading distinction between "Islam" and "custom," I refer to "Swahili religion" as including both. The Swahili themselves distinguish the words *dini* and *mila*. Dini is usually translated as "religion," but it refers only to orthodox Islamic belief and ritual as defined by Muslim scholars and teachers, the entire field of knowledge given to human beings by God; mila is usually translated as "traditional custom," referring to what has often been called "local" knowledge and rite, which is often associated by the more orthodox with non-Islamic or pre-Islamic faiths. Since all Swahili are Muslims, mila cannot include that which is forbidden (*haramu*). In general, dini is associated with theological orthodoxy and "Arab," mila with a less pure orthodoxy and "African," with the many connotations of the dichotomy in purity and reputation, the distinctions between free and slave, patrician and commoner, and in many situations between stone-town and country-town. There are many anomalies, blurrings, and exceptions to these categorizations, and the contents of each category vary from one town to another. Any group in any town may define dini and mila differently from others in the same town, and indeed most groups take care to define their own beliefs and practices as dini and those of their social inferiors as mila. We may also distinguish the more traditional groups who look back to an original Mecca, and the new ones who look forward to a wider Muslim world. The wealthy of a stone-town tend to be strict Muslims in their observance of the shari'a; a few miles away among country-town fishermen, "indigenous" cults and rules are regarded as of equal value and legitimacy. Both sets of communities consider themselves to be faithful and pious Muslims. It is said that *Uislamu na mila aghalabu haupingani,* "Islam and mila are as a rule not incompatible," the emphasis being placed on the word *aghalabu,* "as a rule." There is of course a "lower" limit to mila accepted by all Swahili, where it merges into the practices of neighboring non-Muslim peoples. In all, the general tolerance of Swahili religion has been a crucial factor throughout history, just as have been the regular attempts to introduce reformist movements and interpretations.

Swahili religion is not static but is part of the continual process of change that affects Swahili society as a whole. Throughout this society runs the complementary difference between stone-towns and country-towns. Ideologically, the distinction has been seen in terms of cultural origins, "Asia" as contrasted to "Africa," both essentially symbolic constructs rather than actual historical entities. This ideological division, the boundary between whose parts is never very assured, is expressed particularly in religious adherence and performance. Swahili religion is meaningful only when analyzed as a single whole, but it is a dividuum whose unity is maintained by a belief in the one High God known by two names, Allah and Mungu. Over time the boundary between "Africa" and "Asia" has been moving ever closer to "Asia," and the elements that make up Swahili religion— at least in the last two centuries—have become less local and Islamically more orthodox.

Virtually all of the more educated members of the stone-towns have accepted both dini and many parts of mila, which is increasingly subsumed as "Islamic" and, like people, given more "respectable" Arabian roots. Today formal prayer is given greater place than forms of sacrifice, greater emphasis is placed on the powers of God than on those of spirits, and ancestors are becoming objects of veneration rather than of oblation. Religious knowledge and practice are social resources. As with any other resources, Swahili hold rights in them and they may be exchanged, loaned, and used, like other cultural commodities, to define social boundaries, to claim political power and independence, and to determine the content of and sanctions behind many kinds of social relations. Religious traditions are never static or fixed. Any community continually borrows and discards ritual elements; dogma and orthodoxy are continually reinterpreted; and there are continual redefinitions of truth and error and of new truths and new errors. This is not an argument about theological truth but rather about social knowledge, interpretation, and understanding.[4]

A distinction is often made between the more orthodox as "core" elements and the less orthodox as "peripheral" elements. Most Swahili accept both beliefs of the Koran and those in spiritual forces that appear to be peculiar to the East African coast. In their view, these latter beliefs are complementary to and part of "official" Islam, not in opposition to it, the underlying sanction for them all being the omnipotence of God. All Swahili, including those who are devout Muslims and learned in the Koran, accept the powers of many localized spirits that can be contacted by specialists, and a distinction between "core" and "peripheral" elements of this single religious system is misleading.

Many writers have held that the observances of mila are associated primarily with women, in contradistinction to those of dini, which are associated primarily with men, because the former are in some way considered to be peripheral and inferior in role to the latter—a remarkably ethnocentric view. It is more meaningful to see the rites associated with the dini as essentially having the function of marking, stating, confirming, and validating formally recognized statuses and being concerned with sin as an offense against God; and the rites associated with the mila as having the function of resolving local conflicts and ambiguities in role, of both women and men. Women's roles are seen as more local, with greater variation between towns, less formally defined and more ambiguous; rites that Swahili consider to be associated more with mila are performed more on behalf of women than of men.

Every Swahili settlement has at least one mosque, even if only a small building almost indistinguishable from the dwelling houses amid which it stands. Mosques are used for everyday worship, and the *madrasa* (academies) that typically stand near them are used for children's education and the reading of religious texts for adults. The larger centers may have many mosques, but there is always a main congregational or Friday mosque where the townsmen worship on that day (Ibadhi and Bohra Indians do not worship at the congregational mosques). There are also many privately built mosques, the construction of which is an act of great piety, as is the establishment of a waqf for their upkeep. Periods of prosperity on the coast can often be dated by the sudden building of many new mosques by rich merchants (and also by wealthy women), who wish to transform their wealth into earthly prestige, honor, purity, and later heavenly reward. Each mosque should have an imam for religious duties and an overseer (*msimamizi*), often a madrasa student, whose main duties are to keep it swept and clean and to ensure that there is water for ablutions. There is also a *mwadhini* (muezzin) to call the faithful for prayer five times daily; except in very large mosques, he is often also the overseer. The Friday mosques in the larger towns may each have several preachers (*khatibu*) attached to them. The largest towns also have kadhis or judges to decide on points of law. In most settlements several categories of scholars and teachers give religious lectures to adults, who listen to them read the Koran and religious poems and so partake of the spiritual and social standing earned by religious knowledge. Children do the same by learning the Koran in Arabic by rote in the school (*chuo*). There are two particularly famous religious academies on the coast. One is the Muslim Academy in Zanzibar City, with scholars who have usually come from southern Arabia and may only rarely speak Swahili (the same was true of many Ibadhi judges). The other is in Lamu, the Ribat ar-Riyadh, "The Hospice of the Sacred Meadows," built in 1901. It has a more liberal tradition (for example, in using Swahili for instruction and originally teaching slaves) and has had a great influence throughout the coast. There are several lesser Islamic colleges elsewhere, notably in Mambrui, Kisauni, and Nairobi.

Islam for ordinary Swahili, as distinct from the more learned men, is not an intellectual or theological exercise; rather, it denotes the observance of ritual, the sharing in divine knowledge, and the sense of belonging to a chosen multitude. The shari'a gives a sense of order in the world that is brought about by the wishes and commandments of God and cannot rightly be shaken or disturbed by everyday individual acts. For ordinary Swahili, Islam means mainly the regular observance of prayers, ablutions, and proper family and community behavior, supported and made meaningful by the knowledge that comes from the recitation of the Koran and the life of the Prophet, and listening to poetry. The Omani of

Zanzibar regarded themselves as living in a land which was in religious terms an extension of Arabia and so on the periphery of the civilized world. The Swahili in other towns have seen matters differently. Despite the importance of Arabia in Islam, they see their form of Islam and religion as uniquely their own. Language is an important factor in this attitude. Relatively few Swahili have any fluency in Arabic, and many know only words of formal greeting, the names of the months and festivals, and some verses of the Koran. Yet Arabic is never considered a "foreign" language, but a sacred one, that of the Koran, the chosen language of God and His Prophet. It is the language of knowledge, prayer, ritual, and law, and, of course, of the Swahilis' former rulers, the sultans of Zanzibar. Arabic words have power in themselves, and especially those written in the Koran. If read or heard recited, even without understanding, words written in the Koran impart virtue, identity, and power to the reader or listener; if the words are written on paper or wood and then washed off in water, the mixture when drunk is thought to give success and to cure sickness. Popular belief has it that on the Day of Judgment, when the dead will rise up from their graves, they will speak Arabic. And Lienhardt mentions a belief in Kilwa that all will have light-colored faces and straight hair like Arabs (Lienhardt [1968: 46]). Yet, as I mention below, much worship uses the Swahili language.

I have mentioned the division between dini and mila. This is expressed also in the calendars of ritual performances and the forms these take, and in notions of pollution and purification. Swahili measurements of time lie at the base of all their ritual performances. The main "local" form of measurement is based on a solar calendar, and the more "orthodox" is based on two variants of a lunar calendar.[5] The former is given greater emphasis mainly by sailors and the fishermen and farmers of the country-towns, the latter by the more urban dwellers of the stone-towns. The older of these calendars is the solar calendar, often said to be of Persian origin largely because the name of its New Year, Nauruz, is Persian; it has been used for many centuries by Indian Ocean sailors.[6] It comprises 365 days divided into thirty-six decades (*mwongo*), with an extra five days (*gatha*) added. Its first day is the New Year's Day (*Mwaka*) or Nauruz.[7] Country-towns structure ritual and productive activities by this calendar; they are thus distinguished from more orthodox rites, but considered as complementary and not unorthodox.[8] These rites, which vary along the coast, have mainly to do with fishing, farming, and shipbuilding; they are of long standing and outside orthodox Islam, although care is taken to invoke Allah and to include Muslim readings and prayers.[9]

The lunar calendars are Arabic in terminology and more closely tied to the timetable of orthodox Islamic feasts and fasts. There are two versions. In one, known virtually throughout the coast, the year begins with Id al-fitr at the end of Ramadan and contains twelve months (*mwezi*, "moon," or *mfunguo*, "releasing" of the spirits that were fastened up or imprisoned during Ramadan). The month of Shabaani is also known as *Mwezi wa mlisho* (the month of feasting) and its final day as *mfungo* (the closing), when God imprisons spirits for the coming month. The first nine months are known as the first, second, and later "releasings," and the last three by their Arabic-derived names only, Rajabu, Shabaani, and Ramadani. In the other lunar calendar, rarely used by the Swahili, the year begins with Muharram, the fourth month of the former calendar, and Ramadan is its eighth month instead of its last. The Swahili week begins on Saturday, and the hours begin at dusk, as night precedes day. The first two calendars are used side-by-side in all Swahili towns. The solar calendar is used for times of monsoons and navigation, agricultural and fishing production, and the rites associated with them, and the lunar calendar is used for times of orthodox Islamic rites refer-ring especially to supplication to the Prophet. The choice of which calendar to use reflects differences claimed in ethnicity, and in economy and forms of social organization.

Although many Swahili and Indian Muslims along the coast observe the many "proper" holy days and festivals throughout the year, for most people the year begins with Id al-fitr or *Idi ndogo* ("Little Festival"). Marking the end of Rama-dan fasting, it is a day of feasting when people give food and money to the poor, so observing the Islamic obligation to give alms.[10] Swahili usually call the actual feast day *Siku kuu* ("Great Day"), and on it men go to the special prayers at the mosque wearing formal Muslim attire of long smock and skullcap, even if they do so on no other days of the year. The commemoration of the birth of the Prophet comes in the third month, when the mosques are decorated and there are recita-tions of maulidi, in which details of the Prophet's life are given and processions made around the streets. Maulidi continue to be recited during the month in the mosques and public places of the towns. The word *recite* gives little idea of the ex-citement generated by these rituals, which involve singing, the scattering of rose water, and burning of incense. Women are permitted to attend maulidi, although only separately from the men. Maulidi are also recited on other occasions, par-ticularly the family ceremonies of birth, circumcision, and marriage. After other and lesser holy days[11] comes the last month, Ramadani or *Mwezi wa tumu* (the month of fasting), when food and drink should not be consumed between dawn and sunset. During it evil spirits are "locked away": it is an intercalary month, one that is not a month in the sense of passing of time, when normal moral relations and boundaries are held in abeyance. At sunset immediately after the evening prayer, people eat light foods and it is thought proper and charitable to invite guests to the meal; heavier food may be eaten later in the evening.[12] During Rama-dany there are additional prayers and readings of the Koran, and people go to the mosques daily who may only rarely do so at other times; prayers are considered especially meritorious during this month. On the fifteenth day it is proper to give millet to the mosque official who reads the Koran, as an act of charity. Toward the end of the month comes the "Night of Destiny" (Lailat al-Qadr), commemorating the night when the Koran came down from Heaven. The mosques are filled, as prayers at this time have greater worth than at others. It is believed that on this night the spirits who have been locked away are set at liberty.

A central ritual in all Swahili settlements is the recitation of the maulidi, the celebration of the life of the Prophet. The rite has acquired great political importance in intratown conflicts: factions are often defined by their choice of maulidi and the mosques in which to read them, and the leaders of emerging factions at times introduce new maulidi that they alone perform. There are considerable variations in the choice of versions, the identity of the reciter and the place in which he recites, and the uses made of the occasion to bring into the open and resolve many kinds of social and political conflicts. Although the recitation of the maulidi is today a highly important ritual activity, especially in the more prominent stone-towns, this was not always the case. Pouwels (1987: 196–97) argues persuasively that until the mid-nineteenth century more attention was devoted to rites concerned with local personages, and it was only after the real effects of the Omani overrule were felt that the maulidi became so significant, as part of their cultural hegemony.

Several versions of the maulidi are celebrated, especially during the month in which the Prophet's birth is observed.[13] The traditional patrician maulidi was and is the Maulidi Barzanji, which is read in Arabic without music; it is followed by feasting but is itself quiet and austere. It is also read in Swahili. Its traditional ritual was associated with local ancestral and saintly figures rather than with the Prophet, and after emancipation of the slaves patricians refused to read this maulidi with them. Another maulidi is the Maulidi ya Kiswahili, read widely in the country-towns where sharifu influence is slight. It is accompanied by tambourines (*twari*) and verses are recited or sung in alternate verses of the original Arabic and the translation made in 1748 into the ancient poetical form of Swahili known as kiNgozi. There is also the Maulidi Sharaful Anani (known in Swahili as Maulidi ya Utaya, and recited in either language), which has no instrumental accompaniment and is performed without use of written texts; it lasts some twelve hours and is performed only as an act of great piety. Another is the Maulidi Diriji, performed with tambourines in Pate and Siyu only, and other maulidi are performed elsewhere.

I mention (far too briefly) the histories of these different maulidi because in choosing among them the Swahili express the internal conflicts and external influences in their own history. The situation in Lamu makes the significance of the maulidi clear.[14] The advent of the Omani Sultanate of Zanzibar weakened the coastal towns economically and politically, and there was continual immigration from Arabia of newcomers who came to take over the commerce of the Swahili towns. Slaves increasingly absconded and became free in the later nineteenth century; they wished also to acquire wealth and power, and saw themselves as indirectly helped by the Omani immigrants who had weakened the position of the patricians. Other groups, especially Hadhrami, Comorians, and Indians, were encouraged under the sultanate and introduced new cultural and religious patterns; as competitors of the patricians, they were seen as allies by the ex-slaves and the poor. The second half of the nineteenth century was a period of radical economic, political, and religious turbulence, and for the patricians, in particular, also a time of stagnation and isolation; as part of their battle to retain their position, they stressed their religious exclusivity. The new colonists brought reformist

views and wider aims in trade, religion, and education. The colonized could either
turn their backs on these aims or embrace them: the patricians chose the former,
most of the ex-slaves and the poor the latter. New leaders appeared representing new views and newly developing social groups and categories, as holy men,
religious innovators, and social reformers coming from elsewhere.[15] They were
mostly from Sharufa families and known locally as maSharifu, those who claim
direct lineal descent from the Prophet and the power to purify and bless (*baraka*).
There were then (and remain today) in Lamu and the other stone-towns many
long-settled patrician Sharifu subclans and lineages, but the immigrants stood
apart from the patrician oligarchies, as they came more immediately from Arabia
and could build ties with nonpatricians. The most immediately successful immigrant, and today the best recalled, was Habib Swaleh (properly Seyyid Saleh ibn
Alwy ibn Abdullah Jamal al-Layl), the founder of the famous Riyadh mosque.[16]
He came from Comoro to Lamu about 1880 and acquired fame as a physician.
He lived first in the patrician moiety of Mkomani, but as an mSharifu he mixed
with all levels of society. His main aim was not to reform Islamic beliefs as such
but to establish new institutions to teach those beliefs to those who were largely
deprived of them, the slaves and ex-slaves, the palm-wine tappers, fishermen, and
laborers. He built a madrasa in Langoni, and in 1901 built the mosque of Riyadh.
The patricians refused to read maulidi with slaves present, so Habib Swaleh made
use of forms of dance and song that slaves were normally permitted to see and
hear, since they were considered hardly religious at all. They included the *uta*,
a slave dance that Habib Swaleh greatly liked and performed himself. He also
introduced an acrostic song-poem known as "The String of Pearls" (*Dura Mandhuma*), written by a learned man of Siyu; it was greatly loved by his adherents,
was accompanied by forms of trance, the distribution of food and sweetmeats,
and a carnival-like atmosphere. (It is still recited today).[17] Whereas patricians
could not accept that slaves could acquire purity, Habib Swaleh claimed that
purity came from deeds and thoughts rather than ancestry. The Riyadh mosque
is famous today and usually accepted as the congregational mosque for Langoni.
Habib Swaleh died in 1935 and is venerated as a saint, his tomb in Langoni cemetery being a place of wide pilgrimage. It is significant that he and other reformers
were maSharifu, classless and apart from both traditional and new elites, and
also from the poor; in a sense they were given the role of moral "strangers." The
poor were Muslims but condemned to inferior Islamic instruction and marginal
participation in Islamic ritual; the patricians wanted to keep "their" Islam pure
and unsullied, as their own elite position depended largely on their reputation for
Islamic purity and their near monopoly of Islamic learning and literacy. Habib
Swaleh was nonetheless an mSharifu and as such due honor and respect, and in
time most of the leading families came to support his work. Most of Langoni
moiety is today divided between religious adherence to the two lines of Habib
Swaleh's descendants. One is descended from his son Sharif Idarus, who took over
the Riyadh mosque, the other from another of his sons, Sharif Ahmed Badaawi,

who broke away to develop a rival mosque and school: its mosque, the Mskiti Safaa, has recently been completed.

The maSharifu also play more persistent roles that can be compared to the "routinized" behavior of "prophets" in other societies. They are asked to recite maulidi and to perform other ritual duties. They also settle disputes, both within families (such as between spouses or siblings) and between families. The latter may be taken before either Islamic or secular judges, but their hearings are usually public; whereas maSharifu may settle disputes in private and confidentially by persuasion, supported by their religious qualities and powers. In addition, disputes between persons of different rank are always difficult and are not commonly taken to judges unless one party is non-Muslim. Where both are Muslim, the maSharifu can ignore rank differences, as the parties are equal in the presence of maSharifu, who stand in terms of grace above all ordinary people of whatever rank. Jurally, maSharifu thus occupy intercalary positions between both subclans and ranks. This is structurally more important in stone-towns than in country-towns, where maSharifu are few. It is consistent with another aspect of Sharifu identity: they are regarded as repositories of Islamic piety and grace, an important feature of the stone-towns as places of urbanity (utamaduni).

The mosque is an important factor in the expression of conflicts and disputes between those of different rank and of different claimed ethnic origins (the two being essentially the same but using different idioms). Conflicts are expressed largely in terms of which mosque is accepted as the Friday mosque and which form of maulidi is used. In Lamu, the Mskiti Jumaa was long ago the congregational mosque; after the growth of Langoni as the nonpatrician moiety, the congregational mosque was generally accepted, as it still is by many people, as the Mskiti wa Pwani (Mosque on the Seashore), near the fort in the center of the town today. More recently, the Riyadh mosque has come to be the congregational mosque for many, with the decline of the wealth and power of the patricians. The reaction of many of the latter has been to retain the exclusive Mskiti N'nalalo as "their" congregational mosque, as though simply to deny the existence of Langoni and its nonpatricians altogether. In the country-towns these distinctions and conflicts are few and of little importance, and the congregational mosque is a unifying institution for the entire town. In these towns the moieties still often play what was once their role of dividing the town to provide a sense of balance between two equal segments and thereby make for cohesion of the whole. In recent years, however, many of them have been the scene of a new distinction between the "proper" Swahili as "proprietors" of the towns and new immigrants (mostly from the interior), the descendants of slaves, and "squatters.

The appearance and acceptance of maSharifu reformers have not been haphazard. There is a long history of conflicts between various sections of Swahili society, as well as those involving non-Swahili categories that have wished to belong to coastal society hitherto open to them only as clients or as slaves. Such conflicts became increasingly important at the end of the last century. The first kind has been expressed in terms of competition for moral orthodoxy between traditional and new religious leaders. The second kind has been expressed more in terms of the establishment of and competition between religious brotherhoods. In more recent years, these conflicts have also taken the form of competition between Sunni and Shia (in itself an expression of whether local or international ties should be the more important).

There are in East Africa several Islamic religious orders or brotherhoods, of which the most important are the Qadiriyya and the Shadhiliyya.[18] They include both men and women, although they hold separate meetings, known as *kikundi cha dhikri* ("group of ecstatic performance"); they meet for devotional purposes and attend funerals and other rites involving their members. At meetings they dance, mentioning the names of God and other phrases, with overbreathing and other physical exercises that induce trance and possession. They are led by *shaikhs*, the drinking of whose spittle in sugared water acts as an initiation to the order, and there may be several ranks. Each of the more important leaders has his own "secret" (siri), which provides his special supernatural power and which is often thought to run in families known for their piety. These movements have often been associated with and led by those of non-Arab origins. They played important parts in the early uprisings against the Germans in Tanganyika: not all adherents were Swahili, and they have had a function of widening the traditional scale of Swahili society, in terms of religious adherence and a process of "Swahili-ization" that has spread far into the interior, especially in Tanzania and even Zaire. The brotherhoods are highly organized, even bureaucratized, and as such are in strong contrast to the loosely structured mosque congregations; they provide an effective nontraditional means of amalgamating ethnically and hierarchically diverse elements into Swahili society. The forms of *sufi* ritual and the organization into groups of enthusiasts under innovative leaders have provided a highly efficient instrument for religious conversion and the taking of political power, in which individual emotional conversion experience has played a central part. They have at the same time provided a local neophyte the opportunity to become subsumed as a member in a wide movement in which external power is clearly made manifest as a basis for newly spreading forms of "nontribal" authority and loyalty. And in certain behavioral aspects they share features with the traditional spirit cults.[18]

SPIRITS AND THE LIVING

Part of Islam is the belief in various categories of spirits, ghosts, angels, and other entities created by God. The creatures (*viumbe*, sing. *kiumbe*) that God placed on earth are of many kinds: living people, spirits, and animals, some good and others evil. Men and women live on earth and are visible to all others, whereas the many spirits are incorporeal: some may become visible in certain situations and to certain kinds of persons, and they can come into communication with the living to bring them good or harm. It is sometimes said that the belief in spirits belongs to the mila, the customary element of Swahili religion that is assumed, without much evidence, to have been pre-Islamic and "African" rather than "Arabian" in origin and to stand on the periphery of Islam. This view is mistaken. Beliefs in spirits are found throughout the Islamic world, despite frequent protestations that they are not those of Islam as such but of the preexisting local religions that Islam has incorporated within itself. Are they then pre-Islamic, which might argue that they should vary from one Muslim society to another? Or were they introduced as part of Islam to the local societies in the lives of whose members they have come to play so large a part? The question is of considerable historical importance, yet may well be a false one. In all religions a belief in the Creator or High God is accompanied by a belief in the mystical powers of both living and nonliving intermediaries, the latter including both those who were once living people (such as ancestors and saints) and those who have never been alive (such as most spirits and angels). The identities of these categories, and their relative importance to the living, vary from one society to another. Any local mystical forces found when Islam enters a non-Islamic society are typically given Arabic or Arabic-derived names and conjoined with mystical forces permitted in Islam. The inherent "local" meanings may not change but the names do, or are used side-by-side with the Islamic ones. This may explain the apparent similarity of beliefs in spiritual beings in all Islamic societies. Despite local differences, however, all such beings have one feature in common: they can never be equal to God.

The variations in these beliefs and practices, particularly between stone-towns and country-towns, are partially expressed in the vocabularies used. Some of the terms (*pepo, mzuka, mzimu, koma*) have Bantu roots, whereas others (*jini, shaitani, rohani*) are from Arabic. This should not be interpreted as evidence of different religious traditions that have mingled in the region, but rather as a sign of consistency with different notions of hierarchy and power. The terms in the "Bantu" set are used far more in the country-towns. They refer essentially to mystical forces, mostly linked to ancestry and used mainly to resolve situations of individual ambiguity of status as seen especially by women. The terms in the "Arabic" set are used more in the stone-towns and refer rather to relations of power and of good and evil (which compose another dimension of relations of authority and power)—that is, not to ancestry but rather to commerce and exchanges of rights in property.

The Swahili recognize various categories of nonliving intermediaries. Their names and characteristics vary along the coast and it would be misleading to construct too tidy a schema. Two main kinds are distinguished: the *mizimu* (sing. *mzimu*) and the *majini* (sing. *jini*). The mizimu (also known as *koma*)[19] are everywhere the spirits of the ancestors; but in some southern country-towns they also include the spirits of places, although the distinction is not as clear as the English terms imply. The majini are of several kinds, but all are nonancestral (although they may assume human form). Whereas contact with mizimu is typically by sacrifice and exorcism, that with majini is typically by their possession of the living and by the making of a spirit-contract so that the spirit will serve the living.

The mizimu in the form of ancestral spirits occupy a world of the spirits (*kuzimu* or *mzimuni*) of which the living know little. They may be given shrines, always beneath something, whether a rock, tree, ruin, or small shelter. The dead are offered incense and sometimes food, and a piece of white cloth is typically hung from a tree or other object near the shrine. This is also done at the end of mourning and whenever an ancestral spirit appears in a dream. People refer to these offerings as *sadaka* (see below), and since God and the Prophet are mentioned in the invocation, the rite is considered consistent with Islam and the orthodox practice of giving feasts to commemorate the dead.

The spirits of a locality may also be known as mizimu, particularly in the southern country-towns. They protect a particular place or stretch of land or water, where they control the harvests, whether of grain, fruit, or fish. Contact is made by prayers and offerings of incense placed at their shrines by the town officials known as *mzale* or *mvyale,* who are responsible for all matters having to do with land and the offshore waters. These officials also introduce new settlers or tenants to a town, who offer a small sum of money called ubani (incense) for the spirits to show that they accept the latters' spiritual authority. The shrines are also covered; those for the spirits who are custodians of a stretch of reef and lagoon are placed in caves at the water's edge. Here we may resolve the apparent paradox in nomenclature. Mizimu protect areas of territory. When the living wish to use those areas, they need to propitiate the mizimu by the acts of the mzale, as the territory has now acquired social value. This value is heritable and the basis for the establishment and definition of new descent groups of small span that will later increase in numbers. The mizimu become ancestors not in a genealogical sense but in the sense of permitting, welcoming, and defining the new kin-segment that has obtained its identity by their permission and whose members become metaphorical descendants of the original owning spirit.

The majini are distinct. In orthodox belief as held by the Swahili, they were the first inhabitants of the earth.[20] They were created from fire, whereas the angels came from light and human beings from dust or clay. They lived in Paradise with God, but their leader, Iblisi, argued that he was of higher standing than Adam, to whom God ordered him to bow; he and his followers were expelled from Paradise and made invisible to human beings. Majini are both good and evil. The good ones have learned Arabic, accepted Islam, and inhabit the towns with the living Muslims. The evil ones have never accepted Islam, speak Swahili of a poor kind or only "tribal" languages, and live outside the towns in the bush land with the washenzi (barbarians) and formerly with slaves. Majini are male and female. They can cohabit with and marry human beings, but rules of rank are followed. A Muslim jini can marry a patrician woman but not have children by her, but a patrician male can have intercourse with and marry a Muslim female jini, and she can have spirit-children by him. Also, a patrician male can marry an evil non-Muslim female jini if she converts to Islam, as could the slaves known as *mateka* (war captives), who were "like patricians" in their own country and so could marry good majini. An evil non-Muslim male jini should cohabit only with "barbarians" and slave women, who remained defiled and polluted. The children take the social status of their mother. These jini categories are found mainly in the northern stone-towns and clearly fit into the system of ranking of these towns. The patricians are pure and at the top; they are followed by the good or Muslim majini; at the bottom are the "barbarians," most slaves, and non-Muslim majini.[21] This categorization of majini is not merely a whimsy. To virtually every Swahili I know, the majini are real, and live in the towns and walk in the streets and town-lands. They do not only form a shadow community but are integral to the total society. Part of everyday life, they are accepted as reminders of the spiritual power of the world outside frail human beings.

The majini are usually divided into *pepo* (pl. *pepo;* in some areas also known as *mzuka*);[22] *shaitani* (pl. *mashaitani*); and *rohani* (pl. *marohani*).[23] The last, at least, would seem to be known more in the northern stone-towns than elsewhere, and there is a certain overlap between pepo and mizimu. The pepo (from a root meaning to sway or reel about, as a person does when possessed) are limitless in number, invisible to ordinary people, and not restricted to any one place. They send various kinds of sicknesses, particularly those associated with hysteria or trance-like behavior, to individuals by possessing them, "mounting" them by sitting on their heads. A pepo may seize a person who walks among or near large trees, such as *msufi* (the kapok), and there are many other situations. They live in the bush land, in or near the sea, and at times in towns. The possessed person becomes the "chair or "seat" (*kiti*) of the pepo, which then is likely to possess him or her on future occasions. A family of pepo may occupy a house and be inherited by the human family that lives there, often choosing one or more of the children as their favorites. These are *pepo za nyumbani* (spirits within the house): they cannot be seen but may often be heard moving about. They are not harmful and indeed offer mystical protection and help if treated well by the house owners. The owners should keep themselves and the house clean, sprinkled with rose water and fumigated with incense. At special times, when they might actually become possessed, they should wear a white *shuka* (a piece of calico usually worn as a loincloth), and women should wear a golden finger ring (a man should not wear gold). They should also recite certain verses from the Koran. Should pepo become worrisome, they can be controlled by a spirit-controller, known as their *fundi*, the word for a skilled craftsman who is able to instruct others. The controller can remove the sickness by exorcising the spirit or by appeasing it with gifts, but these are regarded as temporary remedies. The permanent way of dealing with the situation is by initiating the possessed person into a *chama*, a guild or association whose members are the controller and those others who have been possessed by his particular spirit in the past. These groups are found throughout much of the Swahili coast and form social organizations that are not associated with kinship and ancestry but rather with the temperament, occupations, and general social status of the members. Most of those possessed by pepo and who belong to spirit-associations are women, and the controllers are both men and women.[24] These spirits are often disapproved of by strict Muslims as being indigenous to the Swahili coast and so not originally part of Islam. Such people may call these spirits shaitani ("Satan"), but the members of the spirit-associations respond that they are the same as the majini of orthodox Islam.

Other kinds of majini, often confused with pepo, are known as mzuka, shaitani, and rohani. All are or may become visible to human beings. Wazuka and vizuka are specters, the former in the shape of humans and the latter in that of animals. They may strike a viewer with fear but are not otherwise harmful. The mashaitani are evil and the marohani beneficent, but both are considered powerful and potentially very dangerous unless controlled properly and carefully. Mashaitani are in many ways similar to the pepo described above, except that they are harmful. They may live in the bush land, especially in or near large trees and rocks, and like pepo tend to live beneath the rocks or in caves. They are not visible to their victims but are so to *waganga* (doctors), who may control them to harm other people. If a person cuts a tree in which they are living, they will harm him unless he first reads the proper verses from the Koran; then he should clean his room, scatter rose water and incense, and wait there. Later, at night, he will hear the sound of wings and much noise as those mashaitani move to another tree or house.

The third kind of majini are the marohani; there are others, more specialized and found only in particular towns, that I need not discuss here.[25] The rohani is a jini who appears to someone, usually a woman, and may act as "husband" or "wife" to the person whom they may at times possess. Marohani may be called or conjured. A person closes her or his room, hanging it with white sheets and burning incense or aloes and strewing rose water; she or he reads certain Koranic verses for four or seven days. Suddenly, at night, there is a manifestation in the form of a lion, a great snake, or other beast, or of a human being. If the conjuror shows no fear, it will transform itself into a tall man wearing splendid robes and turban or a beautiful and elegantly dressed woman. It will offer advice and take instructions, and requires regular gifts and essences; the conjuror may then perform miraculous acts, or levitate and fly through the air. I was told by one informant, a well-educated young woman, that she was originally possessed by several pepo but has now had a rohani—her husband—for some time. (At first she was unmarried, but now has a living husband as well.) She waits for him in her prepared room for two days each week, the second of which is the Sabbath, Friday, during which days she does not go to her usual job in a modern business house. Her first expenses each week are to purchase the essences of rose water and aloe wood (her spirit-husband dislikes incense) for asperging her room. Her rohani is a Somali, but other women have marohani who are Arab, Orma, Giryama, Pemba, Shambala, and Digo. This is in Mombasa, but in other towns the marohani may come from other neighboring peoples; not all are Muslim (a few are European), but none come from the interior and all are from groups with which the Swahili have had direct mercantile and political ties. Most if not all are said to be dressed in costumes traditionally associated with high office or wealth.

An important aspect of spirit possession is its relationship to power and to spiritual purification, expressed in gifts and essences, respectively, and in the ties of spirit-spouses to certain ethnic groups historically related by trade. Gifts have high symbolic value, and they make or strengthen social relations between people, especially between kin. The essences such as rose water (*marashi*), incense (ubani), and aloe wood (*udi*) are gifts made to spirits, and used in situations involving them. All are expensive and are used for ritual fumigation and aspersion and also as payment for establishing new social relations, as with the "ubani" given as payment by would-be tenants to landowners, and so indirectly to the spirits of the land.[26] The groups mentioned earlier are mostly those with which a joking relationship (utani) is recognized; watani may refer to distant kin whom one may marry, including sons-in-law who are alien merchants. They are marginal, and this form of possession may be seen as a symbolic representation of the traditional uses of marriage and clientship in long-distance trade.[27]

These patterns of gift giving, fumigation, and instruction and control by spirits form a complex of relations of power that run counter to the traditional ones of group, familial, and religious authority, and yet mirror them rather precisely. The associations of women who have been possessed by particular spirits resemble those of men, who exercise formal and overt political, familial, and ritual authority and belong to particular mosques. In both systems structures of hierarchical relations are expressed in similar ways. The belief that a rohani spirit becomes a possessed woman's spirit-husband is accompanied by a form of "marriage payment" similar to the hidaya. This goes to the wife from her father and so in a sense from her to her husband, although its substance remains hers. The spirit-gift is similar: it is demanded by her from her father or guardian and remains hers, although it is shared by the "husband" also, as it makes her wealthy and desirable in his eyes. Typically, this gift is of cosmetics, jewelry, rich foods, and similar personal luxury goods, rather than of a house or furniture; it is a metaphorical representation of the proper hidaya, just as the woman's spiritual marriage is a metaphor of a "real" flesh-and-blood marriage to a living husband.

The woman possessed by a rohani also in a sense "owns" him and so becomes the possessor of an external power that she and she alone can control and bring into the network of relations with the living that compose her social personality. She shows that she has the right to possess her own body and purity and to dispose of them as she sees fit, to remove them from control of her lineage guardians and husband.[28] She could of course do the same by emigrating and marrying elsewhere; but by the spirit-relationship she can do this while remaining at home and at the same time increasing the strength of her individuality, reputation, and personal purity, and indirectly the power of her family. A crucial attribute of a rohani is that it is an individual spirit who is "owned" by a particular woman: no other woman can own him, whereas many women may be possessed by a particular jini and then join a spirit-association devoted to it. People possessed by marohani do not form such groups.

A good deal has been written on spirit possession among the Swahili. The most common view is that women become possessed because they are culturally or materially "deprived." [29] This is too simplistic an explanation and does not fit all the facts. Many of those possessed are not in any meaningful way deprived. They include both women and men, certainly many more of the former; but if we disregard the notion of all Swahili women being deprived—which would presumably mean that all Swahili women become possessed, whereas by no means all do so—this factor is hardly helpful. Neither are all those women who are possessed poor; many are wealthy, well-educated, and in any usual meaning of the words sophisticated and often widely traveled.

I suggest that the notion of social and moral ambiguity is more meaningful than that of deprivation, and it is intertwined with the acquisition and exercise of power. Spiritual power comes from the moral and social periphery and is in itself ambiguous, pertaining to both the social and the extrasocial. As such, it is not surprising that it is more likely to be associated with women, as a facet of the ambiguity of their roles, which is greater than that of men's. By being "invited" and singled out, and perhaps by becoming a member of a spirit-cult, a person is given a new and socially approved spiritual position within the community and has the personal sense of uncertainty and insecurity resolved. Such people are typically those who cannot easily play their expected or proper social roles: a childless or divorced woman who is unable to remarry; a new immigrant to a city who lacks friends and cannot find a job; an ex-slave who, although free, has lost the security (such as it was) of a slave; a young man or woman with little education who feels uprooted without the traditional security of knowing what his or her future career will be.

Spirits are associated either with places, especially stretches of land and sea, or with specific ethnic groups that have been trading partners or military opponents. It is particularly the latter categories that are involved in the possession of women, whose control over land is not as clear-cut as men's. But women are used as links in marriages between subclans and trading partners, and their personal ties with spirits may be seen as metaphorical statements of those links. There is also the factor that a woman, in particular, is able to choose to be possessed by a spirit whose qualities and abilities are those that she lacks: the spirit gives her a place and a competence that she has not had. The help of spirits enables women to control their own lives, especially in new and uncertain situations, in ways and to degrees that are not apparent if we look only at their formal roles. Men are not possessed as are women, but more usually are said to be helped by majini whom they control, especially in enterprises that demand intensive labor or sudden sums of available money: when they are successful, it is usually considered that they have had the help of majini.

Women's roles have always been more ambiguous in Swahili society, perhaps particularly today, when the traditional security of a woman's middle age has largely gone and has not been replaced institutionally. The freedom of younger Swahili women gives way to the uncertain status of married women, especially those who are poor or of slave ancestry. Their only future sense of achievement and security depends on their bearing sons. If they do not do so, their strong sense of failure and their almost hopeless outlook for personal contentment make them into virtual outcasts from both their natal and their conjugal families. They may compensate for this in several ways, one of which is by being "invited" by spirits, whose powers are greater than those of ordinary people, to join spirit-cults in which they can gain a new sense of identity and purpose.

Those people possessed, especially when recurrently so, may in some areas form themselves into organized associations and cults. Swahili spirit- associations (*vyama*, sing. *chama*) are highly institutionalized. This is consistent with the emphasis given to all forms of cross-cutting nondescent associations, the most obvious being men's mosque congregations and sufi brotherhoods. But spirit-associations are not found in every part of the coast. They do not exist among the patricians of Lamu and other northern stone-towns, although they do occur in a weak form among nonpatricians. They were formerly important in Mombasa but have faded today, except for a very few secret cults of which I know little. But they flourish in Zanzibar and all the towns south of Mombasa. The relevant factors here appear to be that in places like Lamu the patrician lineages remain strong and functional; in Mombasa, although a stone-town, the lineage system has been of little importance during this century, and the associations have played a part in uniting both women of free and slave ancestries and those who are Swahili and those who are not, as members of common-interest groups; but in recent years these divisions have lost significance. In the southern towns the prevalence of cognatic descent and the exclusion of unilineality have meant a lack of any formally defined corporate descent groups, and there has been continual intermingling of Swahili and non-Swahili immigrants; spirit-associations have supplied efficient means of defining groupings that have united ethnically different people.

It has often been said of the Swahili that the women's spirit-associations are shadow organizations of those of men, but a more accurate rendition of the Swahili view is to regard them as of equal and complementary validity: they are on the same level of everyday experience and in no way "peripheral." The Swahili belief in the spirit-world is that of a shadow or replicate one, an asocial world of power that is an analogue of the human world of social authority. Spirit-associations and witches' covens (also known as vyama) are analogues of Muslim congregations and brotherhoods. And, as with these latter, women who organize themselves into associations may acquire considerable political and other nonreligious power. It is here also that women may at least temporarily "resolve" their ambiguous status by acquiring a second and public role that does not threaten that of men, and can carve out for themselves a new collective role in the organization of traditional rites of birth, marriage, and death: whoever controls these can exercise great power over the definition and perpetuation of individual and descent-group identity. In transforming traditional hierarchies by linking women of free and slave ancestries as having common interests, Swahili society may partly resolve the perennial contradiction between origins in Arabia and in Africa.

The role of the cult leaders is also in a sense a "shadow" one to that of mosque teachers and officials. These latter are often called "the pillars of the town," due to their Islamic learning and skills in poetry or in high-prestige vocations such as seafaring or carpentry. Cult leaders are rarely included, although they try to be so by claiming Islamic scholarship. They deal with matters such as women's sicknesses and the breaking of taboos, and they may earn large sums of money (which they may later transform into prestige). If women, they do not try to resolve any ambiguity of role but deliberately seek it; if men, they risk being classed with transvestite musicians and other anomalous yet powerful figures who stand outside the formal mosque-centered male networks of scholarship, dignity, and "honor" (*heshima*).

It has been suggested that the high incidence of spirit possession among Swahili women is a direct consequence of their having lost high status during the British colonial era.[30] But this explanation is hardly satisfactory. It implies that the incidence of spirit possession had previously been low or nonexistent; and it is hard to maintain with regard to slave women, whose status became higher under British rule with the abolition of slavery. The colonial presence did not so much lower the status of women, free or slave, as increase their sense of social ambiguity by altering previous relations of economic production and political and domestic authority.[31] Ambiguity in role becomes apparent particularly at times, such as today, when, due to changes in political power, education, and wealth, women are offered choices and constraints that are new, and for which their decisions may run counter to the expectations of the senior members of family and local community.

I do not equate "ambiguity" with "marginality" or "peripherality." Many "core" statuses in terms of power and authority are also highly ambiguous, often sacred, and a locus of unstable power within the context of stable authority. This is especially true of the position of women. There is perhaps some truth in seeing country-towns as not being at the heart of this mercantile society, but that is not the same as referring to individuals as peripheral (and would certainly not be accepted as such by the people of those towns). I suggest that the notions of "core" and "peripheral" in the context of spirit possession be forgotten.

RITE AND PURIFICATION

I have given a sadly cursory account of the religious beliefs held by Swahili people. They provide a framework against which are played out ritual performances and dramas that resolve inherent contradictions and conflicts in this ever-changing society. The Swahili view of the world, despite the many variations between towns and social strata, is based on the acceptance of God's power, compassion, and order, beneath which they are buffeted by the unforeseeable vagaries of God's creatures, both the spirits and the living, engaged in never-ending attempts to gain and exercise power, and even in their pride seeing themselves as God's equals, the greatest sin of all. Even if the experience of perfect happiness cannot be achieved during life, people may seek and hope for some degree of earthly harmony and order. But Swahili see evil, ill health, and moral pollution as being everywhere, and every person and community must continually counter them to purify and so reconstruct flawed sectors of experience.

Men attend the mosques to "beseech God" (*kuomba Allah* or *kuomba Mungu*) and to learn submission to Him, and they may also pray outside; women pray in their homes. Prayer is one of the five duties of Islam, yet Swahili hold that they cannot know its worth or consequences until they die. Prayers go directly to God. Other forms of communication with mystical forces that affect human lives, in particular spirits and living agents of evil, need ritual mediators to be effective.

These mediators are of two main kinds. One comprises orthodox Muslim healers and teachers, the other more "traditional" healers and doctors. It is better to consider their functions rather than the English terms conventionally used for them. Essentially, the former claim to involve God's help and are known as *walimu* (sing. *mwalimu*, "teachers"); whereas the latter invoke, combat, and at times use the powers of spirits, and are known generically as *waganga* (sing. *mganga*, "doctors") and *mafundi* (sing. *fundi*, "those with skill" or "controllers"). But the differences between them should not be exaggerated, and many ritual functionaries exercise both forms of knowledge and skill.

The mwalimu bases his work mainly on the Arabic writings of healing, magic, astrology, and divination, and must know some Arabic and have some arithmetical skills. He is essentially a possessor of Islamic knowledge and can use sacred texts. Power from this knowledge may be used both for good and for evil, but the mwalimu is said to use it for good only, defined not so much by the action itself as by the person who sets it in motion. *Sihiri* (both a noun and verb) refers to forms of magic or enchantment, and is good if performed by someone of known piety and knowledge, but evil if done by others. Divination (*ramli*) and astrology (*uaguzi*) are highly important means of knowing the truth, certainty, and inevitability of God's actions within the uncertainty and turmoil of human experience, and of foretelling the future by finding auspicious dates and times for activities.[33] Most of the mwalimu's curing is done by making gift-offerings (*sadaka*: see below), by medicines known as *kombe* (cup or plate) in which rose water, saffron, or materials used to write Koranic verses are mixed and drunk, and by the making of amulets (*hirizi* or *kinga*).

Whereas the mwalimu acquires power directly from the possession of Islamic knowledge, the power of the mganga has its source essentially in that given to him or her by spirits. Waganga are both male and female, whereas walimu are male only. Most waganga claim that their power comes directly from their use of Koranic texts and prayers, but it is generally agreed that they lack the knowledge that makes a mwalimu. It is accepted that most waganga come from the "African" rather than the "Arab" tradition within Swahili culture and so have deeper popular and "indigenous" roots. This reflects a crucial distinction between the cases they are called to resolve. The walimu work more in the stone-towns, the waganga more in country-towns. The formers' ritual performances are thus complementary to the jural performances of judges and maSharifu and work mainly on cases of healing, problems involving purification during rites de passage, cases of mystical pollution by mashaitani, and certain forms of mystical aggression by other people. The latter work more directly with cases of dispute expressed mainly in terms of witchcraft and sorcery, and with cases of spirit possession by pepo and mizimu. The mganga usually acts as diviner by using the *bao*, a board on which are thrown cowries and other objects, and cures by herbs and medicines of many kinds, including the *tego* (trap), which "catches" an evil spirit or person. The mganga also exorcizes spirits by means of many techniques, and in this role may also be referred to as fundi (controller of spirits). The fundi can contact and control spirits, and can use them on behalf of clients who wish to harm those who harm them. The fundi also organizes spirit-associations and so may play a political role of importance.

At the heart of Swahili religion lie the rites of sacrifice and purification.[34] Their details, aims, and functions vary from one part of the coast to another, and there is much overlapping and confusion, a consequence of the ethnic and hierarchical complexities of the towns, the long process of Islamicization of the coast, and the slow decline of "indigenous" ritual elements. The terms may be confused but the two essential functions of sacrifice remain: gift-offerings to show dependence and respect toward God and lesser mystical powers; and oblation with apotropaic, expiatory, and purifying aims. Much confusion is due to the prohibition on the use of alcohol and the orthodox insistence that all rites should be directed to God and not to spirits and ancestors. Three words are mainly used: *tambiko, sadaka,* and *kafara,* the first of Bantu and the others of Arabic origins. There are others, such as *dhahibu, fidya,* and *akika,* but their uses are more restricted and associated with particular stages in a life-cycle: for example, akika is the feast of goat's meat to mark a child's first tooth cutting, and fidya is a rite to save a very sick person by slaughtering a beast, the meat being given to the poor as charity. Essentially both are forms of sadaka. Tambiko is found mainly in the country-towns where adherence to orthodox Islam is looser, and refers essentially to a blood sacrifice made to the ancestors, mizimu, or koma. It includes a feast (karamu) and traditionally the sharing of beer.[35] Such sacrifices are made to remove sickness and to seek protection by the ancestors, but are disapproved by the strictly orthodox.

Sadaka and kafara are difficult to translate into English. Sadaka refers essentially to a rite that maintains a person or group in harmony by preventing evil or pollution, whereas kafara refers to a rite of expiatory purification which removes evil and pollution that have already come to a person or group. The distinction between them is not rigid, in that more "traditionally" performed rites contain elements of both, whereas more orthodox Swahili Muslims draw a line between them by saying that sadaka refers to the giving of ritual alms, as a public expression of Muslim duty. It refers also to any gift made to children to ask for their prayers (being innocent of sin, children's prayers go more directly to God), to food given to the mosques at the reading of maulidi, and to the distribution of cooked meat at a blood offering, such as is made at the New Year of the meat of the slaughtered bull (see below). Sadaka refers also to the gift or sharing of a particular animal prescribed by a "doctor" to remove sickness sent by certain spirits. Kafara also involves food. The food given is cooked and takes into itself any pollution of the house and its occupants: the gift or oblation takes the pollution and danger with it. When it is thrown into the sea or the bushland, or placed beside a grave, the pollution is safely neutralized. This is done by both walimu and waganga.[36]

A practice found until recently in all Swahili towns, and still today in some remote places, is certainly "pre-Islamic" but also an integral part of the Swahili ritual calendar. This is the New Year purification ritual of a town as a single sacred community, known as Mwaka or Nauroz. Its decline and virtual demise have clearly been due to social, ethnic, and demographic changes that have made traditional hierarchical and dual structures of the towns obsolete, whereas a continually reforming orthodoxy remains relevant for an ever-changing populace.[37] In most towns it has become elided with the orthodox New Year festival of Id al-fitr, which in functional terms plays much the same part in the ongoing life of the community. The traditional rites have been considered an integral part of "true" Swahili civilization, and their condemnation by reformers has merely served to strengthen the ideological distinction between the Swahili towns and external conquerors. Judging from available records, these rites have been very different on the surface throughout the coast, but certain elements are common to them all: a bull being led counterclockwise around the town, followed by its ritual slaughter; the participation of both men and women—and in the past slaves—in leading it and sharing in the feast; and the symbolic deconstruction of the main elements of the town and their reconstruction during the course of the rite.[38] There is no space to enlarge on this important topic. What may be said in summary is that all rites in Swahili religion are performed by or under the direction of a ritual specialist; that most are made to remove harm and ensure it will not befall an individual, although kin usually take part; that all are given the definition of being orthodox as far as possible; that each town or area, as a moral community, has its own body of ritual custom that distinguishes it and helps define its sense of identity and tradition within the frame of Islam; and that rites express the sense of submission, devotion, and truth before God.[39]

An important set of notions found throughout the coast is that of witchcraft and sorcery. The main figure is the mganga, who besides being a healer also combats the evils of witches and sorcerers. Although we need not distinguish them too rigidly, the witch (mwanga) has powers that are innate and even involuntary to harm other people, whereas the sorcerer (*mchawi* or *mlozi*) uses material objects to harm his or her victims.[40] The mwanga is a member of a group of what Johnson (1939: 16) calls "night masqueraders" who are said to devour the corpses of their victims and desecrate graves, whereas the mchawi uses evil "medicines"; the mchawi seems to be the more commonly found, especially in the country-towns. Other terms are used, but the concepts expressed are essentially variants on the themes of eaters and despoilers of corpses and users of medicines or poisons. Witches, in particular, are thought to belong to covens and associations of evildoers known as *chama* (pl. *vyama*),[41] which they join by offering their own children to be eaten. They are thereby initiated and then meet secretly at night to eat human flesh and to plot evil against those whom they hate and envy in their everyday life. The mganga is asked by a victim for assistance and uses his or her skills to divine the identity of the supposed evil practitioner and then to stop or even kill him or her. It is logical that in order to recognize and to harm witches and sorcerers, such a mganga might best be a witch or sorcerer himself or herself: power is morally neutral and can be used for both good and evil. Belonging to a chama whose members are linked by their hatred of others and their willingness to offer their own children shows their total abandonment of the basic social bonds of family and community, of which they are the quarrelsome and deviant members; whereas the chama of possessed women are those who have been spiritually purified by possession. The distinction highlights the spiritual as well as the social ambiguity of women as containing both good and evil. As a means of showing their evil, but to avoid the charge of cannibalism, it is often said that the witches' victims are known as *ng'ombe wa miguu miwili* ("cattle with two legs"). This account is necessarily brief, as I have no detailed record of the local social networks involved between victims and believed witches and sorcerers. But it seems clear that the belief that witches are at least mostly antisocial women is related to beliefs about the possession of women by spirits and their marginal and ambiguous social status. Beliefs in witches and sorcerers seem to be far stronger in country-towns than in stone-towns, where belief in the powers of majini is stronger. The underlying pattern has to do with the ambiguities of hierarchy and gender, both of which affect women more than men.

In Pemba and Zanzibar, at least, it is accepted that some people can turn others into zombies (*ng'ing'inge*)[42] and use them as secret nighttime laborers to acquire wealth. In the early morning, before cock-crow, one may meet gangs of shadowy zombies who have worked all night and are just about to become ordinary human beings again, led by their master, an Omani Arab. This belief is one in the shadow-existence of the former world of slavery and the economic power possessed by slave owners.[43] This is all in the realm of belief. But there is no doubt that many waganga, who are known publicly as healers, do attempt to fight sorcery with their magic in order to help and protect clients. And there is evidence that some people use datura plants to make others do their commands and to kill people when in a state of trance without afterwards remembering that they have done so.[44]

People hold these and other beliefs for many reasons. They attempt to understand and thereby control the various situations of uncertainty, ambivalence, and ignorance of the causes of personal and community ill health, unhappiness, and lack of success; they try to understand why they are on earth and why they die, and what are the wishes and commands of God and spirits; and—a factor that seems to be especially important in a society such as that of the Swahili, in which notions of rank and social diversity are so marked—they try to resolve the many situations of ambiguity in role that befall most people in the course of their lives. Notions of lack of health and success are obviously important in the everyday lives of ordinary people. Sickness and physical accidents are of immediate concern, and people go to a doctor or teacher who uses herbal medicines and Islamic magical remedies, including the making of amulets and charms. Today most people also attend Western-type hospitals and clinics.[45] Behind the many kinds of sickness lies the "social" question of its causes and vagaries. A few Swahili see the problem as one of infection and contagion, but most see it rather in terms of mystical factors such as the anger of God or the dead, the breaking of a taboo, or the spite and envy of living people, witches, and sorcerers. The concept of a cause that lies "behind" permits people to see ill health within a single totality of social and personal experience, and also enables those whose knowledge of medical etiology and curing may be slight to cope with it by repairing the cracks in the social fabric which they take to be the causative factors.

Civilization

and Identity

RANK, ANCESTRY, AND WEALTH

Swahili society, in all its parts but especially in the stone-towns, is one of continual change and differentiation, rift by schisms and buffeted by the predations of outsiders; yet it has retained its basic and stable structure over a very long period. In this chapter I will discuss some of the ways in which people conceive of and try to resolve conflict and change so as to make order and coherence out of the uncertainties that beset both individuals and groups. In the stone-towns these events and processes are seen largely in terms of hierarchical competition; in the country-towns they are seen rather in terms of competition between equals. In the former, patrilineal descent groups and individuals representing these groups compete with each other for wealth and power, and for the rank, reputation, and purity that may be acquired both on their own and also by the transformation of wealth and power. In the latter, competition is between individuals and households seeking wealth and reputation; within their particular descent system, these cannot be translated into changes in marked hierarchical ranking. Unlike the situation in the stone-towns, where subclans and lineages acquire and can retain wealth in many forms, in the country-towns wealth is quickly dispersed among networks of cognatic kin. In both kinds of towns ambitions and changes in status must be validated in religious and moral terms.

In the stone-towns, however rigid the formal hierarchy and traditional patterns of inequality, individuals and families can achieve higher status and change rank. This involves acquiring sufficient economic, political, or religious power, property, prestige, and influence, whether within or beyond one's own lineage, to be regarded as someone whose rank should be increased; to claim a higher lineage ranking than one has had by birth; to move from one part of the coast to another and acquire new rank by claiming higher rank in one's home town than in fact one has had; or, more recently, to acquire high positions in various external governmental or business networks. Even though slavery has been abolished for almost a century, the notions and values associated with it remain important for understanding modern Swahili society, in which claims to free ancestry and the ambiguities of slave ancestry are still discussed, and into which claims and ambiguities many conflicts at various social levels are translated.

There have been various ways to acquire wealth besides the traditional trade in ivory and slaves. The most obvious one was to realize the potential of new exports to overseas, as with sorghum, rubber, or orchella weed at the end of the last century, and to open up new areas of production for export, particularly by establishing new plantations. In Zanzibar these plantations were mainly for cloves, owned by important Omani and worked by slave labor. On the coast itself many entrepreneurs opened plantations for growing grains and other foodstuffs for export to Arabia; they included local men and women, Hadhrami and Omani Arabs, and also freed slaves who took over empty lands near Malindi and further north.[1] Few of these entrepreneurs were accepted as high-ranking members of the total society, and their reputation was local. They could not transform their new wealth into approved ethnic, genealogical, or religious status; nor could they marry into patrician lineages. But they marked the appearance of a new class-like structure that has come largely to supersede the traditional ranking system, a change that became inevitable with the abolition of slavery (Constantin [1987, 1989]). However, these entrepreneurs could transform their wealth into the status of patron. During much of this century there has been money to be made by the import of modern Indian and European consumer goods and provision of services such as insurance, tourist accommodation, and transport. Most of the profits in these areas have been made by Indian, European, Omani, Hadhrami, and "up-country" Africans; many long-settled Swahili subclans, lacking the necessary financial connections, have been kept on the periphery. In all these cases, by acquiring a high reputation and wealth, an individual can build up a body of clients eager for patronage. Most of the patrons are Hadhrami and Indian merchants and officials of central governments and national commercial undertakings, who can build up followings by patronage and occasional marriages. The patricians see the situation largely in terms of financial corruption by the immigrants to the coast, which has taken the place of traditional systems of mercantile exchange. As an elderly high-ranking patrician said to me, "We used to trade in goods, these people trade in one another"—a nice comment on the commoditization of human relations.

Another avenue to wealth has been the careful arrangement of marriages between lineages and between towns. Any patrician genealogy shows many out-marriages for younger and divorced daughters. Most are with distant cross-cousins, whose recognition is usually decided by their known wealth. And non-patricians have always tried to transform new wealth into high status by marrying patrician daughters, a strategy successful only in recent years. There are many cases these days of patrician families marrying their daughters to wealthy husbands in order to gain from the larger "donation" given. But most patrician families have refused wealthy nonpatrician suitors, accepting poor patrician ones instead. A marriage to a wealthy family does not bring in immediate return (since the costs of a fashionable wedding are high), but it does bring in prospective security to the bride and may well lead to valuable commercial contacts.

An important way by which Swahili can raise their social position and redefine their identity is to lay claim to particular categories of ancestry. The origins of the various "free" groups, as distinct from those descended from slaves, are variously claimed to be Shungwaya in Africa, Arabia, and Persia. However, the claims made by a particular group with regard to historical events are by no means consistent, and indeed may change at different periods: claims to origins are used to validate the actual social situation at a given time, whether or not they can be supported by historical evidence.

Patricians, in particular, have mostly claimed Arabian ancestry, a claim that became especially fashionable during the nineteenth century with the rise of the Omani rulers of Zanzibar. As a result, earlier claims to ancient autochthony were seen to be worth less than closeness to the Arabia of the Omani immigrant rulers. I do not imply that all these claims are not historically accurate: many are so; others are clearly dubious. The parts of Arabia claimed as origins by many Swahili are the Hadhramaut (and Yemen) and Oman. If we disregard those recent Arab immigrants who have held low and marginal rank,[2] the earlier immigrant groups are said to have come from the Hadhramaut and later ones from Oman. Descent may be claimed from one of these places in the direct patrilineal line: whether ancestral wives were from Arabia or Africa is irrelevant by Islamic law and convention. This descent implies patrician ancestry, literacy, wealth, and the ownership of stone-built houses. Within these claims there are differences of authenticity and of hierarchy according to the rank and reputation of the descent-name (*nisba*) in Arabia. The period of claimed immigration is a complex matter: for those who are reckoned as of "old Arab" stock, the earlier the better (often an origin in medieval Hadhramaut). For those who claim more modern immigration from Oman, especially if it is linked to the coming of the Zanzibar sultans, the earlier origin cannot be claimed, but this lack of antiquity has been offset by the link to greater political and financial power. In addition, a link to Oman has in recent years often provided the opportunity to migrate there to well-paid posts. (Many inhabitants of Oman today have come from East Africa, and kiSwahili is widely understood there.)

Claimed origins in Persia are rather different. Whereas many claims to Arabian origin do have a degree of historical basis, those to Persian origins hardly appear to do so. Their claimants are mainly the inhabitants of some of the country-towns: besides being Hadimu or Tumbatu or members of other local ethnic groups, they have at times referred to themselves as Shirazi, usually with the Bantu prefix to form the name waShirazi, in contrast to the Arabic prefixes *al-* or *el-*. This usage implies that they are successors to the medieval "Shirazi" kingdoms such as those of Kilwa or Vumba, and that their communities are older than those with Arabian origins. Most of these communities reckon descent cognatically and not unilineally, so cannot claim direct patrilineal lines back to Shiraz. The claims are not to seniority in rank of particular descent groups, but refer to all the members of an ethnic group whose claim is a joint one as opposed to the ruling members of the

Omani Sultanate, who, although politically more powerful, could be shown to have less viable rights to land.

The groups that claim ancestry from Shungwaya are today less central and even marginal in Swahili society, and have low occupational prestige, such as the Bajun.[3] Prins (1967: 39ff) and de Vere Allen (forthcoming) have suggested, with cogency, that in historical fact the presumed "Shirazi" origins are probably those of Shungwaya, whose members later moved southward along the coast and established kingships in places such as Vumba, Utondwe, and Kilwa, their "Persian" origin being taken over by their communities. Since most neighboring non-Swahili groups in the northern hinterland also claim descent from Shungwaya, the Swahili cannot exclusively do the same, and they have changed that claim to one of a Shirazi-Persian origin. All of this buttresses the identification of the Swahili with non-African origins, their main justification (together with adherence to an originally non-African religion) for distinctiveness and superiority.[4] Swahili measure hierarchy and power largely in terms of claimed ancestry and exclusivity of descent and residence. The obverse also holds: that exclusivity of descent may be measured largely by the possession of property and office.

The acquisition and holding of superior position may be achieved by wealth, ancestry, scholarship, and moral reputation. Ideally these should go together, and Swahili oral tradition holds that this was formerly the case, but certainly it has not been so since the rise of the military and colonial hegemony of the Zanzibar Sultanate. Public acceptance of claims to high-status ancestry and position may be achieved by the acquisition of wealth and its transformation by the privatization of public property. The distinction between public and private runs through Swahili cultural values, the private being the end of the process by which what has been in the public domain is removed to the private sphere.[5] The process includes aspects of the acquisition and retention of particular rights in various forms of property, both material and immaterial: houses, farms, mosques, space, ancestry, office and occupation, and educational and artistic achievement. These rights are held by both persons and corporations—in the stone-towns, subclans and lineages—to the exclusion of others; they act both as wealth- and prestige-producing processes and as markers of exclusive corporate identity.[6] In the country-towns most rights are held jointly by the members of a ward and the associated cognatic descent group. I have earlier mentioned the acquisition of status by the building of mosques and the establishment of waqf, thereby establishing new areas of private space, and dwelling houses are made inalienable property by testamentary transference into waqf; and of course property may be created by the building of stone houses. Private rights in property and position are also established by newly formed segments of business lineages, by exclusive forms of marriage and the weddings that are part of them, and by certain kinds of clothing, food, and personal adornment.

In addition, efforts to improve one's social position, by whatever means, must be seen within the wider picture of the decline of Swahili influence in general.

From the days of the Zanzibar Sultanate, overall governmental power has passed to ethnic groups from the interior, most of which are Christian. For centuries these were either trading partners or sources of ivory and slaves, and were considered by the Swahili as "barbarians" (washenzi). Memories run deep and those with power today do not forget the Swahili as slavers and slave owners. The coastal groups have made many attempts to form political parties, especially in Kenya, but although meeting with some initial success, they have in the end failed;[7] and there have been attempts, of which Swahili are very conscious, by central governments to push the Swahili coast into an underprivileged position. The Swahili have protested the situation in many ways while remaining politically unable to do much about it: by redefining and reaffirming a Swahili identity, and by claiming either a morally superior "Asian" identity or a more popular "African" one; by refusing financially advantageous commercial and marital links with more powerful entrepreneurs and government officials; by using scholarship and poetry; and by building and emphasizing ethnic, cultural, religious, and ancestral ties both between Swahili communities along the coast and between them and Muslim societies outside Africa. Some Swahili have taken a separate course, by retreating into a remote world of their own in which too overtly "Arab" or "African" links have been discarded in favor of a unique identity and civilization, threatened by outside changes but of vital unifying importance for the Swahili.

THE PILLARS OF SOCIETY

One means of acquiring high status and prestige is scholarship, the importance of which is a marked feature of Swahili society. To become an Islamic scholar, whether man or woman, may require enough money or personal ties of patronage to pay Islamic teachers. But many scholars do not in fact come from wealthy families: this is a channel to high status that is open to those of many talents and backgrounds. A learned friend told me that scholars and those with Islamic knowledge provide the "pillars" (nguzo) of a town. The pillars form an intercalary status, defined by individual achievement and mobility, that is distinct from rank defined by wealth or ancestry.[8] As repositories of Islamic knowledge, scholars are able continually to repurify everyday behavior by linking it to Islam. In a structural sense, they act as informal arbiters of behavior, both to provide individual links between disparate and often competitive groups and towns, and also to define moral identities and to accept or deny the claims of others to be considered good Muslims and so "proper" Swahili.

Scholarship is expressed in several idioms, the most important being skill in religion, law, and poetry and language. I have mentioned the offices of kadhi, khatibu, and imam. These are religious and legal offices, recognized publicly by a community and conferred for clearly defined abilities. Those holding them may receive payment for their tasks, although few are full-time professionals. There are also several nonprofessional scholarly statuses. One is the widely known scholar, the *mwanachuoni* (literally, "master of Islamic school"), who is by necessity a man, since he must spend much time in the mosque. (A mwanachuoni was rarely a slave, as a slave had no time in which to learn, but some exceptions are remembered.) A second type of nonprofessional scholar is the *mshairi* or *shaha*, a man or woman who knows the skills and techniques of composing *mashairi* (verses or poems), of which there are many kinds, distinguished by both subject matter and rules of prosody. A poet of any distinction writes for himself or herself, but particularly for specific occasions and audiences. Impromptu verbal composition in poetry competitions is a greatly valued skill, whose possessor may acquire prestige and reputation far beyond his or her own town. A third kind of nonprofessional scholar is one who has a deep knowledge of the Swahili language, its usages, history, and meanings. Such a person is known as *bingwa* and seems always to be male: he knows the vocabularies and modes of discourse of many specialists, from fishermen and boat builders to lawyers and religious functionaries. The skill is based on his knowledge of *lugha* (language), with the wider connotation of knowledge of the "civilization" that uses it. The bingwa is an intellectual leader, a teacher, and I have heard him likened to a *nahodha*, the captain of a great dhow, an organizer of men and knowledge.[9] Those with wide reputation for their Arabic learning are known as *ustaadh*, and an elderly man recognized to possess Islamic knowledge (not modern or Western) is addressed as *sheikh* or *shee*. Behind these skills is the ability to use words appropriate to position, age, and gender. This is considered an essential skill for anyone who aspires to high reputation, especially for men. Men should speak carefully, with dignity and the ability to marshal and appreciate arguments in public debate; above all, they must do so in the mosques, where socially important matters are discussed and the fitting use of quotations from the Koran is a necessary step to acquiring public reputation. Other forms of scholarship include the skill of proficient players on the *udi* or other musical instruments, who are known as *masogora* and greatly respected. Finally, there are categories of doctors or healers: mwalimu, *twabibu* (a person who has knowledge of astrology and of Arabic, Indian, and Chinese medicines), and mganga.

The status of a scholar is a quality that owes much to skill, like that of, say, a carpenter (a much respected occupation). But behind or within such skills and social attributes are moral qualities, conferred by God when convinced by a person's outer behavior, so that a person has the general reputation of being a *maarifu* (person of repute). Quasiformal examinations are often held: for example, an apprentice poet may be challenged publicly to compose verses for a set occasion, or a budding bingwa may suddenly be asked to name parts of a ship or of the human body. In these situations acclaim is given publicly by an already recognized scholar of wide reputation, the neophyte thereby being accepted as a learned person.

All these personages, as well as more formally defined and recognized legal and religious officials, are typically given prestige and reputation during their lifetime; they attract followings and pupils and may thereby become wealthy citizens; and they are often recognized after death as saints. Most Swahili towns have in their cemeteries and streets the graves of saints, both men and women, many of whom have a reputation outside their own towns; a few also have reputations beyond the Swahili coast and are the objects of pilgrimages and cults. Pouwels (1987: 87) has suggested that those of the past were almost all from wealthy lineages for the simple reason that only they could afford to own books, and clearly this is an important point. Books have until recently essentially been Islamic texts— copies of the Koran and other religious literature—and these have been owned only by wealthy families due to the great cost of copying them with fine and ex- pensive materials. The patrician pattern has been for one son in each generation to become an Islamic scholar; therefore, learned men tend to be from lineages that already possess wealth and high status. But a substantial minority of scholars have come from country-towns, from the Comoro Islands, and from the ranks of slaves. Also, lineages of maSharifu have long been dispersed throughout the coast and islands, and they have contributed many of the more famous scholars. Great scholarship and reputation have frequently led to the person concerned being at- tributed the power of *baraka*, that of blessing others, by virtue of his piety and purity.

The Swahili give much importance to the status of an expert poet; poetry is considered the paramount form of aesthetic expression. I was told that "poets are divers who go deep into the sea," who use metaphor, metonymy, and allusive and ambiguous meanings in speech and writing that are interpreted by their audiences to elucidate their own problems and situations. When poets are also religious leaders, they have great authority which is exercised by their acting as the mouth- pieces of God and the Prophet. The form of knowledge shown by a religious poet, the "diver who goes deep into the sea," may be seen as comprising the elucida- tion of divine mystery: a poet is a seer as well as a maker of verses. At the same time, the poets' duty is to spread knowledge and learning: to do so implies that they will retain the social order based on differences of rank and knowledge by ensuring that they will have successors. Ordinary people are told the poems, but mastery of the complexities of writing them is beyond the capabilities of any but the most able few. Swahili poetry is extremely complex, both in its use of esoteric and often archaic linguistic forms and vocabulary, and also in its structure, with the use of external and internal rhymes, of the caesura in the middle of lines, and of several kinds of prosody whose rules must rigidly be observed.

The verse, traditionally written in Arabic script and often in an archaic poetical form of Swahili known as kiNgozi, is of several kinds: the main include historical chronicles, poems on Islamic duty and the relationships of man to man and of man to God, love songs, and riddles and proverbs; to these might be added a modern category of poems written for radio and public performances of many kinds. The chronicles comprise the histories and myths of the Swahili towns, often including comments on the vanity of human ambition and the frailty of worldly glory. The Islamic poems include accounts of the lives of the Prophet and his kin, homilies on moral behavior, and accounts of Paradise and Hell in the afterlife. Links with

Arabic verse are close, especially in the case of the older poems, many of which were translations from Arabic into Swahili but with much use of local metaphor. This verse helped to inculcate Islamic and patrician values. Such matters were not considered suitable for servants, slaves, or in some cases women. The love poems and the riddles and proverbs are just those, set both in the context of Swahili culture and in that of the proper observance of Islamic law.[10]

These various kinds of poems are being written today. Others are old and are traditionally "copied" by scribes so that there may be several versions. The copyist should listen to the poet, memorize his verses, and then write them down, not necessarily in exact reproduction. Many poems are known in oral form and may have been old when first written down. How old is difficult to say, since those that may appear to be the oldest deal with essentially mythical events which are the subject of poems of all dates over the centuries. Probably the earliest poets whose verses have come down to us lived in the seventeenth century, although the copies of their poems are of later date.

In Swahili society, to read and write means that one is a Muslim, and all writing is seen as linked to the sacred, to contain qualities that provide and validate proper forms of Swahili style. As elsewhere, to be literate can be to have power, but here this power is seen essentially as coming from God alone and to be an expression not only of binding duty but also of an ultimate moral and jural truth. This helps to explain the immense authority given to judges, teachers, and holy men and the importance given to the written myths and poetry; it has been true not only of overtly "religious" writing but also of written alliances between towns and of mercantile contracts and receipts. The written word lies at the heart of Swahili "civilization" (ustaarabu).

Today, Western forms of education and learning are becoming increasingly open to the Swahili. Until recently, Swahili did not seek Western education: they were protected by the British administrations and feared non-Islamic education as leading to conversion to Christianity. Postcolonial governments have tended to restrict educational and career openings for Swahili. Most administrative officials in the Swahili towns today are non-Swahili and Christian, and few have much sympathy for and understanding of Swahili culture, even though Swahili is now the official language in both Tanzania and Kenya. However, scholars retain high status: many are concerned with developments in education, with finding new and profitable careers for men and women, and recognize the complementarity of both forms of education, providing conversion to Christianity is not a prerequisite to joining the wider world. The "modernization" of traditional learning remains based very largely on the work of traditional scholars.[11]

REPUTATION, PURITY, AND HONOR

Despite its many variations, Swahili society is a single oikumene that is defined by its members in cultural terms. It is given cohesion and strength not only by economic complementarity between its parts but also by the shared notions of ustaarabu and utamaduni. These are used to distinguish the Swahili from members of both alien and marginal or peripheral societies in their world. Ustaarabu refers to the condition of being wise and aware of divine knowledge, of observing behavior befitting members of a society long settled in permanent towns—living in proper houses and knowing how to dress, eat, and comport one-self correctly. All these are necessary conditions for possessing this quality, the opposite of *uhuni* (being a vagabond).[12] Utamaduni is translated in the dictionary as "refinement, civilization," but is better rendered more literally as "urbanity." [13] Those people who occupy a town (mji), and perhaps more particularly a stone-town, are those with ustaarabu and utamaduni, but the occupants of the country-towns also claim these qualities for themselves in contradistinction to non-Swahili groups. They are distinguished, at least by implication, from those without Islam, although this is not always clear, as many neighboring groups are also Muslim. These alien peoples are often called washenzi (barbarians), implying lack of civili-zation, inferiority, and also some sense of the absurd.[14] The word refers to those peoples without attributes of common humanity, but its usage varies between the main parts of the coast. In Zanzibar it was used to refer to raw slaves and to the peoples from whom they were taken; in the north it was disliked, since potential slaves were said still to have been wanadamu ("sons of Adam") who, if enslaved, could be taught some attributes of "civilization," as they were ignorant but not evil.[15]

Many Swahili words refer to the inner moral qualities and states of individuals and their descent groups. Since these qualities, at least in recent years, have been formally associated with Islam, some are basically Arabic terms which, although known to learned people, are rarely familiar to others, especially in the country-towns. The most important of these qualities are *usafi* and *heshima*. The former may be translated as "purity," is an attribute of both persons and places, and is associated mainly with women; the latter may be translated as "reputation" or "honor," and is an attribute of persons, especially men.

Purity is a key concept in the Swahili world view. The notion in itself has little of interpretatory value, since to some degree and in some form or other it is part of all cultures, as both "purity" and its converse, "pollution." The concept stated most baldly as usafi is, superficially at least, much like that found in other cultures, but the particular structure of Swahili society gives it certain aspects that are central in Swahili civilization. At the heart of purity is a moral quality that may be given to human beings—or some of them—by God.[16] Swahili recog-nize that human beings dissemble, lie, and cheat, and may claim for themselves an unjustified purity. It is held that only God can reckon and measure. But His judgments are not available to living people, who can only measure the worth of others as best they can. Purity may be adduced by other living people from cer-tain exterior factors. The stone houses of the stone-towns are spatial and physical representations of one dimension of the purity of the descent groups that own them, and as such must be kept clean, decorated, and adorned; this is tradition-

Figure 6. Veiled women outside their houses, Lamu. Photo: Linda Donley-Reid.

ally the responsibility of the mpambaji, the "adorner" who plays a central role in weddings and also ensures the cleanliness and propriety of the clothing worn by a house's inmates and the propriety of the public and private behavior of its women. One function of the elaborate rites of arusi is to demonstrate the possession of this quality by a newly mature and "complete" woman; and a function of mortuary rites is to restore and again demonstrate her purity after a time of pollution. Other criteria of purity include "good" descent and ethnicity, proper ritual behavior, charity and courage, and skill in certain arts, of which poetry is the foremost.[17] Besides the moral purity of individuals and descent groups, there is also the notion of the purity of the town, in both its physical and social dimensions, a purity renewed by the New Year rites and ensured by the prayers of men in the mosques. The purity of the town derives from that of its inhabitants, in particular of the wenyeji (owners or proprietors), and also from its being a seat of learning, piety, and urbane custom.

This purity, especially of a lineage's house and women, is a key factor in giving its men reputation and honor. Heshima in its sense of "reputation" is an attribute conferred by the living onto men, but it is implicit that a man cannot be worthy of it unless God has willed that his personal character merits it. The quality is given to men who by their behavior acquire Islamic knowledge and compassion and the trust of their fellows, the qualities traditionally claimed by and bestowed upon patricians and summed up in the word *ungwana*. By this last association the quality is removed from being merely an individual one to its being a part of *ustaarabu wa waSwahili* and so of the ongoing community of Islam. Heshima has a second and more complex meaning, that of "honor." [18] Honor is an inner quality: its possession and expression may indeed suggest to others that a person should be given outer reputation, but the two qualities are different, perhaps two sides of one coin but not identical. Heshima is the essential quality of a "true patrician" (*mngwana wa haki*), not merely of a member of a patrician lineage as such. (As I have mentioned, a slave formerly could acquire heshima in certain situations.) It is not a quality of an isolated individual, but an aspect of relations of communication and exchange. By behaving with courtesy, sensitivity, and good-ness toward someone else, a person both acquires heshima himself and bestows it on the person addressed, who, by responding seemingly and graciously, in turn affirms his own heshima and emphasizes its possession by the original giver. As Mauss showed long ago, exchange involves the giving of the essence of the self, and the notion of heshima exemplifies this clearly. Simmel wrote that there can be no honor without shame, and a person who fails to show his own honor or to respect that of another is said both to have haya (shame or embarrassment) and also to give it to the other.

These qualities are attributed to persons and places by the living, although at-tribution is considered effective only if it has God's approval. Other qualities are bestowed directly by God and known only by the material or miraculous actions of those upon whom He has bestowed them. Notions near to that of "purity" are expressed by the Swahili words *baraka* and *karama*, the former more widely known than the latter. Purity is given to women and houses by specialists, the wapambaji; honor is given to men by other people; they are not directly God-given. Baraka and karama, however, are bestowed by God upon people who are thereby marked out by their possession. They are gifts and need not be earned by means that ordinary people can evaluate. Baraka is usually translated as "bless-ing," but "fortune" would be more accurate (at least in the Swahili case). It refers to an increase in fortune, in both senses of the English word, given as a conse-quence of a blessing that came originally from God. [19] It is widely used as an at-tribute of the maSharifu, the direct descendants of the Prophet, but Swahili accept it as being given only to those maSharifu who follow God's words. Karama may be translated as "grace," a gift bestowed by God to someone who will use it to demonstrate His wondrous powers; the recipient may then be known as *walii* and can perform miraculous acts and after death be accepted as a saint whose tomb becomes the object of pilgrimage. [20]

As with kings and most other holders of political office, the ritual compo-nent may be as important as the narrowly social or political: an inner purity and high sense and observance of morality are necessary parts of the role of a mature and reputable person. These qualities are difficult to measure in any individual's overt behavior, and it can be done only by certain means that may be evaluated "objectively." [21] I have mentioned claimed and recognized ancestry as being considered one "objective" measurement; although all Swahili know of individual cases where respected ancestry and quality of moral action do not go hand in hand, in general this has been one accepted measurement of a person's character. Others, closely linked, include rank, wealth, overt expression of religious piety, and Islamic learning. A final measurement, which has always been noted by observers of Swahili society even when they mention little of the symbolic significance of what they see, is that of sumptuary rules and conventions, the overt expression of material standards of living. These, of course, are closely linked to notions of religious purity, ancestry, and the like: the quality of a civilization or of an age has usually been measured by historians in terms of art, music, and other cultural expressions as seen in the lives of those of high rank and great wealth; both can be put onto a measurable and comparative scale of worth. This is true also of Swahili civilization.

The general principle followed among the Swahili has been the obvious one already used in the measurement of ancestry and subject to the same logical paradox: the earlier the origins of one's ancestry, the better, granted that African roots are less desirable than Asian ones.[22] As with ancestry, a group, family, or individual can play sumptuary observances off against each other, juggling them according to the particular situation. Again, the basic notion is that of purity: of men and women, of houses and their contents, of clothing and food. The ways in which this paradox has been met have varied from one period and one part of the coast to another. Until about the mid-seventeenth century, Pate and Mombasa were the wealthy and powerful centers, followed by the rise of Lamu and later of Zanzibar. Pate showed its wealth by using material objects made mainly in eastern Africa (the obvious exception being Chinese porcelain). The later centers did so more by importing and imitating luxury items from India and the Gulf, following the example of the Omani after the decline of Pate and the rise of Lamu and Zanzibar. Today items from Europe, America, and Japan have similar significance.

There is not the space here to list and describe in detail the material objects that go to make, retain, and validate the purity of men, women, and their families and households. Houses should be in good repair, clean, whitewashed, carpeted, hung with tapestries, the wall alcoves filled with beautiful and rare objects. This is traditionally true, at any rate: today poverty among most patrician families of the stone-towns have weakened this aspect of Swahili life, perhaps irrevocably. All the furnishings and objets de vertu represent antiquity of provenance, reflecting that of their owners. Among the most prized and significant have been religious writings and porcelain. Objects of more purely financial value, such as jewelry, may be displayed as part of a woman's ornaments but not otherwise. All these luxury objects have been mainly for ostentation (except perhaps for the religious manuscripts). Few, whether made locally or acquired by the ocean trade, have ever been "trade" objects in the sense of commodities for onward exchange. They are "treasures," and the houses in which they are displayed have been "treasure houses" of wealth, elegance, urbanity, timelessness, and indication of ancient and proper ancestry. The stone-town houses are inward-looking, dull and blackened on the outside: the treasures and purity and glory are inside, beyond the public gaze and the finely carved wooden outer doors that face the public street while both hiding and implying the private wealth and glory within.

We may observe the broader changes in sumptuary behavior.[23] The splendor and wealth of the towns from the fifteenth to the eighteenth centuries were expressed in houses and their furniture and the objects used and displayed in them: the carved doors, rugs and tapestries, chairs, beds, silk and cotton textiles, brass and silver containers, and many lesser household items used more by women than by men, and more ornately decorated than those used only by men.[24] In later centuries the emphasis changed, following Omani fashion in Zanzibar. There came a greater stress on imported luxury items from India and the Gulf: Indian-type beds and other furnishings, Indian-made chests,[25] and boxes of many kinds for the storage (and so implicit display) of items of treasure. It may be suggested that these items have been associated more with men than with women, indicating that the representation of modern entrepreneurial wealth was of paramount importance.[26] All these became more fashionable than locally made objects. They came from outside Africa, and as such were dissociated from the "African" part of Swahili culture, from non-Muslim peoples of "inferior" origins, and from "barbarian" forms of behavior. In fact few were from Arabia, most coming from India, the Gulf, China, and the Levant. It is important to stress, for the patricians in particular, the significance of these possessions as signs of purity and honor rather than of mere wealth: Swahili patricians are fully aware of the vulgarity and pretensions of nouveaux riches.

Much the same history can be seen in other aspects of traditional Swahili life, such as clothing, ornament, cuisine, perfumes, and aromatics. Clothing and adornment are noticeably important cultural factors in all Swahili communities, and would appear always to have been so, as may be seen in the use of cloth and jewelry in both the mythical chronicles of the founding of towns and the medieval accounts of Arab travelers.[27] Cloth and adornment are used as signs and symbols not only to denote status, occupation, age, gender, and other directly observable criteria of persons and groups, but also to denote degrees of moral purity of their wearers within particular statuses and groups. The adornment of house interiors has much the same function. Clothing and adornment are significant not only within and between Swahili communities but also as signs of Swahili civilization in the eyes of their non-Swahili neighbors. The costly and beautifully made clothing of a Swahili man and woman marks them off from non-Swahili, many of whom adopt Swahili dress and may then consider themselves to have become Swahili, although they are rarely accepted by the Swahili themselves (Parkin [1972, 1989]).

But there is rather more to the meaning of Swahili clothing, adornment, food, and other items. The essential notion is that of the persona that is presented to others, including God, a persona that masks the naked individual.[28] It is not a mask of concealment but one that presents a persona by acting as the medium for expressing an inner purity. The problem is to ensure the public recognition of this quality without its being hidden by the "mask" of the clothing and adornment.[29] This is achieved partly by the specifically defined and framed context in which the particular items of clothing and adornment are worn, especially on ritual occasions, and perhaps to a greater extent by the reputation and honor of the participants. The clothing socially defines the person who wears it, in that his or her status is thereby declared to others, including living people, spirits, and God. But it cannot directly indicate the wearer's degree of moral purity. A person without high-status clothing may possess great purity: Swahili history has many holy men of this kind, and of course the maSharifu are generically considered so whatever their outer behavior and clothing. The situation was markedly different in the case of a slave, who might acquire personal respect and prestige and so could be referred to as mngwana (patrician) by virtue of his inner qualities rather than his outer appearance. Nevertheless, a slave was never accepted as a true mngwana; he would be respected as though one by his own owner but not by the community at large. His inner qualities may have been admirable, but purity could never be part of a slave's identity. The past century has seen many efforts by those of slave ancestry to overcome this definition, notably by claiming spirit possession and stressing that African ancestry is as worthy as any other.

There is also the factor of the symbolic meanings of specific cultural items, of certain kinds of clothing, adornment, and food. These items have symbolic resonances and links to other situations of transformation and of statements of purity. Examples include the cloths known as khanga, the cosmetic known as henna (it is said that "henna has many secrets"), and gold, kohl, perfumes, and aromatics, as well as the consumption of certain "hot" and "cool" foods. Properly, all such items should be used only in the making, transformation, and presentation of the self, at initiation, weddings, and mourning; they are not mere ornamentation, although this is often the case today. Great emphasis is placed on the adornment of the human body, and dress, jewelry, cosmetics, aromatics, hairdressing, and the like are all highly elaborated as symbolic means of expressing an inner purity.[30]

During the later part of this century this pattern has been followed, but many of the items used have changed. Most obviously, items from Arabia and India have become obsolescent and those from the West have increased. This has reflected changes in the position of the Swahili coast. With the long decline in the power of both traditional patrician culture and the Zanzibar Sultanate, the sumptuary importance of things such as furniture from Arabia, the Middle East, and India declined. The rise of European colonial rule and of the independent states of Kenya and Tanzania has given increasing importance to objects associated with Europe and the United States, whose mass culture has spread throughout the world. Islamic influence has retained its importance but has also been affected by the cultural Westernization of Saudi Arabia and the Gulf. A modern tape cassette "represents" not only Europe and the United States but also Japan, India, and the Gulf.

This is one side of the coin. The other has been the breaking away of younger people from their elders, their families, and "traditional" Swahili values, and the increasing individual wealth and independence of young men and women—in particular, perhaps, those from poor families, who work as unskilled laborers, "beach boys," prostitutes, and servants in the cities. In these occupations Swahili are outnumbered by non-Swahili immigrants to the coastal towns, so that today East Africa has a single "youth" culture. The tourist industry seems likely to destroy much of Swahili culture, and its operators care for nothing except quick profits, to the exclusion of the Swahili (see Peak [1989]). But this extraneous youth culture is misleading. Throughout the Swahili towns almost every household, including in most case its younger members, retains as much as it can of "traditional" Swahili cultural items and behavior. They are determined to show Swahili distinctiveness in the face of the ever-growing threat of non-Muslim African culture, which appears purely exploitative and corrupt as far as the Swahili towns are concerned. There are many levels of meaning in present-day sumptuary behavior and display.

IDENTITY AND HISTORY

Throughout Swahili culture runs the thread of ambiguity of identity, congruent with the nature of its mercantile history, the complex origins of the society whose boundaries have never been clearly defined, its history of dependence under colonial overrulers for many centuries, and its former dependence on slavery. I have used many "ethnic" and categorical terms as they are used by the Swahili people of the present time—Bajun, Hadimu, patricians, ex-slaves, Hadhrami, maSharifu, and others, including "Swahili" itself—but the contents of these terms change from situation to situation. Certain events—those concerned with differences and relations between these categories—are used as points of reference to redefine and revalidate them. This process has two main parts: to restate history and to change actual usage and identification, and to validate the terms by reference to moral behavior. Behind the ambiguities lie internal difference, conflict, and competition, both between individuals and groups and within and between towns. They are expressed in occasional naked conflict and open competition, but more typically in efforts to gain popular support, in intrigue and gossip, and in the ways Swahili ask for and show validation of status by God, ancestors, and spirits. Certain key features have shaped the lives of the Swahili and their definitions of their own identity and that of others: they have for many centuries formed a mercantile society in which notions of exchange, wealth, and relations of servile production have been central; they have until very recently recognized marked differences of hierarchy, expressed largely in claimed differences of origins; they have long used reading and writing to understand and obey the religious texts and tenets of Islam, to gain knowledge of a believed history, and to make mercantile records and contracts; and they have seen themselves as being of both Africa and Asia, a view that runs throughout their sense of the present and the past and their sense of hierarchy and equality. Mercantilism, literacy, Islam, and questions of origins and history have affected one another, leading to profound ambiguities in Swahili cosmology, law, and everyday social and personal relationships and to perennial attempts to conceptualize and resolve these ambiguities.

Despite the marked differences between stone-towns and country-towns that have provided one consistent theme in this book, I have stressed that these are ideal categories at opposite ends of a continuum on which stand the many diverse Swahili settlements. They are nonetheless actualities, parts of a polythetic series that has its own unities. The various members of the settlements are all conscious of being Swahili, members of one "civilization" that in their view is possessed by no other than Swahili. Every town regards itself as unique, is ever-changing according to its own logic, and affected by the world outside in ways peculiar to itself. Within each town's form of the common "civilization," there is continual difference and conflict that are among its central qualities.

The several behavioral aspects of the mercantile role of the Swahili form a single complex of traits: ownership of permanent and very private houses; the claiming of real or assumed direct lineal ancestry to descent group founders; marriage with as close patrilineal kin as can be made; marriages of daughters with trading partners elsewhere and with those owning land, rights in which may later be passed to wide-ranging categories of descendants; ties of patronage to partners with whom there are trading relations and with whom marriage is not approved; literacy and importance given to learning; the privatization of space and of time (in ancestry); transformation of wealth into reputation and prestige; the giving of public charity; forms of lavish display and consumption; the acquisition and continual renewal of male honor and female purity; and various forms of dignity, sagacity, and courtesy. Not all of these are found among all Swahili, and some at times contradict others. Neither, of course, are they limited to the Swahili alone; but certainly among the Swahili of the stone-towns they form a crucially important complex. The situation in country-towns, not directly involved in this mercantile economy, has been rather different, with emphasis on building and strengthening widespread ties of cognatic kinship, the opening of resources to many kin, and a disapproval of hierarchical differences. All the Swahili see the entire complex of traits as distinguishing themselves from other peoples.

Consistent with these many factors has been the lack of either strong or clearly defined political authority in the Swahili towns, and also the importance given in everyday life to *fitina* (intrigue) and *siri* (secrecy) as part of mercantile and cultural ambition, competition, and social movement uncontrolled by any superior authority.[31] The Swahili descent groups play no such part in everyday relations as their counterparts in the many "segmentary lineage societies" found elsewhere in Africa. The traditional political structure of the towns has been that of a complex pattern of balancing and cross-cutting ties of kinship and affinity, local and descent groups, mercantile cooperation and rivalry, claimed ancestral links, clientship, dialect, religious knowledge and piety, scholarship, sumptuary conventions and fashions, and the interplay of reputation, honor, purity, and grace. Groups within individual towns and the towns themselves have also been linked by their common economic and political subjection to the series of colonial and postcolonial rulers and exploiters, from the earliest times to the present day. The Swahili have only occasionally united to defend themselves against the divide-and-rule strategies of these rulers. Their usual response has been to play external groups against each other, as with pitting the Omani against the Portuguese or British, and also to retreat into cultural isolation and symbolic forms of resistance, such as poetry of subtle and complex metaphor and meaning.

I have tried briefly to describe something of the style of Swahili civilization as the people themselves see it. Despite the hopes and optimism for the future in independent Kenya and Tanzania, much sad wisdom has been gained from centuries of overrule and exploitation by non-Swahili. Perhaps the most famous expression of this nostalgia is the poem about the glories of Pate in its golden past of the late Middle Ages, the *Al-Inkishafi*, put into writing about 1810 or 1820. Its verses give a picture of the life of wealth and learning led by Pate's elite. By the nineteenth century, Pate had decayed into a small settlement of houses clustered near and among the ruins of its former palace and other buildings. The subject of the poem is the contrast between the town's glory and its downfall, as an allegory of the spiritual downfall of men who, obsessed by pride and luxury, ignore the wishes of God, the teaching of His Prophet, and the importance of honor and purity.[32] By contrasting their past cultural wealth with the financial and military power of their adversaries, the Swahili have been able to retain an identity buttressed by pride in their past. As colonized merchants, they have perforce constructed a unique "civilization" and "urbanity" that have been a source of confidence and stability in a world of "barbarism." But their civilization and urbanity are not merely matters of nostalgia for their golden past. They also give strength in the present and for the future; the Swahili use them to acquire new facets of their identity that enable them to make a place for themselves in the new society of eastern Africa. Swahili civilization is not merely backward-looking or a vehicle of silent protest, but a statement of pride in their ability to survive in an oppressive world.

E n d n o t e s

Preface

1   A formal report was submitted to the Fulbright-Hays Committee and the Office of the President of Kenya in 1989. This book is intended to be a fuller report to these bodies, to which I owe much gratitude for help and support.

Chapter 1: The Swahili People and Their Coast

1   The Arabic word also means "edge" or "border" and so might refer to the people on the borders of Arabic or Islamic civilization.

2   In the northern town of Lamu, many Hadhrami, who are today counted as Swahili, used to refer to the earlier-settled patrician subclans and the Bajun groups together as "waSwahili."

3   KiSwahili is a Bantu language, following the grammatical forms of all Bantu languages; its basic vocabulary is comparable in word forms to those of other Bantu languages. It is often said that it is merely a lingua franca, but this is incorrect. There is a considerable literature on the language itself; the most useful short accounts are by Nurse and Spear (1985: chap. 3), Whiteley (1958, 1969), and Prins (1967); other sources include Biersteker (1990), Chiragdin and Mnyampala (1977), Eastman and Topan (1966), Knappert (1970b), Lambert (1957, 1958a, 1958b), Maw (1974), Maw and Parkin (1984), Mohlig (1982), Nurse (1983), Russell (1981), Shariff (1973), and Van Spaandonck (1965).

4   The definition of kiSwahili as a language of exclusion and superiority has been discussed particularly by Eastman (1971, 1975) and Arens (1975). Arens's definition starts from the need for the inhabitants of the noncoastal trading towns to distinguish themselves from neighboring "tribal" groups: it is an "organizational conception" for marking social, economic, and political categories and the boundaries between them. The same strategy can be adapted to situations of ethnic diversity in the coastal settlements proper.

5   See Cassanelli (1982, 1987).

6   Little has been published on the Bajun islands; but see Grottanelli (1955), Elliott (1925–26), and Haywood (1935). For Shungwaya, see especially J. de V. Allen (forthcoming), Nurse and Spear (1985), and Prins (1972).

7   There are several accounts of the Mrima settlements; see especially Sheriff (1981, 1987), P. W. Landberg (1977), W. T. Brown (1971a, 1971b), and Wijeyewardene

(1961, n.d.). For the trades themselves, especially that in slaves, see Alpers (1967, 1969b, 1970, 1975, 1976), Beachey (1962, 1967, 1976), Sheriff (1987: 33–76), Fraser, Tozer, and Christie (1871), Martin and Ryan (1977), Ylvisaker (1982), and Burton (1872). See also J. M. Gray (1950, 1977).

8   Those central to the Swahili economy include rice, coconut, areca, banana, plantain, yam, cocoyam, and other palms and fruits from southeast Asia; the mango, many beans, and hemp from India; onions, garlic, several kinds of pea, and coriander and other spices from southwest Asia.

9   Millets and sorghums, sesame, cotton, and others.

10 Some ancient towns—for example, Pate—have preferred millet as staple rather than rice. Sesame has for centuries been an important oil grain for export, most locally used cooking oil coming from the coconut.

11 Coconut and areca palm, betel, mango, many citrus, banana and plantain, cashew, and others.

12 Clove, pepper, nutmeg, coriander, cardamom, cumin, turmeric, and others.

13 Their most famous sailing vessel was the sewn boat, *mtepe,* built from at least two thousand years ago until the early years of this century. There are today many kinds of sailing vessels, from the *jahazi,* the great square-built lateen-sailed ocean-going ships of up to a hundred tons; through the smaller *mashua,* of basically the same design; to the *dau,* also lateen-sailed but with sloping stem and stern, and very fast. Canoes include the *ngalawa,* the double-outrigger canoe, and the *mtumbwi,* made of a hollowed tree trunk. All are locally made, the finest builders of jahazi today being those of Lamu Island. All have been continually improved and redesigned over the centuries (the "ancient dhows of immemorial custom" are figments of travelers' imaginations). Those called "dhows" by most European visitors are the jahazi and mashua. See especially Prins (1965, 1968, 1984), Nabhany (1979), C. Sassoon (1970), and Villiers (1940).

14 See Prins (1965) and Datoo (1970, 1974, 1975).

15 I mention here only J. de V. Allen (forthcoming), Pouwels (1987), Nurse and Spear (1985), and several contributors to the first volume of *The Oxford History of East Africa,* especially Huntingford (1955, 1963); see also Turton (1975) and Masao and Mutoro (1988).

16 There are several accounts of these "hunting and gathering" groups. The fuller sources include Champion (1922), Declich (1987), Heine (1982), Huntingford (1931), Prins (1960, 1963), Stephen (1978), Stiles (1981, 1982), and Werner (1913, 1919–20).

17 Many sections among the Bajun and other northern Swahili groups still observe taboos on eating fish, which are shared by the pastoralist Cushites. Some, like the Dahalo, would seem to have lost their pastoralist economy and become hunters and gatherers who provided much of the ivory of the ocean trade. They have also left traces in the form of objects such as stone pillars and tombs: the Cushites were a megalithic people. See especially J. de V. Allen (forthcoming).

18 It was used for the many thousands of African slave workers in the marshes of the Euphrates, who rebelled from A.D. 869 to 883. However, their precise origins are not known. De Moraes Farias has argued that the name Zanj was used by early Arab writers to refer to peoples all across Africa, together with the names Habash and Barbara (and variants). They were not ethnic names as such but epithets that referred to trade: the Habash communicated with outsiders by trade and speech, the Zanj by trade only ("silent" trade), and the Barbara were beyond both trade and speech exchanges (Farias [1977]).

19 See Coupland (1938, 1939), Dale (1920), J. M. Gray (1962), Martin (1974), Middleton (1976), Pouwels (1987), and Salim (1973).

20 There were also certain Omani groups that were independent of the two main Omani clusters of the Ghafiria and Hinawia. These were the al-Busaidi and the al-Yoorbi, from both of which came the ruling families, at different periods, of Muscat and Zanzibar; and the people known as Besa, coastal groups in Oman occupying an inferior and semiservile position. See also A. Bujra (1971) and Yalden-Thompson (1958).

21 Local traditions report the coming of groups known as Dibuli and Diba to Zanzibar and Pemba islands in sailing vessels, with cannon. They built wells, stone buildings, and places of worship, the ruins of which may still be seen. They are remembered as cruel: Pujini town was built by Mkama Ndyume, "the milker of men," one of whose sons was Mvunja Pao, "the breaker of rods." Sir John Gray has argued that the Dibuli came from the fourteenth- and fifteenth-century Indian port called Dabhol, and the Diba from the Maldive or Diba islands. Allen suggests that they were rather from the Shungwaya coast (Gray [1962], J. de V. Allen [forthcoming]). For more general accounts of Indians in East Africa, see Delf (1963) and Mangat (1969).

22 When I was in Pemba in 1958, there were several families that claimed Portuguese origins going back several centuries.

23 See Horton (1980, 1984, 1987), Ahmed Badawy (1987), and Horton and Clark (1985). This is today a politically delicate point, as many local scholars deny the possibility that these towns were founded by non-Muslims, even though recent archeological work shows clearly that they predate the coming of Islam. Most writing on this topic takes the literal view that immigrant groups sailed southward and founded Swahili colonies; I here put forward a different hypothesis.

24 See Parkin (1970, 1972, 1989), Bunger (1972), Esmail (1975), Holway (1970), and Swantz (1970).

25 This trading network is described by Chaudhuri (1978, 1985); see also P. Curtin (1984), Kirk (1962), McMaster (1966), Ricks (1970), Romero (1987b), and Sheriff (1975, 1981, 1987).

26 I make the assumption that they have been the "indigenous" peoples of the region, whatever names their predecessors might have used, and have maintained their general form of production over the centuries. See Alpers (1975).

27 This was not a new pattern established by Western colonial powers, although they have usually been considered as the founders of exploitation and impoverishment of eastern Africa, but one that goes back through almost two thousand years of pre-European trade with Asia.

28 See particularly Gray and Birmingham (1970), Alpers (1975), Sheriff (1975, 1987), Lamphear (1970), and Roberts (1968, 1970).

29 For example, although there is plenty of evidence that sections of the Boni (on the hinterland of the Lamu archipelago) have been assimilated into Swahili society, other, more independent sections remain in various forms of alliance and patron-client relationships with the Swahili.

30 See Chaudhuri (1970: 132; 1985: 224) and Polanyi (1957).

31 The account of a central warehouse in Lamu given by el-Zein (1974: 38) is incorrect: his "warehouse" area, Otokuni, was a central market for the display and sale of minor consumer articles imported from Asia and the mainland; goods were not stored there.

32 See Guillain (1856: 3:386); quoted in Sheriff (1987: 119).

33 See Nicholls (1971: 63, 292, 362).

34 Slavery has been perhaps the best-studied of all Swahili institutions. The fullest accounts are by Cooper (1973, 1977, 1980, 1981); other sources include Pouwels (1987), Trimingham (1964), Sheriff (1985, 1987), Nicholls (1971), el-Zein (1974), Lodhi (1973), Beech (1916), P. R. Curtin (1983), Eastman (1988b), Shepherd (1980), Akinola (1968, 1972), and Middleton (1967).

35 See Herlehy and Morton (1988: 25), Sheriff (1987: 59), Nicholls (1971: 204–07, 287–90), and Cooper (1980).

36 The uses of these words vary from one part of the coast to another.

37 I discuss the position of female slaves in chapter 4. See also Strobel (1983) and Burton (1872).

38 The fullest account by far is by Cooper (1980). Middleton (1961) contains material on Zanzibar and Pemba, and Ylvisaker (1979) discusses servile labor on the northern plantations. See also Herlehy and Morton (1988), Mbotela (1956), McDermott (1895), MacDonald (1897), Fitzgerald (1898), Bennett (1964, 1968), and P. R. Curtin (1986a, 1986b).

39 See Landberg (1977) for the Mrima coast.

Chapter 2: The Merchants and the Predators

1 See especially J. de V. Allen (forthcoming), Pouwels (1987), Nurse and Spear (1985), Huntingford (1963), Maveiev (1984), Shepherd (1982), and Wilding (1976).

2 The situation with regard to the sources for the Fumo Liongo epic is sad. They comprised several collections of Swahili poems, formerly in the hands of Swahili scholars in East Africa and in libraries in Europe, of which the largest collection was at the School of Oriental and African Studies in London. Many writers have made use of these materials, including Werner, Hichens, Harries, Knappert, Rozensztroch, and Shariff. However, many of the original manuscripts have vanished. Here, therefore, I depend upon the few published sources. The best-known, by Knappert, comprises snippets taken from different documents, areas, and periods, and is disappointing.

3 El-Zein promised a later analysis of the "Lamu version," but sadly he died before he was able to produce it.

4 His grave is constantly being "discovered" in various ruined sites along the northern coast.

5 Many versions once available of the Liongo corpus were told to European scholars by Swahili literati who themselves represented various strata of Swahili society and so offered versions that were favorable to the standing and aspirations of their interest groups. See Willis (n.d.).

6 Knappert is confused here, believing that the Swahili were matrilineal, a most dubious proposition; see chapter 4.

7 The editions by Knappert (1972, 1979) make little sense here.

8 My views here owe much to those of Rozensztroch (1984).

9 See Prins (1958) for a succinct listing of the chronicles and their versions; also Freeman-Grenville (1962b).

10 These chronicles have often been discussed, especially by Freeman-Grenville (1962b), J. de V. Allen (forthcoming), and Nurse and Spear (1985), and there is no good reason to print them again here in the original words of the chronicles. For editions and discussions of the chronicles themselves, see Al-Bakari al-Lamuy (1938), J. de V. Allen (1982), Chittick (1969b, 1976), Freeman-Grenville (1962b), J. M. Gray (1951–52, 1959–60), Harries (1959), Ingrams (1931), Knappert (1970c), Lambert

(1953), Midani bin Mwidad (1960), Morton (1973), Omari bin Stamboul (1951), Rozensztroch (1984), Said Bakari bin Sultan Ahmed (1977), Stigand (1913), Tolmacheva (1979), Velten (1907), and Werner (1914, 1926–28). See also Pender-Cudlipp (1972).

11 Prins suggests that they sailed from Shungwaya, or that they settled there and their successors moved down the coast (1967, 1972). See also Freeman-Grenville (1962b), Nurse and Spear (1985), Spear (1974, 1977, 1981), and J. de V. Allen (forthcoming).

12 Translations of the Swahili words *washenzi* and *wenye ustaarabu*.

13 The idiom of cloth is complex. Cloth was one of the main trade commodities imported from Asia to East Africa, but the Swahili also made their own cloth from locally grown cotton. White cloth represents purity; colored cloth signifies that its wearers are transformed in their hearts and behavior, like a chameleon: *wajigeukageuka*, "they change themselves from one thing to another" (A. S. Nabhany, personal communication). In addition, "cloth" may refer to trade goods from the northern coast where it was once made, and so the "Shirazi" may indeed have come from Shungwaya. See J. de V. Allen (forthcoming).

14 I do not have the space to discuss the founding myth of Lamu, which is of a different pattern that reflects the traditional form of government in Lamu by an oligarchy rather than a single ruler.

15 I do not know of similar accounts about the coming of the Portuguese in the fifteenth and sixteenth centuries. Either information is inadequate or the Portuguese made little impact on the internal structures of local communities. The Portuguese were not Muslims and so could not make more than impersonal links with the local towns other than with their rulers; they brought many Goan women with them, and local unions seem to have been made by Portuguese soldiers who stayed only for short periods.

16 Most of those who have written about the Swahili have been historians, although that term has covered a very wide field, from early Arab and Portuguese voyagers to nineteenth- and twentieth-century European administrators and missionaries, and to the professional historians and archeologists of recent decades.

17 See Sherriff (1987), Nicholls (1971), Chaudhuri (1985), and Maveiev (1984).

18 I am aware of the difficulties in using this term, which reflects the periodization of European history. Terms such as *prehistoric*, *protohistoric*, and *precapitalist* might be more accurate, but they also connote European history. So I use "medieval" and "Middle Ages" to refer to the coast before the destruction of the great centers of Pate and Kilwa during the seventeenth century, and I refer to later periods merely by particular centuries.

19 There have been many editions. The most useful one is that by Huntingford (1980: 29–31). The description is clearly based on actual visits to the coast, even if not by the writer: it is not a legendary description of wonderful upside-down people of the kind written by Sir John Mandeville, but a working navigational guide.

20 Rhapta has been placed variously on the mainland or in the forlorn reaches of the Rufiji Delta. Horton and Allen have suggested that the *Periplus* includes a later insertion about the island of Menouthias. If we omit that and use the measurement of the sailing distances mentioned in both the *Periplus* and the later work of Ptolemy (Freeman-Grenville [1962a: 3–4]), then the location becomes fairly clear. Rhapta would have been in the Tana River area, which was for centuries the most profitable access to the northern interior, with well-watered offshore islands. Its site has not yet been discovered due to difficulties posed by the swampy terrain.

21   A full listing of archeological reports cannot be given here; among the more important are those by Chittick, Kirkman, Freeman-Grenville, Horton, and Horton and Clark, all listed in the references.

22   For Manda, see Chittick (1984); for Shanga, see Horton (1980, 1984, 1987).

23   The first two items came from the northern interior, crystal being found mainly in the Baringo area. Slaves came mainly from behind the northern coast at this time, especially from Ethiopia, and went largely to Persia until the Zanj revolts of the ninth century.

24   See Spear (1978) and Nurse and Spear (1985).

25   James Allen has written that of 173 Swahili settlements, including those much later ones flourishing in the nineteenth and twentieth centuries, almost 60 percent have or have had good harbors, and almost all are on estuaries or close-by islands (J. de V. Allen [1981a]). Three main factors are important here. For the sailing craft on this coast, a hard bottom that dries out at low tide is more useful than deep-water berthing. Most of the coast has long reefs that protect it from the open sea: a port must therefore lie opposite or near a channel through the reef, as in the cases of Manda, Shanga, Pate, Faza, Kizingitini, Ndau, Malindi, Mombasa, and other towns. And a water supply is crucial. Fresh water has a lower specific gravity than salt water, and a layer of fresh water formed by runoff of rain filtered through sand dunes "floats" on the underlying table of sea water; this means that wells dug near the coast, where are the dunes, are shallower and provide sweeter water than wells dug farther inland. These trading settlements had to be sited in places where exchanges with inland peoples and with overseas vessels could be made, and one of the most important services they could provide was to supply ships with water.

26   There is a considerable literature on coins found on the Swahili coast. Some are from local mints in Shanga, Kilwa, and perhaps a few other places; others are scattered coins from Byzantium, Rome, China, and elsewhere; others are hoards, collections of coins from many places. It is hardly necessary to assume that the presence of exotic coins means that there were actual historical contacts, nor would imported coins normally be used in early trade, as they would have little obvious value. The best accounts are by Freeman-Grenville (1959a, 1962b: 220–24, 1988).

27   Those of the fourteenth and fifteenth centuries were largely of sea-green celadon ware; in the sixteenth century, blue-and-white porcelain became more popular. Glazed earthenware, the yellow-and-green *sgraffito* ware that was the universal Islamic pottery of the late Middle Ages, was also imported from Persia. Other imported pottery included Chinese heavy glossy blue, green, and turquoise bowls; in the seventeenth and eighteenth centuries Portuguese and Spanish blue-and-white pottery became fashionable, followed by painted Dutch and other trade ware. The most useful short account is by C. Sassoon (1975).

28   The Portuguese wrote that the silken cloth from Pate in the seventeenth century, made from imported thread, was the finest in the world (J. de V. Allen [forthcoming]).

29   The immense amount of scattered sources cannot be listed here, but a most useful selection is in Freeman-Grenville (1962a).

30   Ivory was used in China and in India for bangles, combs, dagger handles, sword scabbards, chess and backgammon pieces, and other small consumer goods. African elephants provided larger and harder tusks than did Indian elephants, which were not used for ivory (Freeman-Grenville [1962b: 25–26]).

31   For Ibn Battuta's visit, see, besides his own writing, Freeman-Grenville (1962a: 27–

32); see also Chittick (1967a, 1982), Dammann (1929), Trimingham (1975), and Wansbrough (1970).

32 See Chittick (1963, 1966, 1974b) and Freeman-Grenville (1962b).

33 Some writers have claimed that in the Middle Ages, the period of a misty and heroic past, there was a single great Swahili empire ruled from Pate, or Zanzibar, or another place. This is romantic fancy.

34 There were many differences between the several kingdoms and chiefdoms. The best account remains that by Prins (1967: 92–103) and I have depended largely on his work.

35 The word *shari'a* refers to both Islamic and "civil" law, which are seen as inseparable.

36 Information on the Hadimu kings is sparse and confused. See Prins (1967) and Ingrams (1931).

37 See Prins (1967: 102); also Berg (1968) and Swartz (1979).

38 See Spear (1978), Nurse and Spear (1985), and Parkin (1970, 1972, 1985).

39 All have been succinctly described by Prins (1967: 92ff).

40 See Prins (1967: 94–97), Hollis (1900), W. T. Brown (1971a), Baker (1941, 1949), Dickson (1917, 1921), Lambert (1957, 1958a), Robinson (1939), Mtoro bin Mwinyi Bakari (1981), and Wijeyewardene (1961, n.d.).

41 See below; also J. M. Gray (1962), Nicholls (1971), Sheriff (1987), Flint (1965), and A. Smith (1976).

42 See J. de V. Allen (1976, 1989) and H. Sassoon (1975). The *siwa* and "chair of power" are used also in weddings and other nonroyal occasions: see chapter 6. The finest siwa are the two in the Lamu Museum.

43 There are several accounts of the Portuguese period. Among the more informative are those by Alpers (1975), Axelson (1973), Berg (1974), Boxer and d'Azevado (1960), Chaudhuri (1985: chap. 3), Freeman-Grenville (1962b, 1963a), J. M. Gray (1962), and Strandes (1961).

44 Portuguese relations with the Mombasa Swahili were typically hostile, and each side lived in its own settlement. An account of Mombasa by Pedro Barreto de Rezende in 1634 lists the Portuguese officials in Mombasa. Under the captain of Mombasa were twenty-one customs and fort officials, with a few other customs officials stationed northward along the coast; two military officers, a surgeon, ninety-six soldiers and eighty sailors, with some local troops also; three priests and some nuns of the Convent of St. Augustine; and wives, some from Portugal but most from Goa or Mombasa. The number of officials and military was extraordinarily small for so great a task. Many soldiers and artisans became settlers and even "renegades" under the protection of local rulers, and lived at more or less the same level as local Swahili farmers (probably not less than that of peasants in Portugal). Several hundred settled on Zanzibar and Pemba and stayed behind when the Portuguese finally withdrew, in time losing any separate identity and becoming Swahili. There were also a few priests and nuns up and down the coast, but any traces of Christian communities in the various towns vanished very quickly. See the accounts in Freeman-Grenville (1962a, 1962b) and J. M. Gray (1947, 1958).

45 The most detailed account that has been published concerns the Portuguese "factory" at Sofala in 1513. On average each year the factory received 51,000 pounds of ivory, 139 pounds of gold, 2,000 pounds of copper, 127 branches of amber, 4 grains of seed pearls, 20 pounds of coral, 6 slaves, and some lead. As Freeman-Grenville, from whom these figures are taken (1962b: 198), points out, the amount of ivory represents an

annual slaughter of almost eight hundred animals. The amount of gold is surprisingly low, and much may have been exported illegally or through other ports. Freeman-Grenville estimates that the gold alone, in our terms, was worth something between a quarter- and a half-million pounds sterling. The number of slaves is small, but Sofala exported gold rather than slaves, who went out through Kilwa.

46   The same report mentions that cloth was imported from India, including the scarlet cloth for local royalty. Vast numbers of beads were also imported, the annual amount being over 7,000 pounds of Cambay and other beads, and about 10,000 strings of beads of jet, crystal, and tin. Their value is impossible to work out today. See Freeman-Grenville (1962b: 201).

47   The later history of Mozambique is outside the theme of this book: see Alpers (1967, 1975), Strandes (1961), Boxer and d'Azevado (1960), and Freeman-Grenville (1962a).

48   See Nicholls (1971) and Sheriff (1987).

49   Among the many sources may be mentioned Cooper (1977, 1980), Coupland (1938, 1939), Harlow and Chilver (1965), Ingrams (1931), Landberg (1977: chap. 2), Low and Smith (1976), McKay (1975), Middleton and Campbell (1965), Nicholls (1971), Pearce (1928), Pouwels (1987), Ruete (1987), Sheriff (1971, 1987), and Ylvisaker (1979).

50   The most useful source is Nicholls (1971).

51   Between 1885 and 1902 alone about a hundred thousand firearms were imported (Le Cour Grandmaison [1989: 36]).

52   The British had confirmed the land rights of plantation owners after the abolition of slavery and had also compensated owners for the loss of their slaves. (Since only an owner may manumit a slave under Muslim law, the British government had to purchase them so as legally to free them. This was seen as compensation.)

53   There was also a wave of immigration during the fourteenth to sixteenth centuries.

54   As in Mombasa during the first quarter of the nineteenth century, in Witu, inland from Lamu, where the independent "Swahili Sultanate" was proclaimed in 1856, and in Tanganyika throughout the 1890s, although these were directed more clearly against the German administration of that territory.

55   There were never more than a few hundred Omani in the interior, nor more than a few thousand Swahili (although it is difficult to distinguish them). Some inland settlements were large—Tabora, Ujiji, Kota Kota—but most were small trading and staging posts. There were exceptions. Nyamwezi, ruled by the chieftain Mirambo, sat across the caravan routes: he controlled trade, extorted tolls, and sold ivory and other items at forced prices. In the Upper Congo, where ivory remained plentiful, was the farthest of all Swahili communities, established by Muhammed bin Hamid, known as Tippu Tip and virtually beyond control by Zanzibar or European powers. See B. Brown (1971), Glassman (1988), Hino (1968b, 1968c, 1971), Iliffe (1979), and Lary and Wright (1971).

56   See Brantley (1981), Glassman (1988), and Henderson (1965).

57   Seyyid Khalifa ibn Said, ruled 1888–1890; Seyyid Ali ibn Said, 1890–1893; Seyyid Hamed ibn Thwain, 1893–1896; Seyyid Khaled ibn Barghash, proclaimed and removed, 1896; Hamoud ibn Muhammed, 1896–1902; Seyyid Ali ibn Hamoud, 1902–1911.

58   See Bates (1965), Flint (1965), Grantley (1981), Henderson (1965), Middleton (1965), Middleton and Campbell (1965), and Raum (1965).

59   See Lofchie (1965), Middleton and Campbell (1965), and A. Smith (1976).

60   See Hailey (1950).

61   There is a large literature on the operation of colonial justice in Zanzibar and the East African coast. See especially Anderson (1970), Hailey (1950), Swartz (1979), and Trimingham (1964: 149ff).

Chapter 3: Towns

1   Few attempts to define urbanism are useful for understanding Swahili society. Wirth's classic definition is not, nor is that of Redfield and Singer using a "folk-urban continuum"; these and others are suggestive but do not fit the complexity of the organization of Swahili settlements and the relations between them. See M. G. Smith (1972) and Wheatley (1972).

2   In fact this "stone" is coral, but the word *stone* is always used for a town of this kind, *mji wa mawe* (town of stones). For example, the central and densely occupied half of Zanzibar City is called "Stone Town" and distinguished from the other half of the city, known as N'gambo, "the other side" of the original creek between the two.

3   Some approximate population figures are: Dar es Salaam, 397,000; Mombasa, 247,000 (Old Town, 3,000); Tanga, 77,0000; Zanzibar City, 69,000; Lamu, 13,000; Malindi, 11,000.

4   See J. de V. Allen (1974a, 1981a, forthcoming).

5   It is said in Lamu that its dhows used to sail as far as Madagascar (Buki or Bukini in kiSwahili) to trade in grains and unusual items such as ambergris.

6   See Lewcock (1976) for evidence of cultural links in architectural forms, especially with Muslim trading ports of the western coast of India rather than the more conventionally proposed Arabia and the Red Sea.

7   *Mihrab* is rarely used by Swahili; see Trimingham (1964: 83).

8   A problem with the construction of large mosques is the support of the roof because of the short length of the mangrove poles used in building.

9   In Lamu the Msikiti wa Wanawake (Mosque of Women) is not attended by women; the name refers to the history of its foundation.

10   I discuss the privatization of space by the building of lineage mosques and houses in chapters 5 and 8. See also Berg and Walter (1968).

11   The most useful accounts include Kirkman (1959, 1960, 1963, 1964a, 1964b), Wilson (1978, 1980, 1982), and Garlake (1966).

12   These may have pre-Islamic Cushitic origins, but the matter is unclear.

13   Some large grave coverings are of wood, a sign that the ground is *waqf* (entailed property) leased or borrowed for the purpose by a group not owning the waqf, so that stone structures may not be built on it.

14   My account is necessarily brief, and I would stress that every house that I have seen differs in detail from others. Other accounts are by J. de V. Allen (1979); see also Allen (1973, 1974b), Donley-Reid (1987), Garlake (1966), Ghaidan (1975), and Siravo and Pulver (1986).

15   The word *sabule*, or *sebule*, is sometimes also used for the *ndani*, the private quarters for the house owner and his wife. The basic meaning of sabule appears to be a very private room. Today the word is often used loosely for an anteroom or small room attached to a main room.

16   The galleries are often called *alia* (stripe), i.e., a transverse corridor.

17   The distinction between *msana* and *chumba* is that a gallery is open, whereas a room is closed by a door or heavy curtain.

18   The *ulili* is the "traditional" Swahili bed, without back or arm rests, having a cane top and round carved legs. The same word denotes a high platform used by "doctors" for spirit-offerings. There is also the bed called *kitanda,* which has a back and carved arm rests at either end; it is of Indian origin and when very elaborate is known as *kitanda cha samadari.*

19   The evidence and argument for the purpose of the nyumba ya kati are well given by J. de V. Allen (1979: 20).

20   A cistern is open and has a bowl of Chinese porcelain inset into its floor; even if the cistern is dry, this provides water for small fish kept in the cistern that eat mosquitoes. In some ancient houses, including those in the earliest ruined settlements, there are elaborate internal aqueducts to fill the cisterns.

21   Donley-Reid has suggested that the highly ornamented plaster work in the ndani and the attached bathroom and lavatory has a ritual function of purification (1982, 1984). I have not heard this hypothesis confirmed by the people, but it is certainly consistent with the great emphasis placed in Swahili culture on both physical cleanliness and moral purity (even the poorest houses have separate bathroom and lavatory). Slaves' quarters were not plastered or whitewashed, since they were held to be so polluted that there was no need. I have also been told that when a lime pit is started for the building of a daughter's house, the lime is in time purified "as is the dirt of childbirth."

22   In Lamu they lie along the waterfront and the single streets of shops, the *usita wa mui.*

23   James Allen (1974c: 305) mentions a former stone-town in the far north whose patrician owners moved away during a smallpox epidemic and built a new settlement of palm-matting houses nearby, leaving the stone houses to fall into ruin.

24   J. de V. Allen (1974a: 111); see also Allen (1979: 5).

25   This also explains why patricians occasionally sell houses to Europeans, who stand outside the internal hierarchical and interpersonal system of exchanges; but they steadfastly refuse to sell them to nonpatrician Swahili such as Hadhrami and Omani.

26   See Middleton (1961). I visited Zanzibar briefly in 1988, but the physical deterioration of the roads since 1964 made it difficult to move outside Zanzibar City, and I have no reliable information as to the rest of the island.

27   The largest southern Hadimu town in 1958 was Nganani-Makunduchi, with 6,420 people. Others were Bwejuu with 1,310 and Unguja Ukuu with 1,210. Paje and Dimbani had only 630 people each. However, some larger Hadimu country-towns on the edges of the clove areas supplied labor to the plantations and grew cash crops such as citrus: Chaani had 6,690 people, Makoba 2,660, Uzini 2,200, and Dunga 1,900. The three Tumbatu Island towns together had a population of about 4,500. See Middleton (1961) and Zanzibar Government (1953, 1958, 1960) for detailed figures.

28   The largest, Nganani-Makunduchi and the ancient town of Unguja Ukuu, are each well over a mile across, but with patches of cultivation between their constituent villages.

29   Others include kapok, lychee, jackfruit, breadfruit, ylang-ylang, Java plum, and durian.

30   The most important are raphia, dwarf, areca, and oil palms.

31   See Middleton (1961, 1972). I shall use the vernacular words, and indeed this system of land use and tenure is usually called simply "the kiambo system."

32   *Kiamboni,* "at the kiambo," is often used euphemistically for the place of the dead: *amekwenda kiamboni,* "he has gone home."

33   *Waqf* is a legal institution permitting the dedication of property by its owner for the

present and future support of religious and charitable uses. In everyday parlance the term is used also for the item of property itself. It lies at the heart of the stone-town system of house ownership. See Anderson (1954), Lienhardt (n.d.), Trimingham (1964: 154–55), and Middleton (1961: 69ff). I discuss it in more detail in chapters 5 and 8.

34   I am here writing about the prerevolutionary situation. Changes since then have been considerable, but I have no reliable information.

35   See Caplan (1975), Landberg (1977), and Bujra (1968).

36   See Bujra (1968) and Grottanelli (1955). We have virtually no information about places such as Faza, Kizingitini, Kiunga, or Ndau, all towns of size, importance, and long history.

37   However, see Ylvisaker (1979) on Witu Town, which has something of the same history, although it should be counted as a stone-town.

38   Lamu was regarded by British administrators as either a punishment station or an administrative Shangri-La, remote in either case until the recent tourist industry.

39   For many centuries Lamu was inferior to Pate on Pate Island a few miles to the north. But Pate's harbor has been almost entirely silted up by encroaching mangrove forest (one can easily see the original extent of its great narrow-mouthed anchorage). Lamu took over in the early nineteenth century and has retained its preeminence until the present day.

40   In the 1948 census Lamu was shown as having a total population of 2,300, 81 percent of whom were listed as "Swahili" (as distinct from "Arabs"); this was before the heavy influx of Bajun from the northern islands and of Kikuyu and others from the interior, who have increased the population today to more than 12,000.

41   There is a considerable published literature on the town. The most useful studies include the works of Prins (1965, 1971), J. de V. Allen (1972), Ghaidan (1971, 1975, 1976), Siravo and Pulver (1986), Le Guennec-Coppens (1983), el-Zein (1974), and P. R. Curtin (1982). For Mombasa, see Janmohamed (1976), Kindy (1972), Silberman (1950), and Southall (1989).

42   There is a map of these areas in el-Zein (1974: 133).

43   Except for the Usita wa Pwani ("Street of the Beach"), the open sea front running the length of the town; the Usita wa Mui ("Street of the Town") immediately behind it; and the Teremkoni ("Place of Descending," from the dunes to the sea front), which separates the moieties of Mkomani and Langoni. The latter street lies north of the fort and contains the Msikiti wa Pwani, the main congregational mosque.

44   This factor applies particularly to Lamu and Mombasa Old Town and not, for example, to Pate or Siyu, where there is less overcrowding.

45   The list of names seems never to be completely agreed, but my own list is almost exactly that given by Prins, who may be consulted for the names themselves (1971: 38–39).

46   There are exceptions: for example, Pate has no mikao but only the two mitaa.

47   Prins and others refer to them as "demes" of the same nature as Mkomani and Langoni, but this is a simplification.

48   The famous mwenye mui, Sheikh Zahidi Mngumi of Suudi, who held office in the early nineteenth century, is recalled to have had four hundred slaves (i.e., a great number). He trained them as soldiers and was then selected to continue beyond four years to organize defense against Pate. This sounds rather like an armed coup, but the matter is uncertain.

49   Prins (1971: 46) suggests that Zena was associated with "elegance" and scholarship

and Suudi with commercial enterprise and material success; but I have heard no one speak in these terms.

Chapter 4: Kinship and Descent

1   Most of this material comes from my own research, reported in Middleton (1971); see also Caplan (1969, 1975), Ingrams (1931), and Landberg (1977: chap. 3). Again, I use the ethnographic present tense.

2   The word *kilembwe* has three meanings: great-grandchild (and often great-great-grandchild); the core of bracts at the end of a hand of bananas; and nipple (Sacleux [1939: 375]). The basic meaning is the end of a structure that will reproduce itself as part of a perpetual process.

3   Ufungu comes from the verb *kufunga*, "to close," and implies the closure against nonmembers of the particular group.

4   Such sale is common by sisters and sisters' children who have moved elsewhere, the purchasers being brothers who have remained on the original plot. Even so, it is conditional and not finite: the seller retains the right to be buried in the cemetery of her natal group.

5   See below, this chapter.

6   A more accurate term might be "burgher." But I continue to use "patrician" simply because it has long been the most generally used word and is known to English-speaking Swahili. They are often referred to by both themselves and others as *wazijoho* ("those who wear long embroidered coats"), and there are other terms denoting high cultural behavior.

7   Both are Arabic loanwords, but kabila has become widely used for ethnic group, whereas taifa is considered more "Arabic" and its use is generally limited to the stone-towns.

8   Some writers, most notably Prins (1971), call them lineages; but by conventional anthropological usage they are subclans and segmented into smaller descent groups, these last properly being called lineages.

9   Today this usage is rare, but Swahili people understand it when heard.

10 They are said to be composed of the descendants of shipwrecked sailors and local women. They comprise three local branches: the Famao-Ngamia ("camel," because of their "long necks") who claim Portuguese sailors as ancestors; the Famao-Weli claiming descent from Chinese sailors; and the Famao-Nafasi, who claim descent from Persians. They are more likely to be descendants of immigrant groups who have become submerged in the general population, rather than literally of shipwrecked mariners.

11 The twenty or so years between Prins's and my researches indicates that the generally recognized order of ranking does not change all that rapidly. But certainly I met with rather less certainty about these matters than he seems to have done.

12 Prins's is the fullest and most accurate account of these matters published, and my debt to his work is considerable and obvious. The only other account, by el-Zein, is confused and misleading.

13 Most Wayunbili today claim to be al-Maawi; there are virtually no Kinamte left in Lamu, but some still live in Siyu.

14 They are given by Prins (1971: 56–57) and I need not list them here.

15 The first four words have Bantu roots and do not refer to assumed or claimed historical origins, for which words with Arabic roots tend to be used.

16 This may of course be a sign of the long-standing process of "Arabization" during the twenty years between our researches.

17 From the town of Shihr on the southern Arabian coast; it is significant that they are given the wa- prefix, denoting that they are not reckoned of sufficiently high social standing to be proper Arabs. But because Shihiri is a place-name, the usage is also etymologically correct.

18 See Le Guennec-Coppens (1983, 1989) and Salim (1973).

19 Although most Bajun groups, especially those living in country-towns, reckon cognatic descent.

20 See the interesting hypotheses for the proto-history of the coast adduced from these names by James Allen (forthcoming).

21 *Ma-* is the Swahili plural form for people when referring to them as holders of status or office.

22 See chapter 5. I discuss their religious role in chapter 7.

23 See Needham's discussion of polythetic classification (1971: 10).

24 This and several following points are discussed in chapter 5.

25 For example, Romero (1987a).

26 As for a man: Ahmed bin Sheikh bin Mohammed el-Nabhany; for a women (in this actual case his daughter) Khadija binti Ahmed bin Sheikh el-Nabhany.

27 Meyer Fortes has written that it is erroneous to see the forms of corporate groups as being determined by the nature and kinds of property vested in them: "It is not for the sake of creating, preserving, and transmitting an estate that the corporations emerge; on the contrary, they emerge as fixed, enduring, component units of the politico-jural order" (1969: 308). My argument here is the opposite: that is the existence of certain resources and of new rights that come to be held in them by one group as against others that has determined the identities of Swahili corporate groups.

28 Another word occasionally heard is *uhusiano*, literally, "the condition of being mutu- ally relevant or of mutual concern," which refers to the notion of network interdepen- dence as a principle and not to the groupings themselves.

29 See especially Landberg (1977: chap. 5) for details and household genealogies.

30 As an example, the death of a young man of a prominent lineage in Lamu in 1988 was the occasion for visits of jamaa members from Malindi, Mambrui, Mombasa, and Tanga to the south and from Siyu, Faza, and other island towns to the north; the visits lasted for several days, involved much traveling by bus, and the expenditure of great sums of money in gifts and expenses. The jamaa was that of his deceased father's brother, and not his own, as it was the uncle who arranged the mortuary rites.

 Another striking example is the jamaa of a senior and socially fairly important man in Zanzibar City. Originally from Pemba, his jamaa includes a large number of kin still living in his natal town, together with dispersed kin elsewhere. These include three members of the central government, two in Britain, three in Mombasa, five in the Gulf States, and the wife of one of those state's ambassadors.

 A final example is that of a new settlement of three rows of houses a few miles out- side Zanzibar City built by a wealthy Pemba man (now in Oman) for some forty jamaa members who have migrated from Pemba.

31 The term is in neither Johnson's nor Sacleux's dictionaries; it is found in other East African Bantu languages, e.g., Kikuyu.

32 The terms of formal address for those of senior generation or age or of higher kinship

status all make plurals by the prefix *ma-*, which is used for persons of high status, occupation, or rank; those for the same generation or age use the nonprefix form of the "inanimate" *n-* noun class, as do those for senior generation when used in general reference; those for junior generation or age use the plural form *wa-*, which is the normal plural prefix for living persons of the *m-* noun class. Examples are:

grandfather *babu* (pl. *mababu*)
grandmother *bibi* (pl. *mabibi*; also wife or lady)
father   *baba* (pl. *mababa*)
mother   *mama* (pl. *mamama*)

When used classificatorily, mababa and mamama apply only to those older than one's own parents; for those younger, the *n-* class plural is used (no prefix):

father's sister   *shangazi* (pl. *mashangazi*)
mother's brother *mjomba* (pl. *wajomba*; anomalous, being a reciprocal term)
elder brother   *kaka* (pl. *makaka*)
younger brother *ndugu* (pl. *ndugu*)
elder sister   *dada* (pl. *madada*)
younger sister   *dada* (pl. *dada*)
son   *mtoto* (pl. *watoto*)
daughter   *mwana* (pl. *waana*)
grandchild   *mjikuu* (pl. *wajikuu*)

The term *shemeji*, wife's brother and sister's husband, has as plural the *ma-* form: he is treated with respect but with a certain amount of *utani* permitted: the two are equal in rank. But if there is a divorce, both become "enemies." So perhaps "distance" would be a better term above than "respect." Other affinal terms all take the *wa-* prefix in the plural.

The same rules apply to accompanying adjectival prefixes, and are followed for more distant lineal kin. I should mention that these usages are those of senior and traditionally minded persons; younger people, and non-Swahili using the Swahili language, are rarely aware of them.

33   The Swahili bestow two names on a child: the *jina la kuzaliwa* ("name of being born"), given by the father or father's sister, and the *jina la utani* ("name of familiarity"; see n. 34), given by the father's or mother's mother. The former name should be that of grandparents, and for the first son that of his father's father. This means that the names of a line of first-born sons, which in this context are the most significant, are typically the same alternate generation by alternate generation (e.g., Ali bin Mohammed bin Ali bin Mohammed, and so on back). In the country-towns the sense of a single descent line stretching back in time may easily be lost, and the genealogy's depth cannot easily be shown, a sign that lineal depth is not thought important. Where it is so, as in the stone-towns, details are carefully recorded and recalled even if the names in genealogies are repeated in alternate generations over long periods. In addition, every subclan has its own stock of "family" names.

34   The best account is by Landberg (1977: 11 ff). I use the word *familiarity* as it contains the elements of ambiguity, impropriety, unexpectedness, and freedom from formal jural constraint, as well as of being proper, expected, and even obligatory; all are inherent in the notion of utani. Both "joking" and "cathartic," conventionally used by

anthropologists, refer to only some aspects of the institution. See also Moreau (1941, 1944) and Pedler (1940), who discuss utani between trading groups.

35   As mentioned above, grandparents and grandchildren may address each other as though they were of the same generation.

36   See the Koran, sura 4:23: "You are forbidden to take in marriage your mothers, your daughters, your sisters, your paternal and maternal aunts, the daughters of your brothers and sisters, your foster-mothers, the mothers of your wives, your step-daughters who are in your charge, born of the wives with whom you have lain (it is no offense for you to marry your step-daughters if you have not consummated your marriage with their mothers), and the wives of your own begotten sons. Henceforth you are also forbidden to take in marriage two sisters at one and the same time. Allah is forgiving and merciful" (trans. Dawood [1974]). The sura continues with rules for marriage with concubines.

37   I am well aware of the view that, being a man, I cannot correctly observe and interpret the roles of women. I can say only that most of the material on women in this section has come from Swahili women, but even so may be incomplete. It may be true that male observers have found it difficult to enter the everyday world of Swahili women and so have tended to ignore its complexities, just as female observers have often found it difficult to enter the everyday world of Swahili men. Some observers have maintained that women also hold a "men's" view or state it verbally as a consequence of cultural "brainwashing" by men. But that hardly admits of proof outside psychoanalysis and gets us nowhere.

38   See J. Bujra (1975) and Caplan (1982, 1989).

39   I know of older women in Pate who have never left the town in their lives except to participate in weddings in Siu, six miles away. I know of none who have left Pate to take up their own careers elsewhere, except for occasional marriages, but their children are doing so. I also know of one or two elderly Pate women who had virtually never ventured outside their town, but who recently decided to fly to Mecca on the *hajj*. Today in most towns women walk wearing a veil, although in a few such as Pate veils are worn only in the presence of visiting strangers. Until the 1920s or so, wealthy and important women in the older towns such as Lamu and Mombasa walked beneath a kind of tent (*shiraa*) that covered them and was carried by slaves or servants. I have heard that until her death a few years ago, one old lady in Lamu was so shocked by the British abolition of the shiraa that she had refused to leave her house for over thirty years (Linda Donley-Reid, personal communication). See also Mirza and Strobel (1989) and Romero (1987a).

40   There is much ambiguity about the place of slavery in Islam, which has centered on the problem of the enslavement of Muslims and that of nonbelievers except as part of a *jihad*, or holy war. The Koran states that non-Muslim prisoners taken in war can be enslaved, ransomed, exchanged for Muslim prisoners, in some circumstances executed, taxed, or released as an act of mercy or merit. The problems for Muslim slave-dealers and -owners have been mainly whether purely "commercial" slave raiding was permitted unless it was first defined as a holy war, whether they could take and sell Muslims as well as infidels, and whether they could break the injunction against separating enslaved families.

　　The voluntary conversion of Africans to Islam posed a question as to their availability for enslavement—whether being sons of Ham or being Muslims had priority. After many centuries of adjudication it was accepted that an African Muslim could not be enslaved. A related problem was that of the enslavement of the Swahilis' immediate neighbors and trading partners. Many of the mainland "tribal" peoples embraced Islam. Many devout Swahili might well have doubted the firmness of that embrace, but it did prevent their being enslaved. Peoples such as the Yao, Digo, and Zaramo were thus protected, and some took part in the trade itself as raiders selling to the coastal dealers. The Mijikenda peoples, living along the northern mainland, never accepted Islam but were not enslaved. They were indispensable to the Swahili towns as trading intermediaries in commodities such as ivory and so too precious to enslave, and were tied to the stone-towns by various systems of patronage.

41   However, trusted slaves were armed and also used to walk with their owners in public, dressed in glorious patrician-style clothing (but with the turban tied differently) as a sign of their owners' wealth and reputation.

42   Not the same word as the ethnic name of the rural Swahili of southern Zanzibar.

43   A harsh owner was disapproved of by other owners, and in Zanzibar City, at least, the sultans could and did set slaves free if they had been cruelly treated.

44   See the interesting but confused account by el-Zein (1974: 75ff).

45   Yet in the stone-towns there still remain many patrician women who will have nothing to do with those of slave ancestry.

46   See Strobel (1979), Eastman (1984, 1988a), and Caplan (1989).

47   In conversations with me, many of these women have graciously said that such matters may be spoken of with an elderly foreign scholar, but not with younger ones, whether male or female.

Chapter 5: Perpetuation and Alliance

1   Kuoa is used for men; for women the passive form *kuolewa* is used; to marry (of the official performing the rite) is *kuoza*; and a marriage is ndoa.

2   The plural form is often used: *ndoa za rasmi*.

3   *Makadhi* (judges in Islamic law) are found in only a few larger towns; introduced under the Zanzibar Sultanate, they have lost much of their former importance with ever-growing secularization (or nationalization) of the law in independent Kenya and Tanzania. *Walimu* (teachers) are found in all towns and are of greater everyday importance as practitioners of domestic dispute settlement, interpretation of Islamic rules, education, and healing. There are also in most towns today magistrates, officials of the secular courts. Larger mosques have *khatibu* (preachers).

4   Most of this material is from my own research. There are other accounts, in particular that by Le Guennec-Coppens (1983). This contains excellent descriptions of a woman's life-cycle, although the structural setting is hardly explored. One difficulty is the author's use of quantitative data, in which many figures given are for Lamu as a single unit. However, the actual behavior of patricians, wealthy immigrants such as Hadhrami, and poorer immigrants such as Bajun are all very different from one another. For other accounts, see Arens and Arens (1978), Caplan (1975), Shepherd (1977, 1987), and Tanner (1962, 1964).

5   The point, which I discuss in detail below, is that her first marriage should be to her paternal parallel-cousin, who is of course a member of the same lineage.

6   This word is not listed in either Sacleux's or Johnson's dictionaries. It is mentioned by both Le Guennec-Coppens and el-Zein. It is used in Lamu and Pate and also in Mombasa and Malindi. It may not be used in most country-towns, where notions of inequality are far less marked.

7   Despite popular European reports to the contrary.

8   This term is more often used to refer to marriages elsewhere, as in late medieval Europe (Goody [1983: 151ff]).

9   In Europe they were often made in order to circumvent church rules about marriage being impermissible within certain ranges of kin, and were also seen as marriages of affection rather than of arranged duty (Goody [1983: 148–49]).

10 Le Guennec-Coppens (1983: 148) quotes two Swahili sayings: *Mume ni rafiki tu* ("A husband is only a friend") and *Mume ni mlango wa kanda* ("A husband is only a door of rough matting"). This section owes much to her account of Lamu divorce, although many of the local terms she uses are Arabic rather than Swahili, and so used virtually only by kadhis.

11 Among the Hadimu in 1958 the divorce rate was well over 70 percent.

12 The most detailed study is that by Landberg on marriage in the small town of Kigombe on the Mrima coast of northern Tanzania. Of particular importance is her account of weddings (1977: chaps. 4 and 7). Other valuable accounts include those by Caplan (1975) and Trimingham (1964).

13 See Goody (1983: 110, 213).

14 Le Guennec-Coppens states that it is given after the wedding and may be withheld if the bride is shown not to be a virgin, or if she begins to be unfaithful soon afterward. It may be that the contradiction arises because Le Guennec-Coppens's wealthy but nonpatrician informants have different customs from those of the patricians. She claims that in her sample of Lamu marriages only a minute proportion of marriages are between paternal parallel-cousins; my own figures show a much higher incidence, but I admit that my sample is biased toward patrician marriages.

15 In the myth of Kilwa, mentioned earlier, the indigenous king gave the island to his son-in-law at the latter's marriage to his daughter. I have heard that today this gift may take the form of a partnership in the father's business. Its intent, in all cases, is to define and cement the son-in-law's public persona, whether as well-dressed man or as owner of a productive property.

16 It is perhaps significant that the distinction between the mahari and the kitu in patrician marriages is not made in most southern country-towns, where both kinds of payments are considered mahari. It is tempting to suggest that this is due to the greater Islamic influence in the northern towns. Since Islamic law decrees that the mahari should be of a conventionally fixed amount, this is accepted everywhere; but where economic factors enter, so that there may be a form of inflation in marriage payments, the additional amounts become something other than the formal mahari and are given the name kitu (thing).

17 Some writers, such as Bourdieu, have suggested that there can be no sociological explanation and so the notion of father's-brother's-daughter marriage should be discarded. But, as Holy points out, this is a recognition of failure in analysis rather than a recognition of social and cultural reality. What can be said is that even though father's-brother's-daughter marriage is practiced in many societies (perhaps predominantly in Muslim ones), there is not necessarily any single reason for its occurrence, which is a rather different conclusion. I prefer to seek an explanation in terms of ownership and exchange of rights in property.

18 The best discussion that I know is by Goody (1983), who analyzes aspects of this kind of system in Mediterranean and early European societies. The similarities are striking and can best be understood in social, productive, and mercantile contexts and hardly

in those of cultural diffusion, as historians and anthropologists have too often tried to do in cases of this kind.

19   This is so only of Swahili patricians. Hadhrami (including Hadhrami Sharifu) marriages are virilocal: see Le Guennec-Coppens (1989: 191).

20   I know of two such cases, but in both the new husband had been adopted into the wife's lineage, which had no living sons. Should a woman's second marriage be with a man of own subclan, she may bring the new husband to live with her, but this would not be approved unless he were also to become the head of the lineage and so have the right to occupy that particular house.

Chapter 6: Transformation of the Person

1   Arusi refers only to joyful rites of transformation; neither those of birth nor those of death are so called.

2   See chapter 7.

3   A man is not permitted to observe the wedding ceremonies for a woman. I have been able to discuss them with both older and younger women, who have spoken freely about them, and with many older men who with their wives have arranged weddings for their daughters.

4   This word is given by Le Guennec-Coppens as *aqdi*, the Arabic form (1983: 100).

5   The month of *shabani* or *mwezi wa kulisha* ("the month of feasting").

6   A word that also means bachelorhood or spinsterhood, the condition of being unmarried and living alone.

7   The most detailed published descriptions of marriages in a stone-town are those of Le Guennec-Coppens for Lamu (1976, 1980, 1983: chap. 2). However, her accounts show the official Muslim view held by the kadhis rather than that held by ordinary people, and she tends to ignore the variations between different elements of the town's population. Other valuable accounts are by Strobel (1975, 1979: chap. 1), Donley-Reid (1979), P. R. Curtin (1984), Lambek (1983), and Ottenheimer (1984, 1985).

8   I use this term here rather than the alternative *kungwi*, which is used mostly in Mombasa and farther south. The latter belong to associations (*vyama*) of *makungwi*, but *masomo* in the northern towns do not do so. See Strobel (1979: chap. 8).

9   The latter will in any case almost certainly be a woman of the same lineage, with the prevalence of parallel- and cross-cousin marriage.

10   In some accounts she is regarded as merely some kind of cosmetician, but this is a superficial reading of her role.

11   This is a properly different somo from the one who was in the past a nurse for a patrician daughter and who was usually a trusted slave (*kijakazi*). If a slave, she would been addressed as *dada*, the term for "elder sister." She became a nurse for a young girl and remained with her throughout her life as a trusted servant and confidante. Such a woman would have assisted the newly appointed somo. Today there are few if any such nurses. The term is used also for women bearing the same name, a metaphorical sister of a different kind.

12   But care must be taken to distinguish the different kinds of somo.

13   Translated by Sacleux as "jeune fille dans toute la force de la jeunesse" (1939: 595). The equivalent for boys is *mvulana* in the south and *marubaru* in the north.

14   *Kufuga* is a complex verb. It means both to confine, to domesticate, or to care for, as of bringing up domestic animals, and to shield them from difficulties. *Ukuti* means "beauty" in the sense of an outer expression of an inner moral quality of purity; see

below for discussion of "beauty" and virginity. Here the phrase means to care for and shield the young girl's developing "beauty" so that she will be ready to display it when the proper time comes during her wedding.

15 Vugo are sung and danced by women in the various situations of public and semi-public processions between the two houses; women of both "sides" compete in singing them. The ngoma ya ndani, msondo, and chakacha are sung properly inside the bride's house only, lack the competitive aspect of vugo, and are concerned essentially with the sexual deportment and skills of the future wife. The vugo is described by Le Guennec-Coppens (1980: 26–27).

16 The same term is used in the phrase *siku ya kesha ya mwisho*, "the last day of the formal period of mourning (*matanga*)." It means a ritual vigil that ends a period of literal seclusion, and is held at night.

17 A wide seat with carved back and arms; today a *kiti cha mpingo* ("chair of ebony") is commonly used, but this is traditionally incorrect, as being a chair for men only.

18 Golden jewelry may be worn only by women, never by men. The cloths are of striped patterns known as *debuani* and *subahia*. See also Romero (1987b).

19 Le Guennec-Coppens (1980: 36) writes that they are literally a toothbrush and other toilet articles, but I have no such evidence.

20 Male visitors cannot normally enter the "higher" galleries.

21 The actual defloration is referred to by various expressions, some of which my friends have requested me not to put into print. In everyday speech the usual term is *amekuwa arusi*, meaning that "she has become a (full) bride" and shown by her loss of virginity that she has become a fully mature woman.

22 This sheet is used only for this purpose; an ordinary bedsheet is *'tanga*.

23 The repetition refers to the significance of the blood of menstruation and that of defloration. The one is not caused by human action, the other is brought about by a highly formalized and regulated human act, a distinction analogous to that between a socially unshaped child and a socially shaped and "completed" adult.

24 Today this rite is often, even usually, conflated with the later one called *kutolezwa nde*: see, for example, Le Guennec-Coppens (1980: 47), where they are not distinguished. But properly the words refer to different rites.

25 As in the founding myths of towns, in which the ruler gives his new son-in-law the town itself.

26 The bride stresses the importance of her defloration by her at least symbolic but often very real fear and resistance.

27 The ntazanyao sometimes precedes the defloration in weddings of nonpatrician and country-town families, where this complex of notions is far less important. Traditionally, in any case, a known virgin may not physically be displayed in public, so for the ntazanyao to precede the defloration is tantamount to stating that she is not a virgin. But these days the age of marriage is much later than traditionally, and an unmarried young woman has at least to attend school and so be seen in the streets; this consideration hardly applies today.

28 See chapter 8.

29 A widow in mourning may neither wash frequently nor use cosmetics; her "beauty" is then hidden beneath a mask of dirt.

30 *Makungwi* may be male or female, according to the sex of the initiands.

31 A female Hadimu informant in Zanzibar told me in 1958 that "their penises are not yet ready and they are like girls"; but more information is needed.

32 This material is taken mainly from Caplan (1976), Mtoro bin Mwinyi Bakari (1981: 45–54), Trimingham (1964: 129–30), and Prins (1967: 108–09); see also Cory (1947–48).

33 Whether in the past such elaborate rites were performed in the stone-towns is not known, and the data on the Bajun Islands in the far north are inadequate; however, Prins mentions that the Bajun practiced "late circumcision," as do the Swahili of the Mrima coast (1967: 108). This would imply that the second factor mentioned is significant.

34 Landberg and Caplan provide detailed accounts of these various transfers and expenses; here I give only an outline.

35 See J. de V. Allen (1981c).

36 There are few accounts of pregnancy and childbirth, the best being by Mtoro bin Mwinyi Bakari (1981: 3–18). More has been written on mortuary rites and widowhood, the fullest description being by Landberg (1977: 363–405; 1986).

37 The same word as that used for initiation, when the initiands are also especially vulnerable to evil spirits.

38 A yellow powder imported from India and used also as a woman's cosmetic and perfume.

39 These mikeka are kept in a special store in the mosque and not used as floor matting, which is *msala* or *msali*.

40 *Kipengee* is a window used for passing objects from one room to another but not large enough for someone to walk through. The word is also used for a twisting road, river, or detour.

41 The khanga is given to a poor woman as charity and the mat returned to the mosque.

42 The same word is used for the period of "seclusion" of a woman who has been divorced; it refers essentially to a period when an adult woman must have no sexual relations and is thus symbolically not a full female person.

43 This mixture is *tibu*, the same that is used for a bride-to-be during her prewedding seclusion.

44 The fullest account is by Landberg (1977: 363–405).

Chapter 7: Power, Ritual, and Knowledge

1 I do not here enter into these complex historical arguments. The best account is by Pouwels (1978, 1987); see also Trimingham (1964) and J. de V. Allen (forthcoming).

2 A superb and full account is by Pouwels (1987: 53ff); this contains many Arabic terms that, although comprehensible to those with Islamic learning, are neither understood nor used by ordinary people.

3 There are many approaches to understanding Swahili religion. Here I present an anthropological view of it as seen in the context of the expression of power and authority, rather than of theology or religious history. I am not concerned with the theology of Islam among the Swahili—I would not be so impertinent—but with the ways its adherents are involved with its beliefs and practices in their everyday lives as members of Swahili towns. Much work on Swahili religion has been devoted to listing its elements and tracing their origins to Arabia or a semimythical Africa. These discussions are valuable but stand outside the approach I take here. They tend to revert to earlier histories and ethnographies that have seen the Swahili as merely a congeries of scattered Arab-creole "communities" rather than as a single African society. There has also been a general tendency to study Swahili Islam very much from the viewpoints of

its local learned scholars: Pouwels (1987) uses an esoteric Arabic-derived vocabulary unknown to most Swahili (but is the most detailed source for orthodox Swahili Islam), and el-Zein (1974) is said in Lamu to have used Arabic in his research, as he knew little Swahili.

4   I have space to present only a brief account of this complex set of changing relationships between God, the living, and the spirits. I devote more space to it in Middleton (forthcoming).

5   For more information see Trimingham (1964: 88–93), J. M. Gray (1955), Hirschberg (1974), Ingrams (1931: 280–82, 487–88), and Sacleux (1939: 652–53); see also Freeman-Grenville (1963b).

6   As I mentioned in chapter 1, for "Shiraz" in these accounts we may usually read "Shungwaya." This calendar is also used by the Copts of Egypt and in Ethiopia.

7   New Year's Eve is known as *chonda* (Lamu and northward) or *kibunzi* (Mombasa and southward), and the calendar itself is referred to as Nauruz, chonda, or kibunzi.

8   In prerevolutionary Zanzibar the commemoration of New Year's Day was attended publicly by the sultan and many thousands of people would assemble in the main plaza in front of the palace.

9   A useful list is given by Trimingham (1964: 92–93).

10   Many people fail to keep the fast, especially as the month continues; such a person is mocked as *kobe* (tortoise), a creature that is said to eat continually.

11   An Islamic teacher in Makunduchi told me that these holy days fill in the gaps left by the services in the mosques and so bring "traditional" events and agents under the purifying concern of Allah.

12   See Athman Lali Omar (1989) and Trimingham (1964: 93).

13   See also Pouwels (1987: 196–98), Trimingham (1964: 95–96), Mtoro bin Mwinyi Bakari (1981: 10–12), and el-Zein (1974). There are variations among all these accounts and between them and my own, many of which reflect cultural differences between the several Swahili towns.

14   There is more information about Lamu's past, as well as its present, than for most Swahili towns. See especially el-Zein (1974) and Pouwels (1987).

15   Elsewhere many of them might be considered "prophets," but this is forbidden under Islam, in which since the time of Muhammed there can be only one Prophet.

16   A good deal has been written on Habib Swaleh; see especially Pouwels (1987: 199), el-Zein (1974: 119ff), and Lienhardt (1959). See also Martin (1971).

17   Some writers have called the Dura Mandhuma a maulidi. It is not properly one but a poem of the type known as *kasida*; however, it was often used at the Riyadh mosque in much the same way as a maulidi.

18   See Trimingham (1974), Martin (1976), Nimtz (1980), and Pouwels (1987).

19   Mzimu is in the *mi-* class of animate but nonhuman entities, while koma is in the *n-* class of inanimate objects.

20   The best account of Swahili beliefs and myths about the majini is that by el-Zein (1974), who provides a Lévi-Straussian analysis that appears to represent Swahili cosmology accurately.

21   This account was given to me in Lamu and fits with el-Zein's account. But I was often warned that the latter was based strictly on orthodox belief and is too rigid as far as everyday popular thought is concerned. I was told, for example, that slaves who had been of high status when free in their original societies could marry "good" jini.

22   This is a word of complex meaning. It comes from the root *-zua*, "to make a hole and

to bring to light or to the surface, and so to give light." It has three forms: *mzuka* (pl. *wazuka*), an apparition of human form; *zuka* (pl. *mazuka*), a very bright, large, or powerful spirit; and *kizuka* (pl. *vizuka*), an apparition that is not human. This last form is used also to refer to a widow while in mourning seclusion, when she is not considered a full social being.

23   The plural prefixes *ma-* denote objects and people of great size, importance, or rank.

24   The spirit-controllers are well described for Mombasa by Strobel (1979). Today, however, they play little role in that town, and they have not been reported from the northern towns for many decades. They are still active in Zanzibar and farther south (Giles [1987] and Lienhardt [1968]).

25   See Giles (1987), Trimingham (1964: 114ff), R. Gray (1969), Koritschoner (1936), Lambek (1981, 1988), and Skene (1917).

26   The use of incense is important in all rites that include offering or sacrifice. The living consume the meat and the immaterial forces "consume" the sweet scent of the incense burned with the cooked food: living beings and spirits thus share the offering yet remain distinct entities.

27   A trading partner from Arabia might be married to a daughter, and the rohani husband resembles such a husband in several ways.

28   In the case mentioned, the woman has recently been married: at her ntazanyao rite she became possessed twice by her rohani, who demanded additional gifts from her living husband: the former retained his prior rights over the latter, and it is said that were she to bear a child, he would be deeply angered.

29   See Lewis (1966, 1971, 1986) and Boddy (1989). The explanation is also widely put forward to explain possession in the *zar* cult of Somalia and Ethiopia and the *bori* cult of northern Nigeria.

30   See Strobel (1979), Alpers (1984), Bujra (1975), and Giles (1987).

31   The same may have been so in the earlier colonial periods of the Zanzibar Sultanate and the Portuguese, but data are lacking.

32   In other parts of Africa such people often resolve their difficulties by becoming Christians, but this is hardly possible in this Islamic society unless one wishes to leave it altogether.

33   There is a large literature on Islamic magic; for that on the Swahili in particular see Hock (1987), Lienhardt (1968), Prins (1968), and Trimingham (1964: chap. 4); see also Levy (1957: chap. 10).

34   I cannot here give references to the large literature on this topic, but see Chelhod (1955).

35   The verb *kutambika* refers basically to the fermenting of beer, which explains its substitution by Arabic-root terms by more devout Muslims. See Sacleux (1939).

36   The question of the links between roasting and cooking meat and the removal of sin and pollution, and of the significance of ritual consumption of cooked foods, is highly important but cannot be dealt with here. See Chelhod (1955) and Middleton (forthcoming).

37   There are only a handful of published accounts, the fullest being the brilliant one on the Lamu rite of *Kuzingu kunzinguka ng'ombe* ("the surrounding of the town by the bull") by el-Zein (1974); the other is on Pemba and Zanzibar by J. M. Gray (1955). I have myself witnessed the Mwaka in the Hadimu town of Makunduchi, but too soon after my arrival to have made a more than superficial observation of it. It is still per-

formed annually in Lamu, Pate, and other northern towns, although today in a much attenuated form, as I saw it in 1989.

38   There is no space here to summarize the account by el-Zein, but I do so in Middleton (forthcoming).

39   I have not mentioned Christianity, which has had little direct impact on the Swahili. Christian missionaries have worked on the coast for over a hundred years, although the Portuguese were active as early as the sixteenth and seventeenth centuries (J. M. Gray [1958]). However, they have not been permitted to convert Muslims but only ex-slaves and non-Swahili immigrants (Bennett [1984], Herlehy and Morton [1988], Stovald [1946]). Some early missionaries, such as Taylor and Steere (who translated the Koran into Swahili), were much respected locally as scholars and held public debates with Muslim leaders; but these were regarded as interesting philosophical discussions and did not lead to conversion. In the late nineteenth century Christian settlements were established for ex-slaves, the best-known being Freretown at Mombasa. Today, with increasing up-country immigration, there are sizable Christian communities in the larger Stone-towns, but they have no impact on the Swahili faith. For example, Lamu has some fifteen small Christian churches, but none is used by Swahili.

40   There is no need to enter the tiresome argument as to whether "witch" and "sorcerer" should be distinguished or merged. It depends on the people themselves and not on the ethnographer. Since the Swahili have distinct terms for them, it seems reasonable to accept that they distinguish between them, although their relative importance varies between towns.

41   The same word used for associations of people possessed by spirits.

42   This word, in several forms, was repeatedly given to me when in Pemba and Zanzibar: it is in neither Johnson's nor Sacleux's dictionaries.

43   I should mention the widespread belief in *mumiani* (and other terms), who consume people whom they capture and feed until killing them or draw blood from their heads by piercing them with nails. They are usually claimed to be Arabs and Europeans, those who have had the power to capture Africans.

44   See Lienhardt's long account of the use of datura near Kilwa (1968). I was given similar accounts in discussions with people who claimed to use the drug in the same way in the Hadimu towns of Bwejuu and Paje in southeastern Zanzibar.

45   Devout Muslims often do not like to do this, since the doctors and nurses are usually Christians from non-Swahili areas and so are despised as polluting both in a religious sense, because they are lower in rank as "barbarians," and because it is feared that they might attempt to convert their patients.

Chapter 8: Civilization and Identity

1   See Cooper (1980), Ylvisaker (1979), and Sheriff (1987).

2   There were many in Zanzibar City and Mombasa, as hawkers, coffee sellers, and unskilled laborers. Many died in the Zanzibar revolution of 1964, and the remainder have returned to Oman.

3   The Bajun were long ago almost certainly the builders of towns in the far north, the region of Shungwaya, long ruined and hardly excavated. Under the British many retained high status, often claiming to be "Arabs," but in recent years they have become impoverished, and both men and women travel widely in search of work.

4   There are also certain groups with anomalous origins and ranks, the best-known being

the Wayunbili and the Kinamte, who are attributed the oldest origins of all by virtue of being pre-Arab and pre-Persian. According to the principle of the tie between antiquity of descent and rank position, they should be of the highest rank. But in fact they are given lower rank than the later-coming patrician subclans that took over their earlier political powers; to resolve this paradox these subclans have given the Wayunbili, in particular, attributes of moral impurity.

5   I am using "private" in contrast to "public," not to refer to the "individual" or the "individualistic."

6   Privatization is part of all modern radical changes in Africa, at least, and presumably part of past radical changes—those that involve the widening of social scale, incorporation into wider exchange systems, colonization, "development" (as it is practiced today), and so on. Although these terms are mostly used simplistically to describe highly complex processes, they refer to historical actualities.

7   For example, Mwambao, Kenya African Democratic Union, Afro-Shirazi Peoples' Party. See Salim (1970, 1972, 1976), Lofchie (1965), Middleton and Campbell (1965), and Stren (1970).

8   It is rarely inherited, an exception being in the status of maSharifu, but their innate and inherited quality is the possession of grace rather than scholarship.

9   *Bingwa* comes from the verb *kubingita* ("to carry large loads of many different objects at the same time"), so that a bingwa has many areas of linguistic and cultural knowledge that are brought together in a single person.

10 There are many accounts and collections of Swahili poetry and other literature. Among the more useful are Abdulaziz (1977), Abudu (1978), J. de V. Allen (1977), J. W. T. Allen (1971), Farsi (1958), Freeman-Grenville (1958), Harries (1962, 1971), Hichens (1939, 1948), Knappert (1967, 1970a, 1970c, 1972, 1979), Lambert (1962–63, 1965), Lienhardt (1968), Mbughuni (1982), Nabhany (1979, 1985), Scheven (1981), Shariff (1988), Steere (1870), Taylor (1891), Tolmacheva (1978), Velten (1965), Werner (1932), Werner and Hichens (1934), and Whiteley (1958).

11 For an account of the impact of "Western" education, see Le Guennec-Coppens (1983: 88–98) and, of course, colonial and postcolonial government reports.

12 In addition, the complex of stone-town traits is found, with appropriate cultural translations and modifications, in mercantile societies in other parts of the world with which the Swahili have never been in contact and of which until very recently they can have had no knowledge. See Lapidus (1969).

13 Ustaarabu is from the verb *kustaarabu* (to be wise or knowledgeable) and not from the word "Arab," although many observers have given it this origin; utamaduni has the same root as the Arabian place name Medina.

14 I have heard them also called *waAfrika* ("Africans"), referring particularly to the frequently notorious corruption of many non-Swahili who have recently come to work on the coast.

15 Essentially, washenzi refers to wild animals rather than to human beings, and its greater use in the south is presumably linked to the greater presence there of the actual slave trade with the interior, whereas the northern towns (except in the remote past) mostly bought slaves who had already been captured in the southern interior.

16 I am referring specifically to the Swahili concept of purity. All Muslims hold some such notion or set of notions, but they are not the same throughout Islam. Many writers have fallen into the trap of discussing Swahili moral notions as being those of orthodox Islam wherever it is proclaimed, but this conceals differences of social and historical

reality. The difficulty is that Swahili learned men discuss purity as it is dealt with in the Koran and other writings, whereas the more "ordinary" people, especially in the smaller and more remote settlements, may hold very different ideas, while still claiming to be orthodox Muslims. See especially Pouwels (1987) and Knappert (1970a).

17 Poetry is particularly a skill open to women, of whom the most famous was Mwana Kupona of Lamu: see Werner and Hichens (1934).

18 I am fully aware of the problems of translation in this case.

19 If, for example, a man who makes an investment later receives a return of more than the original sum, this is baraka. It is also due to or signifies his possession of baraka.

20 A famous example is that of Mwana Tau of the town of Siyu. A ship approaching Faza Island began to sink after losing a plank in its side. In Siyu, Mwana Tau was bathing and pulled off a sandal that flew to the ship and replaced the missing plank. After her death she became known as walii, because she possessed such powerful karama.

21 With kings this is typically done by evaluating the physical health of their bodies, which represent both their polities and also their inner moral qualities; by measuring the quality of the "body politic" by the health of the "body natural," and also measuring the latter by the overt glories of the former as seen in pomp, ceremony, and circumstance. The same principle has been and is observable in Swahili life.

22 I am here talking of what we might call the more traditional views of the Swahili. In recent years it has become more desirable for political reasons to stress one's "African" ancestry.

23 The most useful modern account is by J. de V. Allen (1974c, 1981b); see also Donley-Reid (1988) and Hino (1968a).

24 Allen lists trays, coconut graters, mortars and pestles, lavatory clogs, and others.

25 The so-called Zanzibar or Lamu chests of tourist commerce; see Unwin (1987).

26 The same was found among Indian and European members of Zanzibar City at the time.

27 James Allen (forthcoming) has suggested that it was largely the indigenous weaving of cotton cloth that marked the southerly movement of communities from Shungwaya.

28 Even though God can obviously perceive deceit and nonsubmission in an individual, however fine her or his clothing, men and women can honor God by dressing with propriety and neatness; ostentation by itself is prideful and would be a sin.

29 The situation is different in the case of certain rites of transformation in which the person being transformed is in a condition of symbolic seclusion and so at that moment has no moral qualities at all, including that of purity.

30 Other forms of art are few and relatively unimportant. It is forbidden in Islam to portray the human body, and pictorial art is formally decorative, part of the carving on doors, chests, furniture, house walls, and dhows. These, as well as elegant architecture and efficient plumbing, contribute to traditional Swahili style and standards of domestic living.

31 Two notions that quickly become apparent to anyone who lives in a Swahili town are fitina (intrigue or backbiting) and siri (secrecy).

32 This famous epic poem by the Swahili poet Sayyid Abdalla ibn Ali ibn Nasir has been edited and translated by J. de V. Allen (1977), Stigand (1915), Hichens (1939), and Harries (1962).

Glossary

This glossary does not include all words used in the text but mainly those that are used regularly. Only words used in the text are included, not those in the notes. Proper names and other Swahili terms are not included here but will be found in the index.

Arusi   Rites of initiation and weddings

Babu, pl. *mababu*   Grandfather

Baraka   Blessing, grace

Bibi, pl. *mabibi*   Wife, grandmother

Bingwa, pl. *mabingwa*   Scholar, capable person

Chakacha   Women's wedding dance

Chama, pl. *vyama*   Association, coven

Chini (*tini* in kiAmu)   Below

Choo, pl. *vyo*   Bathroom-toilet

Chumba, pl. *vyumba*   Room

Daka, pl. *madaka*   Porch

Damu   Blood

Daraja, pl. *madaraja*   Generation, rank

Dini   "Orthodox" religion

Eda   Seclusion of widow or divorcée

Ezi   Power

Fitina   Intrigue

Fundi, pl. *mafundi*   Master of craft skill or spirits

Fungate   Honeymoon

Harimu   Ritually forbidden, impure

Haya   Shame, embarrassment

Hazina   Treasury

Heshima   Reputation, honor, respect

Hidaya   Marriage gift from bride's father

Ijumaa   Friday, congregation

Jamaa   "Family," kin cluster

Jini, pl. *majini*   Spirit, jinn

Jiwe, pl. *mawe*   Stone

Jumba   Large house

Juu (*yuu* in kiAmu)   Above

Kabila, pl. *makabila*   Clan, "tribe"

Kaburi, pl. *makaburi*   Grave

Kadhi, pl. *makadhi*   Islamic judge

Kafara   Expiatory rite of sacrifice

Kanzu   Men's white attire

Karama   Grace

Karamu   Ritual feast

Kasarwanda   Bridal sheet

Kaya   Capital (Mijikenda)

Kesha   Vigil

Khanga, pl. *khanga*   Women's cloth

Khatibu, pl. *makhatibu*   Preacher

Kiambo, pl. *viambo*   Garden plot of kin group

Kijiji, pl. *vijiji*   Village

Kikao, pl. *vikao*   Ward

Kilemba   "Turban," fee from apprentice

Kirumbizi   Men's stick dance

Kisiwa, pl. *visiwa*   Island

Kitanda, pl. *vitanda*   Bed

Kiti, pl. *viti*   Chair

Kitongo, pl. *vitongo*   Garden plot

Kitu, pl. *vitu*   Groom's donation to bride (lit., thing)

Kiungu, pl. *viungu*   Stone house

227

Kiwanda, pl. *viwanda*   Courtyard, workspace
Kizuka, pl. *vizuka*   Phantom
Kofia, pl. *kofia*   Man's sewn skullcap
Konde, pl. *makonde*   Field
Koo, pl. *makoo*   Descent group
Kufuga ukuti   Rite of "showing beauty"
Kufu   Equality of rank
Kungwi, pl. *makungwi*   Initiation/ wedding teacher
Kuoa   To marry
Kutolezwa nde   Rite of "showing outside"

Lima   Wedding feast
Liwali, pl. *maliwali*   Governor under Zanzibar Sultanate

Maarifu   Person of repute
Madrasa   Islamic school
Mahari   Bridewealth
Matanga   Mourning
Mateka   Slave freed by British
Maulidi   Reading of life of the Prophet
Maziko   Mortuary rites
Mchawi, pl. *wachawi*   Sorcerer
Mchumba, pl. *wachumba*   Betrothed person
Mfalme, pl. *wafalme*   King
Mganga, pl. *waganga*   Doctor, healer
Mgeni, pl. *wageni*   Stranger, tenant
Mgwana, pl. *wangwana*   Patrician
Mhadimu, pl. *wahadimu*   Freed slave
Mila   "Customary" aspect of religion
Mjakazi, pl. *wajakazi*   Female slave
Mjane, pl. *wajane*   Widow, widower
Mji, pl. *miji*   Town
Mjomba, pl. *wajomba*   Mother's brother
Mjumbe, pl. *majumbe*   Headman
Mkao, pl. *mikao*   Ward, deme
Mkeka, pl. *mikeka*   Sleeping mat
Mkoba   Purse, treasury
Mkubwa, pl. *wakubwa*   Senior or important (person)
Mkuu, pl. *wakuu*   Senior or important (person)
Mlango, pl. *milango*   Small kin group (lit. door)
Mpagazi, pl. *wapagazi*   Laborer

Mpambaji, pl. *wapambaji*   Woman who "adorns" bride and house
Mpingo   Ebony
Msana, pl. *misana*   Gallery
MSharifu, pl. *maSharifu*   Descendant of the Prophet
Mshenzi, pl. *washenzi*   "Barbarian" from the interior
Msichana, pl. *wasichana*   Post-menarche girl
Msikiti, pl. *misikiti*   Mosque
Mtaa, pl. *mitaa* (*mtao* in north)   Ward, moiety
Mtani, pl. *watani*   Joking relation
Mtoto, pl. *watoto*   Child
Mtu, pl. *watu*   Man
Mtumwa, pl. *watumwa*   Domesticated slave
Mtwana, pl. *watwana*   Field slave
Mume, pl. *waume*   Husband, male
Mwaka, pl. *miaka*   Year, "New Year"
Mwalimu, pl. *walimu*   Teacher, Muslim healer
Mwalishi, pl. *waalishi*   "Inviter" at weddings
Mwanachuoni, pl. *wanachuoni*   Schoolteacher
Mwanamali, pl. *wanamali*   Post-menarche girl
Mwanamke, pl. *wanawake*   Woman, wife
Mwananchi, pl. *wananchi*   Owner of the land
Mwanga, pl. *waanga*   Witch
Mwari, pl. *waari*   Initiand
Mwenye, pl. *wenye*   Owner
Mwenyeji, pl. *wenyeji*   Owner of the town
Mzale, pl. *wazale*   Ritual official (Hadimu)
Mzalia, pl. *wazalia*   "One born in the country"
Mzee, pl. *wazee*   Old or senior man
Mzimu, pl. *mizimu*   Ancestral spirit
Mzuka, pl. *wazuka*   Apparition

Nasiba   Family name
Ndani, pl. *ndani*   Inner room
Ndoa   Marriage

Ndugu, pl. *ndugu*   Brother, sibling, cousin

Ngao, pl. *ngao*   Alcove in house

Nikaha   Marriage contract

Nisba   Family name

Ntazanyao   Rite of displaying bride

Nyanya   Grandmother

Nyumba, pl. *nyumba* or *manyumba*   House

Pepo, pl. *pepo*   Spirit

Rasmi   Legality

Rohani, pl. *marohani*   Type of spirit

Sabule   Guest room

Sadaka   Act of sacrifice or charity

Samedari   Type of bed

Samosa   Spiced pastry

Shaha, pl. *mashaha*   Poet

Shaitani, pl. *mashaitani*   Evil spirit

Shamba, pl. *mashamba*   Garden

Shangazi, pl. *mashangazi*   Father's sister

Shari'a   Islamic law

Sheha, pl. *masheha*   Town official, "shah"

Sheikh, pl. *masheikh*   Chief, learned man

Shirika   Corporate property group

Siri   Secret

Siwa   Ivory or brass horn

Somo, pl. *masomo*   Initiation/wedding teacher

Suriya, pl. *masuriya*   Concubine

Taifa, pl. *mataifa*   "Tribe," town

Talaka   Divorce

Tamim   Council president (Mombasa)

Tekani   Inner porch

Tumbo, pl. *matumbo*   Small kin group (lit., womb)

Ubani   Incense

Ufuko   Ditch, recess for corpse

Ufungu, pl. *fungu*   Small descent group

Ukoo, pl. *koo*   Cognatic descent group

Uladi   Unilineal descent group

Ulili, pl. *lili*   Type of bed

Unyago   Woman's initiation

Upande, pl. *pande*   Side

Usafi   Purity

Usita   Street (kiAmu)

Ustaarabu   Civilization

Utamaduni   Urbanity

Utani   Joking relationship

Utandu or *utanzu*   Branch of genealogy

Uzawa   Funeral or wedding dues

Vugo   Women's wedding dance

Waqf   Inalienable property, entail

Wikio   Bridge over street

Yumbe   Palace, town hall (of Lamu)

Zaka   Alms, tithe

Zidaka   Wall alcove

References

This is a listing of writings referred to in the text and notes: it is in no way a complete Swahili bibliography. The names of Swahili writers are given in full except when they are conventionally listed under their last names.

Abdalla ibn Ali ibn Nasir. *Al-Inkishafi. See under* J. de V. Allen, Hichens.

Abdulaziz, M. H. 1977. *Muyaka: Nineteenth century Swahili popular poetry.* Nairobi: East African Publishing House.

Abudu, M. 1978. *Methali za Kiswahili.* Nairobi: Shungwaya.

Ahmed Badawy. 1987. *The Shanga panel.* Nairobi: National Museums of Kenya.

Akinola, G. A. 1968. The Mazrui of Mombasa. *Tarikh* 2, no. 3: 26–40.

———. 1972. Slavery and slave revolts in the Sultanate of Zanzibar in the nineteenth century. *Journal of the Historical Society of Nigeria* 6: 215–28.

Al-Bakari al-Lamuy, Shaibu Faraji b. Hamed. 1938. Khabari Lamu. *Bantu Studies* 12: 3–33.

Allen, J. de V. N.d. [1972]. *Lamu.* Nairobi: Kenya Museum Society.

———. 1973. Swahili ornament: A study of the decoration of the eighteenth century plasterwork and carved doors of the Lamu region. *Art and Archaeology Research Papers* 3: 1–14; 4: 87–92.

———. 1974a. Town and country in Swahili culture. Pp. 298–316 in *Symposium Leo Frobenius.* Cologne.

———. 1974b. Swahili architecture in the later Middle Ages. *African Arts* 7: 42–47, 66–68, 83–84.

———. 1974c. Swahili culture reconsidered: Some historical implications of the material culture of the northern Kenya coast in the eighteenth and nineteenth centuries. *Azania* 9: 105–38.

———. 1976. The *Siwas* of Pate and Lamu: Two antique sideblown horns from the Swahili coast. *Art and Archaeology Research Papers* 9: 38–47.

———, ed. and trans. 1977. Abdalla ibn Ali ibn Nasir, *Al-Inkishafi: Catechism of a soul.* Nairobi: East African Literature Bureau.

———. 1979. The Swahili house: Cultural and ritual concepts underlying its plan and structure. *Art and Archaeology Research Papers* (1979): 1–32.

———. 1981a. Swahili culture and the nature of East Coast settlement. *International Journal of African Historical Studies* 14: 306–34.

———. 1981b. The Swahili world of Mtoro bin Mwinyi Bakari. Pp. 211–32 in Mtoro bin Mwinyi Bakari.

―――. 1981c. *Ngoma*: Music and dance. Pp. 233–46 in Mtoro bin Mwinyi Bakari.

―――. 1982. Traditional history and African literature: The Swahili case. *Journal of African History* 23: 227–36.

―――. 1989. The *Kiti cha Enzi* and other Swahili chairs. *African Arts* 22, no. 3: 54–63.

―――. Forthcoming. *Swahili origins: Swahili culture and the Shungwaya phenomenon.* London: Currey.

Allen, J. W. T. 1971. *Tendi: Six examples of a Swahili classical verse form.* Nairobi: Heinemann. *See also* Mtoro bin Mwinyi Bakari.

Alpers, E. A. 1967. *The East African slave trade.* Dar es Salaam: Historical Association of Tanzania.

―――. 1969a. Trade, state, and society among the Yao in the nineteenth century. *Journal of African History* 10: 405–20.

―――. 1969b. The coast and the caravan trade." Pp. 35–36 in I. N. Kimambo and A. J. Temu, eds., *A history of Tanzania.* Nairobi: East African Publishing House.

―――. 1970. The French slave trade in East Africa (1721–1810). *Cahiers d'études africaines* 10, no. 37: 80–124.

―――. 1975. *Ivory and slaves in east central Africa: Changing patterns of international trade to the late nineteenth century.* London: Heinemann.

―――. 1984. Ordinary household chores: Ritual and power in a nineteenth-century Swahili women's spirit possession cult. *International Journal of African Historical Studies* 17, no. 4: 677–702.

Anderson, J. N. D. 1954. *Islamic law in Africa.* Repr., London: Cass, 1970.

Arens, W. 1975. The Waswahili: The social history of an ethnic group. *Africa* 45, no. 4: 426–38.

―――. 1979. *On the frontiers of change: Mto wa Mbu, Tanzania.* Ann Arbor: University of Michigan Press.

―――. 1987. Mto wa Mbu: A rural polyethnic community in Tanzania. Pp. 242–54 in I. Kopytoff, ed., *The African frontier: The reproduction of traditional African societies.* Bloomington: Indiana University Press.

Arens, W., and D. A. Arens. 1978. Kinship and marriage in a polyethnic community. *Africa* 48: 149–60.

Athman Lali Omar. 1989. Festivals and songs of the Bajun of the Kenya coast. Unpublished master's thesis, Council on African Studies, Yale University.

Axelson, E. 1973. *The Portuguese in South-east Africa, 1488–1600.* Johannesburg: Struik.

Baker, E. C. 1941. Notes on the Shirazi of East Africa. *Tanganyika Notes and Records* 11: 1–10.

―――. 1949. Notes on the history of the Wasegeju. *Tanganyika Notes and Records* 27: 16–41.

Bates, M. L. 1965. Tanganyika: Changes in African life, 1918–1945. Pp. 625–40 in Harlow and Chilver.

Beachey, R. W. 1962. The arms trade in East Africa in the late nineteenth century. *Journal of African History* 3: 451–67.

―――. 1967. The East African ivory trade in the nineteenth century. *Journal of African History* 8: 269–90.

―――. 1976. *The slave trade of eastern Africa.* London: Collins.

Beech, M. W. H. 1916. Slavery on the east coast of Africa. *Journal of the African Society* 15: 145–49.

Bennett, N. R. 1964. The Church Missionary Society at Mombasa, 1873–1894. *Boston University Papers in African History* 1: 159–95.

———. 1978. *A history of the Arab state of Zanzibar.* London: Methuen.

———. 1984. *The Arab state of Zanzibar: A bibliography.* Nairobi: Lamu Society.

Berg, F. J. 1968. The Swahili community of Mombasa, 1500–1900. *Journal of African History* 9, no. 1: 35–56.

———. 1974. The coast from the Portuguese invasion. Pp. 115–34 in B. A. Ogot, ed., *Zamani: A survey of East African history.* Rev. ed. Nairobi: East African Publishing House.

Berg, F. J., and B. Walter. 1968. Mosques, population and urban development in Mombasa. Pp. 47–100 in B. A. Ogot, ed., *Hadith* 1. Nairobi: East African Publishing House.

Biersteker, A. 1990. *Masomo ya Kisasa: Contemporary readings in Swahili.* New Haven: Yale University Press.

Boddy, J. 1989. *Wombs and alien spirits: Women, men, and the Zar cult in northern Sudan.* Madison: University of Wisconsin Press.

Boxer, C. R., and C. de Azevedo. 1960. *Fort Jesus and the Portuguese in Mombasa, 1593–1729.* London: Hollis and Carter.

Brantley, C. 1981. *The Giriama and colonial resistance in Kenya, 1800–1920.* Berkeley: University of California Press.

Brown, B. 1971. Muslim influence in trade and politics in the Lake Tanganyika region. *International Journal of African Historical Studies* 4: 617–30.

Brown, W. H. 1985. History of Siu: The development and decline of a Swahili town on the northern Kenya coast. Unpublished Ph.D. diss., Indiana University.

Brown, W. T. 1971a. A pre-colonial history of Bagamoyo: Aspects of the growth of an East African coastal town. Unpublished Ph.D. diss., Boston University.

———. 1971b. The politics of business: Relations between Zanzibar and Bagamoyo in the late nineteenth century. *International Journal of African Historical Studies*: 4, no. 3: 631–43.

Bujra, A. S. 1971. *The politics of stratification: A study of political change in a south Arabian town.* Oxford: Clarendon Press.

Bujra, J. 1968. An anthropological study of political action in a Bajuni village in Kenya. Unpublished Ph.D. thesis, University of London.

———. 1975. Production, property, prostitution: Sexual politics in Atu. *Cahiers d'études africaines* 12: 13–39.

Bunger, R. L. 1973. *Islamization among the Upper Pokomo of Kenya.* Syracuse, N.Y.: Syracuse University Press.

Burton, R. 1872. *Zanzibar: City, island and coast.* 2 vols. London: Tinsley.

Caplan, P. A. 1969. Cognatic descent groups on Mafia Island, Tanzania. *Man* 4, no. 3: 419–31.

———. 1975. *Choice and constraint in a Swahili community: Property, hierarchy, and cognatic descent on the East African coast.* London: Oxford University Press.

———. 1976. Boys' circumcision and girls' puberty rites among the Swahili of Mafia Island, Tanzania. *Africa* 46, no. 1: 21–33.

———. 1982. Gender, ideology, and modes of production on the East Coast of Africa. *Paideuma* 28: 29–43.

———. 1989. Perceptions of gender stratification. *Africa* 59, no. 2: 196–208.

Cassanelli, L. V. 1982. *The shaping of Somali society.* Philadelphia: University of Pennsylvania Press.

———. 1987. Social construction on the Somali frontier: Bantu former slave communities in the nineteenth century. Pp. 216–38 in I. Kopytoff, ed., *The African frontier: The reproduction of traditional African societies.* Bloomington: Indiana University Press.

Champion, A. M. 1922. Notes on the Wasanye. *Journal of the East Africa and Uganda Natural History Society* 17: 21–24.

———. 1967. *The Agiryama of Kenya*. Ed. J. Middleton. London: Royal Anthropological Institute.

Chaudhuri, K. N. 1978. *The trading world of Asia and the English East Africa Company, 1660–1760*. Cambridge: Cambridge University Press.

———. 1985. *Trade and civilization in the Indian Ocean: An economic history from the rise of Islam to 1750*. Cambridge: Cambridge University Press.

Chelhod, J. 1955. *Le sacrifice chez les Arabes*. Paris: Presses Universitaires de France.

Chiragdin, S., and M. Mnyampala. 1977. *Historia ya Swahili*. Nairobi: Oxford University Press.

Chittick, N. 1963. Kilwa and the Arab settlements on the East African coast. *Journal of African History* 4: 179–90.

———. 1965. The "Shirazi" colonization of East Africa. *Journal of African History* 6: 275–94.

———. 1966. Kilwa: A preliminary report. *Azania* 1: 1–36.

———. 1967. Discoveries in the Lamu archipelago. *Azania* 2: 37–68.

———. 1969a. An archaeological reconnaissance of the southern Somali coast. *Azania* 4: 115–30.

———. 1969b. A new look at the history of Pate. *Journal of African History* 10: 375–91.

———. 1974a. The coast before the arrival of the Portuguese. Pp. 98–114 in B. A. Ogot, ed., *Zamani: A survey of East African history*. Rev. ed. Nairobi: East African Publishing House.

———. 1974b. *Kilwa: An Islamic trading city on the East African coast*. Nairobi: British Institute in East Africa.

———. 1976. The Book of Zenj and the Mijikenda. *International Journal of African Historical Studies* 9: 68–73.

———. 1982. Mediaeval Mogadishu. *Paideuma* 28: 45–62.

———. 1984. *Manda: Excavations at an island port on the coast of Kenya*. Nairobi: British Institute in East Africa.

Chittick, N., and R. I. Rotberg, eds. 1975. *East Africa and the Orient*. New York: Africana Press.

Constantin, F. 1987. Condition Swahili et identité politique. *Africa* 57, no. 2: 219–33.

———. 1989. Social stratification on the Swahili coast: From race to class? *Africa* 59, no. 2: 145–60.

Cooper, F. 1973. The treatment of slaves on the Kenya coast in the nineteenth century. *Kenya Historical Review* 1: 87–107.

———. 1977. *Plantation slavery on the east coast of Africa*. New Haven: Yale University Press.

———. 1980. *From slaves to squatters: Plantation labor and agriculture in Zanzibar and coastal Kenya, 1890–1925*. New Haven: Yale University Press.

———. 1981. Islam and cultural hegemony: The ideology of slaveowners on the East African Coast. Pp. 271–307 in P. E. Lovejoy, ed., *The ideology of slavery in Africa*. Beverly Hills: Sage.

———. 1987. *On the African waterfront: Urban disorder and the transformation of work in colonial Mombasa*. New Haven: Yale University Press.

Cory, H. 1947–48. Jando. *Journal of the Royal Anthropological Institute* 77: 159–68; 78: 81–95.

Coupland, R. 1938. *East Africa and its invaders*. Oxford: Clarendon Press.

———. 1939. *The exploitation of East Africa*. London: Faber and Faber.

Craster, J. E. E. 1913. *Pemba, the spice island of Zanzibar*. London: Unwin.

Curtin, P. Romero. 1982. The Sacred Meadows: A case study of "Historyland" vs. "Anthropologyland." *History in Africa* 9: 337–46.

———. 1983. Laboratory for the oral history of slavery: The island of Lamu on the Kenya coast. *American Historical Review* 88, no. 4: 858–82.

———. 1984. Lamu weddings as an example of social and economic change. *Cahiers d'études africaines* 24: 131–55.

———. 1986a. "Where have all the slaves gone?": Emancipation and post-emancipation in Lamu, Kenya. *Journal of African History* 27: 497–512.

———. 1986b. Lamu and suppression of the slave trade. *Slavery and Abolition* 7, no. 2: 148–59.

Curtin, P. D. 1984. *Cross-cultural trade in world history*. Cambridge: Cambridge University Press.

Dale, G. 1920. *The peoples of Zanzibar*. London: Universities Mission to Central Africa.

Dammann, E. 1929. *Beiträge aus arabischen Quellen zur Kenntnis des negerischen Afrikas*. Bordesholm: Nolke.

Datoo, B. A. 1970. Misconceptions about the use of monsoons by dhows in East African waters. *East African Geographical Review* 8: 1–10.

———. 1974. Influence of monsoons on movements of dhows along the East African coast. *East African Geographical Review* 12: 23–33.

———. 1975. *Port development in East Africa: Spatial patterns from the ninth to the sixteenth centuries*. Nairobi: East African Literature Bureau.

Dawood, N. J., ed. 1974. *The Koran*. 4th ed. Harmondsworth: Penguin.

DeBlij, H. 1968. *Mombasa: An African city*. Evanston: Northwestern University Press.

Declich, F. 1987. I Goscia della regione del Medio Giuba nella Somalia meridionale: Un gruppo etnico di origine Bantu. *Africa* (Rome) 42: 570–59.

Delf, G. 1963. *Asians in East Africa*. London: Oxford University Press.

Dickson, T. A. 1917. Notes on the Segeju. *Journal of the East Africa and Uganda Natural History Society* 11: 167–68.

———. 1921. The regalia of the Wa-Vumba. *Man* 21: 33–35.

Donley (-Reid), L. 1979. Eighteenth-century Lamu weddings. *Kenya Past and Present* 11: 3–11.

———. 1982. House power: Swahili space and symbolic markers. Pp. 63–73 in I. Hodder, ed., *Symbolic and structural archaeology* Cambridge: Cambridge University Press.

———. 1984. The social uses of Swahili space and objects. Unpublished Ph.D. thesis, University of Cambridge.

———. 1987. Life in the Swahili town house reveals the symbolic meaning of spaces and artefact assemblages. *African Archaeological Review* 5: 181–92.

———. 1988. Swahili material culture. Pp. 55–66 in E. Linnebuhr, ed., *Transition and continuity of identity in East Africa and beyond*. Bayreuth: Bayreuth University Press.

Eastman, C. M. 1971. Who are the Waswahili? *Africa* 41, no. 3: 228–36.

———. 1975. Ethnicity and the social scientist: Phonemes and distinctive features. *African Studies Review* 18, no. 1: 29–38.

———. 1984. Waungwana na Wanawake: Muslim ethnicity and sexual segregation in coastal Kenya. *Journal of Multilingual and Multicultural Development* 5: 97–112.

———. 1988a. Women, slaves, and foreigners: African cultural influences and group processes in the formation of Northern Swahili coastal society. *International Journal of African Historical Studies* 21, no. 1: 1–20.

———. 1988b. Service (*Utumwa*) as a contested concept of Swahili social reality. Unpublished paper, University of Washington.

Eastman, C .M., and F. M. Topan. 1966. The Siu: Notes on the people and their language. *Swahili* 36, no. 2: 22–48.

Elliott, J. A. G. 1925–26. A visit to the Bajun islands. *Journal of the African Society* 25: 10–22, 147–63, 245–63, 338–58.

El-Zein, A. H. M. 1974. *The Sacred Meadows: A structural analysis of religious symbolism in an East African town.* Evanston: Northwestern University Press.

Esmail, Z. 1975. Towards a history of Islam in East Africa. *Kenya Historical Review* 3: 147–58.

Farias, P. F. de M. 1977. Models of the world and categorical models: The "Enslavable Barbarian" as a mobile classificatory label. Unpublished paper, University of Birmingham.

Farsi, S. S. 1958. *Swahili sayings from Zanzibar.* 2 vols. Nairobi: East African Literature Bureau.

Fitzgerald, W. W. A. 1898. *Travels in the coastlands of British East Africa and the islands of Zanzibar and Pemba.* Repr., London: Dawson, 1970.

Flint, J. E. 1965. Zanzibar, 1890–1950. Pp. 641–67 in Harlow and Chilver.

Fortes, M. 1969. *Kinship and the social order.* London: Routledge and Kegan Paul.

Frank, W. 1953. *Habari na desturi za Waribe.* London: Macmillan.

Fraser, H. A., B. Tozer, and J. Christie. 1871. *The East African slave trade.* London: Harrison.

Freeman-Grenville, G. S. P. 1958. Swahili literature and the history and archaeology of the East African coast. *Journal of the East African Swahili Committee* 28: 7–25.

———. 1962a. *The East African coast: Select documents from the first to the earlier nineteenth century.* Oxford: Clarendon Press.

———. 1962b. *The mediaeval history of the coast of Tanganyika, with special reference to recent archaeological discoveries.* London: Oxford University Press.

———. 1963a. The coast, 1498–1840. Pp. 129–63 in Oliver and Mathew.

———. 1963b. *The Muslim and Christian calendars: Being tables for the conversion of Muslim and Christian dates from the Hijra to the year A.D. 2000.* London: Oxford University Press.

———. 1965. *The French at Kilwa Island.* Oxford: Clarendon Press.

———. 1988. *The Swahili coast, 2nd to 19th centuries.* London: Variorum.

Garlake, P. S. 1966. *The early Islamic architecture of the East African coast.* Nairobi: Oxford University Press.

Ghaidan, U. 1971. *African heritage: The stone houses of Lamu.* Lamu: Lamu Museum.

———. 1975. *Lamu: A study of the Swahili town.* Nairobi: East African Literature Bureau.

———. 1976. *Lamu: A study in conservation.* Nairobi: East African Literature Bureau.

Giles, L. 1987. Possession cults on the Swahili coast: A re-examination of theories of marginality. *Africa* 57, no. 2: 234–58.

Glassman, J. P. 1988. Social rebellion and Swahili culture: The response to German conquest of the northern Mrima, 1888–1890. Unpublished Ph.D. diss., University of Wisconsin.

Goody, J. R. 1983. *The development of the family and marriage in Europe.* Cambridge: Cambridge University Press.

Gray, J. M. 1947. Rezende's description of East Africa in 1634. *Tanganyika Notes and Records* 23: 2–29.

———. 1950. Portuguese records relating to the Wasegeju. *Tanganyika Notes and Records* 29: 85–97.

———. 1951–52. A history of Kilwa. *Tanganyika Notes and Records* 31: 1–28; 32: 11–37.

———. 1955. Nairuz or Siku ya Mwaka. *Tanganyika Notes and Records* 38: 1–22.

———. 1958. *Early Portuguese missionaries in East Africa*. London: Macmillan.

———. 1959–60. Zanzibar local histories. *Swahili* 30: 24–50; 31: 111–39.

———. 1962. *A history of Zanzibar from the Middle Ages to 1856*. London: Oxford University Press.

———. 1963. Zanzibar and the coastal belt, 1840–1884. Pp. 212–51 in Oliver and Mathew.

———. 1977. The Hadimu and Tumbatu of Zanzibar. *Tanganyika Notes and Records* 81–82: 135–53.

Gray, J. R., and D. Birmingham, eds. 1970. *Pre-colonial African trade*. London: Oxford University Press.

Gray, R. F. 1969. The Shetani cult among the Segeju of Tanzania. Pp. 171–87 in J. Beattie and J. Middleton, eds., *Spirit mediumship and society in Africa*. London: Routledge and Kegan Paul.

Grottanelli, V. L. 1955. *Pescatori dell'Oceano Indiano*. Rome: Cremonese.

Guillain, M. 1856. *Documents sur l'histoire, la géographie, et la commerce de l'Afrique Orientale*. 3 vols. Paris: Bertrand.

Hailey, Lord. 1950. *Native administration in the British East African territories*. Part 1, chap. 2, sec. 2; part 1, chap. 3, secs. 8 and 9; part 2, chap. 4. London: Her Majesty's Stationery Office.

Harlow, V., and E. M. Chilver, eds. 1965. *The Oxford history of East Africa*. Vol. 2. Oxford: Clarendon Press.

Harries, L. 1959. Swahili traditions of Mombasa. *Afrika und Übersee* 43, no. 2: 81–105.

———. 1962. *Swahili poetry*. Oxford: Clarendon Press.

———. 1964. The Arabs and Swahili culture. *Africa* 34: 224–30.

———. 1971. Swahili literature in the national context. *Review of National Literatures* 2, no. 2: 38–65.

Harris, J. E. 1976. The Coast African Association: Politics on Kenya's coast, 1940–1955. *Kenya Historical Review* 4, no. 2: 297–310.

Haywood, C. W. 1935. The Bajun islands and Birikau. *Geographical Journal* 85: 59–64.

Heine, B. 1982. Language and history of the Boni. Pp. 106–14 in B. Heine, ed., *Recent German research on Africa: Language and culture*. Tübingen: Institute for Scientific Cooperation.

Henderson, W. O. 1965. German East Africa, 1884–1918. Pp. 123–62 in Harlow and Chilver.

Herlehy, T., and R. F. Morton. 1988. A coastal ex-slave community in the regional and colonial economy of Kenya: The WaMisheni of Rabai, 1880–1963. Pp. 254–82 in S. Miers and R. Roberts, eds., *The end of slavery in Africa*. Madison: University of Wisconsin Press.

Hichens, W., ed. 1939. *Al-Inkishafi: The soul's awakening*. London: Sheldon Press.

———. 1948. *Diwani ya Muyaka bin Haji Al-Ghassaniy*. Johannesburg: University of the Witwatersrand Press.

Hino, S. 1968a. The costume culture of a Swahili people. *Kyoto African Studies* 2: 109–46.

––––. 1968b. The occupational differentiation of an African town. *Kyoto African Studies* 2: 72–108.

––––. 1968c. Social stratification of a Swahili town. *Kyoto African Studies* 2: 51–71.

––––. 1971. Neighbourhood groups in an African urban society: Social relations and consciousness of the Swahili people of Ujiji, a small town of Tanzania, East Africa. *Kyoto African Studies* 6: 1–30.

Hirschberg, W. 1974. Der Suaheli-Kalender an der Ostküste Afrikas. Pp. 215–28 in *In memoriam Antonio Jorge Dias I*. Lisbon: Junta de Investigacaoes Cientificas do Ultramar.

Hock, K. 1987. *Gott und Magie im Swahili-Islam: Zur Beispiel von veröffentlicher und magischer Praktiker*. Köln: Kölner Veröffentlichungen zur Religion Geschichte.

Hollis, A. C. 1900. Notes on the history of Vumba, East Africa. *Journal of the Royal Anthropological Institute* 30: 275–300.

Holway, J. D. 1970. The religious composition of the population of the Coast Province of Kenya. *Journal of Religion in Africa* 3: 228–39.

Holy, L. 1989. *Kinship, honour and solidarity: Cousin marriage in the Middle East*. Manchester: Manchester University Press.

Horton, M. 1980. *Shanga 1980*. Cambridge: Cambridge University Press.

––––. 1984. The early settlement of the northern Swahili coast. Unpublished Ph.D. thesis, University of Cambridge.

––––. 1987. The Swahili corridor. *Scientific American*, Sept.: 86–93.

Horton, M., and Catherine Clark. 1985. *The Zanzibar archaeological survey, 1984–85*. Zanzibar City: Ministry of Information, Culture, and Sport.

Huntingford, G. W. B. 1931. Free-hunters, serf-tribes, and submerged classes in East Africa. *Man* 31: 262–66.

––––. 1955. Bantu peoples of eastern Kenya and and north-eastern Tanzania. Pp. 47–50 in R. A. Hamilton, ed., *History and archaeology in Africa*. London: School of Oriental and African Studies, University of London.

––––. 1963. The peopling of the interior of East Africa by its modern inhabitants. Pp. 58–93 in Oliver and Mathew.

––––, ed. 1980. *The Periplus of the Erythraean Sea*. London: Hakluyt Society.

Iliffe, J. 1979. *A modern history of Tanganyika*. Cambridge: Cambridge University Press.

Ingrams, W. H. 1931. *Zanzibar: Its history and its people*. Repr., London: Cass, 1967.

Janmohamed, K. K. 1976. Ethnicity in an urban setting: A case study of Mombasa. *Hadith* 6: 186–206.

Johnson, F. 1939. *A standard Swahili-English dictionary*. Oxford: Oxford University Press.

Kindy, H. 1972. *Life and politics in Mombasa*. Nairobi: East African Literature Bureau.

Kirk, W. 1962. The north-east monsoon and some aspects of African history. *Journal of African History* 3, no. 2: 263–67.

Kirkman, J. S. 1959. Mnarani of Kilifi: The mosques and tombs. *Ars Orientalis* 3: 95–112.

––––. 1960. *The Tomb of the Dated Inscription at Gedi*. London: Royal Anthropological Institute.

––––. 1963. *Gedi: The palace*. The Hague: Mouton.

––––. 1964a. *The Arab city of Gedi: Excavations at the Great Mosque, architecture, and finds*. London: Oxford University Press.

––––. 1964b. *Men and monuments of the East African coast*. London: Lutterworth.

––––. 1966. *Ungwana on the Tana*. The Hague: Mouton.

Knappert, J. 1964. The chronicles of Mombasa. *Swahili* 34, no. 2: 21–27.

———. 1967. *Traditional Swahili poetry: An investigation into the concepts of East African Islam as reflected in the Utenzi literature.* Leiden: Brill.

———. 1970a. Social and moral concepts in Swahili Islamic literature. *Africa* 40, no. 2: 125–36.

———. 1970b. Contribution from the study of loanwords to the cultural history of Africa. Pp. 78–88 in D. Dalby, ed., *Language and history in Africa.* London: Cass.

———. 1970c. *Myths and legends of the Swahili.* London: Heinemann.

———. 1971. Swahili religious terms. *Journal of Religion in Africa* 3: 67–80.

———. 1972. *A choice of flowers: Swahili songs of love and passion.* London: Heinemann.

———. 1979. *Four centuries of Swahili verse: A literary history and anthology.* London: Heinemann.

Koritschoner, H. 1936. Ngoma ya Sheitani: An East African native treatment of psychical disorder. *Journal of the Royal Anthropological Institute* 66: 209–17.

Lambek, M. 1980. Spirits and spouses: Possession as a system of communication among the Malagasy speakers of Mayotte. *American Ethnologist* 7, no. 2: 318–31.

———. 1981. *Human spirits: A cultural account of trance in Mayotte.* New York: Cambridge University Press.

———. 1983. Virgin marriage and the autonomy of women in Mayotte. *Signs* 9: 269–83.

———. 1988. Spirit possession/spirit succession: Aspects of social continuity among Malagasy speakers in Mayotte. *American Ethnologist* 15, no. 4: 710–31.

Lambert, H. E. 1953. The taking of Tumbe town. *Journal of the East African Swahili Committee* 23: 36–45.

———. 1957. *Ki-Vumba: A dialect of the southern Swahili coast.* Kampala: East African Swahili Committee.

———. 1958a. *Chi-Chifundi: A dialect of the southern Swahili coast.* Kampala: East African Swahili Committee.

———. 1958b. *Chi-Jomvu and Kingare: Subdialects of Mombasa.* Kampala: East African Swahili Committee.

———. 1962–63. The Beni dance songs. *Swahili* 33: 18–21.

———. 1965. Some initiation songs of the southern Kenya coast. *Swahili* 35, no. 1: 49–67.

Lamphear, J. 1970. The Kamba and the northern Mrima coast. Pp. 76–102 in Gray and Birmingham.

Landberg, L. 1975. Men of Kigombe: Ngalawa fishermen of northeastern Tanzania. Unpublished Ph.D. diss., University of California.

Landberg, L., and P. W. Landberg. 1974. Maendeleo: Economic modernization in a coastal community of northeastern Tanzania. Pp. 194–233 in J. Poggie and R. Lynch, eds., *Rethinking modernization.* Westport, Conn.: Greenwood Press.

Landberg, P. W. 1977. Kinship and community in a Tanzania coastal village (East Africa). Unpublished Ph.D. diss., University of California.

———. 1986. Widows and divorced women in Swahili society. Pp. 107–38 in B. Potash, ed., *Widows in African societies.* Stanford: Stanford University Press.

Lapidus, I., ed. 1969. *Middle Eastern cities.* Berkeley: University of California Press.

Lary, P., and M. Wright. 1971. Swahili settlements in northern Zambia and Malawi. *International Journal of African Historical Studies* 4: 547–74.

Le Cour Grandmaison, C. 1989. Rich cousins, poor cousins: Hidden stratification among the Omani Arabs in eastern Africa. *Africa* 59, no. 2: 176–84.

Le Guennec-Coppens, F. 1976. *Les femmes et le mariage dans l'Ile de Lamu (Kenya).* Paris: Institut d'Ethnologie, Musée de l'Homme.

———. 1980. *Wedding customs in Lamu*. Lamu: Lamu Society.

———. 1983. *Les femmes voilées de Lamu, Kenya: Variations culturelles et dynamiques sociales*. Paris: Editions Recherche sur les Civilisations.

———. 1989. Social and cultural integration: A case study of the East African Hadramis. *Africa* 59, no. 2: 185–95.

Lévi-Strauss, C. 1985. On marriage between close kin. Pp. 88–97 in C. Lévi-Strauss, *The view from afar*. New York: Basic Books.

Levy, R. 1957. *The social structure of Islam*. Cambridge: Cambridge University Press.

Lewcock, R. 1976. Architectural connections between Africa and parts of the Indian Ocean littoral. *Art and Archaeology Research Papers* 9: 13–23.

Lewis, I. M. 1966. Spirit possession and deprivation cults. *Man* 1: 307–29.

———. 1971. *Ecstatic religion*. Harmondsworth: Penguin.

———. 1986. The power of the past. Pp. 94–107 in I. M. Lewis, *Religion in context*. Cambridge: Cambridge University Press.

Lienhardt, P. A. 1959. The Mosque College of Lamu and its social background. *Tanganyika Notes and Records* 53: 228–42.

———. 1966. A controversy over Islamic custom in Kilwa Kivinje, Tanzania. Pp. 374–86 in I. M. Lewis, ed. *Islam in tropical Africa*. London: Oxford University Press.

———. 1968. *The medicine man: "Swifa ya Nguvumali," by Hasani bin Ismael*. Oxford: Clarendon Press.

———. N.d. Family waqf in Zanzibar. Unpublished paper, East African Institute of Social Research, Kampala.

Lodhi, A. 1973. *The institution of slavery in Zanzibar and Pemba*. Uppsala: Scandinavian Institute of African Studies.

Lofchie, M. F. 1965. *Zanzibar: Background to revolution*. Princeton: Princeton University Press.

Low, D. A., and A. Smith, eds. 1976. *The Oxford History of East Africa*. Vol. 3. Oxford: Clarendon Press.

Lyne, R. N. 1905. *Zanzibar in contemporary times*. London: Hurst and Blackett.

McDermott, P. L. 1895. *British East Africa or IBEA Co*. London: Chapman and Hall.

McKay, W. F. 1975. A precolonial history of the southern Kenya coast. Unpublished Ph.D. diss., Boston University.

McMaster, D. N. 1966. The ocean-going dhow trade to East Africa. *East African Geographical Review* 4: 13–24.

Mangat, J. S. 1969. *A history of the Asians in East Africa*. Oxford: Clarendon Press.

Martin, B. G. 1971. Notes on some members of the learned class of Zanzibar and East Africa in the nineteenth century. *African Historical Studies* 4, no. 3: 525–45.

———. 1974. Arab migrations to East Africa in mediaeval times. *International Journal of African Historical Studies* 7: 367–90.

———. 1976. The Qadfiri and Shadhil: Brotherhoods in East Africa, 1880–1910. Pp. 152–76 in *Muslim brotherhoods in nineteenth-century Africa*. Cambridge: Cambridge University Press.

Martin, E. B., and T. C. I. Ryan. 1977. A quantitative assessment of the Arab slave trade of East Africa, 1770–1896. *Kenya Historical Review* 5: 71–91.

Masao, F. T., and H. W. Mutoro. 1988. The East African coast and the Comoro Islands. Pp. 586–615 in M. Elfasi and I. Hrbek, eds., *Africa from the seventh to the eleventh century*. Berkeley: University of California Press.

Maveiev, V. V. 1984. The development of Swahili civilization. Pp. 455–80 in D. T. Niane, ed., *Africa from the twelfth to the sixteenth century*. London: Heinemann.

Maw, J. 1974. *Swahili style*. London: Luzac.

Maw, J., and D. Parkin, eds. 1984. *Swahili language and society*. Vienna: Institut für Afrikanistik und Ägyptologie der Universität Wien.

Mbarak bin Ali Hinawiy. 1964. Notes on customs in Mombasa. *Swahili* 34, no. 1: 17–35.

Mbotela, J. J. 1956. *The freeing of the slaves in East Africa*. London: Evans.

Mbughuni, P. 1982. The image of women in Kiswahili prose fiction. *Kiswahili* 49: 15–24.

Midani bin Mwidad. 1960. The founding of Rabai. Trans. L. Harries. *Swahili* 31: 140–49.

Middleton, J. 1961. *Land tenure in Zanzibar*. London: Her Majesty's Stationery Office.

———. 1965. Kenya: Changes in African life, 1912–1945. Pp. 333–94 in Harlow and Chilver.

———. 1967. Slavery in Zanzibar. *Transaction* 4: 46–48.

———. 1972. Patterns of settlement in Zanzibar. Pp. 285–92 in P. J. Ucko, R. Tringham, and D. Dimbleby, eds., *Man, settlement, and urbanism*. London: Duckworth.

———. 1976. The immigrant communities (3): The Arabs of the East African coast. Pp. 489–507 in Low and Smith.

———. 1987. The towns of the Swahili coast of East Africa. Pp. 99–114 in A. Al-Shahi, ed., *The diversity of the Muslim community: Anthropological essays in memory of Peter Lienhardt*. London: Ithaca Press.

———. 1989. Kinship, family, and marriage among the Swahili of the Kenya coast. Unpublished report to Fulbright-Hays Committee and Kenya Government.

———. Forthcoming. *The construction of moral order*. London: School of Oriental and African Studies, University of London.

Middleton, J., and J. Campbell. 1965. *Zanzibar: Its history and its politics*. Oxford: Oxford University Press.

Mirza, S., and M. Strobel, eds. 1989. *Three Swahili women: Life histories from Mombasa, Kenya*. Bloomington: Indiana University Press.

Mohlig, W. J. G. 1982. Field studies in comparative dialect research on Kenyan Swahili dialects. pp. 54–61 in B. Heine, ed., *Recent German research on African language and culture*. Tübingen: Institute for Scientific Cooperation.

Moreau, R. E. 1941. The joking relationship (*utani*) in Tanganyika. *Tanganyika Notes and Records* 12: 1–10.

———. 1944. Joking relationships in Tanganyika. *Africa* 14: 386–400.

Morton, R. F. 1973. The Shungwaya myth of Miji Kenda origins: A problem of late nineteenth century Kenya coastal history. *International Journal of African Historical Studies* 5: 397–423.

Mtoro bin Mwinyi Bakari. 1981. *The customs of the Swahili people: The Desturi za Waswahili*. Ed. J. W. T. Allen. Berkeley: University of California Press.

Nabhany, A. S. 1979. *Sambo ya Kiwandeo (The ship of Lamu Island)*. Leiden: Afrika Studiecentrum.

———. 1985. *Umbuji wa Mnazi*. Nairobi: East African Publishing House.

Newitt, M. 1978. The southern Swahili coast in the first century of European expansion. *Azania* 13: 111–26.

Nicholls, C. S. 1971. *The Swahili coast: Politics, diplomacy, and trade on the East African littoral, 1798–1856*. London: Allen and Unwin.

Nimtz, A. E. 1980. *Islam and politics in East Africa: The Sufi Order in Tanzania*. Minneapolis: University of Minnesota Press.

Nurse, D. 1982. The Swahili dialects of Somalia and the northern Kenya coast. Pp. 73–146 in M.-F. Rombi, ed., *Etudes sur le Bantu oriental*. Paris: SELAF.

———. 1983. A linguistic reconsideration of Swahili origins. *Azania* 18: 127–50.

Nurse, D., and T. Spear. 1985. *The Swahili: Reconstructing the history and language of an African society, 800–1500*. Philadelphia: University of Pennsylvania Press.

Oliver, R., and G. Mathew, eds. 1963. *The Oxford history of East Africa*. Vol. 1. Oxford: Clarendon Press.

Omari bin Stamboul. 1951. An early history of Mombasa and Tanga. *Tanganyika Notes and Records* 31: 32–36.

Ottenheimer, M. 1984. Matrilocal residence and nonsororal polygyny: A case from the Comoro Islands. *Journal of Anthropological Research* 35: 328–35.

———. 1985. *Marriage in Domoni: Husbands and wives in an Indian Ocean community*. Prospect Heights, Ill.: Waveland Press.

Parkin, D. 1970. Politics of ritual syncretism: Islam among the non-Muslim Giriama of Kenya. *Africa* 40, no. 3: 217–33.

———. 1972. *Palms, wine, and witnesses*. San Francisco: Chandler.

———. 1979. Straightening the paths from wilderness: Simultaneity and sequencing in divinatory speech. *Paideuma* 28: 71–83.

———. 1985. Entitling evil: Muslims and non-Muslims in coastal Kenya. Pp. 224–43 in D. Parkin, ed., *The anthropology of evil*. Oxford: Blackwell.

———. 1989. Swahili Mijikenda: Facing both ways in Kenya. *Africa* 59, no. 2: 161–75.

Peak, R. 1989. Swahili stratification and tourism in Malindi Old Town, Kenya. *Africa* 59, no. 2: 209–20.

Pearce, F. B. 1920. *Zanzibar: The island metropolis of eastern Africa*. Repr., London: Cass, 1967.

Pender-Cudlip, P. 1972. Oral traditions and anthropological analysis: Some contemporary myths. *Azania* 7: 3–24.

Polanyi, K., et al., eds. 1957. *Trade and markets in the early empires*. Glencoe, N.Y.: Free Press.

Pouwels, R. L. 1974. Tenth century settlement of the East African coast: The case for Qarmatian/Isma'ili connections. *Azania* 9: 65–74.

———. 1978. The mediaeval foundations of East African Islam. *International Journal of African Historical Studies* 11: 383–409.

———. 1987. *Horn and crescent: Cultural change and traditional Islam on the East African coast, 800–1900*. Cambridge: Cambridge University Press.

Prins, A. H. J. 1956–58. An analysis of Swahili kinship terminology. *Journal of the East African Swahili Committee* 26: 20–28; 28: 9–16.

———. 1958. On Swahili historiography. *Journal of the East African Swahili Committee* 28: 26–40.

———. 1960. The Somaliland Bantu. *Bulletin of the International Committee on Urgent Anthropological and Ethnological Research* 3: 28–31.

———. 1963. The didemic diarchic Boni. *Journal of the Royal Anthropological Institute* 93: 174–86.

———. 1965. *Sailing from Lamu: A study of maritime culture in Islamic East Africa*. Assen: Van Gorcum.

———. 1967. *The Swahili-speaking peoples of Zanzibar and the East African coast*. Rev. ed. London: International African Insitute.

———. 1969. Islamic maritime magic: A ship's charm from Lamu. In H. Greschat and H. Jungraithmayr, eds., *Wort und Religion*. Stuttgart: Evangelischen Missionsverlag.

———. 1971. *Didemic Lamu: Social stratification and spatial structure in a Muslim maritime town*. Groningen: Instituut voor Culturele Antropologie der Rijksuniversiteit.

————. 1972. The Shungwaya problem: Traditional history and cultural likeness in Bantu North-east Africa. *Anthropos* 67: 9–35.

————. 1982. The *Mtepe* of Lamu, Mombasa and the Zanzibar Sea. *Paideuma* 28: 85–100.

————. 1984. *Watching the seaside: Essays on maritime anthropology*. Groningen: Rijks-universiteit Groningen.

Pulver, A., and F. Siravo. 1985. Lamu: A conservation plan for Kenya's oldest living town. *Kenya Past and Present* 18: 17–31.

Ranger, T. O. 1975. *Dance and society in eastern Africa, 1890–1970: The Beni Ngoma*. London: Heinemann.

Raum, O. F. 1965. German East Africa: Changes in African tribal life under German administration, 1892–1914. Pp. 163–208 in Harlow and Chilver.

Ricks, T. M. 1970. Persian Gulf seafaring and East Africa: Ninth to twelfth centuries. *International Journal of African Historical Studies* 3: 339–57.

Roberts, A. D., ed. 1968. *Tanzania before 1900*. Nairobi: East African Publishing House.

————. 1970. Nyamwezi trade. Pp. 39–74 in Gray and Birmingham.

Robinson, A. E. 1939. The Shirazi colonization of East Africa: Vumba. *Tanganyika Notes and Records* 7: 92–112.

Romero, P. 1987a. Mama Khadija: A life history as example of family history. Pp. 140–58 in P. Romero, ed., *Life histories of African women*. London: Ashfield Press.

————. 1987b. Possible sources for the origin of gold as an economic and social vehicle for women in Lamu (Kenya). *Africa* 57, no. 3: 364–76.

Rozensztroch, M. 1984. Liongo Fumo: Légende et signification politique. Unpublished doctoral thesis, University of Paris.

Ruete, E. 1886. *Memories of an Arabian princess*. Ed. P. Romero. Repr., New York: Markus Wiener, 1989.

Russell, J. 1981. *Communicative competence in a minority group: A sociolinguistic study of the Swahili-speaking community of the Old Town, Mombasa*. Leiden: Brill.

Sacleux, C. 1939. *Dictionnaire Swahili-Français*. Paris: Institut d'Ethnologie.

Said Bakari bin Sultan Ahmed. 1977. *The Swahili chronicle of Ngazija*. Trans. L. Harries. Madison: University of Wisconsin Press.

Salim, A. I. 1970. The movement for Mwambao or coast autonomy in Kenya 1956–63. *Hadith* 2: 212–28.

————. 1972. Early Arab-Swahili political protest in colonial Kenya. *Hadith* 4: 71–84.

————. 1973. *The Swahili-speaking peoples of Kenya's coast, 1895–1945*. Nairobi: East African Publishing House.

————. 1976. Native or non-native? The problem of identity and the social stratification of the Arab-Swahili of Kenya. *Hadith* 6: 65–85.

Sassoon, C. 1970. The dhows of Dar es Salaam. *Tanzania Notes and Records* 71: 185–99.

————. 1975. *Chinese porcelain in Fort Jesus*. Mombasa: National Museums of Kenya.

Sassoon, H. 1975. *The siwas of Lamu*. Nairobi: National Museums of Kenya.

————. 1980. Excavations at the site of early Mombasa. *Azania* 15: 1–44.

Scheven, A. 1981. *Swahili proverbs*. Washington, D.C.: University Press of America.

Shariff, I. N. 1973. Waswahili and their language: Some misconceptions. *Kiswahili* 43: 67–75.

————. 1988. *Tungo zetu: Msingi wa Mashairi na Tungo Nyinginezo*. Trenton, N.J.: Red Sea Press.

————. 1991. The Liyongo conundrum: Reexamining the historicity of Swahilis' national poet-hero. *Research in African Literature* (in press).

Shepherd, G. 1977. Two marriage forms in the Comoro Islands: An investigation. *Africa* 47, no. 4: 344–58.

———. 1980. The Comorians and the East African slave trade. Pp. 73–99 in J. L. Watson, ed., *Asian and African systems of slavery*. Oxford: Blackwell.

———. 1982. The making of the Swahili: A view from the southern end of the East African coast. *Paideuma* 28: 129–48.

———. 1987. Rank, gender, and homosexuality: Mombasa as a key to understanding sexual options. Pp. 248–70 in P. Caplan, ed., *The cultural construction of sexuality*. London: Tavistock.

Sheriff, A. M. H. 1975. Trade and underdevelopment: The role of international trade in the economic history of the East African coast before the sixteenth century. *Hadith* 5: 1–23.

———. 1981. The East African coast and its role in maritime trade. Pp. 551–67 in G. Mokhtar, ed., *The UNESCO general history of Africa*. Vol. 2. London: Heinemann.

———. 1985. The slave mode of production along the East African coast, 1810–1873. Pp. 161–81 in J. R. Willis, ed., *Slaves and slavery in Muslim Africa*. London: Cass.

———. 1987. *Slaves, spices and ivory in Zanzibar*. Athens: Ohio University Press.

Silberman, L. 1950. The social survey of the Old Town of Mombasa. *Journal of African Administration* 2: 14–21.

Siravo, F., and A. Pulver. 1986. *Planning Lamu: Conservation of an East African seaport*. Nairobi: National Museums of Kenya.

Skene, R. 1917. Arab and Swahili dances and ceremonies. *Journal of the Royal Anthropological Institute* 47: 413–34.

Smith, A. 1976. The end of the Arab Sultanate: Zanzibar, 1945–1964. Pp. 196–211 in Low and Smith.

Smith, M. G. 1972. Complexity, size and urbanization. Pp. 567–74 in P. J. Ucko, R. Tringham, and G. W. Dimbleby, eds., *Man, settlement and urbanism*. London: Duckworth.

Southall, A. W. 1989. The African port city. *Economic Development and Cultural Change* 38, no. 1: 167–89.

Spear, T. T. 1974. Traditional myths and historians' myths: Variations on the Singwaya theme of Mijikenda origins. *History in Africa* 1: 67–84.

———. 1977. Traditional myths and linguistic analysis: Singwaya revisited. *History in Africa* 4: 229–46.

———. 1978. *The Kaya complex: A history of the Mijikenda peoples of the Kenya coast to 1900*. Nairobi: Kenya Literature Bureau.

———. 1981. Oral traditions: Whose history? *History in Africa* 8: 165–81.

Steere, E. 1870. *Swahili tales, as told by the natives of Zanzibar*. London: Bell and Daldy.

Stephen, H. 1978. Hunting and gathering as a strategic adaptation: The case of the Boni of Lamu District, Kenya. Unpublished Ph.D. diss., Boston University.

Stigand, C. H. 1913. *The land of Zinj: Being an account of British East Africa, its ancient history and present inhabitants*. London: Constable.

Stiles, D. 1981. Hunters of the northern East African coast: Origins and historical processes. *Africa* 51: 848–62.

———. 1982. A history of the hunting peoples of the northern East African coast. *Paideuma* 28: 165–74.

Stovald, K. E. 1946. *The C.M.S. in Kenya: The coast*. Nairobi: East African Literature Bureau.

Strandes, J. 1961. *The Portuguese period in East Africa*. Nairobi: East African Literature Bureau.

Stren, R. 1970. Factional politics and central control in Mombasa, 1960–69. *Canadian Journal of African Studies* 4, no. 1: 33–56.

Strobel, M. 1975. Women's wedding celebrations in Mombasa, Kenya. *African Studies Review* 18, no. 3: 35–45.

———. 1979. *Muslim women in Mombasa, 1890–1975.* New Haven: Yale University Press.

———. 1983. Slavery and reproductive labor in Mombasa. Pp. 111–29 in C. Robertson and M. Klein, eds., *Women and slavery in Africa.* Madison: University of Wisconsin Press.

Strong, S. A., ed. 1895. The history of Kilwa. *Journal of the Royal Asiatic Society* 27: 385–430.

Sutton, J. E. G., ed. 1970. *Dar es Salaam: City, port, and region. Tanzania Notes and Records* 71 (special issue).

Swantz, M.-L. 1970. *Ritual and symbol in transitional Zaramo society: With special reference to women.* Studia Missionalia Uppsaliensia 16. Uppsala: Gleerup-Lund.

Swartz, M. 1979. Religious courts, community, and ethnicity among the Swahili of Mombasa. *Africa* 49, no. 1: 29–41.

———. 1982. The isolation of men and the happiness of women: Sources and use of power in Swahili marital relationships. *Journal of Anthropological Research* 38: 26–44.

———. 1983. Culture and implicit power: Maneuvers and understandings in Swahili nuclear family relations. Pp. 19–38 in M. J. Aronoff, ed., *Culture and political change.* New Brunswick, N.J.: Transaction Books.

Tanner, R. E. S. 1962. Relationships between the sexes in a coastal Islamic society: Pangani District, Tanganyika. *African Studies* 21, no. 2: 70–82.

———. 1964. Cousin marriage in the Afro-Arab community of Mombasa, Kenya. *Africa* 34, no. 2: 127–38.

Taylor, W. E. 1891. *African aphorisms, or Saws from Swahili-land.* London: Sheldon Press.

Tolmacheva, M. 1976. The origin of the name "Swahili." *Tanganyika Notes and Records* 77–78: 27–37.

———. 1978. The Arabic influence on Swahili literature: A historian's view. *Journal of African Studies* 5: 223–43.

———. 1979. "They came from Damascus in Syria": A note on traditional Lamu historiography. *International Journal of African Historical Studies* 12: 259–69.

Trimingham, J. S. 1964. *Islam in East Africa.* Oxford: Clarendon Press.

———. 1975. The Arab geographers and the East African coast. In H. N. Chittick and R. Rotberg, eds., *East Africa and the Orient.* New York: Africana.

Turton, E. R. 1975. Bantu, Galla, and Somali migration in the Horn of Africa: A reassessment of the Juba/Tana area. *Journal of African History* 16: 519–37.

Unwin, S. 1987. Dhow trade chests. *Kenya Past and Present* 19: 34–43.

Van Spaandonck, M. 1965. *Practical and systematic Swahili bibliography: Linguistics, 1850–1963.* Leiden: Brill.

Velten, C. 1905. *Desturi za Waswahili.* Gottingen: Vandenhöck and Ruprecht. *See* Mtoro bin Mwinyi Bakari.

———. 1965. *Swahili prose texts: A selection from the material collected by Carl Velten from 1893 to 1896.* Ed. and trans. L. Harries. London: Oxford University Press.

Verin, P. 1982. L'introduction de l'Islam aux Comores selon des traditions orales. *Paideuma* 28: 193–200.

Villiers, A. 1940. *Sons of Sinbad.* New York: Scribners.

Wansbrough, J. 1970. Africa and the Arab geographers. Pp. 89–101 in D. Dalby, ed., *Language and history in Africa*. London: Cass.

Werner, A. 1913. Some notes on the Wapokomo of the Tana Valley. *Man* 12: 359–84.

———. 1914. Swahili history of Pate. *Journal of the African Society* 14: 148–61, 278–97, 392–413.

———. 1926–28. The Swahili saga of Liongo Fumo. *Bulletin of the School of Oriental and African Studies* 4: 247–55.

———. 1932. *The story of Miqdad and Mayasa*. Medstead, England: Azania Press.

Werner, A., and W. Hichens, eds. 1934. *Utendi wa Mwana Kupona* (Advice of Mwana Kupona upon the wifely duty). Medstead: Azania Press.

Wheatley, P. 1972. The concept of urbanism. Pp. 601–37 in P. J. Ucko, R. Tringham, and G. W. Dimbleby, eds., *Man, settlement and urbanism*. London: Duckworth.

Whiteley, W. H. 1958. *The dialects and verse of Pemba*. Kampala: East African Swahili Committee.

———. 1969. *Swahili: The rise of a national language*. London; Methuen.

Wijeyewardene, G. L. T. N.d. Administration and politics in two Swahili communities. Unpublished seminar paper, East African Institute of Social Research, Kampala.

———. N.d. Kinship and ritual in the Swahili community. Unpublished seminar paper, East African Institute of Social Research, Kampala.

———. N.d. Mambrui: Status and social relations in a multi-racial community. Unpublished seminar paper, East African Institute of Social Research, Kampala.

———. N.d. A preliminary report on tribal differentiation and social groupings on the southern Kenya coast. Unpublished seminar paper, East African Institute of Social Research, Kampala.

———. 1961. Some aspects of village solidarity among KiSwahili-speaking communities of Kenya and Tanzania. Unpublished Ph.D. thesis, University of Cambridge.

Wilding, R. 1976. *Swahili culture: A bibliography of the history and people of the Swahili-speaking world*. Nairobi: Lamu Society.

Wilkinson, J. C. 1981. Oman and East Africa: New light on early Kilwan history from the Omani sources. *International Journal of African Historical Studies* 14: 272–305.

Willis, J. N.d. Fumo-Liongo: A confusion of histories. Unpublished paper, School of Oriental and African Studies, University of London.

Wilson, T. H. 1978. *The monumental architecture and archaeology north of the Tana River*. Nairobi: National Museums of Kenya.

———. 1979. Swahili funerary architecture of the North Kenya coast. *Art and Archaeology Research Papers* 1979: 33–46.

———. 1980. *The monumental architecture and archaeology of the central and southern Kenya coast*. Nairobi: National Museums of Kenya.

———. 1982. Spatial analysis and settlement patterns on the East African coast. *Paideuma* 28: 201–19.

Yalden-Thompson, D. 1958. A paper on the Oman Arabs in Zanzibar Protectorate. Unpublished paper.

Ylvisaker, M. 1979. *Lamu in the nineteenth century: Land, trade, and politics*. Boston: African Studies Center, Boston University.

———. 1982. The ivory trade in the Lamu area, 1600–1870. *Paideuma* 28: 221–31.

Zanzibar Government. 1953. *Notes on the census of the Zanzibar Protectorate, 1948*. Zanzibar: Government Printer.

—————. 1958. *The report of the Supervisor of Elections on the elections in Zanzibar, 1957.* Zanzibar: Government Printer.

—————. 1960. *Report on the census of the population of Zanzibar Protectorate (taken on the night of the 19th and 20th March, 1958).* Zanzibar: Government Printer.

I n d e x

Academies, Islamic, 164
Adoption and fostering, 90, 108, 126
Agriculture: Hadimu, 69ff.; labor, 103;
  organization, 82; production, 23
al-Busaidi clan, 34, 43, 47f.
Al-Inkishafi (poem), 200
al-Masudi, 38
Alcohol, 180
Allen, J. de V., 65, 68, 187
Alliances, 44, 102
Amulets, 179
Ancestors: in ritual, 163; as spirits, 171f.
Ancestry, significance of, 83, 90, 96, 102,
  184ff., 195
Arab: immigrants, 2, 12f.; marriage, 131;
  travelers, 38f.
Arabic, significance of, 162, 165
Archeology, research, 36, 203*n*23
Architecture, 2, 11, 60ff., 62ff., 209*n*6
Arms, import of, 16, 48
Art, 225*n*30
Arusi. See Initiation; Weddings
Associations, 53, 81, 173, 177
Astrology, 82, 179, 189
Authority: Lamu descent groups, 96;
  Hadimu kin groups, 87
Autochthonous groups, 12

Bajun people, 58, 72, 77, 79, 97f., 108f.,
  116, 124, 134, 138, 187
Baluchi, 43, 91, 97
Barbarism (*ushenzi*), notion of, 32, 102,
  113
Beauty, notion of, 145, 149, 151, 218*n*14

Beni associations, 81
Betrothal, 122, 142, 154, 226
Blessing (*baraka*), 190, 194
"Blood" in kin reckoning, 86
Bondei people, 7
Boni people, 6, 16, 29
Brava town, 5
Bridewealth: contributions, 74, 85; in
  country-towns, 154f.; patrician, 123,
  128, 132; size, 132
Brotherhoods, Islamic, 170

Calendars, 165
Capitalism, 17, 35, 47
Caplan, P. A., 88, 154
Carpentry, 189
Cemeteries, 56, 61, 78, 158
Charity, 138, 150, 193, 127, 129
Childbirth, 156ff.
Childhood, rites in, 157
Chinese, trade, 13, 38
Christianity, 223*n*39
"Chronicles," 27f., 30
Circumcision, 141
Civilization (*ustaraabu*), notion of, 54, 97,
  102, 113, 191f.
Clans, 98
Class differences, 185
Clothing: significance of, 2, 11, 115, 166,
  187, 195ff; at weddings, 148f., 153
Cloves, 7, 25f., 72, 89. *See also* Planta-
  tions
Coast, geography of, 3, 5ff.
Cognatic descent, 85ff.

249